A History of Everyday Life in Medieval Scotland, 1000 to 1600

A History of Everyday Life in Scotland
SERIES EDITORS: CHRISTOPHER A. WHATLEY AND ELIZABETH FOYSTER

Volume 1: A History of Everyday Life in Medieval Scotland, 1000 to 1600
Edited by Edward J. Cowan and Lizanne Henderson

Volume 2: A History of Everyday Life in Scotland, 1600 to 1800
Edited by Elizabeth Foyster and Christopher A. Whatley

Volume 3: A History of Everyday Life in Scotland, 1800 to 1900
Edited by Trevor Griffiths and Graeme Morton

Volume 4: A History of Everyday Life in Twentieth-Century Scotland
Edited by Lynn Abrams and Callum G. Brown

A History of Everyday Life in Medieval Scotland, 1000 to 1600

Edited by Edward J. Cowan and Lizanne Henderson

Edinburgh University Press

© editorial matter and organisation Edward J. Cowan and Lizanne Henderson, 2011
© the chapters their several authors, 2011

Edinburgh University Press Ltd
22 George Square, Edinburgh
www.euppublishing.com

Typeset in 10/12pt Goudy Old Style by
Servis Filmsetting Ltd, Stockport, Cheshire, and
printed and bound in Great Britain by
CPI Antony Rowe, Chippenham and Eastbourne

A CIP record for this book is available from the British Library

ISBN 978 0 7486 2156 9 (hardback)
ISBN 978 0 7486 2157 6 (paperback)

The right of the contributors to be identified as authors of
this work has been asserted in accordance with the Copyright,
Designs and Patents Act 1988.

Published with the support of the Edinburgh University
Scholarly Publishing Initiatives Fund.

Contents

Figures

Series Editors' Foreword

Elizabeth Foyster and Christopher A. Whatley

The four books in this series examine the ordinary, routine, daily behaviour, experiences and beliefs of Scottish people from medieval times until the present day. Their focus is on the 'common people', that is, most of the population, the ordinary folk below the ranks of the aristocracy, substantial landowners, opulent merchants, major industrialists, bankers and financiers, even if it is true that people from relatively humble beginnings have managed periodically to haul themselves into the ranks of the nation's social elite. Contributors in each volume describe the landscapes and living spaces that formed the familiar contexts for daily life. The events and activities that determined how individuals spent their time are explored, including the experiences of work and leisure, and ranging in duration from those that affected the passage of a single day, through those that impinged on peoples' lives according to the calendar or the seasons and weather, to those that were commonly experienced over the course of the life-cycle. Scottish people made sense of their everyday lives, it is argued, through ritual and belief, by their interactions with others and by self-reflection.

As a whole, the series aims to provide a richer and more closely observed history of the social, economic and cultural lives of ordinary Scots than has been published previously. This is not to suggest that accounts and analyses of the everyday in Scotland have not been written. They have.[1] And this present series of four volumes overlaps with the publication of the fourteen volumes of the *Scottish Life and Society* series, sponsored by the European Ethnological Research Centre in Edinburgh, led by Alexander Fenton. The first volume in this series was published in 2000, with others following at intervals through to 2008. Unlike the series of which this volume is part, which is structured by chronological periods in which selected broad themes are studied, each of the books in the *Scottish Life and Society* series has been organised around a particular topic, including: farming and rural life; domestic life; boats, fishing and the sea; and religion.[2] They are substantial, multi-authored volumes, and eclectic in the range of subjects and sub-topics covered, entirely befitting the series subtitle, *A Compendium of Scottish Ethnology*. It represents a monumental resource for future researchers.[3] Where appropriate, contributors to this series *A History of Everyday Life in Scotland* have drawn upon the *Scottish Life and Society* team's findings. Rather than clashing, however, or overlapping to the point of repetition, the two series complement each other, with ours concentrating more on continuities and change, and historical explanations for this, and written, mainly but not entirely, by professional historians. Together, both series offer readers a heady mix of historical information, and an array of approaches, analytical styles and depths and insights.

The everyday had a context, or contexts. At the individual level what was everyday altered across time and often differed according to class, gender, age, religion and ethnic group. It was also shaped by national and regional surroundings, and could vary between urban and rural environments, highland and lowland, inland and coastal settings, the northern and western islands.[4] Contributors pay attention to regional and local variations and peculiarities, especially with regard to language, dialect, practices and customs. The series reveals aspects of the everyday that were distinctively Scottish, but it also shows how the everyday lives of Scots were influenced by other cultures and nations. This resulted from travel, trading relations, or migration by Scots who lived and worked abroad, both temporarily and permanently. Indirectly, Scots read and learned of the shared or conflicting ideas and practices of everyday life in near and distant lands. Contributors to the series can point to international differences and similarities because of the pioneering work on the everyday that has been conducted by historians on other countries across a range of periods. While relatively little has been published specifically on the everyday in Scotland or even Britain, we are fortunate to be able to draw upon an extensive body of historical research for Europe and the Americas.[5]

The roots of this historical endeavour, and the approaches that this series takes, lie in a range of developments within the discipline. In Britain, the interest of social historians – often with a Marxist perspective – in writing 'history from below', has brought the lives of working-class people to centre stage.[6] In Scotland the study of 'new' social history was pioneered by T. C. Smout, with his seminal *History of the Scottish People, 1560–1830* (1969), although Smout's approach was liberal rather than leftist.[7] This was followed in subsequent decades by a surge of research on a range of topics, and a plethora of publications written by a small army of historians examining different historical periods, including the same author's *Century of the Scottish People, 1830–1950* (1986).[8] Furth of Scotland, *Annaliste* historians, such as Fernand Braudel, focused attention on the material culture of daily life, and a later generation of French and then Italian historians narrowed the scale of study to produce 'microhistories'. These examined in detail the history of one individual, village or incident in order to understand the wider *mentalité* of the societies of which they were a part.[9] Historians in Germany have addressed the issue of the everyday most directly, where the concept of *Alltagsgeschichte* ('the history of everyday life') was conceived, and continues to be the source of lively debate.[10] Preceding, running alongside and occasionally influencing historical work has been the study of everyday life by academics in other disciplines, including ethnology, sociology, social anthropology, geography, psychology and cultural theory.[11] Academics from these disciplines contribute to some of the volumes of this series.

What can the reader expect from this series, and how does the content of the books that comprise it differ from other social histories of Scotland?

First, by uncovering the everyday, we provide fresh insights into a diverse range of historical topics. Whereas much social history can focus on the structures, ideals or prescriptions that were intended to govern daily living, this series examines the practices and realities of life experience. Although not the primary purpose of the series, people's experiences of major change, like wars, famine and environmental disaster, are incorporated. The result is to demonstrate how the extraordinary affected the ordinary. But as Alexander Fenton correctly observed of Scottish rural society some years ago, broad trends, big ideas and eye-catching technologies only explain so much; how they impacted on the everyday depended on local conditions and responses. As important for understanding the everyday lives of ordinary people, and the pace and nature of change, were, for example, how small-scale pieces of equipment were adopted and used, and how things were done in the home or barn or yard far from power centres that passed legislation or, from which sprang – as in the case of Edinburgh and east-central Scotland in the early eighteenth century – models for and aids to agrarian improvement. But on Orkney even in the later eighteenth century weighing machines – the pundlar and the pindlar – weights and measures, and the commonly used, one-stilt plough, had been in use since Viking times.[12] Change on the ground was invariably slow, piecemeal and indigenous rather than spectacular.[13]

Examples and case studies of aspects of everyday life in these volumes also enhance our understanding of some long-standing subjects of debate within Scottish history. Hence, readers will gain new insights about the role of the kirk in social and moral discipline, the impact of enclosure and the Clearances in the Lowlands as well as the Highlands, the struggles between popular and elite forms of culture, standards of living, and the significance of 'public' and 'private' spaces in daily life. In addition, the exploration of the everyday has allowed our contributors to cover less familiar historical territory – some of which has posed considerable challenges. We discover how Scottish people's fears, anxieties and perceptions of danger changed over time, we learn about the importance of gestures as well as forms of verbal and written communication and we begin to recover how ordinary Scots experienced their sensory worlds of taste, sound, sight and touch. The everyday enables historians to engage with important emerging topics within the discipline of history, for example, the history of the Scottish landscape and the environment. Chapters in the books in the series explore the changing relationship with and impact of Scots upon their natural environment.[14] The series also demonstrates how women, whose lives were once considered too everyday and mundane to merit serious academic study, played a central part in the negotiation and management of particularly home and family daily life.[15] In addition, women could play an active role in everyday life beyond the domestic scene, as recent research has begun to reveal.[16] Scottish men's gendered identities were also constructed and experienced in the context of the everyday.

The contributors to this series have been able to write these histories not, on the whole, because they have discovered vast quantities of new evidence in the archives, although much original material has been uncovered. Rather, a new history has emerged because they have asked novel questions of material with which they were familiar, and have pieced together a wide range of what was often unused information from both primary and secondary sources. Undoubtedly, writing the history of the everyday presents unique problems of evidence for the historian. These problems can vary with historical period; those researching the everyday in medieval times can face a dearth of written sources, while it is easy to be overwhelmed by the mass of information available for the twentieth century. However, there are also more fundamental issues of evidence at stake that have to be faced by all historians of the everyday. As Braudel recognised, 'everyday life consists of the little things one hardly notices in time and space'.[17] Everyday life could be so banal, repetitive, tedious, boring, easily forgotten or taken for granted that our predecessors rarely bothered to record it. Sometimes this means we have to read 'against the grain' of the sources that do survive. In other words, examining the exceptional incident or object to deduce its opposite. For the most part, however, writing about the everyday necessitates the laborious sorting through and amalgamation of fragments of the past: written, visual and material. Contributors to this series have found evidence of the everyday in artefacts, archaeological sites, buildings, diaries, letters, autobiographies, polite and popular literature, trial records of church, burgh and state courts, estate papers, directories, prints, maps, photographs and oral testimony. It is the incidental comment, remark or observation, chance survival, brief glimpse or snapshot that often contains a clue to and even the core of the everyday. The historian's task is to put these details together, 'as in a jigsaw puzzle', so that we can present to readers a picture of the everyday.[18]

What the reader will not get from the series is a complete or comprehensive compendium of everyday life. This, as indicated earlier, is to be found elsewhere. It has not been our intention to list or describe all everyday objects and occurrences, even if this were practicably possible. Rather, our purpose is to explain and analyse the everyday as well as record it. The methodological tools used by contributors are diverse, and reflect their differing disciplinary backgrounds. This is especially the case in the twentieth century volume, where interdisciplinary approaches are most widely employed.

The second distinctive contribution of this series to our understanding of the Scottish past is concerned with what it reveals about historical change.

Across the series the reader can expect to find enduring continuities within everyday life, but also transformations, some rapid, but most long and drawn out. These can be observed by the historian; how far and in what ways they were experienced by ordinary people is harder to know. Yet it is clear that, over time, changes did occur in everyday life, as new ways of working, forms of social organisation, products, sights and sounds expanded the experiences of ordinary Scots. Even the fundamentals that comprise everyday life – what people ate and drank, where they slept, what they wore, where they worked and how they travelled from A to B – were indisputably transformed. Even so, these volumes also present evidence of elements of everyday life stubbornly resistant to change. The consecutive volumes in this series do not signify a set of breaks with the past, or a turning point in all aspects of the everyday. Hence, to take some examples: Scots continued to trust self-administered and home-made cures for illness even as medicine became professionalised and institutionalised; oral culture continued to thrive long after literacy had become the norm; and families and their communities continued to mark birth, marriage and death as significant rites of passage. Ale is still widely drunk at the start of the twenty-first century; and walking and other earlier forms of transport, the use of the bicycle, for example, are growing in popularity. The enduring qualities of everyday life have attracted comment. For the Marxist cultural theorist Henri Lefebvre, the everyday in more recent times offered a glimmer of hope in capitalist societies, because it revealed 'a corrective to the spectacularizing discourse of modernity'. Despite industrial and technological change, the humdrum and main concerns of everyday life for many people remained little altered.[19] Historians have noted people's determination to maintain the routines of daily life in the face of dramatic change, such as during periods of crisis and conflict.[20] Our predecessors shared our need for food, drink and shelter, and our yearning for love and affection, but when other parts of their lives faced serious disruption, the relative importance of fulfilling these needs had to be adjusted. Scots could be proud of 'making do' in times of hardship, and of the fact that daily life 'went on' despite the havoc and destruction around them. This series looks more closely at why particular aspects of the everyday were so hard to disrupt.

By so doing, revealing perspective is provided upon the meaning for ordinary Scots of 'great events', such as wars, which traditionally have been seen as the key moments of change in Scottish – and other nations' – history. Arguably, it was in the context of the 'non-event-ness' of the everyday that the vast majority of Scots spent their lives.[21] Indeed, as Dorothee Wierling has observed, 'most persons have *nothing but* . . . ordinary everyday life'.[22] Studying the history of everyday life is about retrieving the history of what most people did most of the time.

The series demonstrates that the speed of change in everyday life could vary between that experienced within the space of a generation, to barely perceptible shifts across centuries. However, the series also offers some explanations for what brought about change when it occurred. More important is how change was accommodated within the everyday; this was a social process. The seeds for change in Scottish society were frequently contained within the everyday. The everyday was often 'political'. Studying the everyday allows us to see how ordinary people could exercise power over their lives to resist, counter, accommodate or adapt to the changes they encountered. As Ben Highmore has observed, everyday life often serves in helping people to cope with 'the shock of the new'. The everyday becomes the setting:

> for making the unfamiliar familiar; for getting accustomed to the disruption of custom; for struggling to incorporate the new; for adjusting to different ways of living. The everyday marks the success and failure of this process. It witnesses the absorption of the most revolutionary of inventions into the landscape of the mundane. Radical transformations in all walks of life become 'second nature'.[23]

In short, it is by examining the minutiae of people's daily lives that we can uncover the significance of historical change as this affected ordinary people.

Above all – and this is our third aim – the series aims to provide an accessible history that will interest, excite and engage with the reader. This should not be difficult to achieve given the degree of public interest in the everyday. From the popularity of 'reality' TV shows where individuals are exposed to reconstructed life as their Iron Age ancestors might have lived it, for instance, to the fact that it is often the kitchens and servants' living quarters of stately homes which attract the most visitors and curiosity, it is clear that there is an appetite to find out more about the everyday. This is because the history of the everyday is one to which most people can relate, or at least with which we can empathise. It is the bread and butter of life in the past. This is not to suggest that the reader will find any straightforward or single narrative of everyday life in these volumes. The history of the everyday is complex in the extreme: the range of experience is immense, what evidence we do have is often contradictory and there are enormous black holes in our knowledge and understanding. The books in the series reflect all of this, but they have also identified patterns and processes that make some sense of the everyday life of the Scots over the centuries in all of its diversity.

Notes

1 A classic in its time was H. G. Graham, *The Social Life of Scotland in the Eighteenth Century* (London, 1899), while Marjory Plant's *Domestic Life of Scotland in the Eighteenth Century* (Edinburgh, 1948), and Marion Lochhead's *The Scots Household*

in the Eighteenth Century (Edinburgh, 1948), broke new ground in revealing much about everyday life in and around the home. It was Alexander (Sandy) Fenton, however, who led the way in Scotland in modern exploration of the everyday, particularly that of rural society: see, for example, A. Fenton, *Scottish Country Life* (Edinburgh, 1976, 1977; East Linton, 1999), and *The Northern Isles: Orkney and Shetland* (Edinburgh, 1978; East Linton,1997).

2 *Scottish Life and Society: A Compendium of Scottish Ethnology*, 14 vols (John Donald, in association with The European Ethnological Research Centre and The National Museums of Scotland).

3 Perhaps the most enduring research tool deriving from the project will be H. Holmes and F. Macdonald (eds), *Scottish Life and Society: Bibliography for Scottish Ethnology*, vol. 14 (Edinburgh, 2003).

4 For a fine study of the impact of environmental factors and changing international conditions upon a locality, and aspects of everyday life in the northern isles, see H. D. Smith, *Shetland Life and Trade, 1550–1914* (Edinburgh, 1984).

5 See, for example, C. Dyer, *Everyday Life in Medieval England* (London, 1994); S. Wilson, *The Magical Universe: Everyday Ritual and Magic in Pre-Modern Europe* (London, 2000); R. Sarti, *Europe at Home: Family and Material Culture 1500–1800* (New Haven, 2002); R. Braun, *Industrialisation and Everyday Life*, trans. S. H. Tenison (Cambridge, 1990); S. Fitzpatrick, *Everyday Stalinism. Ordinary Life in Extraordinary Times: Soviet Russia in the 1930s* (Oxford, 1999); 'The Everyday Life in America series' edited by Richard Balkin; and M. Wasserman, *Everyday Life and Politics in Nineteenth-Century Mexico: Men, Women and War* (Albuquerque, 2000).

6 The work of E. P. Thompson was especially important in this regard, notably his seminal *The Making of the English Working Class* (London, 1965). See also the collection of his essays in *Customs in Common* (London, 1991). Thompson pays little attention to Scotland; more inclusive – and comparative – is Keith Wrightson's *Earthly Necessities: Economic Lives in Early Modern Britain* (New Haven, 2000), which contains much on everyday lives and how these were affected by the emergence of the market economy.

7 Marxist analyses of Scottish society appeared later, for example, T. Dickson (ed.), *Scottish Capitalism: Class, State and Nation from before the Union to the Present* (London, 1980); Dickson also edited *Capital and Class in Scotland* (Edinburgh, 1982).

8 Some sense of what has been achieved over the past half century or so can be seen in the bibliographies that accompany each of the chapters in R. A. Houston and W. W. Knox's *New Penguin History of Scotland from the Earliest Times to the Present Day* (London, 2001).

9 See, for example, F. Braudel, *Civilization and Capitalism 15th–18th Century*, vol. I, *The Structures of Everyday Life: The Limits of the Possible*, trans. S. Reynolds (London, 1981); E. Le Roy Ladurie, *Montaillou: Cathars and Catholics in a French Village 1294–1324*, trans. Barbara Bray (Harmondsworth, 1980); and C. Ginzburg, *The Cheese and the Worms: The Cosmos of a Sixteenth-Century Miller*, trans. J. and A. Tedeschi (Baltimore, 1980).

10 See, for example, A. Lüdtke (ed.), *The History of Everyday Life: Reconstructing Historical Experiences and Ways of Life*, trans. W. Templer (Princeton, 1995).

11 See, for example, A. J. Weigert, *Sociology of Everyday Life* (London, 1981); J. M. White, *Everyday Life of the North American Indian* (New York, 2003); T. Friberg, *Everyday Life: Women's Adaptive Strategies in Time and Space*, trans. M. Gray (Stockholm, 1993); G. M. Davies and R. H. Logie (eds), *Memory in Everyday Life* (Amsterdam, 1993); H. Lefebvre, *Critique of Everyday Life*, 2 vols (London, 1991 and 2002); Michel de Certeau, *The Practice of Everyday Life*, trans. S. Rendall (Berkeley, 1984); and M. de Certeau, L. Giard and P. Mayol, *The Practice of Everyday Life Volume 2: Living and Cooking*, trans. T. J. Tomasik (Minneapolis, 1998).

12 W. S. Hewison (ed.), *The Diary of Patrick Fea of Stove, Orkney, 1766–96* (East Linton, 1997), pp. 21, 24.

13 Fenton, *Scottish Country Life*, p. v.

14 See T. C. Smout, *Nature Contested: Environmental History in Scotland and Northern England Since 1600* (Edinburgh, 2000); and for a study which looks more closely at the relationship between one element of the environment, trees, and aspects of everyday life, T. C. Smout (ed.), *People and Woods in Scotland: A History* (Edinburgh, 2003).

15 For discussion of the links between women and the everyday see, D. Wierling, 'The history of everyday life and gender relations: on historical and historio-graphical relationships', in Lüdtke, *History of Everyday Life*, pp. 149–68.

16 See, for example, E. Ewan and M. M. Meikle (eds), *Women in Scotland, c.1100–c.1750* (East Linton, 1999); L. Abrams, E. Gordon, D. Simonton and E. J. Yeo (eds), *Gender in Scottish History since 1700* (Edinburgh, 2006); W. W. Knox, *Lives of Scottish Women: Women and Scottish Society, 1800–1980* (Edinburgh, 2006). A pioneering if eccentric account of women's role in popular protest was J. D. Young's *Women and Popular Struggles: A History of Scottish and English Working-Class Women, 1500–1984* (Edinburgh, 1985).

17 Braudel, *Civilization and Capitalism*, p. 29.

18 Sarti, *Europe at Home*, p. 1.

19 J. Moran, 'History, memory and the everyday', *Rethinking History* 8:1 (2004), pp. 54–7.

20 See, for example, N. Longmate, *How We Lived Then: A History of Everyday Life During the Second World War* (London, 1971).

21 The concept of 'non-event-ness' is taken from B. Highmore, *Everyday Life and Cultural Theory* (London, 2002), p. 34.

22 Wierling, 'The history of everyday life', p. 151; the emphasis is in the original.

23 Highmore, *Everyday Life*, p. 2.

Introduction

Everyday Life in Medieval Scotland

Edward J. Cowan and Lizanne Henderson

The modern study of the history of the medieval everyday could be said to have begun with Fernand Braudel. Of course, there had been earlier studies of everyday life but they read somewhat like catalogues rather than as investigative histories.[1] It was Braudel who introduced 'everyday life, no more, no less, into the domain of history . . . Everyday life consists of the little things one hardly notices in time and space.'[2] The everyday exists in the context of 'material life' or 'material civilization', the world of the infra-economy, shifting barely perceptibly over time, almost stagnant; the phenomenon dubbed by historians of the Annales School, the *longue durée*. This means that in real terms – diet, shelter, communications and a thousand other facets of life – the philosopher David Hume (1711–76) had much more in common with Duns Scotus (1265–1308) than with anyone living now.

It may be modestly suggested that this collection represents a totally new way of looking at medieval Scotland. As one commentator asserts, everyday history is 'integral history': 'an endeavour that seeks to identify and integrate everything – all relevant material, social, political, and cultural data – that permits the fullest possible reconstruction of ordinary life experiences in all their varied complexity, as they are formed and transformed'.[3] Such a claim may appear rather pompous, perhaps, because the goal is, in reality, unattainable, though we would all agree that the attempt should be made, as completely and honestly as possible.

The focus of this study is on the folk of Scotland, that is, the total population. In Scots, 'folk' is used of the people, or humankind, collectively; it can also refer to the inhabitants of a place, to members of a person's family, kindred, clan, or community, as a collective for the servants, workers and employees on a farm, and as a term for human beings as opposed to animals or supernaturals. It is thus an all-embracing and non-exclusive term which incorporates all ranks and classes within society. In this, the present volume differs from others in this series because the record of the everyday in medieval Scotland is overwhelmingly aristocratic or elitist. If this book concentrated on 'the common people' as defined by the series editors, it would be very short indeed. As a consequence, the historiography of medieval Scotland has not been greatly concerned with everyday life. In fact, some might claim that the topic has been entirely ignored. This is understandable because tracing the history of Scottish everyday life is not an easy task.

The everyday in Scotland was traditionally taken to mean that which pertained to all weekdays but not the Sabbath.[4] Although the word is classless, because all, from peasants to princesses, share certain basic functions and experiences, it also came to mean 'common' which, in the sense of 'common to all', is useful but less so if it is indiscriminately applied to the 'common folk'. More helpful Scots words are 'commonty' or 'commonalty' which could be used in the sense of the whole community, the community at large, or for a section of it, as when John Knox addressed the 'Commonalty of Scotland' on the eve of the Reformation (see below). Even if some topics, such as warfare, childbirth or famine, did not figure, in everyone's everyday experience, they were part of everyday communication.

For some eighty years, if not longer, there has been considerable debate about the relationship between the two cultures, that of the learned, the 'Great Tradition', and that of the people at large, the so-called 'Little Tradition'. Clearly these labels were invented by self-regarding academics who mislabelled both, for the so-called Great Tradition is the less inclusive of the two while the other, which gives rise to irritatingly patronising descriptors such as the 'Little people', (even worse the 'Wee Folk'), is all-inclusive, irrespective of birth, rank or status.[5] It could be said that the everyday involves all that is common to most of humanity, embracing such matters as food, drink, weather,[6] shelter, gender, birth, children, love, courtship, marriage, death, religious belief, superstition and so on; the list is potentially endless. At the same time, one person's everyday is not necessarily another's. Women often enjoyed their own exclusive cultures as did men occupationally, such as soldiers, sailors, students, agriculturalists, miners, fishermen, hunters, or woodsmen, to mention but a few.[7] The survival of information about such cultures is often a matter of chance, scraps of evidence concerning the banal and the exotic, rather like the objects mislaid or thrown away to be rediscovered by later generations, as described by the late Jenny Shiels and Stuart Campbell in their fascinating discussion (Chapter 3) of medieval material life.

Not surprisingly, most surviving artefacts are post-medieval, as is the case with documentary evidence. Archaeology can teach us a great deal. It would be quite possible to write a more satisfying account of everyday life in Roman Scotland (assuming we are permitted to take in Hadrian's Wall) than it is to produce such a study for Robert Bruce's Scotland. In recent years, there has been much exciting archaeological investigation of the Scots, the Britons, the Picts, the Angles, the Vikings and of the early Church but, after much soul-searching, we decided to restrict the period covered by this volume, broadly from the end of the first millennium AD to 1600, with Fiona Watson alone expertly reviewing the earlier period in her overview of landscape and people (Chapter 1). Coverage of the period is not complete. Many gaps remain but we are grateful to all those who rallied to the cause in helping to chart pathways for what remains in Scotland seriously underinvestigated territory.

THE NATURE OF SCOTTISH SOCIETY

The various peoples of the early medieval period came together in the kingdom of Scotland which emerged at the end of the first millennium. The everyday experiences of one of these, the Vikings, a people unique in the coincidental survival of their literary and archaeological heritage, is the subject of Ted Cowan's contribution (Chapter 2). Scottish kings from Malcolm Canmore to Alexander III moulded a nation for which many fought to the death in the Wars of Independence, 'this poor little Scotland beyond which there is no dwelling place at all'.[8] Despite its supposed reputation for violence, the country remained predominantly peaceful throughout the twelfth and thirteenth centuries before the commencement of the seemingly interminable strife with England which continued into the sixteenth century. Renaissance ideas led to reformation of religion accompanied by new notions and theories about kingship and the constitution. In common with much of Europe, Scotland experienced prosperity in the thirteenth century which was reflected in the development of burghs, impressive castles and accomplished church architecture. A cooling climate wrought havoc with crops and diet during the fourteenth century when a series of plagues attacked livestock and the Black Death devastated the human population. Thereafter, as Richard Oram fully demonstrates (Chapter 9), ever-present fears about plague, disease and death led to changing attitudes towards religion. The late Audrey-Beth Fitch indicates (Chapter 12) that the cult of the Virgin Mary remained strong and vital on the very eve of Reformation, suggesting an increasing popular demand for spirituality.

Medieval Scottish history often seems to consist of a struggle between monarchy and aristocracy, the latter claiming to control the former, a principle enunciated in the Declaration of Arbroath in 1320.[9] For several centuries the people of Scotland are largely invisible. They gradually emerge in tracts about political thought, often regarded as a somewhat dull subject, but in reality concerned with analysis of the nature of society. Further information is to be gleaned from creative writers of the fifteenth and sixteenth centuries; for example, Robert Henryson (1425–1508) and William Dunbar (1460–1520). A tract known as *The Porteous of Nobility* (1508) reminded the aristocracy that their duty was to serve the king and defend the people, also making the point that birth alone did not confer nobility, which had to be earned. John Mair, the internationally regarded philosopher and historian, agreed: 'there is no true nobility but virtue and its acts'. Although critical of the nobility, he staunchly defended their political role. 'It is from the people, and most of all from the chief men and the nobility who act for the common people that kings have their institution.'[10] The view that the folk could not be trusted to act on their own was widespread in the Middle Ages but they could be said to have truly entered the Scottish political dialogue with the performance of Sir David Lindsay's *Ane Satyre of the Thrie Estaitis* in 1552, featuring the memorable champion of the Scottish commons, Jock o the Commonweal. He appears in other literary sources as Jock Uppaland, or John Upon-the-land, from a poem of *c.*1520 through to a tract of 1597, always in the same role. Jock's attitude to the commonalty can be favourably compared with that of Dame Scotia who figures in the excellent *Complaint of Scotland* (1550). The Dame urges her sons, the three estates, to abandon their arguments with one another because they are destroying the kingdom. She reserves a special venom for her oldest son, the commons, the predecessor of the two other estates, nobility and clergy, who originally shared his humble origins. The son protests, in language very like that of Jock Uppaland, that he suffers from cruel exploitation as he sinks into poverty. The Romans used to appoint a tribune of the people to defend their freedom and liberty against the nobles and the senate but there is no such official in Scotland. According to the Dame none of the common sort should enjoy liberty but should be daily daunted and held in subjection because their hearts are full of malice, ignorance and inconstancy. There is nothing more deplorable in the world than to listen to the judgement of the common people who lack sense and reason.[11]

Just how representative of sixteenth-century women Dame Scotia may be must be left to others to decide. There has been of late quite a spate of publication on Scottish women's history in the medieval period. It is still easy to agree with Robert Wedderburn, however, that we remain lexically impoverished when discussing gender. He observed that the Latin term *homo* signifies both man and woman; 'bot ther is nocht ane Scottis terme that signifies baytht man ande woman'.[12] Rebecca Boorsma tenaciously quarries the two great poems on the Wars of Independence to elicit information about the role of women in these struggles (Chapter 7). Lizanne Henderson explores changing ideas, predominantly male, about witchcraft in sixteenth-century Scotland (Chapter 10).

Following on from *The Complaynt* it remained for John Knox to take a rather more charitable view of the commons of Scotland. Having vainly besought crown and nobility to bring about perfect reformation, he was forced to appeal to the commonalty as a last resort:

> Albeit God hath put and ordained distinction and difference betwixt the king and subjects, betwixt rulers and common people, in the regiment and administration of civil policies, yet in the hope of the life to come he hath made all equal . . . to you it doth no less appertain, than to your king or princes, to provide that Christ Jesus be truly preached amongst you, seeing that without his true knowledge can neither of you attain to salvation. And this is the point wherein, I say, all men is equal.[13]

When *The First Book of Discipline* (1560–1) stated it 'appertaineth to the people and every several congregation to elect their own minister' the Scottish people had truly arrived, along with Reformation.[14] They had, of course, been present all along. Elizabeth Ewan, who has done much to pioneer Scottish women's studies, contributes an excellent study on everyday town life in all its richness and diversity (Chapter 5). Ted Cowan (Chapter 11) uses the twelfth-century *Life* of Glasgow's St Mungo as a lens to investigate the attitudes and assumptions of the city's inhabitants. Mark Hall (Chapter 6) tellingly explores the role of games in the everyday.

ETHNOLOGISTS AND GAELS

A group of distinguished sixteenth-century historians displayed a remarkable interest in sociology or even ethnology, paralleling the activities of Lindsay and Knox.[15] Nicola Royan expertly discusses the potential pitfalls in using their material (Chapter 8). As she rightly points out, the most influential of the group was probably Hector Boece, whose *Scotorum Historia* was published at Paris in 1527. A native of Dundee, Boece studied at Aberdeen and at Paris where he encountered the great Renaissance figure, Erasmus. On returning to Scotland he became principal of King's College, Aberdeen. In the introduction to his chauvinistic 'History' he wrote of how the world and everything in it was subject to change; nothing was permanent. He soon revealed two of his other prejudices. He deplored the alleged gluttonous capacity of the Scots for rich food and strong drink, overindulgence in which led to illness and early death. Also, like his fellow historians/ethnologists, he was a great admirer of the Gaels, who, in his view, preserved values which his contemporary fellow Scots – he had Lowlanders in mind – had lost.

Boece oversaw the translation into Scots of his History by John Bellenden, reflecting a current demand by some of the Scottish folk for a history in the vernacular. Indeed, according to fellow historian John Leslie, of whom more below, the translation was 'recited to the greit furderance and commoun weill of the hole natione'.[16] Bellenden's version opens with the arresting statement that the Scots desired 'to schew the ancient blude of thair lang begynnyng'.[17] He went on to discuss 'the new Maneris and the auld of Scottis', offering powerful arguments and evidence to demonstrate that the Scots were no longer the people they once were. Much of this was inspired by Boece's reading of classical literature in which savage peoples were often favourably compared with effete Romans. Like the latter, contemporary Scots were drowning in all manner of avarice and lust. Boece undoubtedly had an agenda in producing his polemical material, such that his reliability can legitimately be questioned. His, after all, is only one voice, which should be heard as one of antithesis. His positive statements about the attributes of the 'Auld Scots', still retained for the most part by sixteenth-century Gaels of whom he approves and flatters, were condemning of contemporary

Lowlanders. Everything he applauded in the everyday of Gaeldom was, by implication, absent in Lowland Scotland. For example, the heroic ancestors practised temperance, the fountain of all virtue. Moderation was paramount in sleep, eating and drinking. The populace consumed plain bread made from native cereals. Hunted meat was consumed half raw. 'Thair stomok wes nevir surfetly chargit' because they ate only two meals per day. They consumed whisky, 'nocht maid of costly spicis, bot of sic naturall herbis as grew in thair awin yardis'; otherwise they were content with ale or water. Warriors brought their own oatmeal on campaigns. In Boece's view all of these virtues and practices are now absent so far as Lowlanders are concerned, yet still present, at least to some degree, among the Gaels.

In the past everyone exercised regularly and strenuously. Baldness was unknown because no one wore hats or bonnets, and folk went barefoot except in the coldest weather. Clothes were made from home-grown materials. From their earliest years children were taught to sleep on the ground uncovered. Mothers nursed their own children. 'The wemen thocht thair barnis wer not tender nor kindly to thaim, bot thay war nurist als weill with the milk of thair breist, as thay wer nurist afore with the blude of the wambe.' Breastfeeding was to be preferred to wet-nursing, an observation most likely influenced by his friend Erasmus, the great humanist and theologian, who made the same argument in the *Colloquies*. It should be pointed out, however, that few women in the *Gàidhealtachd*, or anywhere else in Scotland, were in a position to engage a wet-nurse, a practice associated with the nobility and the better off. As Boece proceeds with his litany he appears to cast his net ever wider, perhaps straying from the reality of everyday Scotland.

For example, when he reaches the topic of warfare, not an everyday occurrence but a subject of perennial fascination, he seems to be no longer discussing either the Auld Scots or Auld Scotia. Injury to one affected all, compensation being sought in blood. All were prepared to die for their chiefs. Deserters were killed without trial, while scourging was reserved for those who failed to maintain, or to engage, their weapons. Unless they were pregnant, women fought alongside the men. The army on the march would slaughter the first beast it encountered, each warrior dipping his sword in its blood before tasting it.

There seems little or no corroboration for the claim that anyone affected with the 'falling evil', or madness, was castrated, 'that his infeckit blood shuld spreid na forthir', though there may be some truth in the assertion that women who were menstruating, or who suffered any blood disorder, were banished from male company. More doubtful is the allegation that, if they conceived in this condition, both they and their children were buried alive. Equally doubtful is Boece's offhand remark that persons perceived to be incurable gluttons or drunkards were permitted to eat or drink their fill for one last time before they were drowned. And so the list went on.

Figure I.1 *William Daniell's drawing of Alexander 'Crotach' MacLeod's tomb, St Clement's Church, Harris. MacLeod, who embodied all of the supposed virtues of the 'Auld Scottis', built the church in the late fifteenth to early sixteenth centuries. © National Library of Scotland. Licensor www.scran.ac.uk.*

Boece's admiration for Gaels extends to their language: When Lowlanders acquired the Saxon tongue they lost the old language, even though it was superior to that of other peoples. About the time of Malcolm Canmore (1058–93), owing to increased interaction with the English, the old ways became contaminated, so generating Scotland's present predicament.

> For quhare our eldaris had sobriete, we have ebriete and dronkinnes; quhare thay had plente with sufficence, we have immoderat cursis [courses] with superfluite; as he war maist noble and honest, that culd devore and swelly [swallow] maist; and be extreme diligence, serchis sa mony deligat [luxurious] coursis, that thay provoke the stomok to ressave mair than it may sufficiently degest.

People now consume twice as many meals so that fish, fowl and animals are endangered species because of voracious consumption. The current craze for foreign foods and wines, drugs and medicines has a debilitating impact upon health and well-being, the material displacing the spiritual, though paradoxically he thought the Scots were becoming more religious.

John Leslie, Bishop of Ross also studied at Paris, becoming a professor at

Aberdeen. His *Historie* was first written in Scots, translated into Latin and then retranslated back into Scots. He was heavily influenced by Boece. He, too, was fascinated by the awareness that the auld manners were precisely the same as those among the people who, in his own day, spoke Gaelic. Gaelic institutions, language, clothing and way of life had been preserved uncorrupted for over two thousand years. The Gaels sustained good health by consuming 'sik fude as they mycht have of the grunde', that is, home-grown produce. They had a preference for oat bread and they liked their meat running with blood because it was 'mair sappie' and more nourishing. Fish was also favoured but they ate only once a day, hating gluttony, thus preserving health and banishing illness so that most died of old age.

Their chiefs were the first to attack the enemy in order to inspire their followers who were unpaid. In the intervals between fighting they practised running, fencing, wrestling and hunting. Children were brought up in similar pursuits and were encouraged to note the example of men of renown in whose footsteps they might follow. The whole society was keen on revenge so that 'deidlie fade [feud] was nevir put in the buke of oblivione'; never forgotten, it was ever present.

The unshowy clothing of the Auld Scots was adapted for war; plaids were worn throughout the day and used as blankets at night. Leslie described their wool coats, designed with wide sleeves to facilitate the launching of missiles. 'Breickis [breeches] they had verie slichte, and indeed mair to hyd thair memberis than for ony pompe or pryd.' Women also wore decent, modest clothing. The chiefs would put on their best clothes to visit court but would revert to the country manner of dress as soon as they returned home. Most of them remained true to the Catholic faith. On the downside the Highlanders were vehemently committed to sedition and strife, despising farming and crafts, because all wished to be thought noble, or bold men of war; 'of this cumis thair pryd and hichtiness, and bosting of thair nobilitie; quhen sum writeris in thame noted sik vices thay spak no altogither raschlie'.

Leslie protested that he had described the manners of his countrymen at some length because of the unusual insolence of certain persons who had maliciously tried to disparage 'what was to our praise'. Such criticism blackened the character of all Scots. His point seems to be that people differ from one another and one cannot be made to stand for all. There would be those in other parts of the country who were guilty of the alleged sins of the Gaels but malicious generalisation was not helpful. He supplied an example of what he meant in a section of his *Historie* which discussed the Borders. Some writers had stated that the Scots ate human flesh. Leslie asserted that such a practice could not be attributed to all Scots but only to those of Annandale! Furthermore he appears to suggest that any lads of Annan Water returning home from defeat in battle were likely to be killed by their stout wives. 'Bot the alde crueltie of a fewe sulde nocht be ascrivet to the hail Scottis natione.'[18] The good bishop was thus aware of the dangers of stereotyping.

George Buchanan was a native of Killearn and a Gaelic speaker, the foremost Scottish intellect of his generation.[19] His *Rerum Scoticarum Historia* was printed in 1582, the year of his death, though parts of it had previously circulated in manuscript. Buchanan made many of the same observations about the Gaels as Boece and Leslie. In the past they had favoured plaids of bright variegated colours but in his own day they favoured dark brown, 'imitating nearly the leaves of the heather, that when lying upon the heath in the day, they may not be discovered by the appearance of their clothes'.[20] He described how the Highlanders would still bed down in their plaids to sleep in snow or the severest storms. At home in their houses they also lay on the ground, on ferns or heather. He, too, discussed their weapons but highlighted their fondness for music, for harps strung with brass or catgut, adorned with silver and gems, or crystals. 'Their songs are not inelegant, and in general, celebrate the praises of brave men, their bards seldom choosing any other subject.'[21] All of these writers were fascinated by 'manners', which have normally been considered a concern of Enlightenment thinkers. Biased though they may be, they provide much valuable information about the everyday.

THE EVERYDAY OF ROMANCE

We turn now to some examples of how it may be possible to recover snippets of everyday life from disparate sources. Throughout medieval Christendom the everyday was more similar than different, in part because the Church imposed a kind of monolithic culture upon Europe. Of course, there might be variations from one country to another, particularly concerning politics and polity, the conflict between Crown and papacy, or the pope's recognition of Scotland's special status as a 'daughter of the see of Rome', but such things mattered little at a grass-roots level. Church law was likewise pretty uniform; much of that governing the Scottish Church was identical to, or indeed, copied from England and repeated over the centuries. While it is true that the legislation tells us more about the Church's obsessions concerning the possible sins and misdemeanours of its lay flock, the folk were also subjected to a steady flow of information and diktats intent upon cultivating innate assumptions and truths. For example the Form of Excommunication was to be 'published and fulminated four times a year', a kind of blanket inclusion cataloguing all the sins that people should avoid. Thus, the ban included those 'schismatics and infamous persons' who schemed against their bishops, who bore false witness in cases of matrimony, disturbers of the king's peace, thieves, withholders of tithes, usurers, and witches and their clients.

Clerics were to wear becoming attire, avoiding clothes with coloured stripes, or which were immodestly short. Priests were forbidden to cohabit with their mistresses or to provide houses for them and any children they might have. They must not alienate their tithes or indulge in business.

Sanctuary was refused to the *depopulatores agrorum*, those who laid waste lands by night, and highway robbers. Tithes (*Scottice* teinds), the tenths of individual incomes claimed by the Church, were to be scrupulously levied on everything, namely all produce which was renewed annually, such as corn, hay, fish, wool, milk, cheese, butter, peats, coppiced wood, fruit, hunting and hawking; even stillborn calves, complete with skin and entrails, were to be teinded. Withholding of tithes was considered extremely serious. Singing and dancing at funerals was banned, 'since it does not become us to laugh at the weeping of others, but in a case of the kind rather to grieve as they do'. Sports and wrestling were outlawed in churches and churchyards. Women were to attend church at the beginning of their ninth month of pregnancy for confession and sacrament but all women were specifically forbidden to enter the choir in time of mass.

Priests who had relationships with females in their congregations were to be severely dealt with. Those in good standing should have tidy haircuts and decent clothing. They should avoid taverns or mixing with 'open tipplers', as well as dicing and other games when travelling. At St Andrews, churchyards were to be fully enclosed all the way round, 'so that no access be open to unclean and brutish beasts, for sacred places should be kept clean'. As late as 1549 it was decreed that priests should shave off beards and wear the tonsure in order to distinguish them from laymen.[22]

The Aberdeen statutes of the thirteenth century permitted laymen to baptise children in extremity, that is, when no priest was present. The same privilege was sometimes extended to midwives because, in the warped view of churchmen, unbaptised children were damned. They were, however, to use 'the Roman or even the English tongue'. The learned editor of the *Statutes* observes that, because other languages, such as Gaelic, Scots or Norse, were not specified, many people were thus excluded.[23]

One such group might have been the Gaelic-speakers of Galloway, the province which is the setting, in part, of the romance, *Fergus of Galloway*, composed about 1200. It might seem an unlikely source of information about the everyday, concerned as it is with its eponym, a historical, but heavily fictionalised lord of Galloway who died in 1161 and who, reincarnated by the poet as a chivalric anti-hero, yearns for a place at the court of King Arthur. There are good reasons for identifying the romance's author, Guillaume Le Clerc, with William Malveisin who was successively Archdeacon of Lothian, Bishop of Glasgow and Bishop of St Andrews. Authorial intent seems to have been comedic.[24] Fergus is depicted as a second Perceval, a brash and rustic simpleton from a remote part of the world, Galloway, populated by barbarians like himself. In common with much literature *Fergus* is concerned with what is *not* everyday or common. It delights in rendering an historical figure unhistorical, in enchanting an otherwise recognisable Scottish landscape and in depicting the marvellous, the fantastical and what is known in Scots as the 'eldritch', the weird or other-worldly. Information

Figure I.2 *Grave slab depicting priest in Eucharistic vestments. Kilmory Knap, Argyll, fourteenth to fifteenth centuries. This individual is suitably clad in 'becoming attire'.*
© *Royal Commission on the Ancient and Historical Monuments of Scotland. Licensor* *www.scran.ac.uk.*

about the everyday is to be discerned in what falls through the cracks in the text, in the unremarkable, in what is taken for granted.

The romance begins and ends, auspiciously, on the Feast of St John the Baptist, 24 June and Midsummer's Day, which remained an important Scottish popular festival until the nineteenth century.[25] The story opens at Arthur's court in Wales but the king soon announces that he wishes to hunt a white stag in a forest near Carlisle. There follows an exhilarating wild hunt as the stag leads his pursuers all over the south of Scotland through the Borders to Jedburgh, the Lammermuirs, the Forest of Glasgow and Ayr, 'the home of fair women of whom none are more beautiful in all the world', eventually fetching up in Galloway. There is little in the account of the hunt, except the distance, that those in aristocratic circles would have found unusual. On rising in the morning, the king washes his hands, mouth and eyes. It has long been fashionable to regard the Middle Ages as dirty, even filthy,[26] but there is fairly frequent reference to personal toilet.

In Galloway the entourage comes upon a motte and bailey castle owned by a wealthy peasant named Somerled, the father of three sons, two of whom are shepherding in the mountains while the eldest is ploughing, 'dressed in a short, shaggy jerkin roughly made from lambskins, a pair of rawhide shoes on his feet. Such was the work they were engaged in every day.'[27] He carried a club for such was the Galloway custom when working.[28] There and then he decides he wants to join Arthur and the knights of the Round Table. Unhitching the horses and oxen – which suggests a joint draught team – he picks up the ploughshare and coulter (the plough irons)[29] – and runs with them to the castle, sweating so profusely as almost to collapse. When the father is informed of his son's court fascination, he attacks him with a stick, to be physically restrained by the mother. There follows a neat little vignette of intra-familial exchanges. Ranting in peasant fashion, Somerled cries 'son of a whore', where did he get such ideas? His job is in the fields. The wife interjects that he has no reason to accuse her of whoredom. Furthermore their son's courtly inclinations are probably due to the many knights in his ancestry – on *her* side of the family! Somerled relents, ordering armour and arms, somewhat rusted with age, to be handed over to his son. The iron leggings are put on over white linen breeches but he wears no other hose. He is provided with a fine plump horse, one of the Galloway breed noted for their ability to move more swiftly over boggy ground than any man could travel on foot. There is much humorous detail about his antiquated weapons but the time comes to depart, his mother kissing him more than a hundred times, rightly fearful that she will never see him again.

Arriving in Carlisle, Fergus announces that he has come to join the Round Table, so eliciting a venomously sarcastic response from Kay who is subsequently reprimanded by the ever-sympathetic Gawain. Having been accepted, and feeling like Roland himself, Fergus goes off in search of

Figure I.3 *Buittle church, thirteenth to fourteenth centuries, in Galloway, dedicated to St Colman, was one of the largest parish churches in medieval Scotland. © John R. Hume. Licensor www.scran.ac.uk.*

lodgings in a persistent drizzle that penetrates his armour and soaks him to
the skin. He receives shelter from a damsel, daughter of the king's chamberlain, who explains that, if her father disapproves, he must leave. Fergus's face
is bruised from the unaccustomed wearing of a helmet; otherwise he is still
dressed in his ploughing gear. Both he and his hostess wash before and after
dining. When the chamberlain arrives, he welcomes his guest and arranges
for him to be dubbed knight with all modern chivalric accoutrements.
Fergus is given a richly equipped single bed in an ornately painted chamber.
In the morning he is apparelled in splendid clothes, 'complete with hose and
shoes laced on' in place of his sockless hide shoes.

It is noteworthy that the chamberlain asks Fergus whether he has been
given lodging or whether 'he has been foolish enough to appropriate quarters and a lodging'. The latter is possibly a reference to the much resented
convention known as *surdit de sergeants* which gave the sergeants or officials,
representing the lords and barons of the area, the right to billet themselves
and their men on local householders. They could also accuse individuals
of crimes and, in some cases, they had powers to administer capital punishment. The practice was outlawed by Alexander III but it survived in
Galloway where a document of 1300 declared that everyone living in the
Glenkens, in the Stewartry of Kirkcudbright, was freed from the burden. A
few years later the 'Community of Galloway', a very interesting descriptor,
felt the need to petition for the end of the pernicious practice which had supposedly been banned everywhere in Scotland a generation earlier. It would
appear to have been as deeply unpopular in 1200 as it was a hundred years
later.[30]

Leaving Carlisle he heads for the castle of Liddel where he meets Galiene
who would turn out to be the love of his life. The romances are imbued
with love and stacked with lovers but this lady has no equal; she is the very
epitome of feminine beauty, with her laughing eyes, smallish brows and a
lily-pale complexion with a flush of crimson:

> She had a shapely mouth as pretty as if adorned with roses. Her teeth, small and
> completely even, were whiter than ivory or crystal. Her shoulders were a trifle
> broad, her arms long, her hands tiny but not immoderately so; for Nature's atten-
> tion to her formation had been so close that she made not the slightest error in it.
> She had small breasts just like two little apples, and her flanks were graceful and
> shapely . . . [she was] wise as well as fair.

Such a vision of beauty was probably fairly universal irrespective of class or
daily reality. Fergus, 'handsome in body and flanks, large in the shoulder and
with fine hands', with long arms and massive fists, has had little training when
it comes to courting but he need not worry for she is smitten. Cupid, having
an interest in modern gadgetry, fires a bolt from his crossbow (one with a
windlass no less) and hits his target. Several pages describe her anguish; she
sobs, she yawns, tosses and turns, weeps, laughs, and contradicts herself.

She determines to confront the object of her desire though she is ashamed to be 'so brazen as to tell him what she has in mind'. So it is that she visits the room wherein Fergus is fast sleep, 'without any thought of her; nor does he know what love is, never having experienced its pain'. Shedding hot tears, she lifts his blanket and, kneeling, places her hand on his chest. Fergus awakes only to reject her! Further bouts of consternation follow. Fergus must complete his quest ahead of surrendering to love; his task completed, he too is penetrated by Cupid's bolt. Love conquers him, accuses him, blames him and burns him with its spark. He convinces himself that a fool such as he who 'flings underfoot what he can hold in his hands' does not deserve to live among normal people. 'I'm stupid to dabble in love. My father never in all his living days indulged in that sort of thing!' The implication is that only those with knightly sensitivities or of a certain rank are capable of experiencing love; his father, after all is a peasant, albeit a wealthy one. Only physical hunger relieves his obsession with Galiene. Eventually he is a starving wanderer, never eating bread or cooked meat, consuming raw game when he feels the urge, thin faced, unshaven and unshorn, clad in rags, skinny and emaciated. Truly a parlous state but one not entirely unknown to many of the poorer commons in the twelfth and thirteenth centuries. But Fergus is not as other men. He has many knightly adventures, conquering the Black Knight, acquiring a shining shield, defeating an evil king in combat and participating in a tournament, all in a recognisable Scottish landscape. Most importantly of all he wins the love of his life, the smitten, assertive Galiene, a beauty with a mind of her own and certainly possessed of more gumption than Fergus. At their wedding, clouds of smoke rise from the kitchens in preparation for the feast. Love has conquered all and the pair presumably lives happily ever after.

One who had a well-honed taste for romances was Scotland's hero king. After the battle of Dail Righ near Tyndrum in 1306, Robert Bruce retreated southwards across Loch Lomond to the friendly shelter of the Lennox before taking to the Clyde and sailing to Rathlin Island off the Irish coast, where he probably wintered. Ironically, John Barbour, in his great poem *The Bruce* depicts the periods between defeats as almost idyllic, perhaps an attempt to salvage something of the aristocratic everyday, however improbable. Douglas organised deer hunts and the provision of 'engines' to catch fish, everything from salmon to minnows. Bruce found time to encourage his troops with tales of Roman valour, citing 'ancient stories of men who were placed in various difficult circumstances, whom fortune opposed strongly, but who in the end won through'. Equally surreal was the female contingent vacationing in the Highlands before being sent off for safe keeping to Kildrummy Castle where they faced the ineluctable actuality of subsequent capture. Deadly serious was their later barbarous incarceration in cages. Before embarking upon Loch Lomond, Bruce read his followers the romance of *Fierabras*.[31]

CALENDAR CUSTOMS

As previously mentioned, the *Romance of Fergus* makes much of Midsummer which conveniently falls into the Church calendar, rendering the festival a fascinating blend of Christian and non-Christian practice. Modern scholarship often seems to suggest that the folk had their own distinct calendar customs which the Church did not always recognise though, in fact, the two did quite often intersect because Christians had a long history of deliberately hijacking pre-existing celebrations. The fifteenth-century Church statutes list a total of forty-four days (Sundays not included) which 'ought to be observed by resting from servile work by clergy and people'.[32] In addition, there were many other fast days. The question arises of how the populace responded to the clause in the reformers' *First Book of Discipline* which stated that all saints' and holy days 'such as had been invented by the papists' were to be 'utterly abolished' from the realm.[33] Few, presumably, were very happy about the proposed removal of so many holidays at the stroke of a pen. It was asserted that Good Friday was the day on which all of the world's salvation is founded, 'without which all other festivals would be in vain'.[34] It has been said that, in medieval times, people spent most of their time discussing festivals that had recently taken place while looking forward to those yet to come but, since there were so many in the calendar, there has to be some doubt about this, especially if the non-Christian dates are added. The big festivals were Yule and Easter. *Orkneyinga Saga*, for example, tends to mark the years with reference to Christmas feasts though it mentions numerous other Christian dates as well. We have several excellent studies of calendar customs but these tend to be atemporal and chronologically unrooted. It is well known that festivals, like flowers, come and go whereas certain authorities seem to suggest that, if we know of a festival existing in 1750 and 2010, then celebration must have been continuous or, less forgivably, must have been around since time immemorial, linked in some cases to the stone monuments of the Neolithic era. Even in a small nation like Scotland, all festivals were not observed in all parts of the country. Some were quite localised and others, such as the Rood Fair, the festival of the cross, were celebrated on completely different dates in Dumfries and in Aberdeen. To confuse matters further, practices associated with one festival were sometimes transferred to another. To take just one example: Christmas guising was shifted to Halloween as were certain other traditions. Folk believed that the future was as knowable as the past.[35] Prophecy and prognostication were popularly practised and believed in, so much so that festivals were used as an excuse for that purpose so that earlier ideas that one festival was better than another for certain predictions – about such topics as marriage or life expectancy – became blurred and confused.

Yule and Midsummer were dictated by the sun, following very soon after their respective solstices, so they were probably celebrated, even unconsciously, from earliest times. Fire remained an important part of the festivities. William Wallace was said to have set Scotland alight from Solway to Pentland Firth, a spectacle that allegedly was almost replicated annually on 24 June when hilltop, Midsummer fires were lit throughout the length and breadth of the country, though weather must sometimes have placed a literal damper upon some of these events. The other big festivals were Candlemas (1 February) and Michaelmas (29 September), the first devoted to St Bride, the other to St Michael. It was a good idea, though, to select a propitious date for a special event because some were better than others for battles, weddings or the most mundane of occasions.

BORDER REALITIES AND BALLAD MENTALITIES

It used to be a widely held view that the border ballads were simply a debased form of medieval romance[36] but they represent an important literary genre in their own right, one which has long been thought to preserve something of the voices and attitudes of the tenacious inhabitants of the Scottish Border country.

Perhaps one of the most interesting features of the Border past concerns the Debatable Lands of the West March, known as *Terra Contentiosa* because they were claimed by Scotland and by England and ruled by neither. The inhabitants were a law unto themselves. They refused to recognise the legislation of either country while allegedly attracting others of criminal disposition who sought refuge from order. The most memorable description of Borderers at this time was of 'a lawless people, that will be Scottish when they will, and English at their leisure'. Earlier they had been encouraged to act as a kind of buffer between England and Scotland but, by the sixteenth century, they were increasingly taking matters into their own hands. It is true that some of the worst border atrocities took place in this region but, on the other hand, the Borderers shared grazing rights, they traded with each other, they played sports together and attended feasts. Scots married English people and vice versa even though such was a capital offence. Borderers on both sides sometimes banded together against both kingdoms or warned one another of incursions by the Wardens of the Marches. They occasionally conspired to free one another from such prisons as Carlisle Castle. The Grahams were originally Scottish, becoming English by adoption, yet they still sometimes called upon the Earl of Montrose, as head of their name, to intervene on their behalf. Borderers were reluctant to die in great battles such as Flodden or Solway Moss. They created their own identity and culture and, though their society was undeniably bloody and violent, it was subject to a complex system of checks and balances.[37]

So desperate had the situation become in the eyes of the authorities that, in 1551, the Wardens of both countries issued a proclamation which uncompromisingly stated that 'all Englishmen and Scottishmen are and shall be free to rob, burn, spoil, slay, murder and destroy all and every such person or persons, their bodies, buildings, goods and cattle as do remain upon any part of the said Debatable land, without any redress to be made for the same'.[38] This was, of course, outrageous, if interesting as an early development of what would become British colonial and imperial policy. But what has been missed by the commentators is that the Debatable Land, which could be regarded as a microcosm of the Borders in general, in effect acted as a human frontier as opposed to a geographical or physical one, a system that arguably would have operated perfectly well but for the state interference of Scotland and England.

Something is to be learned about the everyday attitudes and concerns of Borderers from their surviving ballads, originally existing in the oral medium but written down (or as some would argue written from scratch) from the seventeenth century onwards. In seeking to discover and to ascertain the assumptions of a past age, however, we must jettison some of our own. For many of today's readers or listeners – for the ballads were, and are, meant to be sung – ballads are mainly about reiving and cross-border disputes. Scrutiny of what is now regarded as the standard collection of ballads, however,[39] indicates that there are almost twice as many Robin Hood ballads as there are Riding or Feuding ballads.[40] About one-third of the corpus may be said to be centrally concerned with women who, of course, are not entirely absent from other examples. Many of these show women triumphant, outwitting their male protagonists or unnatural creatures. Yet, victorious or otherwise, women and men inhabited a cruel and unforgiving world in which violence was ever present.

When Percy fought Douglas at the battle of Otterburn 'They swakked their swords till sair they swat, / And the blood ran them between.' In the brutal ballad, *Edom o' Gordon*, the lady of the castle requests that the attacking captain allow her son to go free. He invites her to lower the boy over the wall only to reveal his hideous treachery: 'Wyth sped, before the rest, / He cut his tonge out of his head, / His hart out of his brest'. Wrapping them in a cloth he tosses them back to the distraught mother who, with her other children, was burned to death when the castle was subsequently torched. In another historical burning, *The Fire of Frendraught*, Rothiemay is trapped as melting lead from the window is pouring over his head and his feet are on fire.

> My eyes are seething in my head,
> My flesh roasting also,
> My bowels are boiling with my blood;
> Is not that a woeful woe?

In the song, *Jamie Telfer of the Fair Dodhead*, we are given the gratuitous, and exact, information that, while fighting, a man was shot through his left testicle.

> The Captain was shot through the head,
> And also through the left ba-stane;
> Tho he had lived this hundred years,
> He'd never been looed by woman again.

In both examples, the stunningly superfluous observations in the last lines
are absolutely typical of the folk tradition which seldom hesitates to state the
obvious. The ballads are also much concerned with sex and sexual relations,
as well as with affective relationships or the absence thereof. Premarital sex
occurs so frequently as to suggest that sex precedes courtship rather than the
reverse, the women usually proving complicit. Consummation comes before
introductions:

> O syne ye've got your will o me,
> Your will o me ye've taen,
> Tis all I ask o you, kind sir,
> Is to tell to me your name.

Pregnancy often results. In one case the mother was eleven years old, one
year younger than the permitted marriage age.[41] Such premarital adventures,
however common, were not widely approved and they frequently led to
tragedy. Girls' fathers and brothers often objected – occasionally with incestuous overtones. *The Douglas Tragedy* preserves a neat example of Scottish
non-sentimentality. The doomed lovers are buried at St Mary's churchyard,
roses entwining above their graves to symbolise their love. But the Black
Douglas was having none of it. He rode by, pulled up the roses and flung them
in St Mary's Loch. Another irate father kills Clerk Saunders while the two
lovers sleep together, the woman mistaking her man's blood for his sweat.

It has been unconvincingly suggested that an absence of affective relationships between parents and children in this period may have driven the latter
towards incest.[42] Only some half-dozen ballads are concerned with this sad
topic. It is difficult to know whether we are supposed to respond to the
following with disgust or laughter. 'It is nae wonder', said Brown Robyn,

> Altho I dinna thrive,
> For wi my mother I had twa bairns,
> And wi my sister five.

It is just possible that the ballad was responding satirically to ecclesiastical
obsessions about incest which the populace at large did not share. In his
contribution to this volume David Sellar (Chapter 4) addresses the subject
of the forbidden degrees in his illuminating contribution on the family, an
institution curiously ignored in Scottish historiography.

Rape is a rare topic but *Prince Heathen* offers a clear example:

> He's taen her in his arms twa,
> Laid her between him and the wa,

An ere he let her free again,
Her maidenhead frae her he's taen.

The vile deed was intended all along in *Willie's Lyke-Wake* in which the eponym arranged his own wake to entice his victim. When she appeared he 'took her by the waist sae neat and sae sma / And threw her atween him and the wa', recalling the terminology of *Prince Heathen*. Another lass conceals her lover at the side of the bed against the wall to protect him from her vengeful father. *Captain Wedderburn's Courtship* reiterates the theme that the captain wishes to bed his lady 'neist the wa', a position which she steadfastly resists even after marriage. It is obvious that the outside edge of the bed was the woman's natural position; otherwise she felt constrained and dominated.

Elopement with Gypsy laddies could bring bliss or disaster depending presumably on whether or not the balladeers favoured the Romanies or 'Lords of Little Egypt' who maintained a significant presence in the Scottish Borders and Galloway from the sixteenth century onwards. *The Gypsy Laddie* tells of a lady who went off with the raggle-taggle Gypsies under a spell to be cruelly abused, inverting the romance of most Gypsy ballads. Abduction often equated with elopement in a society which frowned upon freedom of action especially in opposition to parental wishes. Almost the sole example of wife beating in the ballads resulted from a domestic dispute involving Lord and Lady Wariston. This was based on a well-documented historical episode of 1600 when the wife was executed following her murder of the husband.[43]

Lusty, confident, clever women were no strangers to medieval literature. One woman, spurned by her supposed beau after a love-making session when he tells her that he will not marry her against the wishes of his family, retorts 'If I binna gude eneugh for yer wife, / I'm our-gude for yer loun' [if I'm not good enough to be your wife, I'm too good to be your mistress]. Another tells the 'coof' who has jilted her that just as he turns to other women so will she look to other men, eventually haunting him into submission. One of the most bold and sexy of all ballad women appears in *Tam Lin*. Janet actively seeks out Tam, intrigued as she is by his wicked and other-worldly reputation. Finding herself pregnant, she opts to become a single mother rather than be married off to some dupe or other in her father's retinue. She briefly considers abortion because of her lover's supposed fairy origins but, on learning that he is a mortal, abducted like Thomas the Rhymer, by the fairy queen, she determines to rescue him on Halloween. Clinging to him while he undergoes several shape-shiftings, she triumphs, a sturdy heroine, as we may think, admired by women and men alike.

It may be that the ballads as much represent the world view of women as they do of men. While it is anachronistic to attempt to determine 'female topics', it is hard to believe that men were the source of information on such subjects as childbirth or midwifery, both of which were clearly reserved female issues. Furthermore, the near absence of themes such as witchcraft, the witch-hunts, rape and wife beating, might suggest that the ballads represent woman's idealised view of her world with much of the pain expunged. As one of us has suggested, the ballad genre provides an entire cosmos with its own inherent system of checks and balances. Intriguingly the ballad evidence presents an almost mirror image of the conventional view of the submissive female enduring the patriarchal system. Thus, the popular tradition completely contradicts the 'official' view, the documented evidence of Church and state, as well as those of contemporary historians and commentators.

There were still references to the Debatable Land as late as 1604. By that time, the Scottish king was king of England, suffering the ignominy of a border that ran straight through the middle of his domain. He therefore mounted a campaign of state terror to take out the traditional societies of his Scottish kingdom – the Borders, the Highlands and Islands and Orkney and Shetland. Families like the Grahams were transported to Ireland and, when they returned home, to Germany. Finally in desperation they were transported to America or the Caribbean and certain early death. It was at this period that most of the Big Border Ballads came into being, memorials to a society that was finally doomed. The rhetoric of government detected little difference between the 'clannit folk', or the clans, of the Highlands and the Lowlands. Just as troublesome Gaels harboured 'infamous bykes of lawless limmers' so the Borderers consisted of bangsters and gangsters, the latter term first used in this context.[44] It is ironic that James VI, who saw himself as the bearer of an imperial crown, should have begun his English reign by launching vicious attacks on the traditional societies of his native kingdom.[45] So far as he was concerned, the everyday assumptions of his subjects, so often encouraged in the past by the crown, were now anathema to the point that he waged war on his own people. It is remarkable that, in the case of families such as the Armstrongs, Maxwells and Johnstones, or such clans as the MacGregors and the MacDonalds, crown policy was genocide in all but name, and the targets cultural as well as political and social.

This volume deals with a somewhat intractable subject. All of the contributors would like to have expanded on their topics but were limited by time and scarcity of evidence. At the very least they hope to have indicated some possible avenues of future enquiry because, without some understanding of how folk reacted to the everyday, we can have little hope of comprehending how history had an impact upon the folk themselves.

Notes

1 For example, the very influential series written for children but frequently consulted by adults, Marjorie and C. H. B. Quennell, *A History of Everyday Things in England*, 4 vols (London, 1918–34). For a much profounder example see Christopher Dyer, *Everyday Life in Medieval England* (London and New York,

2000) though the same author's *Making a Living in the Middle Ages: The People of Britain 850–1520* (London, 2003) has little discussion of Scotland despite the promise of its title.

2   Fernand Braudel, *Civilization and Capitalism 15th–18th Century*, vol. I, *The Structures of Everyday Life: The Limits of the Possible* (New York, 1981), pp. 28–9.

3   B. S. Gregory, 'Review Essay: Is small beautiful? Microhistory and the History of Everyday Life', *History and Theory* 38 (1999), p. 102.

4   *Scottish National Dictionary*, loc. cit.

5   Lizanne Henderson and Edward J. Cowan, *Scottish Fairy Belief: A History* (Edinburgh, [2001] 2007), p. 10, discussing Robert Redfield, *Peasant Society and Culture* (Chicago, 1956), Peter Burke, *Popular Culture in Early Modern Europe* (New York, 1978) and Carlo Ginzburg, *The Cheese and the Worms: The Cosmos of a Sixteenth-Century Miller* (Harmondsworth, [1976] 1982).

6   See now Alastair Dawson, *So Foul and Fair a Day: A History of Scotland's Weather and Climate* (Edinburgh, 2009).

7   For some exploration of this theme see Edward J. Cowan and Mike Paterson, *Folk in Print: Scotland's Chapbook Heritage 1750–1850* (Edinburgh, 2007), *passim*.

8   Edward J. Cowan, *'For Freedom Alone': The Declaration of Arbroath 1320* (Edinburgh, [2003] 2008), p. 148.

9   Cowan, *For Freedom Alone, passim*.

10 John Major, *A History of Greater Britain*, A. Constable (ed. and trans.), (Edinburgh, 1892), p. 215.

11 *The Complaynt of Scotland (c.1550) by Mr Robert Wedderburn*, Intro. A. M. Stewart (Edinburgh, 1979), pp. 98–110.

12 *Complaynt*, p. 13.

13 D. Laing (ed.), *The Works of John Knox*, 6 vols (Edinburgh, 1895), vol. 4, pp. 528–9.

14 Edward J. Cowan, 'Scotching the Beggars: John the Commonweal and Scottish History', in Alexander Murdoch (ed.), *The Scottish Nation Identity and History. Essays in Honour of William Ferguson* (Edinburgh, 2007), pp. 1–17.

15 For full documentation of this section see Edward J. Cowan, 'The Discovery of the Gàidealtachd in Sixteenth Century Scotland', in *Transactions of the Gaelic Society of Inverness* lx (1997–8, 2000), pp. 259–84.

16 John Leslie, Bishop of Ross, *The Historie of Scotland*, E. G. Cody (ed.), 2 vols (Edinburgh, 1888), vol. 2, p. 223 note.

17 John Bellenden, *The Chronicles of Scotland Compiled by Hector Boece Translated into Scots by John Bellenden*, R. W. Chambers, Edith C. Batho and H. Winifred Husbands (eds), 2 vols (Edinburgh, 1938, 1941), vol. 1, p. 21.

18 Leslie, *Historie*, vol. 1, pp. 89–100. Boece makes the same point, see *Works of John Bellenden*, vol. 1, p. xxvii.

19 I. D. McFarlane, *Buchanan* (London, 1981), John Durkan, *Bibliography of George Buchanan* (Glasgow, 1994).

20 James Aikman, *The History of Scotland Translated from the Latin of George Buchanan with notes and a continuation to the Union in the Reign of Queen Anne*, 4 vols (Glasgow, 1827), vol. I, p. 40.

21 Aikman, *History of Scotland*, vol. I, p. 41.
22 David Patrick, *Statutes of the Scottish Church 1225–1559* (Edinburgh, 1907), pp. 3–93.
23 Patrick, *Statutes*, p. 30 note.
24 Tony Hunt, 'The *Roman de Fergus*: Parody or Pastiche?', in Rhiannon Purdie and Nicola Royan (eds), *The Scots and Medieval Arthurian Legend, Arthurian Studies* lxi (Cambridge, 2005), pp. 55–69.
25 M. Macleod Banks, *British Calendar Customs Scotland*, vol. III, June to December *Christmas The Yules, Publications of the Folk-Lore Society* (London and Glasgow, 1941), pp. 15–28.
26 For example, John Warrack, *Domestic Life in Scotland, 1488–1688 A Sketch of the Development of Furniture and Household Usage*, Rhind Lectures in Archaeology, 1919–20 (London, 1920), p. v.
27 Guillaume le Clerc, *Fergus of Galloway: Knight of King Arthur*, D. D. R. Owen, trans. with intro. and notes (London, 1991), p. 6.
28 There is no reason to think that Scots were any less contemptuous of the peasantry than any other nation but, given the scurrilous nature of the language normally used to describe them, Fergus got off lightly. Paul Freedman, *Images of the Medieval Peasant* (Stanford, 1999), pp. 133–73.
29 This may be the earliest Scottish written description of a plough. On ploughs see Alexander Fenton, *Scottish Country Life* (Edinburgh, 1976), pp. 27–49, especially 29–31.
30 Daphne Brooke, 'The Glenkens 1275–1456 Snapshots of a Medieval Countryside', in *Transactions of the Dumfriesshire and Galloway Natural History and Antiquarian Society* lix (1984), p. 44.
31 John Barbour, *The Bruce*, A. A. M. Duncan (ed.) (Edinburgh, 1997), pp. 108, 132.
32 Patrick, *Statutes*, 78.
33 *John Knox's History of the Reformation in Scotland*, ed. William Croft Dickinson, 2 vols (Edinburgh, 1949), p. 281.
34 Patrick, *Statutes*, pp. 78–9.
35 Edward J. Cowan, 'The Discovery of the Future: Prophecy and Second Sight in Scottish History', in Lizanne Henderson (ed.), *Fantastical Imaginations: The Supernatural in Scottish History and Culture* (Edinburgh, 2009), pp. 1–28.
36 Edward J. Cowan, 'The Hunting of the Ballad', in Edward J. Cowan (ed.), *The Ballad in Scottish History* (East Linton, 2000), p. 4.
37 On Border history see Rev. George Ridpath, *The Border History of England and Scotland Deduced From The Earliest Times to The Union of The Two Crowns* (1848) (Edinburgh, 1979); John Graham, *Condition of the Border at the Union Destruction of the Graham Clan* (Glasgow, 1905); D. L. W. Tough, *The Last Years of a Frontier. A History of the Borders during the reign of Elizabeth I* (Oxford, 1928); Thomas I. Rae, *The Administration of the Scottish Frontier 1513–1603* (Edinburgh, 1966); George MacDonald Fraser, *The Steel Bonnets: The Story of the Anglo-Scottish Reivers* (London, 1974).
38 James Logan Mack, *The Border Line From The Solway Firth to the North Sea Along The Marches of Scotland and England* (Edinburgh, 1924), p. 87.

39 F. J. Child (ed.), *English and Scottish Popular Ballads*, 5 vols (Boston and London, 1882–98). Ballad references in the text are to this edition.

40 Edward J. Cowan, 'Sex and Violence in the Scottish ballads', in Cowan, *Ballad in Scottish History*, p. 95. See this article for full documentation of this part of the present chapter. It must be stressed that the figures quoted above are somewhat imprecise owing to problems of classification. See Natascha Wurzbach and Simone M. Salz, *Motif Index of the Child Corpus: The English and Scottish Popular Ballad* (Berlin, 1995).

41 Monsignor John C. Barry (ed.), *William Hay's Lectures On Marriage* (Edinburgh, 1967), p. 111. This work provides much corroboration of ballad content.

42 Lawrence Stone, *Family, Sex and Marriage in England 1500–1800* (rev. ed. London, 1979), pp. 87–8. The notion that love between parents and children was uncommon has been challenged by a large number of historians including Jean-Louis Flandrin, *Families in Former Times. Kinship, Household and Sexuality* (Cambridge, 1979), p. 160.

43 Keith Brown, 'The Laird, his Daughter, her Husband and the Minister: Unravelling a Popular Ballad', in Roger Mason and Norman Macdougall (eds), *People and Power in Scotland. Essays in Honour of T. C. Smout* (Edinburgh, 1992), pp. 104–25, and 'Memorial of the confession of Jean Livingston, Lady Waristoun, with an account of her execution, July 1600', in C. K. Sharpe (ed.), *Lady Margaret Cunninghame, Lady Waristoun* (Edinburgh, 1827).

44 *Historical Manuscripts Commission* (London: Stationery Office), vol. IV, Argyll MSS, App. 489: G. M. Fraser, *The Steel Bonnets: The Story of the Anglo-Scottish Border Reivers* (London, 1974), p. 49.

45 Edward J. Cowan, 'James VI King of Scots and the Destruction of the Gàidhealtachd', in *Triade 8, Ecosse des Highlands Mythes et realité* (Brest, 2003), pp. 149–66.

Chapter 1

Landscape and People

Fiona Watson

INTRODUCTION

For most medieval Scots, male or female, high- or low-born, the land was
– almost literally – one of the most mundane aspects of their lives. As with
the rest of medieval Europe and elsewhere, it underpinned the entire social,
economic and political structure of the kingdom, as well as supporting a
whole range of occupations even beyond the farming engaged upon by the
vast majority in a way that no other aspect of their lives – up to and including
the king himself – could touch. Yet, even these bold statements are only the
beginning of any analysis of the complex and conflicting bonds that developed between the Scots and their land between AD 500 and 1500. During that
period, Scotland itself was born and developed into an enduring political
entity; the apparatus of government, at both a local and national level, grew
more complex; the climate shifted from the 'medieval optimum' towards
'the Little Ice Age'. And yet, in other ways, there is a sense that, in this most
fundamental of relationships, there was much that remained unchanged.

This is not meant to imply, however, any necessary or essential back-
wardness about Scottish agriculture and the economic structures that
depended upon it in this period. It should be remembered that, as late as the
mid-eighteenth century, parts of rural France were just as remote and unre-
sponsive to the outside world, including the tentacles of central authority,
as they had been when the Romans marched in over 1500 years before.[1] The
apparatus of the state and the sophistication of the royal court are only one
measure of the ability of a nation to make the most of the natural resources
that were bestowed on its people. It is also debateable whether taxation –
in this period, the share of the land's produce taken by the state as well as
the profits of trade – is the best means, in a comparatively uncentralised
kingdom like Scotland, of gauging the country's land-based wealth.

On the other hand, there is no doubt that Scotland's exports continued
to be largely unfinished 'products', such as fish, cattle, wool and hides. This
suggests an abundance of particular natural resources but a lack of the political or economic savvy to invest in the infrastructural means to exploit them
fully by exporting finished goods. Nevertheless, there is evidence, across the
country and at many societal levels, of a degree of entrepreneurialism that

is rarely appreciated. Despite the periods of warfare that afflicted Scotland, particularly in the Border regions, after 1296, the desire to exploit the land – and, of course, the seas and the rivers to which it is inextricably linked – is abundantly evident.

As a result, the landscape we are about to explore was not some untapped wilderness, however formally uncharted it may have been. The mark of human activity, though flimsily structured,[2] lay everywhere in forest and valley, moor and upland, absent perhaps only on the highest hills. Scotland was criss-crossed by dykes, ditches and lades, scattered with houses and agricultural buildings, dug up, dug out, enriched, encircled, some things kept in, others kept out, alive with the noise of all manner of beasts. The land was also loved, in intricate, well-kent detail, and feared, not least when it turned its back on its people, as it often did. The sovereign may have favoured his relationship with his subjects in describing himself as king of Scots but it was the land of the Scots that ultimately shaped them all.

THE LAND

It is, of course, a historical accident that the term 'Scotland' – with all the cultural, political and historical connotations that go with it – should happen to pertain to the northern third of the island of Britain. Nature pays little heed to the artificial borders with which humans have scattered the globe. Nevertheless, the fact that a distinctive legal framework has applied over this particular 30,000 square miles has had a definite effect on what was – or was not – likely to happen on the ground.

'It is the combination of soils, topography and climate which determines the potentialities and limitations of the Scottish environment with reference to human occupation and food production.'[3] Given the obvious topographical differences in Scotland – from the mountainous regions of the north and west and parts of the borders to the rich floodplains of the east – the basic raw materials with which Scots have had to contend for their survival have most certainly not been evenly distributed. Modern assessments of land capability indicate that at least half of the country is covered in peaty soils of one kind or another, a product of the wet, oceanic climate, which often results in problems of drainage. Only about 17 per cent is currently described as 'prime agricultural land' (meaning good for arable production) with another 11 per cent considered passable. Some 70 per cent of Scotland's land is capable of sustaining pastoral production, though the greater part (48 per cent) comes under the category of 'rough grazing', meaning, in effect, that it is only just good enough for that.

Although these are modern assessments, 'the same relative contrasts in land quality would have existed since the first arrival of people in Scotland'.[4] Modern technologies, however, are far less able to deal with steep slopes or rocky outcrops than the more primitive implements of earlier Scots and, thus, land that would today be regarded as entirely unsuitable for cultivation might well have been brought under, for example, the foot plough (*cas-dhìreach* or *cas-chrom*). The economics of the labour market were also entirely different in the past, when applying large numbers of people to any potential difficulty was not, generally speaking, a problem.

Finally, we should be careful when applying any subjective analysis of land quality that might view arable production as intrinsically 'better' than the rearing of animals. There is plenty of evidence to suggest that, through-out much of Scotland, the latter was at least as important an element of the agricultural system, having a positive impact, too, on the social and economic status of individuals and on the country as a whole. In Scotland, the farmer and the cowman (or the sheepman) were friends simply because they were often the same person. Equally, while it is true that selling animals in times of dearth was essential so as to be able to buy grain, it can also be argued that, for many medieval Scots, arable farming was the subsistence element of the economy while pastoral farming was the way to improve one's situation. In other words, accumulating livestock was considered a good route to becoming wealthier.

Climate plays a crucial role in determining what can and cannot be grown, and where, as well as affecting the success or failure of the growing seasons in any given year. Though the climate of north-west Europe has been viewed as essentially stable since c.630 BC, when the current sub-Atlantic period began (bringing with it a decline in summer temperatures by as much as 2 °C, an increase in rainfall totals and mild winters), there have also been some slight variations. The comparatively dry period, known as the Medieval Warm Epoch, reached its zenith between AD 1000 and 1250, before worsening in the fourteenth century with a series of catastrophic years that combined flood-ing, animal diseases and poor harvests, as in 1315–21. Increased storminess was also a feature, though the Little Ice Age itself is not deemed to begin until the very end of the Middle Ages.[5]

It is well known that vineyards flourished in the south of England before 1300 but there is also reference to one in Dumfriesshire as late as 1507, along with the tantalising association of vines with an orchard in Renfrewshire in 1483. The fact that this reference to grapes was ultimately deleted perhaps implies that they had once grown there but that this was no longer the case, a possibility that would accord with the changing climate.[6] Climate change is an inevitable part of life on this planet but the potential impacts of any such fluctuations are extremely varied and mediated not only by other natural phenomena, such as soil quality, topography and aspect,[7] but by human ingenuity and adaptability.

THE PEOPLE

The main purpose of the land for most of human history has been – quite simply – to sustain the people living on it, and status, at the elite end, was accorded to those who could protect the majority, whether that meant taking up arms or interceding with the unruly elements. At the beginning of the Middle Ages, the kingdoms occupying what would eventually become Scotland were already organised hierarchically, implying that their primary assets – the land and its associated waterways, together with what could be produced on or in them, as well as coincidentals such as precious metals – were controlled, to some degree at least, by the few. Those few – society's leaders and the specialist craftsmen who accommodated their needs – were able to abrogate their direct, personal responsibility to engage in the eternal struggle with the land that shaped the lives of everybody else. But their wealth and status came from the land nonetheless.[8]

The spectacularly successful Scandinavian colonisation of eastern England, however, along with the Northern Isles, parts of the northern and western Scottish mainland, the Western Isles, and parts of Ireland may have been the catalyst – as it was in Charlemagne's Frankish kingdom – for a wholesale restructuring of the land and its resources somewhere between AD 800 and 1000. Because there is no written record for this period, it is proving impossible to establish exactly when the *dabhaichean* – the units of land into which late Pictland/early Scotland was divided to ensure that 'a specific community or communities possessed access to every economic resource required throughout a year' – came into being. Although only Moray, in north-east Scotland, has been systematically examined, the evidence never-theless suggests that this was a wholesale process, implying the workings of an embryonic state with the requisite bureaucracy to see it through.[9]

It is certainly highly likely that an external threat, such as that posed by the Vikings, would provide the kind of impetus for such a revolutionary endeavour. At the same time – again in common with other parts of north-ern Europe – this also marked a considerable shift in thinking as the king began to promote the idea that all land within the kingdom was his and, as a result, he was owed a proportion of all his subjects' annual produce. This contrasted with the previous way of thinking whereby those members of the elite who acknowledged the king as their overlord paid tribute to him but there were no necessary implications for the concept of land ownership. At the same time, the *daibhechean* were almost certainly also created to provide a predetermined level of military service.[10]

Although society's leaders may have eschewed the notion of toiling on the soil, their status as warriors, so heavily imbued in the literature of the early centuries of the Middle Ages, relied on daring exploits often designed to relieve the enemy of one essential commodity: cattle. For the men of the Gododdin, their lands under threat from the advancing Anglo-Saxons, the purpose of one such mission in the sixth century, described by the poet Aneurin, was to attack 'in full force for eastern herds'. The site of the Gododdin's last stand was no broad plain but a ford, a most dangerous, but essential, place to defend for those with beasts in tow.[11] Six hundred years later, an anonymous writer, in a poem retrospectively set in the sixth century, also describes a raiding party heading south into Anglo-Saxon territory, before returning – successfully this time – to 'ford-filled Alba'.[12]

THE KINGDOM

Even as the Middle Ages began to come to a close, however, this imperative remained very much alive. In 1430, the Scottish parliament legislated as to 'what men shall do when they come home [*from England*] with their prey', urging those driving sheep or cattle north to leave the animals and return to their leaders if they came under attack, with the clear implication that this was something they were most unwilling to do.[13] The better part of a millennium separates the first example from the last but the basic dynamic seems to have remained the same. It was cattle, above all – often combined with his ability to acquire it from his enemies – that marked out a man's status.

The land and the people working it did ultimately provide the king with taxation in kind (predominantly livestock and grain) as well as periodic hospitality, even beyond the lands he controlled directly himself. In addition, customs duties on trade – again largely the unfinished natural resources produced on the land – also came to the king to allow him to 'live of his own' – a perennial problem for the cash-strapped monarchs of later medieval Scotland. As a result, he did take some considerable interest in making sure that the sources of his income were being properly looked after, and that the best use was being made of them. As a result, there was a role for the Scottish parliament to play in setting out ground rules for a standard approach to certain key aspects of land management. Of the forty-four pieces of legislation passed up to 1504 directly concerned with the organisation and/or exploitation of the land and its resources, the earliest and by far the most numerous are concerned with fishing. To begin with, this was essentially salmon but, by 1424, the crown had become aware of, and extremely interested in, the potential – in terms of customs revenue – of the herring fishing of the Irish Sea.[14] By 1487, there is explicit reference to this as a form of industry, though the impetus almost certainly came from local landowners, such as the Earl of Argyll, given the imprecation to the king not to grant any of this fishing out 'to foreigners nor to others'.[15]

The other acts concerned themselves with muir-burn, which was banned from April to November largely to safeguard the arable crop, the protection of wild deer and hares, the extirpation of wolves, wild birds, some of which, such as rooks, crows and birds of prey like buzzards, kites and 'mittels', did damage to the corn and to wildfowl, and others, such as plovers, partridges, ducks and grouse, which were 'grown to eat for sustenance of man', the preservation and, indeed, expansion, of woods and hedges and the protection of other aspects of a lord's policies, including orchards, rabbit warrens, beehives and doocots. The concern for Scotland's woods, however, evident in parliament from 1425, was not sufficient to prevent the heartfelt lamentation of 1504, when it was bemoaned that 'the woods of Scotland are utterly destroyed'.[16]

The agricultural productivity of the people of Scotland was obviously of national concern to make sure that there was sufficient food and other essentials to go around, and also to contribute to the wealth of the country as a whole through internal and external trade. Parliament would certainly legislate to protect people in time of dearth, and also to exhort more effective production.[17] In times of national emergency, too, the qualification for military service was reduced to that most basic and essential of commodities – one that even the poorest widow could contribute – one cow or its equivalent.[18] By the later Middle Ages, taxation was levied on everyone's produce. In the fourteenth century, only white sheep (but not black or dun-coloured ones), broken-in horses and oxen, and household utensils were exempted.[19] By the fifteenth century, there was less emphasis on sheep, and the exemptions were crops still in the ground or what the lord used for his own household. The rates levied in 1424 were:

a cow for 5 s.,
a wether or a yew for 12 d,
a goat, a gimmer or a dinmont for 8 d,
a wild mare with her young for 10 s.,
a colt of three years of age or more for a merk,
a boll of wheat for 12 d,
a boll of bere, rye or peas for 8 d,
a boll of oats for 4 d[20]

COURTS AND THE COUNTRYSIDE

Despite the king's own interest in his people's behaviour and productivity, the average Scot was predominantly regulated in terms of his or her daily life by the owner of the lands on which they lived.[21] The barony court was the principal mechanism of control in the later Middle Ages, as well as the forum for promulgating legislation. Some of this legislation may have been inspired by acts of parliament; some would relate to local needs, at least as interpreted by the owner who would usually preside over the court himself.

Most of the evidence for the workings of the barony court comes from the early modern period, but its basic concerns are unlikely to have changed significantly. As pointed out in the *Black Book of Taymouth*, with regard to the Campbell estates in highland Perthshire and Glenorchy:

> The acts and proceedings of the Baron Courts, collected in 1621, will be found to present a fair view of the rural economy of the district. There are regulations for muirburn, summer pasture, peat-cutting, mills, smithies, and ale-houses; laws against poaching on moor and river; a rule that smacks of superstition, against

cutting briars [except] 'in the waxing of the moon'. Swine are proscribed; no quarter is given to rooks, hooded crows, and magpies. The Laird shows his determination to have trees about his tenants' houses by numerous regulations; and tenants are bound, under high penalties, to give their cottars the comforts of fuel and kail-yards, 'with corns conform'. Agriculture is stimulated by rules for sowing 'uncouth' oats, or seed better than the common black oat of the Highlands; for collecting of 'middens'; even for irrigating 'drawing water through the land' long before the grand discovery of draining had been made. To avoid the devastation of Highland 'speats' [floods], the green sward on the banks of rivers and burns is not to be broken. To save a different devastation, every tenant was obliged to make yearly four 'croscats of iron' [probably some sort of dog spear] for slaying of the wolf.[22]

As the above clearly indicates, most of the regulations promulgated in these courts were concerned with 'good practice' for the careful and effective management of the land and its resources. They were explicitly issued, on the estates of the Laird of Glenorchy, at least, 'with the advice of the commons and inhabitants of the country for the weal thereof', suggesting a degree of discussion.[23] Those presiding over the courts were also required to practise the wisdom of Solomon in judging misdemeanours – which might often result in 'effusions of blood' – that often stemmed from the fact that different uses of the land took place side by side. In 1592, for example, 'the whole cottars and poor folk of the country complain upon the honest men in the country for holding of swine which is to their great hurt and wrack'.[24] Animals straying into cornfields or muir-burn getting out of control were other potential flashpoints that could lead to neighbour falling out seriously with neighbour.

The agricultural system was underpinned by the steelbow system which operated by means of a donation of animals and seed from the landowner to the tenant in return for a percentage of the annual 'increase' (that is, the number of young or the crop produced). From a modern point of view, such a system is hugely problematical, because, as Adam Smith said: 'That land could never be improved to the best advantage by such tenants. 1st., because stock could not, without the greatest difficulty, accumulate in their hands; and 2dly., because if it did accumulate they would never lay it out in the improvement of the land, since the lord, who laid out nothing, was to divide the profites with them.'[25] From a medieval point of view, however, the ancient sense that the elites had a responsibility to look after their people, as well as sharing in the profits of their labour, played a greater role than more modern tendencies to look at good and bad fortune as invested in the individual. Medieval communities, as with more ancient ones, rose and fell – in theory at least – together, and the only reason that some few could take on more specialised roles, up to and including the king himself, was because the bulk of the population remained as farmers. This was a symbiotic relationship in which the distribution of the wherewithal to produce this year's livestock and arable crop from those who controlled the land to those who worked it remained deeply symbolic.

CONCLUSION

This chapter has attempted to give some idea of how the people of medieval Scotland interacted with the land, something that, by the very nature of farming, they did every single day, even if some periods were less busy than others. The seasons controlled the year and the religious festivals into which the calendar was divided often reflected that fact – Rogation Sunday, for example, marked the beginning of 'a period of supplication for the harvest'.[26] The experience of those who spent most of their working lives outside not only provided an instinctive sense of the time of day but also a detailed understanding of local weather systems and interpretations of a vast plethora of omens to predict what one should or should not do to safeguard crops and livestock.[27]

Whatever the theory, too, the impression from the parliamentary record is that women played a prominent role in controlling and working the land. They were certainly summoned to court to answer for their actions and took others to court to defend their rights.[28] It is also clear that, by the end of the medieval period, the cases heard by the lords auditors in parliament were becoming overwhelmingly concerned with the destruction or taking away of either livestock or crops. Such activities were very damaging indeed to the 'common weal' which the king was sworn to protect. The issue was complicated, however, by the fact that removing a person's movable goods – predominantly livestock, but also cut grain – was the best means of legitimately extracting debts.

It was asserted earlier in this chapter that, contrary to conventional wisdom and prevailing trends elsewhere in medieval Europe, it was livestock husbandry, rather than the growing of crops, that meant most to the majority of medieval Scots. This is not meant to imply that arable production was not essential; it most certainly was, and any crop failure could have catastrophic results. But there is evidence to suggest that livestock was equally important and perhaps even that this was ultimately what wealth was measured in throughout many parts of Scotland. Indeed, despite the fact that the taking of 'calps' (a gift made to a superior in return for protection) was banned in 1489/90, such practices continued in the Highlands for decades to come. Here the calp was more explicitly described as 'the best for futit beist being in thair possessionis the tymes of thair deceiss [the best four-footed beast being in their possession at the time of their decease]', and it seems likely that this was the same practice proscribed in Galloway and Carrick at the end of the fifteenth century.[29] The Gododdin would surely have understood the point of such a show of obedience – and wealth – to one's lord.

Figure 1.1 *Holy Isle from Larybeg Point, Arran. © St Andrews University Library. Licensor www.scran.ac.uk.*

Living off the land in medieval Scotland was hard and yet, despite the warfare, the famine and the disease, there seems to have been a desire to make the most of all the possibilities. There is the occasional hint, too, that this land was loved and appreciated for its beauty as much as it was feared for its capricious harshness. The poem, 'Arran', written by an unknown author in the twelfth century, paints an idyllic picture of the island.

Frisky deer on its mountains,
moist bogberries in its thickets,
cold waters in its rivers,
acorns on its brown oak-trees

. . .

Fine for them when good weather comes –
trout beneath its river banks;
gulls reply round its white cliff –
fine at all times is Arran.[30]

Those of us who have lived in or visited Scotland have probably known days like that, all the more precious because of their rarity.

This chapter has only scratched the surface of a huge topic that requires much more work from scholars than has been the case for far too long. It would pay historians, too, to engage with those from other disciplines – archaeologists, soil scientists, pollen specialists, dendrochronologists,[31] climatologists – who are working on very similar issues. Above all, we must remember that history is not a linear march of progress out of the terrible conditions of the distant past towards more enlightened ideals. Thus, the damning indictments of later writers, such as those responsible for the Agricultural Reports of the nineteenth century, cannot be taken at face value, especially when their fire was turned on the Highlands. They certainly cannot be automatically applied to earlier periods. Working the land *was* the everyday story of medieval Scotland but it was neither trivial nor simple.

Notes

1   Graham Robb, *The Discovery of France* (London, 2007), p. 4.

2   Sadly, the dearth of archaeological evidence for medieval Scotland – as indicated by Historic Scotland's determined efforts to try to recover some of it in their Medieval Or Later Rural Settlement project – attests to the fact that most of the structures of this period were extremely flimsy, indeed, often of turf and/or timber.

3   D. A. Davidson and S. P. Carter, 'Soils and their Evolution', in Kevin J. Edwards and Ian B. M. Ralston (eds), *Scotland after the Ice Age* (Edinburgh, 2005), p. 49.

4   Davidson and Carter, 'Soils and their Evolution', pp. 52–3.

5   G. Whittington and K. J. Edwards, 'Climate Change', in Edwards and Ralston, *Scotland After the Ice Age*, pp. 13–14; I. G. Simmons, *An Environmental History of Great Britain* (Edinburgh, 2001), pp. 69–70.

6   T. C. Smout, 'Woodland History before 1850', in T. C. Smout (ed.), *Scotland since Prehistory* (Aberdeen, 1993), p. 42; National Archives of Scotland (hereafter NAS), *Register of the Great Seal*, lib. xvi, 83; NAS, PA2/4, f. 28v–29r.

7   'Aspect' in this context essentially means which way a site is facing, with implications for the amount of sunshine it is likely to get, or corresponding frosts.

8   See, for example, K. Forsyth, 'Scotland to 1100', in J. Wormald (ed.), *Scotland: A History* (Oxford, 2005), pp. 22–3.

9   Alasdair Ross, *The Province of Moray, c.1000–1232*, unpublished PhD thesis, University of Aberdeen (2003), pp. 46–51; p. 229; Alasdair Ross, 'The *Dabhach* in Moray: A New Look at an Old Tub', in Alex Woolf (ed.), *Landscape and Environment* (St Andrews, 2006), pp. 57–74.

10   Ross, 'The *Dabhach* in Moray', 57–74.

11   Aneirin, 'The Gododdin', in Thomas Owen Clancy (ed.), *The Triumph Tree: Scotland's Earliest Poetry, AD 550–1350* (Edinburgh, 1998), Re cattle: A-text, verse 40; B-text, verse 28; Re the ford: A-text, verse 17; verse 53; B-text, verse 9.

12   'The Birth of Áedán mac Gabráin', in Clancy, *The Triumph Tree*, p. 181.

13   *Register of the Privy Council of Scotland* (hereafter *RPS*), 14 vols (Edinburgh 1877–98), 1430/46.

14   *RPS*, 1424/14.

15   *RPS*, 1487/1/23.

16   *RPS*, 1424/22; 1478/6/86; A1493/5/19; A1504/3/116; *RPS*, 1401/2/14; 1425/3/14; 1428/3/6; 1458/3/36; 1458/3/37; *RPS* 1424/21; 1458/3/33; 1428/3/13; 1458/3/32; *RPS* 1425/3/11; 1425/3/12; 1458/3/28; 1458/3/31; A1504/3/116.

17 See, for example, *RPS*, 1450/1/23; 1468/6; 1426.39.

18 *RPS*, 1318/29.

19 *RPS*, 1357/11/2.

20 *RPS*, 1424/1424/25; 1424/29.

21 See G. W. S. Barrow, *Kingship and Unity*, 2nd edn (Edinburgh, 2003), pp. 64–5, for a discussion of the basic royal revenue stream. The desire to have the king 'live of his own' was a source of contention between Crown and tax-payers from at least the time of Robert I (1306–29). See NAS SP13/8. If the king was the landowner, then he, or his lieutenants, would deal with the same issues but not through a barony court.

22 Cosmo Innes (ed.), *The Black Book of Taymouth* (Edinburgh, 1855), pp. xxviii–xxix. In fact, the documentary record for Breadalbane courts goes back into the sixteenth century, NAS GD112/17.

23 NAS GD112/17 1576.

24 NAS GD112/17, 7 November 1592.

25 Adam Smith, 'Of the cultivation of the antient metayers, or tenants by steelbow', in R. L. Meek, D. D. Raphael and P. G. Stein (eds), *Glasgow Edition of the Works and Correspondence of Adam Smith*, vol. 5, *Lectures On Jurisprudence* (Indianapolis, [1762] 1982).

26 Malcolm Barber, *The Two Cities* (London, 1993), pp. 6–7.

27 See 'The Celtic Year', in John Gregorson Campbell, *The Gaelic Otherworld*, Ronald Black (ed.) (Edinburgh, 2005).

28 See for example, *RPS* 1479/3/7; 1479/3/12; 1479/10/44; 1482/3/39; 1483/3/27;1483/10/81.

29 *RPS*, 1489/7/7; 1490/2/24; 1490/2/25; GD112/24/3.

30 'Arran', in Clancy, *The Triumph Tree*, p. 187.

31 These use tree rings as a guide to environmental conditions on an annual basis.

Chapter 2

The Worldview of Scottish Vikings in the Age of the Sagas

Edward J. Cowan

INTRODUCTION

December 1263 brought death to King Hakon of Norway in the Bishops' Palace, Kirkwall, Orkney. As a devoted Christian, he had the lives of the saints in Latin read to him until, tired by the mental effort of translation, he switched to the sagas of the saints in Old Norse. Thereafter he heard the kings' sagas all the way from the protohistorical times of Halfdan the Black down to the reign of his immediate predecessor, Sverre, whose saga was read out day and night whenever the king was awake. Just after midnight, soon after the saga ended, the mighty Hakon died.[1] With him the age of the sagas could also be deemed to have come to a close, as did five hundred years of a Viking presence in Scotland. Hakon had just led a mighty armada to Scotland to retain possession of the Hebrides, an enterprise which came to grief in the equinoctial storms of the Firth of Clyde and an indecisive conflict at Largs. Three years later the Western Isles were ceded to the Scots in the Treaty of Perth. Orkney and Shetland were to be ruled from Norway for a further two hundred years until pawned to Scotland as part of a royal dowry.

The word *víkingr* is not a flattering term in Old Norse, or West Norse, the Germanic language spoken in Norway and her colonies, notably Iceland. A Viking was a pirate or brigand, later romanticised in much the same way as his English cognate. It was a Scot, George Chalmers, engaged in his massive *Caledonia* project (1807), who first introduced the term to English; 'Thorfinn commenced his career as a vikingr'. He was closely followed by the Paisley poet and ballad collector William Motherwell, who produced the unmemorable 'Love-song of Jarl Egill Skallagrim', a proud 'vikingir'.[2]

PLUNDERING THE SOURCES

Arguably, more is known about the Vikings than any of the other peoples of early Scotland. In the last forty years or so their culture has enjoyed the boon of extensive archaeological investigation, not only in Scandinavia, but also in Orkney, Shetland, the Hebrides and parts of the Scottish mainland, as well as many other areas of Scandinavian settlement outside the homeland, shedding much light upon everyday life in particular.[3] There has also been

significant study of Norse place names which often convey useful economic
information though much remains to be done.[4] Place names also give a good
impression of Viking settlement throughout the country. For example, they
are dominant in Shetland and Orkney, less so in Caithness.[5] They are very
numerous in Lewis and well represented throughout the Outer Hebrides,
Skye and the western seaboard though more thinly scattered in the rest of
the Inner Hebrides. Despite assertions and assumptions to the contrary,
they are not numerous in Galloway,[6] while those in the Borders and the
eastern Lowlands are probably a result of migration from England rather
than primary settlement. A great deal of excellent research on Viking ships
has been achieved.[7] Viking military skills and abilities have been subjected
to scrutiny.[8] Chronicles and histories have been made available in new editions and modern translations. Very little has survived in the way of record
or charter evidence for Scandinavian history before the thirteenth century;
the situation for Scotland is slightly better. Most important of all, so far as
historians are concerned, is the incomparable legacy of Old Norse literature,
the poems and sagas in which the Vikings enshrined their views of themselves and their world.[9] Such texts have proved highly, indeed ridiculously,
controversial in certain quarters, mainly among scholars who mistakenly
cling to the outmoded view that objectivity in historical research is still possible. Honesty and transparency in the use of sources, however diverse, are
essential but much-invoked objectivity is often code for the very opposite –
extreme subjectivity employed in support of invincible omniscience.

The Scandinavian world in the High Middle Ages preserved and produced some of the finest and most exciting literature in all the medieval era.
Iceland proved especially productive, in part because it was unique, having
been founded as a kingless colony in the late ninth century, traditionally to
escape the tyrannous ambitions of Harald Fairhair of Norway, it required
a history and an identity. The point was well made in one manuscript of
Landnamabók, The Book of Settlements:

> People often say that writing about the Settlements is irrelevant learning but we
> think we can better meet the criticism of foreigners when they accuse us of being
> descended from slaves and scoundrels, if we know for certain the truth about our
> ancestry. And for those who want to know ancient lore and how to trace genealo-
> gies, it is better to start at the beginning than to come in at the middle. Anyway
> all civilised nations want to know about the origins of their own society and the
> beginnings of their own race.[10]

Scotland was not Iceland but Orkney belonged to the Scandinavian world
that shared such concerns, hence the legendary introduction to *Orkneyinga
Saga* which firmly splices the pre- and protohistory of the Northern Isles into
that of Norway.

The history of the kings of Norway was the concern of the consummate
Icelandic historian, Snorri Sturluson, in his lengthy classic, *Heimskringla*,

literally 'the orb of the world'. In his preface he noted that the poems composed by skalds at the court of Harald Finehair were still known by heart in
the thirteenth century, as were songs about Norwegian kings made during
the previous three hundred and fifty years. 'We rest the foundations of our
story principally upon the songs which were sung in the presence of the
chiefs themselves or of their sons, and take all to be true that is found in
such poems about their feats and battles.' Although skalds were notorious
for praising their patrons, he writes, 'no-one would dare to relate to a chief
what he, and all those who heard it, knew to be false and imaginary, not a
true account of his deeds because that would be mockery, not praise'.[11] The
author, or authors, of *Orkneyinga* who composed the work some time before
Snorri picked up his pen, shared his opinion, making liberal use of poems as
anchors for their story: for example, the compositions of Arnórr Jarlaskáld,
who celebrated the deeds of earls Thorfinn and Brusi.[12] Confusingly to
modern readers, such poets often made use of elaborate metaphorical
expressions, known as kennings, based on the older corpus of legendary
skaldic poetry, which is the major source of information about Norse
mythology, cosmology and the deeds of the gods. This Orcadian interest is
reflected in the career of Bjarni Kolbeinsson, Bishop of Orkney from 1185 to
1223, sometimes thought to be the compiler of *Orkneyinga Saga* but known
to have definitely composed the lengthy poem, *Jómsvíkingadrápa*, which cel-
ebrates the deeds of the Jomsvikings, a *drápa* being a praise poem. Bjarni's
literary interests extended to other legendary material which clearly enjoyed
something of a revival during his lifetime.[13]

  In compiling his unrivalled history, Snorri Sturluson employed the myth-
ological and legendary material to distance the remote from the more recent
past. He was also author of *The Prose Edda*, a book of poetics concerned
with the creation of the world and humankind, and the doom of the gods,
but with other matters as well. Therein he recounted how Ginnungagap
(the great void) was situated between ice-bound Niflheim and Muspell, the
region of heat; where these two met, life appeared in the drops of running
water which grew into the likeness of a man.[14] Snorri was well aware that the
poetry preserved competing accounts of the creation of the world as well as
a great deal of information, some of it rather obscure, about Norse pagan
belief. Writing as a thirteenth-century Christian, he attempted to make sense
of this confusing and patchy material by creating a cosmology parallel to that
of Christendom.

  It is now recognised that Nordic religion of the pre-Christian era incorporated elements from circumpolar peoples such as the Inuit and the Sámi
of Finland and northern Scandinavia.[15] As in other Christian cultures, some
of these pagan beliefs survived conversion. Christian writers still sometimes
display a tendency to dismiss non-Christian beliefs as childlike nonsense or
as a kind of monolithic competitor to Christianity itself but Scandinavians
remained remarkably tolerant of, and interested in, the ideas of their pagan

forebears. What might be distinguished as the pagan mindset was deployed to great effect by the sagamen who first committed the Icelandic prose narratives to vellum.

Sagas originally circulated in the oral medium. Some may have been quite well developed while others were little more than anecdotes or short stories mostly concerning the first settlers who took up land in Iceland, as described in *Íslendingabók* and *Landnámabók*, both of which were written in the vernacular Old Norse and thus, significantly, were intended to be accessible to those who spoke that language, to a much wider readership than the few who were Latinate, but not intended for the international community who obviously had no knowledge of Old Icelandic. These texts were concerned with settlers who came largely from Norway but who also brought with them, in some cases, wives, concubines and slaves from the Hebrides and Ireland, so accounting for the new colony's acquisition of a Celtic infusion which, thanks to DNA research, is now known to have been much larger than the literary evidence would seem to imply. It was thus for ancestral reasons that later sagas, fortunately, provided a good deal of information about Scots, an interest which Icelanders retained through Orkney and its earls but also through shared affinities and experiences with the Norwegian kingdoms of the Hebrides until the mid-thirteenth century.

Like poems, sagas would be recited or declaimed at national assemblies (meetings of the Althing), in chiefly halls and in individual households. Sagas fell into at least three loose categories. First 'Sagas of the Inside World' dealt with Iceland and its history. Often described as 'Sagas of Icelanders', they recounted the adventures and struggles of personalities who lived during the settlement period. Others recorded contemporary happenings in the twelfth and thirteenth centuries until the demise of the Old Icelandic Commonwealth in 1262, when it reverted to Norwegian rule. 'Sagas of the Outside World' were concerned with Greenland and Vinland (America) but most of all with Norway whose kings Icelanders fled from and feared while remaining a source of perennial fascination. Icelanders and Norwegians deserve credit for the preservation of sagas about the kings of Norway culminating in Snorri's *Heimskringla* and the productions of his nephew Sturla Thordarsson, notably *Hakon's Saga* and *Magnus Saga* of which only a fragment now remains. One of the oldest of the historical sagas is *Orkneyinga Saga*, which, it should be noted, nowhere survives as a unified text but rather is scattered throughout several different manuscripts. Modern editions and translations suggest a unity which may be illusory though, like *Heimskringla*, it is tempting to see it as a treatise on the successful ruler. A final category would be 'Sagas of the Other World' about legendary kings and heroes inhabiting a world not dissimilar to that of the French romances, several of which were translated into Icelandic together with much other literature. These divisions are not precise and they often overlap but what cannot be doubted is that the sagas in the first two categories were conceived as historical, as containing genuine information about the past. The sagamen would have argued that there were different ways of communicating that past, that the story was the important part of *historia*. The check on the accuracy of their material was the audience who had heard the sagas many times before and thus could not, and would not, tolerate novelty or invention in the content, while perhaps accepting both in the telling. It was said of Sturla Thordarsson that he told a saga 'better and more knowledgeably' than it had ever been heard before, 'a good story very well told'.[16]

One other literary form, tantalising, intriguing and frustrating in equal measure, is that of runic inscriptions. Runes represent a lineal alphabet adapted for carving on wood, stone and other objects. Rune sticks were used by merchants in York, Dublin and Bergen to place orders for merchandise. In Scotland, they exist mainly, though not exclusively, as carvings on stones. As is well known, the largest collection of inscriptions in Scotland is found on the walls of the astounding Maeshowe tomb in Orkney, now five thousand years old, into which Jerusalem-farers, crusaders or pilgrims, broke, in the 1120s, when Earl Hakon was about to go on pilgrimage to the Holy Land to atone for his murder of St Magnus, or in the early 1150s, at the start or end of Earl Rognvald's Mediterranean cruise. All runic inscriptions intrigue because of the immediacy factor. The reader confronting the stone is engaged with, or if s/he is lucky, may even be in touch with, a message written almost nine hundred years ago. They tantalise because we cannot be absolutely sure in all cases that we are understanding what we are reading, so cryptic are the messages. And they are frustrating because we usually know nothing about the inscribers or those commemorated on the stones. The greatest modern authority on the Orkney runes has described the Maeshowe collection as 'graffiti', for understandable reasons. They were inscribed by bored warriors probably sheltering from atrocious weather. One modest individual wrote: 'These runes were carved by the man most skilled in runes west of the ocean.' Another pined for 'Ingigerd the most beautiful of women'. A message with strong sexual connotations was, 'Ingibjorg, the fair widow. Many a woman has gone stooping in here. Very arrogant'; Ingibjorg is presumably humbled in the carver's imagination, if not in real life. Quite explicit is 'Þorny fucked. Helgi carved.' That at least one woman was present is indicated by a 'signed' rune – 'Hlif, the earl's housekeeper, carved'. The word for 'housekeeper' is *matselja* 'slavewoman who distributed food in the household', translated by Barnes as 'steward'. Six inscriptions refer to treasure. Four of these appear to be in sequence as each carver picked up where the previous one left off, and are all carved close to one another in the tomb: 'In the northwest is hidden a great treasure'; 'It was long since a great treasure was hidden here'; 'Happy is he who can find great treasure of gold'; 'Hakon bore this treasure alone out of this mound'. A Norwegian scholar has wittily characterised the foregoing as the products of an internet chatroom![17]

There are another fifteen runes from Orkney, five from Shetland and three from Caithness. A stone from Iona exhibits the text, 'Kali Olivsson laid this stone over [his] brother Fugl'. In 1263 a member of Hakon's expedition scratched out 'Vígleikr stallari reist' ['Vígleikr the marshall wrote'] on a cave wall on Holy Island, off the coast of Arran. The famous Hunterston brooch bears the runic inscription, 'Melbrigda owns this brooch'. The carver had a Celtic name but knew Norse runes. Runes were not everyday because not everyone could write or read them but they undoubtedly preserve the everyday thoughts of some folk.

EVERYDAY LIFE IN VIKING SCOTLAND

There is a substantial literature on everyday life in the Viking age, much larger than can possibly be addressed in a short chapter.[18] Archaeology continues to throw up new evidence. At present it is known that Viking males were generally between 5 feet 7 inches (170 cm) and 5 feet 11 inches (180 cm) in height; women were a little shorter, one burial in Lewis measuring 5 feet 3 inches (160 cm). At age twenty, life expectancy for men was 40.4 years, for women 38.1. Infant mortality has been calculated at 260 deaths per thousand, for children aged up to one year, a high figure. A woman in the fascinating boat burial at Scar, Sanday in Orkney was in her seventies, however.[19]

At the time of writing, there are no towns in Scotland which are known to be Viking foundations outside of Shetland and Orkney. There are no equivalents to York and Dublin though Dumbarton may have served as a trading centre after Olaf and Ivar conquered it in 870, carrying off large amounts of booty and large numbers of captives who were subsequently enslaved.[20] Kirkwall awaits full investigation.[21]

It used to be believed that Viking house design was informed by ship technology, that their houses like their graves, were boat shaped but it is now understood that they were often rectangular in plan. All the domestic buildings excavated so far have been farms of one kind or another, from fairly humble structures to the rather grand *stofa*, or hall, of Duke Hakon of Norway at The Biggings, Papa Stour, with its timber-planked floor, dated to between 1013 and 1156. The Vikings, as is known from as far away as Newfoundland and illustrated on many other sites, were pragmatists. They tended to settle on or near previously occupied sites. Thus, at Jarlshof and Underhoull in Shetland, at almost all the Viking sites so far excavated in Orkney, at The Udal, North Uist and possibly at Drimore, in South Uist, there is evidence of pre-existing native settlements. At Buckquoy there is a suggestion of a Pictish house modified for Viking occupation, while the excavator of the prestigious complex at The Udal has speculated that natives were violently displaced by the newcomers who remained until the buildings were abandoned because of the Hebridean ravages of Magnus Barelegs, king of Norway, at the end of the eleventh century. At many sites, the artefactual evidence shows a blend of cultures though whether as a result of conquest or

Figure 2.1   *Late Norse house, Unst, Shetland. © Shetland Museum. Licensor www. scran.ac.uk.*

peaceful coexistence is still a matter of debate. It should be noted, however, that to judge from the evidence presented in the early poems and in the sagas, the Vikings were undoubtedly a bloodthirsty lot, fixated on violence and conflict, which must, at times, have been everyday preoccupations, if not everyday experiences.

All excavations show evidence of agricultural activity. Cattle, sheep and pigs are conspicuous, as are byres and barns for threshing, drying or storing grain, mainly oats and barley. Sheep were sometimes milked while cattle become more numerous in the later period, providing an estimated 95 per cent of the meat consumed. It is hypothesised that some kind of meat processing took place at Pool, Sanday. The bones of rabbit, red deer and seal have occasionally been found in middens. Some buildings have been interpreted as stables. The main dwelling often exhibits a central hearth with lateral benches or sleeping platforms. A horizontal or click mill has been discovered at the Earls' Bu, Orphir. There is considerable evidence of metalworking and some of smithies, the one at Jarlshof preserving a suggested stone anvil. In Shetland, good use was made of steatite (soapstone) for pots, dishes and containers. The Brough of Birsay revealed boat rivets, perhaps indicating that boat timbers had been reused in at least one domestic building. Line sinkers for fishing are commonly found. Fish played an important role in the Norse diet, cod, saithe and ling proving the most popular catches, though eel, haddock and ray were also consumed. It has been suggested, based upon evidence from Shetland and Caithness, that by the thirteenth and fourteenth centuries fishing was taking place on something of a commercial scale. Seabirds and their eggs supplemented the food supply, both harvested from the cliffs.[22]

Loom weights have turned up everywhere as have bone pins and pieces of Pictish and Viking bling. Wool was the most common textile but flax was grown to produce linen for clothing, ropes and sails. Hides and fleeces were also processed. Buckquy produced a *hnefatafl* board and two other unspecified game boards. Intriguingly, the same site yielded an infant burial thought to be a possible foundation deposit, placed when house building began. The same site also preserved a pagan burial. Many of these farms in the areas of Norse settlement were continuously occupied well into the medieval period.

Pagan burials are full of interest because, unlike the Christian variety, they contain grave goods. Items that might be useful in the afterlife, or which might confer status, were mainly favoured. Bodies were deposited fully clad, female remains often being found in association with pins or brooches, males with weapons or tools. Unusually for Scotland, Oronsay burials preserved evidence of what looked like a boat burning. One of the females wore Norwegian brooches and an Irish ringed pin while the other's adornment was made from Celtic shrine mounts. A Colonsay grave yielded a boat and a horse. The man was buried with a sword, axe, spear and shield, and two arrows, as well as a pair of scales and lead weights. Portable scales, found at several sites, were used to weigh hacksilver which was employed as currency, though these balances need not necessarily be associated exclusively with merchants because any person of status would most likely use them. A man and a woman were excavated at Ballinaby, Islay. The man was accompanied by his sword, shield, spears, axes, a fishing spear (used for hunting salmon), a blacksmith's hammer and tongs, a drinking horn and a cauldron, the woman reposing with a heck (used in spinning), a linen smoother, a needle case, two brooches, an impressive silver pin fastener and a bronze ladle. A concentration of burials has been found at Broch of Gurness, Orkney. One woman had a Thor's hammer around her neck. Another grave contained a folding bronze balance. An impressive cluster has also been investigated at Pierowall, Orkney. The earliest graves, of the thirty-two discovered at Westness, were Pictish, so it appears the Vikings took over the site which proved immensely rewarding, yielding two boat burials and some other boat-shaped graves. One warrior had a set of gaming pieces, another a sickle and ploughshare. A further boat burial was discover at Scar on Sanday, a probable family group of man, woman and child. Apart from the boat itself, which there is reason to think was built in Norway, the most elaborate find, positioned at the woman's feet, was an amazing whalebone plaque, thought to have been used for linen smoothing. Close to her right side was a high-status brooch. Balnakeil in Sutherland preserved the grave of a boy aged between eight and thirteen who was buried with a full-size sword among other objects.[23]

Unfortunately, not much is known about what these grave goods actually signified. Did warriors headed for Valhalla (which seems in any case to have been reserved for persons of very high status) require their weapons there, or a horse, or a burned-out boat? Valhall, the Hall of the Slain, seems to have been mainly concerned with endless fighting and feasting, the dead of the day returning for the drink of the evening. A note to one of the poems asserts that the pagans used to believe in the possibility of reincarnation which is dismissed as an old wives' tale. Perhaps it was somehow the spirit or the essence of the object that travelled with the spirit of the deceased to the next world, or perhaps the depositing of treasured items in a person's grave was seen as a mark of respect to the ancestors from whom these artefacts had been acquired. It is to be hoped that the dead escaped at least one everyday torment. Almost all graves contain combs which were used to remove lice from the head and probably other parts of the body also.

EVERYDAY LIFE IN ORKNEYINGA SAGA

Orkneyinga Saga, or as it used to be known, *The Sagas of the Earls* was composed around 1200 by an Icelander with Orcadian connections.[24] Almost forty years ago I suggested that the saga should be read as a treatise on the good ruler, and I still believe that to be the case, while acknowledging that it is about many other things as well. The question has sensibly been asked about whether the Vikings believed in their history as related in the sagas; 'How much trust did they place in their veracity, and how important was this to them?'[25] To judge from *Orkneyinga* it would seem that the answer to all three queries would be 'very little', because the characters in the saga are very suspicious about what they are told. Truth about the past is dependent upon the trustworthiness or otherwise of the informant, which is to be read in her or his face, expression and tone. Folk in sagas hear words but they also observe character and gesture. Sagamen do not pretend to know what goes on in a person's mind for they are not novelists but they do permit themselves to speculate on such matters by observation of externals. Their perception often verges on the cinematic, using long shots, such as distant views of ships at sea, or close-ups of, say, sweating men engaged in individual combat, to communicate their view of reality. To coin a phrase, all human life potentially is there. But not all sagas are equally exciting, colourful and well observed. As it happens, *Orkneyinga* is heavily political and much taken up with the violent deeds of great men, sometimes, it must be said (*pace* Orcadians), to the point of tedium. The idea in this part of my discussion is to indicate how useful, or otherwise, the saga may prove in preserving information about everyday life. We will be guided by the topics which the saga has chosen to emphasise and highlight. Obviously it has much to impart about the daily lives and concerns of the earls but it is to be hoped that it can also shed light on those of humbler inhabitants of

Shetland, Orkney and Caithness, places central to the saga world but often ignored in modern Scottish historiography. The temptation to transpose aspects of Viking activity in other parts of the Scandinavian common-wealth to Scotland will be resisted unless there is good reason for doing so. Orkney's links with Norway remained very close until the mid-thirteenth century, the regular visits of the earls creating many opportunities for cul-tural reinforcement, literary or otherwise, while connections with Iceland were also fairly frequent.

The Icelandic tradition insisted that Scotland, or a large part of it, belonged to the Norwegian 'empire'. *Landnámabók* as well as *Heimskringla*, *Laxdale Saga* and the *Saga of Eric the Red* all recount that Ketil Flatnose, a great, ninth-century, Hebridean chieftain and his wife, Auð the Deep-Minded, had a son, Thorstein the Red, who campaigned alongside Sigurd the Mighty. Together they conquered Caithness and Sutherland, Moray and Ross, Thorstein becoming a king of Scots before he was betrayed and killed. Auð and her household subsequently migrated to Iceland and the Breidafjord district which was to become something of a saga production centre, guaranteeing the memorialisation of Auð's family and their great deeds, real or invented.

Despite their Hebridean background Auð and her kindred enjoy high status. There is much to be learned about Norse social attitudes and assump-tions from an unfinished poem entitled *Rigsþula* in which the god Heimdal is credited with the creation of Norse society. Adopting the name, Rig, from Irish *rí* 'king', he sets off on a procreative journey. He first visits the house, door ajar, of Great-grandfather and Great-grandmother who feed him a 'coarse loaf, thick and heavy and stuffed with grain', and boiled calf meat. He then sleeps between the two for three nights. Nine months later Great-grandmother has a baby whom she names Thrall (slave);

> He began to grow and thrive well;
> On his hands there was wrinkled skin,
> Crooked knuckles,
> Thick fingers, he had an ugly face,
> A crooked back, long heels.

As he grows, he learns to make baskets and to carry home brushwood all day long. He marries Slavegirl, who is bandy legged, has muddy feet, sun-burned arms and a bent nose. They have many sons with such names as Rough, Badbreath, Stumpy, Fatty and Lout; 'they established farms / put dung on the fields, worked with swine, / looked after goats, dug the turf'. Their daughters were Podgy, Bulgy-calves, Bellows-nose, Great-gabbler and Raggedy-hips. Such names of those deemed to be the ancestors of 'all the race of slaves', give some impression of qualities and characteristics considered undesirable by the Norse.

Rig moves on to a house with a door on the latch:

The man was whittling wood for a cross-beam.
His beard was trimmed, his hair above the brows,
His shirt close-fitting, there was a chest on the floor.

On it sat a woman, spinning with a distaff,
Stretching out the thread, preparing for weaving;
A head-dress was on her head, a smock on her body,
A kerchief round her neck, brooches at her shoulders.

In due course they have a son and they name him Farmer; his offspring have such names as Soldier, Thane, Smith, Yeoman, Lady, Sensible, Wise, Shy and Sparky.

The third result of Rig's exertions is the birth of Lord whose parents are Father and Mother, dwelling in a hall, door half open with a ring on the latch. When first encountered, they gaze into one another's eyes; they have leisure for love, a commodity apparently denied lesser mortals. Father makes bows and arrows, his wife admiring her clothing, smoothing down her sleeves, straightening her headdress, a pendant on her 'shining breasts'; she wears a short cape and a blue-stitched blouse, 'her neck whiter than freshly fallen snow'. She produces a an embroidered white linen tablecloth and a fine white loaf, silver dishes, and ornamented goblets for wine. They dine on pork and roast birds. Their son grows up learning to handle weapons, to ride, hunt and swim. Rig teaches him runes, names and adopts him, tells him to acquire property and settlements. He goes off on a quest through the dark wood and over frost-covered mountains, hurling his spear, wielding his sword. Significantly, 'he started a war, he reddened the plain with blood, / dead men fell, he fought for the land'. He was earning his place in Valhalla. And, of course, his youngest son was to become known as 'King'.[26]

THE EARLS AND THE FARMERS

(Farmer) began to grow and to thrive well;
he tamed oxen, worked the harrow,
he built houses and threw up barns,
made carts and drove the plough. *Rigsþula* [27]

As early as Chapter 5 of *Orkneyinga*, an important element is introduced, namely the earldom's farmers who remain front and centre throughout the saga. The latter's complaints about losses from Viking attacks, against which Earl Hallad should be defending them, lead him, unable to satisfy them, to return home to Norway. 'This excursion made him a laughing stock.' His successor was Turf-Einar, so named because he was the first to cut peat for fuel at Tarbat Ness, Easter Ross, because firewood was scarce in the islands. In fact, unsurprisingly, he was not the first, for the monks at Portmahomack also used peat, as did many before them, but Einar's action suggests some kind of territorial jurisdiction. It has been convincingly shown that one-eyed Einar, the unpromising progenitor of the comital house of Orkney, is also associated with one-eyed Odin, so providing one more legendary strand, linking Orkney to Norway.[28] The spectacular results from the monastery's excavation suggest that it did not outlast the Viking incursions.[29] Furthermore it is now quite well accepted that the ancient Pictish province of Fortriu was situated in Easter Ross rather than further south as had long been thought.[30] *Orkneyinga* thus preserves suggestive, if sometimes elusive, material on Viking–Pictish relations, the echoes of which rumble on to the end of the saga.

When King Harald went to Orkney following the death of Halfdan he taxed the island sixty gold marks. Einar took the opportunity to pay the fine himself with the agreement of the farmers, thus increasing his hold over them; the wealthy would redeem their lands later while the poor were, in any case, unable to pay. Earl Sigurd the Stout, in turn, surrendered these land rights to the farmers in return for their support. The severe levies imposed by Einar, Sigurd's son, to the point of causing famine, were resented but those who lived under the rule of his brother Brusi enjoyed great prosperity. An enraged Einar threatened to kill Thorkel the Fosterer for submitting a plea on behalf of the farmers who rebelled against comital extortions. On learning that Einar planned treachery, Thorkel took offensive action, following a feast designed to promote conciliation. The two men were supposed to leave together; Einar sat on a bench beside the fire while Thorkel prepared for departure. When Thorkel, accompanied by an Icelandic visitor named Hallvard, walked through the hall, Einar asked him if he was ready yet. 'I am now' he responded, landing a blow on the head of Einar who collapsed on the open hearth. 'I've never seen such a useless lot,' said Hallvard. 'Can't you pull the earl out of the fire?' He hooked his curved Icelandic axe around Einar's neck and heaved him up on to the raised sleeping platform that was essential furniture in all great halls. Thorkel escaped for it was his destiny that he should triumph.

When Brusi consulted King Olaf (the saint) about his dispute with Thorfinn concerning the division of the islands, he was forced to acknowledge the king's overlordship, swearing an oath of loyalty and becoming his man. A similar agreement was imposed upon a reluctant Thorfinn. It often seems as if there was a popularity contest on the part of the earls to win over the farmers. Because they were enjoying peace, they did not relish the return of Hakon, Paul's son from Norway, fearing that 'bad feeling and violence' would follow him, but they were pleased when Magnus, his cousin, arrived. Holdbodi, a Hebridean farmer, was witness to the final discussion between Hakon and Magnus before the latter's martyrdom. Magnus suggested alternatives to death – pilgrimage to the Holy Land, exile in Scotland, mutilation or imprisonment, the last appealing to Hakon. At that point the chieftains jumped to their feet, vowing to kill one or the other because they would tolerate no more joint rule. 'Better kill him then,' said Hakon. 'I don't want an early death; I much prefer ruling over people and places.' It was said that he brought strong rule to the islands and new laws which found great favour with the farmers. When Hakon died, they had grave concerns about how his heirs, Harald and Paul, would get on together but, after Harald's demise, they unanimously supported Paul as sole ruler. The same problem recurred during the troubled joint chieftainship of Earl Rognvald and Earl Paul. Some folk advised Paul to share the rule 'but most of the leading men and farmers too, wanted him to buy Rognvald off with money to go away, even offering to make contributions of their own'. Others advised fighting. In the event Paul was murdered but there was still considerable opposition to Rognvald such that 'no condition the farmers laid down was a matter for blunt refusal' and he held regular assemblies with them. Such was his relationship that, when he ran out of funds for the building of Kirkwall Cathedral, he allowed the farmers to purchase their holdings. 'Farmers who were friendly to both sides' attempted to bring about conciliation between Earls Erlend and Harald Maddadsson, persuading Harald to hand over his share of the islands for good. Erlend summoned farmers from all over Orkney to an assembly asking them to give him their allegiance, which they did. The agreement stipulated that, if Rognvald returned from his trip to the Holy Land, Erlend would hand over to him the part of the islands that was rightfully his but, if he claimed more than half of the earldom, the farmers would back Erlend. When Rognvald returned, intermediaries tried to arrange a settlement between him and Erlend, while the farmers invoked the recent agreement which stipulated that Erlend should not withhold Rognvald's portion of Orkney. A reconciliation was agreed two days before Christmas. Clearly the Orkney farmers were a power in the land and were not to be taken for granted. Indeed, their support was essential to the success of any individual earl.

THE MOVING WHEEL ON THE RESTLESS AXLE

> The petty kings, having rent the realm asunder will quickly divide the loyalty of the people who inhabit the land, both of the rich and the poor and each of these lords will then try to draw friends about him as many as he can . . . Soon immorality begins to multiply, for God shows his wrath in this way that where the boundaries of the territories of the chiefs touch, he places a moving wheel on a restless axle. After that each one forgets all brotherly love and kinship is wrecked. *The King's Mirror*[31]

The entire saga could be viewed as an extended essay on comital rule, the warrior ethos and even, perhaps, masculinity. A few observations may be in order by glancing at the careers of Earl Rognvald and his alter ego, Svein Asleifarson. At first sight, Earl Rognvald Kolsson might have some claim to be regarded as the greatest of the Orkney earls. He walks on to the saga stage to boast of his own enviable attributes, reminiscent of Lord's accomplishments in *Rigsþula*:

> At nine skills I challenge –
> A champion at chess:
> Runes I rarely spoil,
> I read books and write:
> I'm skilled at skiing
> And shooting and sculling
> And more! – I've mastered
> (Harp) music and verse.

What is missing, oddly, is any mention of his military prowess. This man was born a Norwegian, starting life as a trader who poetically commemorated Grimsby in England, as 'wet, filth and mud'. Returning from his trip he was stylishly dressed in fashionable attire, something of a dandy, in fact. He owed his grant of half of Orkney to Norwegian royal patronage and the circumstance that he was regarded as the heir of his martyred uncle, St Magnus. Because his cousin, Earl Paul, refused to surrender any part of the isles, Rognvald sought an alliance with the sinister Frakkok and her kindred in Sutherland. He also started to build a power base in Shetland though, during his first summer, he proved a rather inept naval commander. His father Kol thought rather better of him but he advised that to win over support he should capitalise on his relationship with St Magnus to whom he should make a vow that, if he was successful in his bid to take over Orkney, he would dedicate a 'stone minster' to the saint in Kirkwall. The vow was solemnly sworn, a shrewd suggestion because Rognvald gained Church support thereby. He gradually made headway as he gained experience and built up his power base. On a visit to Norway it was suggested he might like to undertake a pilgrimage to the Holy Land. Returning to Shetland he was shipwrecked. The main point of this incident seems to be to demonstrate Rognvald's strong spirit, cheerfulness and optimism. The same is true of his fishing expedition around Sumburgh Head, dressed in a cowl, after which he distributed his catch to the poor. He caused great merriment, one woman bursting into laughter when he slipped while climbing up on a rope from the beach, tumbling back to the bottom of the slope.

> Wittily the woman
> Mocks my wear,
> But she laughs overlong,
> And may not laugh last.
> Early I sailed out,
> Eagerly, and all fully
> Furnished for fishing.
> Who'd figure me for an earl?

This poem gave rise to the expression that 'not many people know an earl when he's dressed as a fisherman'. This episode is presented as genuinely good natured, communal and to Rognvald's credit. He definitely possessed something of the common touch.

This is not the place for an analysis of the pilgrimage to the Holy Land, 1151–35 but a few observations may illuminate our theme. A voyage which included Narbonne, Galicia, the Mediterranean, Acre, the banks of the River Jordan, Byzantium, Italy and Norway could hardly be described as 'everyday' at present, let alone in the twelfth century. It was unusual in the experience of most people, though not unknown. What is interesting is that these men of the north took their assumptions with them to the warmer climes of Europe. They were led by a great poet, Rognvald, a man well trained and expert in skaldic verse yet open to the new troubadour poetry of the south which emerged around 1100. 'Troubadour poetry was, like skaldic verse, a wholly courtly art-form, practised by kings and noblemen or at their courts, and was again often of great elaboration even though its content was wholly distinct from that of skaldic verse.'[32] Obviously Rognvald and the poets who accompanied him already had some knowledge of the genre. At Narbonne the voyagers encounter the dazzling Ermengard, the unattainable woman of the troubadours. She was a well-established historical personality,[33] though whether her meeting with Rognvald took place as depicted in the saga may be doubted. It relates that her kinsmen persuaded her to invite the earl to a banquet, promising that 'if she were to welcome men of such high rank, travelling from distant lands, it would add to her reputation far and wide'. She appeared in her finest, hair loose in the manner of virgins, topped by a golden tiara. The earl sat her on his knee and made a verse.

> I'll swear, clever sweetheart
> you're a slender delight
> to grasp and to cuddle,
> my golden-locked girl.
> Ravenous the hawk, crimson-
> clawed, flesh-crammed –
> but now, heavily hangs
> the silken hair.

Skaldic poetry is almost untranslatable. Compare Paul Bibire's version of the same stanza:

> Truly your tresses, wise lady,
> surpass (the hair) of most women
> with locks of Frodi's milling. The
> hawkland's prop lets hair fall on to
> her shoulders, yellow as silk – I reddened
> the greedy eagle's claw.[34]

Whatever the poet intended to convey he clearly was taken with Ermengard's magnificent hair. The juxtaposed, and intrusive, crimson-clawed predator seems to come out of the north as a metaphor for her golden tiara.

That the conventions were not entirely understood may be indicated by Armod's concupiscent composition: 'I'd bed her gladly, even once would be worth it, a wish come true.' Thereafter, at least part of the pilgrimage becomes a courtly quest on behalf of Ermengard; castles are conquered, pagans plundered and storms at sea endured, in her name. Eventually the pilgrims swim the Jordan tying knots in the brushwood to encourage others to follow.

In an environment such as Orkney, there would have been talk for years about a local expedition to the Jordan and about the alleged exploits of the earl at the court of the most beautiful woman in Christendom. In societies based on kinship and lordship, the achievements of the earl reflect well on everyone, instilling a sense of belonging in the followers and fostering social cohesion. Rognvald's poetry would not have been confined to his immediate entourage any more than his saga would have been. His court was his drinking and feasting hall where he entertained chieftains who were also farmers and who hosted their own social events, doubtless retelling the tales and reciting the poems they had heard. Celebration of the earl's accomplishments, literary, historical, or architectural in the building of the magnificent Kirkwall Cathedral, became part of everyday pride and of what it meant to be an Orcadian.

The less spectacular saga episodes can also prove illuminating. In September 1152, Earl Harald and his men spotted a hostile longship approaching off Cairston near Stromness. They all took refuge in the nearby castle but one individual was so panicked that he ran all the way to Kirkwall to seek the sanctuary of the cathedral. Arni Hrafsson became stuck in the church door because of his shield, still attached to his back. A man called Thorgeir could vouch for the truth of this because he was in the kirk at the time. When the earls arranged one of their many (often futile) peace meetings at Kirkwall, one man was excluded from the settlement until he promised to marry his pregnant girlfriend. Jon Wing bore the loss of frostbitten toes fleeing into a frozen night to escape the wrath of Svein Asleifarson. Earl Rognvald, despite his great deeds and talents, suffers a somewhat ignominious death, overshadowed by the more colourful hunting down of his attacker, Thorbjorn Clerk. Nor was he celebrated as one of the three most powerful of the Orkney earls. Perhaps the ideal man in the eyes of men was Reginald, King of Man, who had an Orkney mother. He was described as the greatest fighting man in all the western lands; 'For three whole years he had lived aboard longships and not spent a single night under a sooty roof.'

James Barrett has emphasised the suspicion with which various scholars have regarded *Orkneyinga*, especially archaeologists like himself who strive for interpretations 'unbiased by this evocative but potentially misleading category of evidence'. Having 'rediscovered' the value of biography, however, he has now challenged the view that Svein Asleifarson is considered an anachronism in the saga, suggesting instead that he is an acceptable illustration of chieftainship. The two perspectives are not necessarily contradictory. Many chiefs in Scottish history have proved the personification of anachronism and they continue to do so. Svein's exploits were certainly colourful and memorable but they were largely responsible for the failure of Earl Rognvald's lordship; his effectiveness as a ruler was called into severe question by his inability to control Svein whose actions are frequently criticised by the sagaman. Svein represented the warrior ethos, and he was undoubtedly a man's man, if not necessarily one that other men wished to emulate.

He is described twice in the story as *ójafnaðar-maðr*, an unjust overbearing man, a man of iniquity.[35] Such does not make him anachronistic but it does render him undesirable. He was a shrewd man, with a talent for seeing into the future, but ruthless and violent. The account of his looting of the monastery on the Isle of May after seven days of monkish hospitality, followed by his visit to David I to receive a friendly welcome and fine hospitality, even after he has admitted to the plundering, simply beggars belief and must be intended to be comic. It is diagnostic when Rognvald says, 'I expect Svein in Orkney at any moment and all the more so when he talks about going somewhere else.' Earl Erlend's men thought Svein 'a very odd character'. At one time he thought there was nothing he could not do but at others he was scared into complete inactivity. Many folk considered that he would always be causing trouble unless sent into exile. The alleged planned burning of his own house on Gairsay leaves him bereft of any respect or sense of morality. Earl Harald Maddadsson has to tell him to discontinue his greatest pride and pleasure, namely his Viking expeditions, on which he depends to support his retinue. In the final two chapters, in which Svein figures, he is described in one by the Dubliners as 'the greatest trouble-maker known . . . in the western world' while the other reports, 'people say that apart from those of higher rank than himself, he was the greatest man the western world has ever seen in ancient and modern times'. He was different things to different observers, a great chief, a great troublemaker, a mass of contradictions and an unwanted anachronism.

FOSTERAGE

When Hakon was past his infancy, Svein Asleifarson offered to foster him, so he was brought up on Gairsay and, as soon as he was strong enough to travel with grown men, Svein began to take him on Viking expeditions every summer, doing all in his power to build up Hakon's reputation.[36]

Fosterage was an important and useful means of social cohesion in Norse and Gaelic society. It was obviously a matter of great prestige when Earl Thorfinn was fostered by his grandfather, Malcolm, king of Scots. There could be no higher aspiration. Equally there was much advantage in a person fostering someone of a higher social standing than himself, as was the case with Thorkel the Fosterer who gained his soubriquet by also fostering Thorfinn. He first came to prominence by attempting to intervene with Earl Brusi on behalf of the farmers, thus risking his life. He was placed in further danger when he collected tribute from the Orcadians on behalf of Thorfinn. He was well received at the Norwegian court and he had to return there after he despatched Earl Einar. Thorkel also advised Thorfinn that, since his brother and rival, Brusi, had become King Olaf's man, then he better do the same. He did so, though with ill grace because he was reluctant to surrender his ancestral lands to men with no birthright or entitlement; but the successful Vikings were pragmatists. King Olaf judged that Thorkel must agree compensation with Thorfinn and Brusi for his killing of their brother. He preferred to take his chances with Thorfinn, however, rather than the Norwegian king and so, laying his head on Thorfinn's knee, he announced that he could do with him as he liked. The earl concluded that Thorkel must stay with him, never leaving him without permission, and must accede to his every wish – for life. Thus, fosterage and lordship were thoroughly cemented. Thorkel was in attendance throughout Thorfinn's campaigns against Macbeth.[37] In time, Brusi's son Rognvald grew to manhood, having been fostered by King Olaf (Haraldsson). Thorkel was given the credit for killing him on the seashore of Papa Stronsay, 'because no one else would do it; but then, he had sworn to do anything Thorfinn believed would add to his power'. Thorkel's subsequent career is unrecorded though he may have been confused with another Thorkel the Fosterer who survives for a mere eight lines in the saga before he is killed. But that is the saga way. The question of how any of us are influenced by people whom we meet momentarily or for a very short time is still an intriguing one. Svein Asleifarson became foster-father to Hakon, son of Earl Harald. He did all that he could to enhance the young man's reputation which is exactly the function of the fosterer.

CUSTODIANS OF THE FATES OF MEN[38]

> From (Yggdrasill) come three girls, knowing a great deal,
> From the lake which stands under the tree;
> Fated one is called, Becoming another –
> They carved on wooden slips – Must-be the third;
> They set down laws, they chose lives,
> For sons of men the fates of men (*Voluspa*)

Women are quite conspicuous in Old Norse literature. In his poem 'High One' (Odin) compares the love of a faithless woman to a smooth-shod horse on slippery ice, to sailing rudderless in a wild storm at sea, and to a lame man chasing after reindeer on an icy hill. Their hearts were fashioned on a potter's wheel; 'the words of a girl no one should trust / nor what a woman says'. Lest he be considered sexist, he admits in the following stanza that 'men don't keep faith with women; we speak fair words when we think most falsely'.[39] The first woman to figure in *Orkneyinga Saga* is the dreaded Ragnhild, daughter of Eric Bloodaxe, a woman who inherited her father's bloodlust and a taste for Orkney earls. She plotted the death of her first husband and, having married his brother, she led the latter's nephew, Einar, to believe that she would be the reward, if he would dispose of his uncle. He retorted that she, a respectable woman, should not suggest such things but, of course, he succumbed only to have Ragnhild deny that she had any part in the affair. Indeed, she urged vengeance on Einar, her dupe. Once again she betrayed the man who allied with her in expectation of gaining the earldom and 'other things just as important' from Ragnhild herself. She married Ljot. It was their grandson, Sigurd the Stout who, when challenged to battle by a Scottish earl, was so fearful of the consequences that he consulted his mother, Eithe, who was both the daughter of an Irish king and, fortuitously, a sorceress. 'Had I thought you might live forever I'd have reared you in my wool-basket. But lifetimes are shaped by what will be, and not by where you are,' she retorted, handing him a raven banner which she had made herself and which was fatal to whoever carried it. Such was Sigurd's task at the battle of Clontarf. He died a Christian, however, because, in the meantime, King Olaf of Norway (St Olaf) had offered the earl the stark choice of baptism or instant death.

Thora, mother of the recently martyred Earl Magnus, had invited him and Earl Hakon to a feast after what was supposed to be a meeting of reconciliation. She 'attended to the guests, serving drink to [Earl Hakon] and the very men who had taken part in the murder of her son'. She waited until the drink began to affect Hakon and then, weeping gently, she accosted him.

> I was expecting the two of you but now only you have come. Will you do something to please me in the eyes of God and men? Be a son to me and I shall be a mother to you. I'm sorely in need of your mercy, so let me have my son taken to church. Hear my prayers now, just as you yourself would hope to be heard by God on the Day of Judgement. Hakon, wracked with guilt 'looked at her and wept'. 'Bury your son', he said, 'wherever you wish.' His reward was to die in his bed a popular ruler.

Less gentle females were Helga and Frakkok, the daughters of Moddan of the Dales in Caithness; their Celtic heritage doubtless informed their evil scheming as they conspired in the creation of a poisoned shirt, designed for Paul but mistakenly worn by Harald. The latter interrupted the ladies busy at their needlework on the newly made shirt, stitched with gold thread. As he made to put it on, disregarding their warnings, they 'pulled off their bonnets', tearing their hair, to no avail. Paul subsequently banished them back to whence they came, Kildonan in Sutherland. When Earl Rognvald entered the story, he allied with Frakkok against Earl Paul, to no great effect despite her many powerful friends, marriage connections, in-laws and kinsmen. As I have previously suggested,[40] Frakkok is an intriguing character who straddled the Celto-Norse worlds but who was to die ignominiously in a house burning contrived by Svein Asleifarson.

Frakkok was the aunt of Margaret, sister of Paul the intended shirt wearer; she arranged Margaret's marriage to Maddad, Earl of Atholl, their son being Harald Maddadsson, whom Margaret schemed to have recognised as Earl of Orkney when he was only three years old. When Earl Paul heard of this suggestion, he vowed to quit Orkney and retire to a monastery. He suggested that Svein Asleifsson should spread a rumour that he (Paul) had been blinded and maimed. Some folk said that it was actually Margaret who hired Svein to blind and imprison her brother, eventually employing someone else to murder him. After her husband died, she moved to Orkney, having a child with Gunni, Svein Asleifarson's brother. Her son was obviously disgusted by his mother's behaviour but more was to come from this most self-reliant woman. She was abducted by Erlend the Young. Because he had already unsuccessfully sought permission from her son to marry her, complicity in the elopement can be assumed. The couple fled to Shetland, settling in the Broch of Mousa, now the most complete and impressive surviving example of this type of fortified, Iron Age structure. There they were besieged by Earl Harald who was eventually persuaded to permit marriage in return for Erlend's support which, because he had been raised a Scot, he somewhat lacked in the islands. Margaret is thus the means of pacification or feud quenching, perhaps atoning for any earlier role she may have played in creating mayhem. She is last heard of departing from Mousa en route to Norway, remembered as 'a very beautiful woman but full of her own importance'.

Both Paul and Rognvald encountered another distinguished woman, the mother of Thorstein, Ragna, who farmed on North Ronaldsay and who also had a property in Papa Westray. Paul accepted an invitation to a feast and then stayed the night owing to bad weather, thus affording the opportunity for conversation on many subjects with this intelligent female. She counselled Paul on the necessity for great leaders to cultivate strong allies. He had made some bad choices in the past but now he should reach an agreement with Svein Asleifarson. Paul retorted that Ragna was a sharp woman, 'but you're not the earl of Orkney yet and you're not going to rule in this land'. Pretending anger, he vowed he would not bribe Svein to defeat Rognvald whom he had never knowingly wronged nor even met. The meeting with Rognvald went rather better. It arose from a visit to North Ronaldsay by an Icelander, Hall Thorarinsson, who sought a place with Earl Rognvald and who hoped that Thorstein might be of assistance in approaching him; to no avail. Hall made a bitterly ironic poem in which he celebrated Thorstein's 'clever accomplishment', namely outright rejection of himself, and which ended with Rognvald telling him to 'go swallow your sausages', a reference to the reputed fondness of Icelanders for fat. Shortly thereafter, Ragna, wearing a red headdress made of horsehair, went to see Rognvald who made a teasing humorous verse in court metre (*drottkvætt*) in her honour:

> So, no sweet-talk;
> time surely was when
> the queenly ones covered
> heads with a kerchief?
> Now this merry matron
> Ties a mare's
> Tail – she's teasing me –
> To her top-knot.

Ragna retorted that his words bore out the old saying 'no man knows all'; her headpiece came from a stallion not a mare. 'Then she took a silk kerchief and as she put it on her head she carried on talking about her business.'[41]

This puzzling exchange has recently been elucidated by Bo Almqvist who explains (as have others) that the word for Ragna's eye-catching head-gear, *gaddan*, is the same as Gaelic, *gadan*, a flexible twig or withy used for binding. Almqvist compares this story to other Scottish tales in which the educated speaker confronts the simpleton with, 'Amn't I lucky, I have a horseshoe!' The other then replies 'Isn't learning wonderful? I wouldn't known this wasn't a mare's shoe!' Ragna thus outwits Rognvald but then creeps back into his good books by donning the kerchief as she continues to plead for a position for Hall.[42] She succeeds. There is flirtatious sexual tone to the exchange as in anything to do with horses or, indeed, hair, mares' tails, topknots, or for that matter, merry matrons but the gender reversal is intriguing – it is she who uses stallion's hair! Earl Rognvald proved quite taken with Ragna. He not only accepted Hall but he and Ragna jointly composed the *Háttalykill*, *The Old Key of Metres*, illustrating each type of metre with five verses. 'These days only two are used as the poem was thought too long.' Such a collaboration on poetry is a unique and unexpected example of twelfth-century gender equality even though, historically, it was Hall Thorarinsson who collaborated with Rognvald. By deliberately manipulating this information, the sagaman shows that he truly considered Ragna a remarkable woman to be credited with sharing an activity so very dear to Rognvald's heart.

The earl's empathy for one less fortunate, spiced up with a little flirtation, is illustrated in the episode following his shipwreck in Shetland. The lady of the house brought him a fur to warm him in front of a blazing fire. A servant girl entered the room, shivering with cold and mumbling something that no one could understand. Rognvald, however, claimed to know what she was saying and he made a poem to express the words she wanted to say:

You sit steaming, but Asa's
s-soaked to the skin;
f-f-far from the fire,
I'm freezing to death. (143)

The suggestion is that she should have his place, or a seat beside him, or perhaps she too should be under the fur with him!

DRINK: 'THE MIND-STEALING HERON WHICH HOVERS OVER FEASTS / WAITING TO SEIZE MEN'S WITS'

Beer isn't such a blessing to men
As it's supposed to be;
The more you swallow, the less you stay
The master of your mind.

The poems celebrate the appeal of imbibing; 'from the best carousing a man will come / to his senses soon again', but they also contain health warnings; when a man takes a drink 'what wit he has collapses'.[43] Thor was famously challenged to down the contents of the drinking horn in three draughts at most but, despite swallowing fabulous amounts, he made little impact on the contents. He was tricked, however; the other end of the horn was in the sea and his vast consumption created the ebb tide.[44] Ale often wrecked feasts:

Even friends fond of each other;
Will fight at table;
Nothing will ever bring to an end
The strife of men at meals.

But greed or 'the stupidity of stomachs' were also factors. Violent eruptions were frequently caused by drinking, leading to killings and, in some extreme cases, prolonged feuding.

The main beverage was beer made from malted barley, or its inferior sibling, bere. Mead made from honey was also on offer. Wine, which of course had to be imported and was thus expensive, was regarded as the drink of luxury and status. The folk of the Orkney earldom – occasionally women as well as men[45] – were no more immune to alcohol than the rest of their Scandinavian cousins. They drank on ships, in taverns, at home and in great halls. Indeed, whenever not otherwise occupied they reached for the cup. Earl Thorfinn the Mighty feasted his men and other guests throughout the winter on meat and drink, much as other notables would entertain their followers at Christmas, 'so there was no need for anyone to search for taverns' in order to drink their 'draughts, glory-drenched'. Earl Rognvald Brusison was killed when he went to Papa Stronsay to collect malt for the Christmas ale. His killer. Thorkel the Fosterer, thoughtfully loaded a ship with the malt for the return trip to Kirkwall, hanging Rognvald's shields along the prow.

The ship was eagerly welcomed with its promise of Christmas cheer which, unsuspected, also brought certain death.

King Magnus of Norway was eating on his ship when a white-hooded figure stepped aboard and helped himself to bread, accepting a cup as well. Thorfinn had come to make terms. A few days later on another visit, Thorfinn and Magnus 'began to drink and enjoy themselves' when a man appeared demanding satisfaction for his brother killed by Thorfinn at Kirkwall. 'Perhaps you haven't heard that I'm not in the habit of paying compensation for the men I've killed. You'll learn that I seldom kill anyone without good reason.' On this occasion the earl fled to avoid the king's anger. There was imbibing after the slaughter of St Magnus. Earl Rognvald is barely introduced into the saga before he is engaged in a pub crawl in Bergen, favouring a tavern owned by a lady of good family named Unn. On both occasions, he befriended the bright young son of a landholder, Jon Peterson. One night the two men retired to bed after drinking but a number of others continued the session, among them, Brynjolf, one of Jon's retainers, and Havard who was in Rognvald's retinue. As the drink flowed, tempers rose, leading to arguments about who were the greatest landholders in Norway. As was almost inevitable on such occasions, Havard bashed Brynjolf's head, rendering him unconscious. Later Brynjolf slew Havard. Rognvald and Jon were no longer friends. From then on the whole situation deteriorated as the situation became more complicated, sucking others into the vortex of feud. Eventually King Sigurd of Norway, sitting in judgment, settled the issue. Woundings and killings were balanced against both sides and, in addition, Jon married Rognvald's sister Ingirid. All parted the best of friends and Jon subsequently became Rognvald's loyal companion accompanying him on pilgrimage. At Imbolum in Turkey[46] there was time for a little refreshment. One drunken retainer fell off the pier into the harbour silt, celebrated in one of his leader's verses; 'mucked up in mud . . . not covered in glory . . . ditched at Imbolum and dripping with dirt'. Jon Peterson disappeared one night after a very heavy session, his wounded corpse being recovered next day. Thus inebriated, he ignominiously exited the saga.

One of the best-known, beer-fuelled killings took place at Orphir during the Christmas feast held by Earl Paul. Svein Asleifarson showed up having just suffered the loss of his father in a burning. He was soon to learn also that his brother had been drowned at sea. The earl 'asked people not to do any-thing to annoy Svein over Christmas as he already had enough on his mind'. Also present, with his kinsman Jon, was Svein Breast-Rope, Earl Paul's fore-castleman; his obscure soubriquet was probably nautically inspired. He is described as *úhamingjusamliger*, 'unlucky looking'. He was, furthermore, an 'outsitter', one who communed with trolls and spirits. The two Sveins were to engage in a great drinking competition in the hall at Orphir on Christmas Day. Each was attended by plate servers and cup-bearers. There had long between bad blood between the two. Breast-Rope, got it into his head that his cup was being filled up more often than that of Asleifarson which often was not even empty. When they switched to drinking horns, Breast-Rope was convinced that his was larger than the other, eventually demanding that they swap horns. Asleifarson was given a large horn which he passed to his rival who sinisterly muttered, 'Svein will kill Svein and Svein shall kill Svein.' When the earl retired, Asleifarson accompanied him from the hall while Breast-Rope went on drinking with his kinsman, Jon. Asleifarson, standing in the shadows with an axe, awaited Jon and Breast-Rope, who always carried a sword even when everyone else was unarmed. Svein Asleifarson struck him a fatal blow but, with his dying breath, Breast-Rope sliced his sword through the head, 'right down to the shoulders', of the man he mistakenly assumed in the darkness to be his assailant. In fact, it was his kinsman, Jon.

Svein went drinking in Atholl, on one occasion in the presence of entertainers. Less welcome was the lock-in each night of Svein and his retainers, so untrustworthy were they considered. He drank on Gairsay and in Damsay where he spent the nights imbibing in the great hall but sleeping on board ship. One day he was invited to sample ale brewed by a friend. When Rognvald and Harald attacked Damsay, Earl Erlend was so dead drunk that his would-be rescuer was able to lift him bodily and jump overboard with him into a dinghy. Erlend's corpse was later discovered, with a spear through it, in a pile of seaweed.

Svein's drinking hall on Gairsay was the largest in all Orkney. While plundering in Ireland, he looted two merchant ships of wine and mead which were used to lubricate a feast with Earl Harald. When Svein's two sons divided his inheritance between them after his death in Dublin, however, they erected partition walls in his great drinking hall. The glory days were over. The drinking, of course, was not. In 1230 Snaekoll Gunnisson and Hanef, the steward of the king of Norway, together with other supporters went drinking in Thurso. Quarrels often erupted on those drunken evenings but on one such, when Hanef was becoming quite merry, word arrived that Earl John Haraldsson of Orkney planned to attack them that very night. All the men, pleasantly intoxicated, thought it was a good plan to arm and strike first. The earl was caught in his basement and despatched. He died beside a tun, a large barrel for storing wine or beer.[47]

OTHER FOLK'S BELIEFS

It is noteworthy that, Svein Breast-Rope apart, there is not a great preoccupation with what might be called superstition in *Orkneyinga Saga*. Frakkok and a few others practise witchcraft but the sagaman does not dwell upon the subject. Hakon Paulsson, future earl and the slayer of St Magnus, consults a soothsayer about his personal destiny. The two have an interesting exchange, for Hakon is supposedly a Christian yet he does not consider that he and the seer need be envious of one another because of talents or beliefs.

His consultant finds it odd that Christians fast and keep vigil in the hope of discovering the future but 'the more there is at stake the less they find out'. Folk like himself, unburdened with penances can easily discover important things 'that our friends want to know, so that they're not kept in the dark'. In a sense the soothsayer is correct because most of the superstition in the saga is of the Christian variety. A massive wave presages St Magnus's death; his miracles are efficacious and a blinded bishop has his sight restored at St Triduana's shrine.

Magnus quickly became the focus of a cult, as folk flocked to his tomb at Birsay and then Kirkwall, seeking miracles, much to the embarrassment of the Bishop of Orkney and the surviving earl, both of whom remained staunchly opposed to translation and canonisation until they had no option but to comply with popular demand. Dedications to Magnus are not numerous but there are several in Shetland whence many of the pilgrims attending his shrine were said to have come. The section of the saga describing the Magnus cult is taken from a Latin miracle book which confirms the impression that the saint was particularly venerated in Shetland, possibly because he was regarded as somehow anticomital like the Shetlanders themselves. Bergfinn Skatason, a blind farmer from Shetland, took two cripples with him when he visited the shrine of the saint who appeared to them in person. Bergfinn could then see well enough to distinguish one hand from the other but, on a return trip, his full sight was restored; the cripples straightened up. The farmer seems to have figured prominently in the development of the cult. One Shetlander was cured of leprosy and another of insanity. An Orkney farmer fell from his barley rick badly hurting himself but was cured at the shrine. A man from the Faeroes had his crippled hand restored. Thord Dragon-Jaw, a tenant of Bergfinn's, refused to stop working thus infringing St Magnus Mass, a sin for which he was rendered insane, recovering only after his landlord paid a fee to the shrine and organised a three-day vigil for him. Bergfinn tended to another islander whose skull was fractured by a falling crossbeam, offering pilgrimage to Rome, the freeing of a slave or a gift of money should the man recover, as he did when the money was duly paid. Three Shetland women, all named Sigrid were also cured. The first, blind from infancy, was given her sight back when her father paid 'a great deal of money' to the shrine. A second had a broken leg restored. The third went mad, having to be restrained until a pilgrimage to Rome was pledged on her behalf. Insanity was apparently not uncommon. Magnus, in a fashion rather worldly for a saint, intervened on behalf of a compulsive gambler in England who bet his cargo boat and everything he possessed on a final throw. His opponent threw two sixes but Magnus caused the dice to split showing 'two sixes and an ace', so he won, later donating large sums to the Church. This Magnus was a somewhat mercenary saint! A man possessed by the Devil was sewed up in a cowhide and cured on a visit to Kirkwall. Thus were the everyday fears of the folk reflected in the miracles of Magnus.

Pagans as well as Christians understood the purifying properties of fire but burnings seem unduly prominent in the saga. When Rognvald sets his house alight, Earl Thorfinn narrowly escapes, breaking through a partition wall with his wife Ingibjorg in his arms. Womenfolk and slaves had already been allowed to leave. Thorfinn swiftly retaliated in kind. Two kinsmen of Svein Asleifarson burned Thorkel Flayer and eight of his men in his house. Frakkok was burned at Helmsdale and one of her burners, Svein Asleifarson, actually considered burning his own house on Gairsay, even though it contained his wife and children, because he thought his enemy, Earl Harald, was inside.[48]

LISTENING TO THE VALKYRIES

Let him who listens
To our Valkyrie song
Learn it well
And tell it to others.

Njáls Saga includes the *Darraðarljóð*, along with other material concerning the battle of Clontarf in 1014. A man named Dorruðr in Caithness, on the morning of the battle (Good Friday), looked through the window of an outhouse to see twelve women who had set up a ghastly loom on which they were weaving Odin's web, the fates of men; 'men's heads served as loom-weights, and intestines from men as weft and warp, a sword as the beater, and an arrow as the pin beater'. Herein is the perfect metaphor of an extremely familiar everyday object representing other-worldly activities. The technical aspects of an upright loom and the various parts that it comprises have been meticulously investigated to great effect.[49] A couple of strophes will give the flavour of the whole. It is now accepted that the poem should be dated to the early tenth century. It is possible that it was composed in Caithness.

Far and Wide
With the fall of the dead
A warp is set up:
Blood rains down.
Now, with the spears,
A grey woven fabric
Of warriors is formed.
Which women friends
Of Randvér's killer [i.e. Odin]
Complete with a red weft.

The fabric is warped
with men's intestines
and firmly weighted

with men's heads;
blood-stained spears serve
as heddle rods,
the shed rod an iron-bound axe
and arrows are pin beaters.
With our swords we must beat
This fabric of victory.

The valkyries are named as Hildr (Battle), Hjorþrimul (Sword-Noise),
Sanngríðr (Very Violent or Cruel), Svipul (Unstable), Gunnr (War), and
Gondul (Wolf or Staff-Bearer). At the end of the poem they tear apart the
woven cloth, 'each one retaining the piece she was holding' and, mounting
their horses, they ride off bareback, six to the north and six to the south.[50]
The song appears to foretell the victory of a young, kingly, Norse warrior
over the Irish who 'will undergo grief / which will never fade / in men's
memories: / now the fabric is woven / and the field dyed red; / the tidings of
men's destruction / will travel through the land'.

Now it is fearsome
To gaze around
As blood-red clouds
Gather in the sky:
The heaven will be stained
With men's blood
When our prophecies
Can spread abroad.

The poem, taken with others as well as the testimony of the sagas, confirms
Viking culture as one devoted to the celebration of violence and warfare.
Herein, once again, is preserved the memory of an older pagan world, the
bloodiness and violence of which survives, like a curse, into the twelfth-
century earldom.

In Norse cosmology *veröld*, world, translates as 'the age of humankind'.
People and gods lived in Midgarðr while Útgarðr was the space beyond,
inhabited by giants and nonhumans, corresponding to *innangarðs*, the farm-
yard and the *utangarðs*, the land beyond, Scots infield and outfield. Such,
briefly, was the concept of horizontal space; the vertical was represented by
Yggdrasill, the world tree, the ash tree of existence, which linked the human
world to the abode of the gods at the top of the tree, and with the dead in
Hel below its roots.[51] This wonderful concept was long ago characterised by
Thomas Carlyle as having its roots

deep down in the kingdom of Hela or Death; its trunk reaches up heaven-high,
spreads its boughs over the whole Universe . . . Is not every leaf of it a biography,
every fibre there an act or word? Its boughs are the histories of nations. The rustle
of it is the noise of human existence onwards from of old . . . It is the past, the

present and the future; what was done, what is doing, what shall be done; the infinite conjugation of the verb To Do.[52]

These worlds end in the chaos of Ragnarok, the doom of the gods, an age of carnage in which gods fight one another, or battle monsters, while the elements operate in unison, until eventually calm returns as the Earth sinks into the sea. But then Earth reappears, a brave new world rising from the waves, 'eternally green; / the waterfall plunges, an eagle soars over it, / hunting fish on the mountain'. The good gods return to meet and remember the events of the past; their golden chess pieces are rediscovered. The suspicion that all the calamities will be repeated, through the devastating combination of history, memory and the archetypal war game, is confirmed by the sinister appearance of the dark dragon, Nidhogg, bearing corpses as he flies over the plain. In the Norse world Time, as revealed by mythology and genealogy, was cyclical; the past was reborn in the present, just as Spring followed Winter and children inherited ancestral characteristics.

The Viking legacy included the extension of the geographical horizons of Shetlanders, Orcadians, Caithnessians and Scots in ways that were without precedent. In the great halls of the earls of Orkney, it would have been possible to meet people who had travelled from the American continent and Greenland, who knew of Svalbard (Spitzbergen) far to the north. Merchants might pass through who were familiar with North Africa. The earls themselves had travelled to Byzantium and the Holy Land, placing them within reach of the Silk Road to China. Others possibly reached the same destination by following the river systems and portages of Russia. By the twelfth century, Orkney was truly at the centre of a brave new world whose furthest reaches were gradually becoming part of the everyday.

Notes

1 *Icelandic Sagas*, 4 vols (Rolls Series, 1887–94); Sir George Webb Dasent (trans.), *The Saga of Hacon and a Fragment of the Saga of Magnus with appendices*, 2 vols (rep. Felin Fach, 1997), vol. 2, pp. 366–7. See also Edward J. Cowan, 'Norwegian Sunset – Scottish Dawn: Hakon IV and Alexander III', in Norman H. Reid (ed.), *Scotland in the Reign of Alexander III 1249–1286* (Edinburgh, 1990), pp. 103–31.

2 Edward J. Cowan, 'Scotland's Nordic legacy The Harvest of Battles and Beddings', in J. M. Fladmark (ed.), *Heritage and Identity: Shaping the Nations of the North* (Shaftesbury, 2002), p. 80.

3 The best books on Scotland are indicated in the Annotated Bibliography.

4 W. F. H. Nicolaisen, *Scottish Place-names: their Study and Significance* (London, 1976); Barbara E. Crawford (ed.), *Scandinavian Settlement in North Britain: Thirteen Studies of Place-Names in their Historical Context* (Leicester, 1995).

5 Doreen Waugh, 'Caithness An Onomastic Frontier Zone', in C. Batey et al., *Viking Age*, pp. 120–8.

6 Edward J. Cowan, 'The Vikings in Galloway: A Review of the Evidence', in

Richard D. Oram and Geoffrey P. Stell (eds), *Galloway Land and Lordship* (Edinburgh, 1991), pp. 63–75.

7 See general texts in Annotated Bibliography. All have sections on ships. Also Judith Jesch, *Ships and Men in the Late Viking Age. The Vocabulary of Runic Inscriptions and Skaldic Verse* (Woodbridge, 2001); Mark Merrony, *The Vikings Conquerors, Traders and Pirates* (London, 2004); Ole Crumlin-Pederson and Birgitte Munch Thye (eds), *The Ship as Symbol in Prehistoric and Medieval Scandinavia* (Copenhagen, 1995).

8 Paddy Griffith, *The Viking Art of War* (London, 1995); Ian Peirce, *Swords of the Viking Age* (Woodbridge, 2004).

9 On sagas and medieval Icelandic literature see Annotated Bibliography.

10 Hermann Pálsson and Paul Edwards (trans.), *The Book of Settlements Landnámabók* (Winnipeg, 1972), p. 6. See also Diana Whaley, 'A Useful Past: Historical Writing in Medieval Iceland', in Margaret Clunies Ross (ed.), *Old Icelandic Literature and Society* (Cambridge, 2000), pp. 161–202.

11 Snorri Sturluson, *Heimskringla History of the Kings of Norway*, Lee M. Hollander (trans.) (Austin, 1964), p. 4.

12 Diana Whaley, *The Poetry of Arnórr jarlaskáld An Edition and Study* (Turnhout, 1998).

13 Paul Bibire, 'The Poetry of Earl Rognvald's Court', in Barbara E. Crawford (ed.), *St Magnus Cathedral and Orkney's Twelfth-century Renaissance* (Aberdeen, 1988), pp. 223–4.

14 Snorri Sturluson, *The Prose Edda Tales From Norse Mythology*, Jean Young (trans.) (Berkeley, 1954), p. 33.

15 Thomas A. Dubois, *Nordic Religions in the Viking Age* (Philadelphia, 1999); Neil S. Price, *The Viking Way Religion and War in Late Iron Age Scandinavia* (Uppsala, 2002). For a different approach see Jens Peter Schjodt, *Initiation Between Two Worlds. Structure and Symbolism in Pre-Christian Scandinavian Religion* (University of Southern Denmark, 2008).

16 Julia McGrew (trans.), *Sturlunga Saga*, 2 vols (Boston, 1970, 1974), vol. 2, p. 489.

17 Terje Spurkland, *Norwegian Runes and Runic Inscriptions* (Woodbridge, 2005), pp. 143–9; Michael Barnes, 'The Interpretation of the Runic Inscriptions of Maeshowe', in Batey et al., *Viking Age*, pp. 349–69; Michael P. Barnes, *The Runic Inscriptions of Maeshowe, Orkney* (Uppsala, 1994), *passim*.

18 For a selection of general books on the Vikings see Annotated Bibliography.

19 Graham-Campbell and Batey, *Vikings in Scotland*, pp. 50–1. The remainder of this section draws heavily on chapters 10 to 12 of this study.

20 A. O. Anderson, *Early Sources of Scottish History*, A.D. *500–1286*, 2 vols (Edinburgh, 1922), vol 2. pp. 302–3.

21 Raymond Lamb and Judith Robertson, 'Kirkwall: Saga, History, Archaeology', in Owen, *World of Orkneyinga Saga*, pp. 161–91.

22 On this subject see John Randall (ed.), *Traditions of Sea-Bird Fowling in the North Atlantic Region* (Port of Ness, 2005).

23 Graham-Campbell and Batey, *Vikings in Scotland*, pp. 113–54. See also Olwyn

Owen and Magnar Dalland, *Scar: A Viking Boat Burial on Sanday, Orkney* (East Linton, 1999).

24 Finnbogi Gudmundsson, 'On the Writing of *Orkneyinga Saga*', in Batey, et al., *Viking Age*, pp. 204–11; Peter Foote, 'Observations on *Orkneyinga Saga*', in Crawford, *St Magnus Cathedral and Orkney's Twelfth-century Renaissance*, pp. 192–207.

25 Price, *Viking Way*, p. 30.

26 Carolyne Larrington (trans.), *The Poetic Edda* (Oxford, 1996), pp. 246–52.

27 All references are to Hermann Palsson and Paul Edwards (trans.), *Orkneyinga Saga. The History of the Earls of Orkney* (London, 1978), hereafter *Orkneyinga* unless otherwise indicated. A useful index obviates the need for too much cluttered referencing throughout this chapter.

28 Else Mundal, 'The Orkney Earl and Scald Torf-Einarr and his Poetry', in Batey et al., *Viking Age*, pp. 248–59.

29 Martin Carver, *Portmahomack. Monastery of the Picts* (Edinburgh, 2008), pp. 144–6.

30 Alex Woolf, 'Dun Nechtain, Fortriu and the Geography of the Picts', in *Scottish Historical Review* 85.2 (2006), pp. 182–201; Alex Woolf, *From Pictland to Alba 789–107*, Roger Mason (ed.), *New Edinburgh History of Scotland*, vol. 2, pp. 10–13 and index.

31 L. M. Larson (trans.), *The King's Mirror* (New York, 1917), p. 199.

32 Bibire, 'Poetry of Earl Rognvald's Court', p. 220.

33 Fredric L. Cheyette, *Ermengard of Narbonne and the World of the Troubadours* (Ithaca and London, 2001).

34 Bibire, 'Poetry', p. 232.

35 Foote, 'Observations', p. 196.

36 *Orkneyinga*, p. 190.

37 Edward J. Cowan, 'The Historical MacBeth', in W. D. H. Sellar (ed.), *Moray Province and People* (Edinburgh, 1993), pp. 117–41.

38 On Norse women see Judith Jesch, *Women in the Viking Age* (Woodbridge, 1991) and Jenny Jochens, *Women in Old Norse Society* (Ithaca and London, 1995).

39 Larrington, *The Poetic Edda*, pp. 6, 25–6.

40 Edward J. Cowan, 'Caithness in the Sagas', in John R. Baldwin (ed.), *Caithness A Cultural Crossroads* (Edinburgh, 1982), pp. 34–6.

41 *Orkneyinga* pp. 133–4; Alexander Burt Taylor, *The Orkneyinga Saga: A New Translation with Introduction and Notes* (Edinburgh, 1938), p. 389 note.

42 Bo Almqvist, 'What's In A Word? Folklore Contacts Between Norsemen and Gaels As Reflected in *Orkneyinga Saga*', in Owen, *World of Orkneyinga Saga*, pp. 34–6.

43 Patricia Terry (trans.), *Poems of the Vikings. The Elder Edda* (Indianapolis and New York, 1969), pp. 14–15.

44 Sturlyson, *The Prose Edda*, pp. 77–8.

45 For an interesting discussion of female drinking habits see Jochens, *Women in Old Norse Society*, pp. 105–11.

46 Imbolum is thought to have been a suburb or street of Byzantium.

47 *Hacon's Saga*, vol. 1, pp. 155–6.

48 Cowan, 'Caithness in the Sagas', p. 37.
49 R. G. Poole, *Viking Poems on War and Peace. A Study in Skaldic Narrative* (Toronto, 1991), pp. 116–56.
50 Price, *Viking Way*, pp. 331–41.
51 On Norse cosmology see Kirsten Hastrup, *Culture and History in Medieval Iceland. An Anthropological Analysis of Structure and Change* (Oxford, 1985), pp. 145–51. It is, of course, not permissible to transpose Icelandic ideas about such matters to Orkney without sound evidence for so doing.
52 Thomas Carlyle, *On Heroes, hero-worship, and the heroic in history* (London, 1840: 1889), pp. 199–200.

Chapter 3

Sacred and Banal: The Discovery of Everyday Medieval Material Culture

Jenny Shiels and Stuart Campbell

INTRODUCTION

Our knowledge of everyday life in medieval Scotland has been significantly enhanced in recent years by the recovery of thousands of objects and coins from agricultural land, most probably derived from the dumping of nightsoil and from refuse from households, markets and fairs. The recovery of these artefacts by people using metal-detecting machines has shown that coins and objects in considerable numbers can be readily retrieved when modern farming methods bring them into the ploughsoil. These losses and discards are proving to be a rich source of information on medieval material culture and represent a random cross-section of the types of items in everyday use and circulation across the country.

The material under discussion here is entirely new to the archaeological and historical record and its recovery through the use of metal detecting machines remains controversial.[1] None of the artefacts discussed here would have come to light at all, however, but for the efforts of a handful of individual enthusiasts who have been responsible for the majority of these new finds made in the past ten years. Their compliance with the Scottish laws of Treasure Trove[2] means that a new set of data is now available for study and research from find spots which would never have attracted archaeological investigation, these being generally featureless fields but which are now proving to be surprisingly rich in medieval evidence.

BEFORE THE BURGHS

While towns as distinctive entities may not be obvious as upstanding archaeology before the twelfth century, there is ample evidence for activity on many burgh sites and rural settlements which long predates their final manifestations as built environments. Sites which have recently produced significant numbers of medieval objects and coins from metal-detecting, including Dornoch, Fortrose, Crail, Culross, Aberlady, Maxton near Kelso and St Combs near Fraserburgh are all notable in having also produced pre-Roman, Roman and, significantly, early historic and Viking/Norse objects which are

Figure 3.1 *Viking silver ingots and an ingot mould from sites on the River Tweed.*
© *Crown copyright reproduced courtesy of the Treasure Trove Unit.*

scant in the archaeological record. These locations represent every type of
locale from Highland, Lowland, coastal, inland, burgh and rural settlement,
and there is little doubt that they have all been occupied, albeit intermittently
and probably seasonally, over several millennia and that the evidence which
remains today for medieval presence represents only one short phase in
lengthy site activity. It is no surprise, then, that the landscapes in which prehistoric settlements were sited remained attractive for medieval settlement.
The land clearance which began some four thousand years previously in the
Neolithic period and continued into the Bronze Age had prepared Scotland's
most fertile land for cultivation, and the proximity of sites to the sea or to
major river systems established communication and trade routes from the
Continent thousands of years before the inception of the burghs.

   If we consider the material culture evidence immediately prior to the
establishment of Church and State in the twelfth century, we can detect the
traces of those multicultural influences which precede the establishment
of Anglo-Norman institutions. Until the eleventh century and possibly
beyond, bullion in the form of small portable ingots were in use in Scotland
in place of, and alongside, coinage. Discoveries in the past few years of silver
ingots which are directly comparable to types found in Viking hoards have
been found at Maxton and Sprouston on the River Tweed along with a stone
mould for casting such ingots from the banks of the Tweed in the vicinity of
Old Melrose (Figure 3.1). These three sites date to the Anglian occupation
of Northumbria, and each has produced everyday Anglo-Saxon objects but
the Viking-type ingots point to these sites continuing in use with possibly a
Scandinavian presence from the tenth to the twelfth centuries, indicated by
the siting of Norse hogback gravestones on the tributaries of the Tweed.[3]
The importance of Berwick-on-Tweed as the entry and exit point to the

North Sea is clear, and it is here that we might expect exceptional material evidence for the preceding centuries of cultural influences that can be demonstrated at the sites referred to above. Alas, this is not the case, and a different law of Treasure Trove in England and Wales has resulted in an absence of comparable evidence of everyday things from this important Scottish medieval town.[4]

Fragments of Viking hacksilver, so-called because it comprises broken silver objects which have been hacked or cut up to melt and reuse, have recently been found at Crail, Culross and Aberlady; significant numbers of ninth-century Northumbrian coinage[5] and decorative metalwork are testament to the activity and importance of these sites in the period immediately prior to their medieval manifestation. The so-called 'Dark Ages', then, are proving to be not so dark, as we can now demonstrate thanks to these emerging new discoveries that are proving instrumental in understanding the origins of a number of medieval sites and settlements.

EVIDENCE OF CHANGE

In comparing the material culture of the preceding phases of activity with that which is recognisably medieval and pan-European in character, it becomes possible to determine the ways in which this new identity was formed. Indeed, it is often the appearance in the archaeological record of seemingly mundane objects that can chart the monumental changes occurring in a society that herald the very beginnings of change. By the twelfth century, Scottish material culture had begun to show a strong European influence. In some ways, this is part of a familiar story involving the founding of monasteries, the introduction of a formal monetary economy and the use of royal and personal seals. These developments are well known, representing as they do notions of kingship, legality and the nation state familiar to conventional historiography. Less obvious to the historian are those everyday objects reflecting concepts of self-representation and belief which demonstrate a shift in attitudes throughout the population as a whole rather than those rarefied concepts of government and property confined to the elites. In this sphere, it seems clear that the Scottish population had begun to consume – or adopt – a standard west European material culture. The importance of these finds is not simply that they show contact with the wider world for that is clearly demonstrated in the import of Continental pottery to many Scottish burghs.[6] Equally so, the propensity of the elite to exhibit and entrench their status by the import and consumption of exotic and luxury goods is nothing new. Rather, while many exotic imports were prized precisely because of their rarity, the objects discussed here do not remain unusual but instead take their place within the currency of everyday life.

However exotic coinage may have first been, it rapidly became commonplace in everyday life. A silver sterling of David I, minted at St Andrews by

Mainard, the Fleming, also responsible for building the burgh, was discovered in a ditch at Preston in Berwickshire in 2003. One of only eight examples
to survive, it belongs to the very first coins to be minted in Scotland under a
Scottish king, and marks the start of an independent Scottish coinage.[7] Large
numbers of coins, both English and Scottish, along with a smattering of continental issues dating across the entire medieval period, have been recovered
from fields surrounding Dornoch and Crail, and chart the fortunes of these
sites. At Dornoch, coinage appears to have been common in the thirteenth
century despite it not achieving burgh status until the seventeenth century,[8]
and presumably the wealth generated by the cathedral lands is responsible
for this phenomenon. At Crail a high proportion of early coins, but very
little by way of late medieval small change,[9] indicates a peak of activity in the
thirteenth and fourteenth centuries which is paralleled in the types of everyday objects found from the same vicinity and which include small personal
effects such as buckles datable to this period.

DRESS AND SECULAR CULTURE

By the late twelfth century, an emerging interest in ornament and display
can be demonstrated by the appearance of various forms of jewellery across
Europe, typified by the finger rings in a hoard from Lark Hill, Worcester,
containing six silver rings which can be dated to the late twelfth century by
the coins which also formed part of the hoard.[10] Among the simplest of these
rings is a plain silver band decorated with a series of cruciform panels, and
the discovery of two of these in Aberdeenshire[11] indicate that Scotland was
among the earliest adopters of this new trend (Figure 3.2). The discovery
of an identical ring in copper alloy on the Isle of Lewis indicates that this
fashion was sufficiently popular both to reach across the political and cultural divides between the Hebrides and the mainland kingdom as well as to
be reproduced in a non-precious metal, a point that will be discussed later.

Figure 3.2   Twelfth-century rings in an identical style in silver and bronze from
Inverboyndie, Aberdeenshire (left) and the Isle of Lewis (right). © Crown copyright
reproduced courtesy of the Treasure Trove Unit.

These rings are also found outside the British Isles, for example in Denmark, this time in both gold and silver.[12] The appearance of the same objects across Europe at the same time is surprising and sudden and often interpreted as indicating increasing economic prosperity. While this is undoubtedly a factor, it does not seem to explain the contemporary appearance of identical forms in societies which otherwise had little in common.

While it is tempting to conclude that the appearance of such objects reflects the emerging Anglo-French influence on Scottish society, it remains the case that such objects are not part of Anglo-French culture, and their emergence is just as sudden elsewhere in the British Isles. Equally so their appearance in areas culturally and politically distinct from England and France, from Denmark to the Isle of Lewis, suggests that the primary cause for their appearance is not Anglo-French acculturation. Nevertheless, given the nature of the transformations started by David I and the international nature of the monastic orders, such changes undoubtedly acted as vectors for the spread of the new material.

Although an apparently trivial artefact, the Lewis ring represents a clear break with the past. Earlier objects of adornment tended to be elaborate and expensive items intended to advertise the status of the wearer. By way of contrast, the Lewis ring sums up the nature of this new material; a style which appears in both precious and non-precious metals suggesting use by a wider range of social classes and for reasons other than prestige. An interest in secular display and adornment is by no means a constant in the past and, in the eleventh century, there was very little of this type of material, and the appearance of such jewellery in Scotland at the same time as in the rest of Europe suggests that Scotland is sharing in an overall change in attitudes about secular ornament. The sudden popularity of these new items appears not to be concerned with reasons of fashion although the importance of fashion should not be discounted. Rather, such items were often inspired by a complex mix of ideas and beliefs, beliefs that did not originate in Scotland. If a simple phrase can be used to describe this new material culture, it would be replete with meaning; this meaning can be social, religious, sexual or political and, in most cases, the meaning of the piece is the prime reason for wearing it.

The best example of this new internationalism is perhaps the annular brooch. The use of a brooch or metallic clasp to fasten clothing at the neck can first be seen in sculptures and manuscripts of the late twelfth century and, by the thirteenth century, the use of an annular brooch was widespread in Europe, from Scotland to the Balkans and north to the Baltic coast.[13] These brooches often developed symbolic and social associations and were often given as gifts. Perhaps it is not surprising that a brooch used to fasten garments at the breast soon became bound up with notions of female modesty and propriety. Writing in 1184, the poet Johannes de Hauville spoke for many husbands when he declared:

Figure 3.3   *An inscribed gold fourteenth-century brooch from Falkirk and a bronze example from Luce Sands, Dumfries and Galloway. © Crown copyright reproduced courtesy of the Treasure Trove Unit.*

> My bride shall wear a brooch – a witness to her modesty and a proof that hers will be a chaste bed. It will shut up her breast and thrust back any intruder, preventing its closed approach from gaping open and the entrance to her bosom from being cheapened by becoming a beaten path for any traveller, and an adulterous eye from tasting what delights the honourable caresses of a husband.

Accordingly a number of brooches bear amatory inscriptions, presumably a gift from a husband, whether actual or intended. A fourteenth-century gold brooch recently discovered from near Falkirk bears the inscriptions *OR ME NE VBLIE NI DEV* 'don't forget me or God' and *JE SVI : ICI EN LV DE AMI* 'I am here in place of a lover' (Figure 3.3).[14] These inscriptions are in Norman French, indicating both an influence from within the British Isles and a wider influence from Continental Europe where French was widely used for such inscriptions as the language of courtly love. Objects such as this comprise an excellent example of the changing influences in Scottish society, the adoption of new forms of dress and adornment, and the influence of the rules and ideals of courtly love central to many medieval concepts of self.

It may seem odd in a discussion of everyday life to deal with a precious metal object espousing an ideal of romance most often associated with the nobility yet, as will be seen below, such cultural ideals were not confined to those who could afford gold to pledge their devotion. Examples also exist in pewter and bronze, and similar items pertaining to the relationships between the sexes are not uncommon, especially those concerning the central relationship of marriage. *Fede* (faith) rings became fashionable and their bezels

Figure 3.4 Fede *rings in both bronze and silver from Moray. © Crown copyright reproduced courtesy of the Treasure Trove Unit.*

in the form of clasped hands made them multi-purpose as objects associated with religious piety and as betrothal rings. The use of these rings appears to have been a constant throughout the medieval period, first appearing in the late twelfth century along with those rings discussed above. The majority are in silver but surviving examples vary greatly in the weight of metal used, suggesting they were produced to cater for a range of financial means. Unsurprisingly, this affordability is continued to its logical conclusion, with examples in bronze (Figure 3.4) also known as well as a stone mould from Perth intended to cast pewter versions.[15] This latter is the nearest medieval crafts came to mass production, and suggests that the use of such rings was widespread. The discovery of moulds from Perth raises an important point: however exotic such objects may initially have been they were not imported but manufactured here.

In many ways such objects are not too distant from modern engagement and marriage rings although we should not forget the explicit sense of male prerogative and conjugal entitlement that such objects embody. At the same time, brooches as well as rings could be inscribed with a religious text, most commonly an appeal to Christ or the Virgin Mary or an excerpt from the Gospels. These inscriptions are not simple expressions of piety but rather represent a specific belief in the efficacy of certain formulaic texts to protect the wearer from harm, in effect a magic spell. It is important not to view such ideas as crude superstition, because the rationale for this belief was a respectable intellectual position held by, among others, St Thomas Aquinas.[16] In the medieval Christian cosmology, such everyday magic was considered a vital link between the heavenly and earthly realms in a world where divine intervention – in the form of miracles – was actively expected. Like similar beliefs concerning the magical power of precious stones, these ideas were spread across Europe by the writings of clerics and philosophers, the original Latin being translated into local languages,[17] and it is an illustration both of the influence and speed of transmission of these beliefs that such jewellery appeared in Scotland at the same time as these ideas gained prominence.

Although one of the best collections of amuletic brooches is the precious metal group held by the National Museums of Scotland,[18] such brooches are also known in pewter[19] in the Netherlands, and examples in copper alloy are frequently found. What is most remarkable about such pieces is how unremarkable and commonplace they were, and the pewter and bronze examples provide a useful illustration of how an exotic philosophy could be rapidly assimilated into the local culture and disseminated throughout the populace.

The appearance of the same objects in precious and base metals is a constant throughout the period, and it is rare indeed to find an item of jewellery or personal adornment that does not also exist in pewter or bronze. The consistency of this makes it unlikely that this is simply a copying without understanding but rather reflects a genuinely widespread desire for these items fuelled by a full awareness of their intended functions. The ubiquity of these low-cost alternatives does challenge the notion of the medieval population as too impoverished to afford such goods; while a gold brooch might be commissioned by a rich patron at the other end of the market, the inexorable law of economics must hold sway. The archaeological evidence from burghs such as Perth suggests a large-scale industry devoted to producing affordable alternatives to precious metal objects.[20] Indeed, the efforts involved in producing such cut stone moulds makes sense only if sufficient quantities of the finished product can be sold. The popularity of these objects in turn implies a widespread understanding of the symbolic roles these objects played and the cultural ideals which lay behind them.

These base metal counterparts should not be despised as inferior copies, for they are on the whole well made, and the technical skill of the lettering on many base metal objects surpasses that of the precious metal brooches. Their popularity attests not so much to an unthinking desire to copy the dress of one's social betters but rather to the notion of a uniform material culture that crossed social boundaries and that was used and understood by all classes of society. In one sense, however much the people were divided by social hierarchy, they were united by common perceptions and beliefs which functioned independently of social position.

In concluding this section, the authors should emphasise that they are not arguing the case for a medieval society dominated by sex and superstition – far from it. It is not that such ideas dominated medieval life at the expense of other ideals but rather that they formed an integral and perhaps unremarkable part of it.

MATERIAL CULTURE AND CONSUMPTION IN THE HIGHLANDS AND LOWLANDS

The use of metal detectors around settlements with medieval antecedents has revealed that many are surrounded by a thick scattering of artefacts in the ploughsoil. For the archaeologist this material represents a fascinating snapshot of what the medieval inhabitants were using and wearing. The objects recovered range from buckles and fittings used in everyday dress to those objects used in the domestic sphere. As such they reflect the nature of medieval manufacture; if not quite mass production, then clearly intended to produce large quantities of objects at affordable prices.[21] Much of this detecting has been carried out around burghs in the north of Scotland, such as Dornoch and Fortrose, and has recovered an impressive quantity and range of material.

Reflecting the methods of production and use, these artefacts conform easily to broad categories and tend to follow a repetitive and even predictable pattern. Such predictability might appear uninteresting but it is the quantity and unchanging nature of the material that demonstrate that it was worn widely, and the appearance of the same material on sites from the East Neuk of Fife to the north of Scotland demonstrates the universality of its use. Such material has been found in Scotland before but, as many excavations have concentrated on the power centres of secular and ecclesiastical elites, such material could be seen as part of a wider assemblage of exotic and imported goods in sites such as castles and royal burghs.[22] The value of the metal-detected evidence is that it shows how commonplace such material really was. Like the brooches and finger rings discussed above, the objects recovered have good European parallels. In this sense it becomes clear that the influence of European material culture is not restricted to single items of jewellery but was truly widespread.

The material in Figure 3.5 has been assembled from a number of settlement sites in the Black Isle and is representative of the personal items which tend to be found. In general, the material tends to follow the major trends in European dress and consumption; for example, the strap end buckles and belt mounts are from decorated girdles used in the thirteenth and fourteenth centuries while the lace chape is from the laces used to fasten the tightly fitting clothing popular in the fourteenth and fifteenth centuries.[23] It is important to note that these objects are diagnostic of particular forms of clothing and suggest that, in many ways, the population was dressing in a fairly generic European style. Overall the evidence suggests that particular trends and forms of dress arrived in Scotland at the same time as in the rest of Europe, and the material from sites such as Fortrose tallies well with that recovered from London and Amsterdam. In stressing the clear foreign influences, it is important not to lose sight of one obvious point: the clear cultural differences one might expect between northern and southern Scotland are not generally reflected in this material, and the majority of the dress accessories and other items recovered from the sites in the Black Isle could as easily have come from a site in Fife or the Scottish Borders.

The general quantity and range of material recovered indicate a level of consumption which compares well with the rest of Europe. While

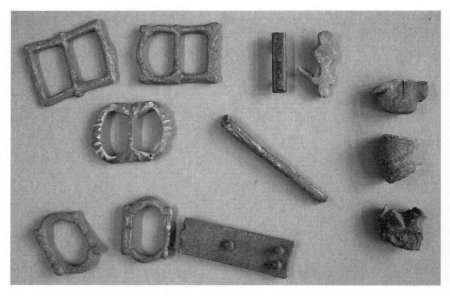

Figure 3.5 *A variety of medieval dress accessories. Bottom left, the buckles for girdles of the thirteenth and fourteenth centuries; centre right, a lace chape of fourteenth- to fifteenth-century date.* © *Crown copyright reproduced courtesy of the Treasure Trove Unit.*

archaeologists are often guilty of viewing the recipients of such goods as passive partners in their acquisition, there is sufficient evidence to suggest that the burghs were part of a network which could easily attract such goods. The quantity of medieval coins around such sites as Dornoch and Fortrose suggests an economy fully integrated into a wider trading network and with the financial means to participate in that network.[24] Equally, other finds demonstrate the ability to acquire wares from some distance away. The remains of a twelfth- or thirteenth-century pewter candlestick from near Fortrose are tangible evidence of such connections (Figure 3.6). When complete, the candlestick would have been an impressive object and demonstrates no little skill on the part of the maker. Examples from the same mould are known from London and Dublin,[25] a useful illustration of the wide-ranging network of which sites such as Fortrose were part.

A most striking aspect of the material found by metal detecting is the extraordinary amount of lead and lead alloy objects in use for everyday purposes and, indeed, we can only speculate as to the consequences on the population of this daily exposure to such a hazardous metal. If plastic is the cheap, ubiquitous and multi-purpose hazardous material of our times, then lead was undoubtedly its precursor in the medieval period in terms of

Figure 3.6 *The fragmentary candlestick from Fortrose.* © *Crown copyright reproduced courtesy of the Treasure Trove Unit.*

its popularity as a cheap and adaptable material employed for a plethora of purposes.

From Crail in Fife lead objects recovered by metal detecting demonstrate an extraordinary range of purpose and use, from line and net weights and

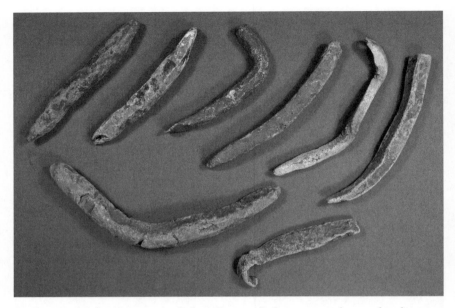

Figure 3.7 *Medieval writing leads from Fortrose. © Crown copyright reproduced courtesy of the Treasure Trove Unit.*

sounding weights all used in fishing, spindle whorls and loom weights for use in spinning and weaving, seal matrices, writing leads or styluses, trade tokens and weights, and for buttons and pilgrim badges, papal bulls and small mortuary crosses for burial with the dead. This cheap and malleable metal, resistant to corrosion, was easy to obtain and use by unskilled people in a domestic or semi-industrial capacity, and was almost limitless in the ways it could be used.

From the twelfth century, the use of lead for writing is commonplace, and writing leads are some of the most common metal-detected finds from the sites under discussion (Figure 3.7). They take the form of lead strips, similar in style to a short pencils and are either round or square in section, sometimes with a hole pierced at one end so that they could be hung round the neck on a string. Like graphite pencils, they made grey marks which could then be rubbed out or written over in ink.[26] Dozens of these have been recovered from sites across the country, and we can assume that they were in use by the clergy and by merchants from the twelfth century onwards and, along with bookstraps and book clasps and hinges, they indicate a surprisingly widespread literacy, albeit most probably reserved for certain members of society (Figure 3.8).

Crail became a royal burgh in the late twelfth century, and herring fishing

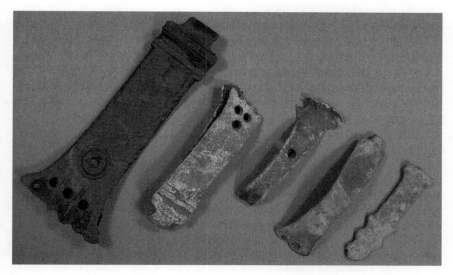

Figure 3.8   *A selection of fifteenth- to seventeenth-century bookclasps from Fortrose.*
© *Crown copyright reproduced courtesy of the Treasure Trove Unit.*

was a major source of its wealth. Evidence of this fishing heritage comes in the form of crudely cast lead hogback-shaped net and line weights which also turn up on sites as diverse as the hamlet of St Combs in Aberdeenshire, West Haven in Angus and from excavations at Whithorn in Galloway,[27] indicating a distribution round the coast of mainland Scotland (Figure 3.9), and there is anecdotal support for this style of weight continuing in use until comparatively recently. Lead sounding weights used to judge sea depth belonged to the standard kit on all vessels in the early navigation of harbour and other shallow waters, and those from Roman shipwrecks in the Mediterranean are identical in shape and form to those recovered from Crail and West Haven in Angus.

WOMEN'S WORK

Household industry has produced one of the most ubiquitous everyday items in the form of the decorated lead spindle whorl, a circular weight with a hole which is placed at the end of a spindle to give it the momentum to keep spinning. The spinning of flax and wool, essential to the ordinary household economy, was practised by women of every social class, and decorated and undecorated lead and lead alloy whorls have been found across Scotland from rural sites to burghs as well as in burials. The sizes and weights of these whorls vary in accordance with whether wool or flax was being spun and whether coarse or fine yarn was required. The decoration of the whorls is

Figure 3.9 *Medieval and post-medieval lead fishing line and net weights from Crail.*
© *Crown copyright reproduced courtesy of the Treasure Trove Unit.*

usually restricted to combinations of radial lines and dots or applied pellets, closely conforming to the stone and bone versions, although their mode of manufacture and their similarities in decorative ornament are comparable with the tokens and buttons of the fourteenth and fifteenth centuries (Figure 3.10). Examples of spoiled castings of these whorls have come from Redcastle near Inverness and from a site near Dornoch, known locally as the 'tinker's track', which may suggest that some production at least was in the hands of itinerant smiths travelling with their moulds and melting and recasting scrap lead as required.

It is rare that archaeological objects can be identified as gender-specific outside of a burial context but the distribution of these decorated whorls suggests they were popular across Scotland, and as far south as the Humber and into Lincolnshire, although they appear not be a southern phenomenon because they are absent from the London and Winchester excavations.[28] The excavation of a late medieval burial of a young woman at Coldingham Priory in the Scottish Borders found one of these decorated whorls placed with her in the grave,[29] and it is tempting to speculate that, in some cases, these may have been the only personal objects that some women owned. The inclusion of spindle whorls in burials is widespread, from Scandinavia to Ireland, and their burial with males and infants from the thirteenth to sixteenth centuries in England can be interpreted in a variety of ways as linking the dead with the owner or in relation to their use in popular cures.[30]

Figure 3.10   *Medieval lead spindle whorls from Crail. © Crown copyright reproduced courtesy of the Treasure Trove Unit.*

Customs and superstitions surrounding women and their spinning and weaving abound, from the Greek myths relating to Ariadne to contemporary Hebridean waulking songs (Gaelic call and response songs), and we can only speculate as to how these were used and perceived by medieval women across Scotland.

PERSONAL IDENTITY AND AUTHORITY

As the institutions of state and religion became established, individual identity as a mark of authority came to be represented in the form of seal matrices. These were a necessity for conducting everyday business and as a means of communication in a largely illiterate world, and were used to authorise all manner of transactions by impressing the seal into wax. A wide variety of seal matrices has been recovered by metal detecting in recent years, ranging from those belonging to people of the highest rank down to the lowliest cleric making do with an off-the-peg lead seal. It was common to cancel a personal seal upon the death of the owner to prevent misuse. This was done either by scoring or by breaking the seal, and many seals are, indeed, broken and therefore difficult to decipher. It is a broad rule of thumb that ecclesiastics and women most often owned oval-shaped seals while the male laity had circular seals. As seals had to be understood at a number of levels by both the literate and illiterate population, they carried a symbol or device in the centre of the seal and an inscription or legend around the outside. Wealthy and powerful individuals owned large and often intricate seal matrices bearing their personal heraldic devices, and these were made from moulds intricately carved by skilled goldsmiths.

Merchants' seals, bearing marks peculiar to the individual, were used from the fourteenth century although the scarcity of records in Scotland again make these difficult to decipher.[31] A highly visible ranking hierarchy is evident both in the expertise of execution of the matrix and in the type of metal used in casting the matrices. Two examples from Crail show that, even with everyday off-the-peg lead seals, there existed a difference in quality with one being a very crude lead oval blank, which has been scored with lines round the edges to imitate a legend and a rough incision in the centre for a device, while the other, though now broken, has been cast from a well-executed mould with part of the legend still legible in high relief (Figures 3.11 and 3.12). Later seal matrices, cast in the form of a flower, are a purely Scottish phenomenon and date to the sixteenth and seventeenth centuries.[32] A broken example from Dunfermline has a centrally placed heraldic shield as a device and what remains of the legend reads '. . . ARD 'S' RASTOUN' (Figure 3.13). The reverse bears a ribbed stalk where it joins the 'flower' and an incised arrow to indicate the correct orientation of the seal, while the stalk or handle is cast in the form of a trefoil with a casting seam along its length. A Scottish lead seal matrix in the British Museums collections bears an identical handle, and impressions on documents date it to 1571 and 1572.[33] It is unclear why this type of seal matrix is found only in Scotland although they are manufactured in the same way as lead buttons of the period and would therefore have been cheap and easy to produce as blanks which could then be incised with whatever legend or device the owner requested.

Figure 3.11   *A complete crudely made lead seal matrix from Crail. © Crown copyright reproduced courtesy of the Treasure Trove Unit.*

Figure 3.12 *A broken lead seal matrix from Crail. © Crown copyright reproduced courtesy of the Treasure Trove Unit.*

Figure 3.13 *A Scottish lead seal matrix from Dunfermline. © Crown copyright reproduced courtesy of the Treasure Trove Unit.*

PILGRIMAGE AND DEVOTION

Pilgrimage became popular in the twelfth century with the murder of Thomas Becket, and Canterbury quickly became one of the most popular and important shrines in Europe. New opportunities for travel arose for the wealthy, and for the rural poor the possibility of making pilgrimages to local shrines as well as contact with the wider world, as pilgrims journeyed to shrines such as St Andrews. The discovery in a field at Crail of a lead pilgrim souvenir badge of St Andrew (Figure 3.14) in the form a scallop shell

Figure 3.14   *A pewter scallop-shell pilgrim badge of St James and a lead pilgrim badge of St Andrew from Crail. © Crown copyright reproduced courtesy of the Treasure Trove Unit.*

from the shrine of St James of Compostella at Santiago in Spain illustrates one common means of the transmission of information and news beyond the local level, with pilgrims throughout Christendom making their way to St Andrews. A pilgrim who had made the long arduous journey to Spain could signal this through wearing a readily recognisable badge, and must have attracted considerable interest and curiosity among the people encountered en route. Earlsferry in Fife was the medieval crossing point from North Berwick for pilgrims on their way to St Andrews, and the nuns from the Cistercian house at Haddington received income from the ferry and from the production of St Andrew pilgrim badges.[34] The crudely executed lead St Andrew badge from Crail does not compare with the fine openwork pewter versions found in England and on the Continent, and it is tempting to see these as early versions of the tourist souvenir, hastily turned out to meet a growing demand.

Pilgrim souvenirs remain rare finds in Scotland, and it is unclear whether this is simply an absence of evidence or whether in fact pilgrimage to shrines such as St Andrews was rather less common than is estimated in comparison with major English and Continental sites. However, The widespread destruction of all such idolatrous objects, following the Scottish Reformation, has undoubtedly robbed Scotland of many examples of Christian art and devotion although easily hidden objects, such as these small badges, continue to turn up. A simple lead fleur-de-lis pilgrim souvenir, again from Crail, is similar to two found at Hertogenbosch in the Netherlands, dated to the fourteenth or fifteenth century,[35] and is probably more typical of the type of souvenir associated with local pilgrimage where the fleur-de-lis as the universal symbol of Mary is likely also to have associations with the parish church at Crail to whom it is dedicated.

Small metalwork items for everyday use in liturgical practices hint at what may have been common currency prior to the Scottish Reformation, and small cast bronzes depicting animals in grotesque style parallel the Romanesque and Gothic ornamental stonework on abbeys and churches. Discoveries from find spots across the country, including Auldearn and Lhanbryde in Moray, Crail, Culross and Kingsbarns in Fife, Birnam in Perthshire and Cockburnspath in the Scottish Borders, demonstrate their widespread use and distribution. The fine bronze swivel ring from Cockburnspath (Figure 3.15) depicting biting beasts is what remains of a larger object and most probably belonged to the accoutrements of the medieval church there, and it has direct parallels with a large composite swivel object from Cirencester dated to the twelfth century. From Lhanbryde (Figure 3.16), a small animal head cast in the round is probably a strap end for attachment to the leather straps that were used for fastening psalters, and a similar example from the excavations at the Abbey of Bury St Edmunds again dates these to the twelfth century.[36] It is no surprise that these small objects, which were easy to conceal or indeed to lose or destroy, continue to turn up in the vicinity of pre-Reformation churches.

Figure 3.15 *A twelfth-century Romanesque-style bronze swivel ring from Cockburnspath.*
© *Crown copyright reproduced courtesy of the Treasure Trove Unit.*

Figure 3.16   *A Romanesque bronze strap end from Lhanbryde. © Crown copyright reproduced courtesy of the Treasure Trove Unit.*

CONCLUSION

To the archaeologist, objects are an active part of everyday life, a material culture that can tell us a great deal about the user; objects are social and cultural signifiers which might demonstrate belonging to a particular social group or indicate an individual's status and position within that group.

The archaeological excavation of Scotland's burghs has produced a wealth of architectural and structural evidence for medieval life, along with a rich variety of organic objects including wood, bone, leather and some ironwork. Comparatively small quantities of the types of metalwork discussed here have been recovered in excavations, however. The many thousands of metal-detected finds reported for Treasure Trove assessment in the past decade have therefore added a new and important dimension to artefact studies. The material discussed in this chapter has been restricted to a few common categories owing to considerations of space but many thousands of objects, both complete and fragmentary, now await further study in Scotland's museums where they have been claimed by the Crown under the laws of Treasure Trove. This chapter offers the first insights into the potential of this material as a resource for historians and for archaeologists.

Notes

1 Many professional archaeologists are concerned at the widespread use of metal-detecting machines by hobbyists seeking treasure and, in the process, destroying or damaging sites and evidence from archaeological layers.

2 Individuals and landowners in Scotland have no legal title to antiquities they find, and all such finds must be reported to the National Museum Scotland for assessment as Treasure Trove. Any object and coin, of any date up to the present, made from any type of material, including bone, stone and precious metal, can be claimed under these laws in Scotland, thus protecting the archaeological heritage, www.treasuretrovescotland.co.uk.

3 J. T. Lang, 'Hogback monuments in Scotland', in *Proc. Soc. Antiq. Scot.* 105 (1972–4), pp. 206–35.

4 Treasure Trove law in England and Wales allows finders to keep what they find, other than gold and silver, and with no obligation to inform museums, so that we must assume much evidence is lost to private collections.

5 N. M. McQ. Holmes, 'The Evidence of Finds for the Circulation and Use of Coins in Medieval Scotland', in *Proc. Soc. Antiq. Scot.* 134 (2004), pp. 241–80.

6 D. Hall and S. Hennery, 'New evidence for early connections between Scotland and Denmark? The chemical analysis of medieval greyware pottery from Scotland'. *Tayside and Fife Archaeological Journal* 11 (2005), pp. 53–69.

7 Holmes, 'The Evidence of Finds for the Circulation and Use of Coins in Medieval Scotland'.

8 Holmes, 'The Evidence of Finds for the Circulation and Use of Coins in Medieval Scotland', p. 271.

9 Holmes, 'The Evidence of Finds for the Circulation and Use of Coins in Medieval Scotland', p. 271.

10 George Zarnecki, Janet Holt and Tristram Holland (eds), *English Romanesque Art, 1066–1200* (London, 1984), p. 293.

11 S. Campbell, *Inverboyndie, Medieval Ring*, Discovery and Excavation Scotland, 11 (Council for Scottish Archaeology, 2004); S. Campbell, *Turriff, Medieval Ring*, Discovery and Excavation Scotland, 17 (Council for Scottish Archaeology, 2004).

12 F. Lindahl, *Symboler i guld og sølv; Nationalmuseets fingerringe 1000–1700-årene* (Copenhagen, 2003), p. 79.

13 D. A. Hinton, *Gold and Gilt, Pots and Pins: possessions and people in medieval Britain* (Oxford, 2005), pp. 188–9.

14 Pers. comm. Philip Bennet.

15 C. Moloney and R. Coleman, 'The Development of a Medieval Street Frontage: Evidence from Excavations at 80–86 High Street, Perth', in *Proc. Soc. Antiq. Scot.* 127 (1997), pp. 707–82.

16 R. W. Lightbown, *Medieval European Jewellery: with a catalogue of the collection in the Victoria and Albert Museum* (London, 1992), pp. 98–9.

17 Lightbown, *Medieval European Jewellery*, p. 96.

18 V. A. Glenn, *Romanesque and Gothic: Decorative Metalwork and Ivory Carvings in the Museum of Scotland* (Edinburgh, 2003), pp. 58–9.

19 H. J. E. van Beuningen, A. M. Koldeweij, and D. Kicken, *Heilig en Profaan 2 laatmiddeleeuwse insigne suit openbare en particuliere collectives*, Rotterdam Papers 12 (2001), pp. 469–70.
20 Hinton, *Gold and Gilt, Pots and Pins*, p. 180.
21 A. R. Goodall, 'The Medieval Bronzesmith and his Products', in D. W. Crossley (ed.), *Medieval Industry*, CBA Research Report No. 40 (London, 1981), pp. 63–71.
22 J. H. Lewis, 'Excavations at St Andrews, Castlecliffe, 1988–90', in *Proc. Soc. Antiq. Scot.* 126 (1996), pp. 605–8, A. Cox, 'Backland Activities in Medieval Perth: Excavations at Meal Vennel and Scott Street', in *Proc. Soc. Antiq. Scot.* 126 (1996), pp. 733–822.
23 G. Egan and F. Pritchard, *Dress Accessories, 1150–1450* (London, 2002), pp. 55–6, 284–5.
24 Holmes, 'The Evidence of Finds for the Circulation and Use of Coins in Medieval Scotland'.
25 G. Egan, *The Medieval Household* (London, 1998), pp. 135–7.
26 M. Biddle and D. Brown, 'Writing Equipment and Books', in Martin Biddle (ed.), *Object and Economy in Medieval Winchester*, Winchester Studies 7ii (Oxford, 1990), pp. 729–59.
27 P. Hill, *Whithorn and St Ninian: The Excavation of a Monastic Town, 1984–91* (Stroud, 1997), p. 395.
28 Egan and Pritchard, *Dress Accessories*.
29 J. Franklin, 'The Finds', in Simon Stronach, 'The Anglian Monastery and Medieval Priory of Coldingham: *Urbs Coludi* revisited', *Proc. Soc. Antiq. Scot.* 135 (2005), pp. 395–422.
30 R. Gilchrist and B. Sloane, *Requiem: The Medieval Monastic Cemetery in Britain* (London, 2005), p. 102.
31 J. Cherry, 'Seal matrices', in P. Saunders and E. Saunders (eds), *Salisbury and South Wiltshire Museums Medieval Catalogue* (Salisbury, 1991), pp. 29–39.
32 D. H. Caldwell, 'Lead Seal Matrices of the 16th and Early 17th century', in *Proc. Soc. Antiq. Scot.* 123 (1993), pp. 373–80.
33 Caldwell, 'Lead Seal Matrices of the 16th and Early 17th century', p. 380.
34 Peter Yeoman, *Pilgrimage in Medieval Scotland* (London, 1999), p. 59.
35 Van Beuningen, *Heilig en Profaan*, p. 424.
36 Zarnecki, *English Romanesque Art*, p. 250.

Chapter 4

The Family

David Sellar

INTRODUCTION

Much ink has been spilt on the history of the European family in the Middle Ages. Historians and anthropologists, lawyers and sociologists have all contributed to the research. Key topics have been the structure of the family, the institution of marriage and the role of women. Among the many distinguished scholars who have contributed to the debate, the French historian Georges Duby and the English anthropologist Jack Goody have been particularly influential.[1] Duby, working mainly from French sources, has pointed to the emergence of the aristocratic 'lineage' from wider family groups around AD 1000. He has also emphasised the tension which existed for many centuries between the ideal of Christian marriage expounded by the Church and a much older secular model of marriage. Goody compared 'western' or 'occidental' family structures with those which he termed 'eastern' or 'oriental'.[2] He describes the system of descent in the oriental model as 'strictly patrilineal', and contrasts this with a western 'bilineal' model which places greater emphasis on paternal and maternal kin and on marriage alliances. He suggests that the oriental kin group typically derives from 'a segmentary tribal system' based on 'the agnatic lineage [that is, a lineage related through males] clearly defined in time and space', in contrast to the western model which emphasises bilateral descent and 'does not exist in itself but only in relation to each individual, having therefore no continuity in time, nor cohesion in space'.[3] As to marriage, Goody suggests that the oriental kin group has 'strongly endogamous tendencies', that is, a tendency to marry within the patrilineal kin – while the western bilineal model exhibits a 'tendency towards exogamy'.[4]

There has also been a revolution in Irish historical studies in the last generation, especially as regards Gaelic history and culture. Here one can point particularly to the publication in 1972 of Kenneth Nicholls's seminal *Gaelic and Gaelicised Ireland in the Middle Ages*.[5] The Irish Annals, contemporary with the events which they describe from the seventh century onwards, and the old Irish law tracts, first committed to writing around the same time, provide exceptionally rich source material. Irish scholars have emphasised the kin-based nature of Gaelic society in Ireland, and the fundamental importance, politically, legally and socially, throughout the medieval period, of agnatic lineages tracing their descent in the male line from a common ancestor or eponym. For example, the dominant lineage in the midlands and north of Ireland from the sixth to the eleventh centuries was the *Ui Neill* (the descendants of Niall), named from their eponymous ancestor, Niall 'of the Nine Hostages', who would seem to have flourished shortly after AD 400, but whose historicity has sometimes been questioned. Over the centuries a successful lineage might segment and give rise to further patrilineal groupings. Thus, many later Irish ruling families claimed descent in the male line from the *Ui Neill*, including the O'Neills of Tyrone (whose eponymous Neill was a tenth-century member of the *Ui Neill*), the O'Donnells of Tyrconnell, and the O'Melaghlins in Meath. Kenneth Nicholls has compared such lineages to oriental kin groups, and has pointed to the phenomenon of the 'expanding clans', the process by which a successful ruling lineage could expand both numerically and territorially over several generations, gradually displacing earlier ruling families with branches of their own lineage, until a substantial proportion of the population of a territory descends, quite literally, from a common ancestor in the male line.[6] Recent DNA-based genetic research in Ireland, focused partly on surnames believed to descend from Niall of the Nine Hostages, has borne this out. Indeed, it suggests that a surprisingly high percentage of the modern Irish population shares a Y chromosome inherited from an ancestor in the male line who may have lived up to 1600 years ago.[7] If Niall of the Nine Hostages did not exist, modern science would find it necessary to invent him! A parallel can be made here with the results of DNA research in Asia which has identified the Y chromosome of Genghis Khan and shown that his living descendants in the male line are to be numbered in tens of thousands.

In Ireland, as elsewhere in Europe, much work has been done on the history of the institution of marriage. This, too, has emphasised the contrast between marriage according to the canon law and an older secular model. The early Irish law tracts disclose an approach to marriage completely at odds with the later canonical ideal. They allow for polygamy and concubinage, and for divorce available to both sexes on a number of grounds. At first, there appears to have been genuine polygamy, including provision for a 'chief wife' who was accorded special privileges. In later centuries, polygamy was serial, with spouses being divorced and replaced in rapid succession. As in Western Europe generally older customs of secular marriage were tenacious and long survived the coming of Christianity. Although Ireland was Christianised early, traces of older marriage customs survived until very late. The historian Donncha Ó Corráin has written that, Irish dynasties, as the laws and other sources conclusively prove, were polygamous from the earliest period until the collapse of the Gaelic System';[8] while Kenneth Nicholls has commented with pardonable exaggeration that,

In no field of life was Ireland's apartness from the mainstream of Christian European society so marked as in that of marriage. Throughout the medieval period, and down to the end of the old order in 1603, what could be called Celtic secular marriage remained the norm in Ireland and Christian matrimony was no more than a graft onto this system.[9]

Any history of the family in Scotland needs to take into account both the Irish and the more general research into the European family. Scotland has not been short of family or 'clan' histories yet the history of the family as an institution has been rather neglected. The theories of Duby, Goody and others have attracted little comment in Scotland, with the exception of the lively field of women's history. Perhaps this is not so surprising. The surviving evidence for Scotland in the Middle Ages is poor compared to that for Ireland, England and much of the Continent. In addition, the story of the family in Scotland is far from straightforward. In some respects, it appears to be comparable to the Western European model described by Duby and Goody but, in others, it resembles more the lineage-based model described by Irish historians. The contrast often made between Highland and Lowland culture, between Gael and Gall, is relevant here. Highland society has often been represented as 'kin based', 'clannish' and 'patriarchal', in contrast to the feudal society of the Lowlands, although this is certainly to oversimplify. The Historiographer Royal, Chris Smout, has commented memorably that, 'Highland society was based on kinship modified by feudalism, Lowland society on feudalism tempered by kinship', although even this statement needs further refinement.[10] There is the additional complication that, as late as the twelfth century, the kingdom of the Scots was an amalgam of several different peoples: by the reign of King David I (1124–53) the Picts may have been a distant memory but David and his successors regularly addressed the men of their realm as *Francis* (a description which included French, Normans and Bretons), *Anglis* and *Scottis*, and sometimes also as Cumbrians and Galwegians. There were, in addition, Scandinavians of largely Norwegian extraction in the Isles and the north-west mainland, and Scandinavians of Danish descent in the Borders.[11]

This then can only be a preliminary survey hedged by caveats. One further difficulty, which inevitably distorts the picture, is that the records that do survive in the period under review (1200–1600) are almost exclusively concerned with the upper levels of society: the aristocracy, the gentry and wealthier townspeople. Only in the sixteenth century does a fuller picture of everyday life begin to emerge, vividly described by Margaret Sanderson among others.[12] One key source throughout the period, however, applicable to rich and poor alike, at least in theory, is the law: the common law of the kingdom of Scotland on the one hand; and the common law of the Church, the canon law, on the other.

This brief survey will concentrate on two main areas: clanship and kinship; and the law of marriage. These provide the indispensable background for understanding the history of the family in Scotland in the late medieval and early modern periods.

CLANSHIP AND KINSHIP

The word 'clan', borrowed into English from Gaelic *clann*, has several levels of meaning. The primary meaning of *clann* is 'children' although it can also be used of descendants of a common ancestor, for example, a great-grandfather. But the term came to be used to describe an agnatic lineage which might be many generations deep. At a further level, *clann* could describe a powerful and well-established kin group which wielded considerable political power: a polity as much as, or more than, a social group. By way of definition, it has been suggested that, 'in medieval Highland society the term *clann* was used to describe a patrilineal kindred the members of which descended in known steps from a named ancestor'.[13] This definition underlines two points believed to be true of the clan in Scotland and in Ireland: namely, that the members of the true clan were related to one another through the male line, and that the eponym or name father of the clan was a historical, and not a mythical, character. The term 'clan' has, of course, passed into wider anthropological usage and has been used by anthropologists to describe kin groups that may not conform to the above definition as regards either patrilineal descent or the historicity of the eponym.

The earliest known appearance of the word 'clan' in Scotland, in its secondary meaning of a kin group, occurs in the eleventh century in the notes or *Notitiae* recording grants of land to the monastery of Deer in Buchan. The grantors' names included Comgell, '*toisech* of *Clann Chanann*' and Donnchad (Duncan), '*toisech* of *Clann Morgainn*'.[14] There is no further record of Comgell or Duncan or their respective clans. There is no reason to believe, however, that the use of the term *clann* in the *Notitiae* marks the rise of a new type of social or political unit; rather, it seems to have taken the place of older kinship terms, such as *cinel*, which had much the same import. The fact that the clans named in the *Book of Deer* operated in or around Buchan is a reminder that Gaelic language and culture were to be found over a wider area in the eleventh century than in the later Middle Ages: not only Buchan but also Fife, Carrick and Galloway were to remain Gaelic-speaking for centuries to come. Indeed, the royal chancery had a set style for the appointment of a *capitaneus* or chief of a clan in Galloway.[15]

Although the clans mentioned in the *Book of Deer* remain obscure, many other clans which flourished from the thirteenth century onwards can readily be identified. From Somerled, king of the Hebrides, killed invading Scotland at Renfrew in 1164, descend the Clan Dougall who take their name from his son Dugald, the Clan Donald from his grandson Donald, the MacRuairis from another grandson Ruairi, and also the MacAllisters.

The Campbells take their name from a thirteenth-century ancestor with the byname *cam beul* or 'twisted mouth'. The MacLeods and the Lamonts are also named from thirteenth-century eponyms, while other clans, for example, the MacGregors, are named for ancestors who lived in the fourteenth and fifteenth centuries, or even, as in the case of the Farquharsons, the sixteenth. Some clans, such as the MacKenzies, MacFarlanes and the Robertsons, are of indigenous Gaelic descent. Others, such as the Frasers and the Chisholms, descend from incomers. The Campbells and Galbraiths claimed ancient Strathclyde British descent, while the MacDonalds and the MacLeods descend from the mixed Norse-Gaelic blood of the Isles.

Clans could vary greatly in size and function from a few individuals to the mighty Clan Donald, descended from kings and able to challenge the Crown itself. The more powerful clans were able to attract smaller clans into their following: for example, the Macraes followed the MacKenzies. As surnames came to be more widely used in the Highlands towards the end of the Middle Ages, dependants of powerful clans came to adopt the surname of the chief, whether they were related to him by blood or not. Sometimes these newly adopted clansmen attracted opprobrious bynames: such as 'the boll of meal Frasers' who were allegedly persuaded to take the name of Fraser in return for a measure of meal.[16] Over the generations, however, a significant number of those on the land at a lower social level are likely to have been direct male descendants of the chiefs, legitimate or otherwise. In a society which set so much store by lineage, there was a tendency for younger branches of the chief's family to displace older established families, only to be displaced themselves some generations later by more recent offshoots of the chiefly line. As already noted, the same phenomenon has been observed by historians of Gaelic Ireland and validated by DNA research. In Scotland, the DNA research of Bryan Sykes has demonstrated that a substantial proportion of the many contemporary MacDonalds, MacDougalls and MacAllisters carries the Y chromosome of their founding father Somerled.[17]

Kin solidarity remained strong throughout Scotland, not just in the Highlands, until well after 1600. The word 'clan', though Gaelic in origin and associated with Gaelic culture, was borrowed early into Scots. An Act of Parliament of 1587 even referred to many prominent Borders families as 'clans', and poets such as Dunbar used the word as synonymous with 'kin' and kindred'.[18] For many, the patrilineal kin group, rather than the nuclear family, functioned as the basic social unit. Members of the name looked to their head or chief for protection and assistance. Chiefs, in turn, were conscious of their responsibilities. In 1433 Robert Lamont, chief of the name, entered into an agreement with his 'deyr [dear] cosyn and man', Finlay Ewynsone (or Lamont), that he would be 'leyl and a gud lorde as his lorde and cheff of kyn acht [ought] for to be to thar neyr cosen and man'.[19] In 1488, the elderly chief of the Rosses made a grant to his grandson and heir of 'the haill rule of his persoun, his house and place of Balnagown, kin, men and friends'.[20] Heads of families, Highland and Lowland, played a role in conflict resolution both internal to the clan or family and external. Thus, in 1599, leading Murrays agreed to submit 'any action or cause either civil or criminal' arising among them to 'eight of the most wise, well affectioned, and most efficient of the surname'.[21] In 1576 the Earl of Glencairn, as head of the Cunninghams, and the Earl of Argyll, as chief of the Campbells, agreed that any slaughter or dispute between their kin or dependants would be settled by them with the advice of their 'friends'.[22] In 1609 'the haill kin of Clanchattan' – Macintoshes, MacPhersons, MacQueens, MacPhails, MacBeans, Macleans of Dochgarroch and others – entered into a Band or Bond of mutual support and defence.[23]

On occasion, action might be taken against a kin group and all its members. Thus, in 1528, 'Letters of Fire and Sword' were issued against the unruly Clan Chattan: 'considerand the grete harmys and contemptionis done be the said kin of Clanquhattane', the king and his council determined, 'to mak utir exterminatioun and destruction of all that kin, thair assistaris and parte takaris'. Seven sheriffs, the lieutenant general of the north and many others were commanded to invade the Clan Chattan, 'to thair utir destruc-tioun, be slauchtir, byrning, drowning, and uthir wayis; and leif na creatur levand of that clan, except preistis, wemen and barnis'.[24] Fortunately for the Clan Chattan, this blood-curdling enterprise was not vigorously prosecuted. More successful was the well-known proscription of the Clan Gregor. The whole name of MacGregor was proscribed in 1603 after the battle of Glen Fruin, by Loch Lomond, and it became a capital offence to bear the name of MacGregor. Much persecution followed. This proscription was not lifted until 1661, only to be reimposed after the Jacobite Rising of 1715, until finally lifted again in 1774. As a result, many MacGregors adopted other surnames, such as Stewart, Graham, Campbell and Murray: the famed Rob Roy MacGregor doubling also as Campbell.[25]

One area in which the kin played a crucial role was in connection with the legal process of 'assythment' or compensation for slaughter or mutilation. Such actions were commonplace in Scotland throughout the Middle Ages and beyond. Their function was to prevent a blood feud. Sir James Balfour of Pittendreich notes in his *Practicks*, compiled c.1574–83, that,

> Assythment or kinbut [compensation payable to the kin] is that satisfactione quhilk is maid or adjudgit to be payit be the committaris of slauchter, to the kin, bairnis, and freindis, of ony persone that is slane, in contentatione of the damage and skaith [harm] quhilk they sustaine through wanting of the partie slayn, and for the pacefieing of their rancor . . . [26]

Assythment, according to Balfour, fulfilled the dual purpose of compen-sation and of pacifying the rancour of the kin. After agreement as to the appropriate amount of compensation had been reached, 'Letters of Slains' were issued on behalf of 'the kin, bairns and friends' of the party killed or injured, recording that due compensation had been paid in the name of 'kinboot' and assythment, and remitting all rancour towards the perpetrator.[27] It is significant that, even although the primary role in settling the feud and fixing compensation was played by the paternal kin, maternal relatives were not excluded. Balfour notes that 'Ane letter of slanes sould be subscrivit by the principal persounis of the four branches of him that is slane'; that is, by the kin of the four grandparents of the dead man.[28] Illegitimate children, too, were allowed to participate in the assythment to the extent of a half share although they could not raise an action.[29] It is also worth noting that the word 'slains', surprisingly, has nothing to do with the English verb 'to slay', but comes from Gaelic and Old Irish *slan* meaning 'indemnity' or 'compensation', a term clearly borrowed from Celtic law into Scots, and an indication of the great antiquity of this method of settlement.[30]

Peter Stein, in writing about the kin and the survival of the blood feud in the broader European context, has noted that,

> It is sometimes assumed that when courts are introduced retaliation disappears . . . Retaliation is seen as an irrational exercise of revenge. Recent studies have shown that this approach is incorrect. The principle of compensation is as prominent as that of retaliation even in the simplest societies. They are seen as complementary rather than opposed to each other.[31]

Although Stein was not writing about Scotland, this is conspicuously true of the process of assythment. As Jenny Wormald observes in similar vein in her seminal article 'Bloodfeud, Kindred and Government in early Modern Scotland', the long survival of the action of assythment in Scotland also runs counter to the widely held belief that 'public and private order, represented by government and kindred respectively, conflict because they are essentially incompatible': and again, that 'Scottish society offers little support for the view that powerful lordship is exercised at the expense of kinship'.[32]

MARRIAGE BEFORE THE REFORMATION – CELTIC SECULAR MARRIAGE

As already seen, George Duby and others have drawn attention to the tension which existed for centuries in Western Europe between an older secular model of marriage and the ideal of Christian matrimony as taught by the Church, refined and regulated by papal decree in the twelfth and thirteenth centuries, and set out in the *Corpus Iuris Canonici*. Typically, the secular model paid greater regard to the wishes of the families concerned than to those of the actual parties to the marriage. It allowed for ready divorce and a succession of spouses. In marriage as expounded by the canon lawyers, on the other hand, the crucial element in the formation of marriage was the willing consent of the parties; and marriage was for life with no dissolution of a valid marriage being permitted. Eventually the canon law model prevailed throughout Western Europe, though the process took centuries. French historians have pointed to many examples of earlier secular marriage custom; for example, the chequered marital history of the Emperor Charlemagne (d.814) and the marital affairs of the eleventh- and twelfth-century counts of Anjou. Others have pointed to descriptions of marriage according to Scandinavian custom (sometimes referred to as marriage *more Danico*) and the memorable descriptions of love, marriage and divorce to be found in the Icelandic sagas.

One of the best-documented examples of the secular model of marriage in medieval Europe, and one of the longer lasting, is 'Celtic secular marriage' in Ireland, discussed above. Although the Scottish record is poor compared to Ireland, there is every reason to believe that such marriage customs were practised in Gaelic Scotland, at first in the mainstream of Scottish life, and surviving later in the Highlands and Islands.[33] Two late practitioners of Celtic secular marriage were Hugh MacDonald of Sleat in Skye who died in 1498 and who had six sons, each by a different mother, and Ranald MacDonald of Benbecula who died in 1636. Ranald was indicted for 'Murder and Polygamy' in 1633. The indictment lists his various wives, some of them having been 'putt away' (that is, dismissed) and concludes that, 'sua at this present hour he hes thrie mareit wyiffes alive'.[34] Article One of the 'Statutes' of Iona of 1609 refers to such marriage practices when it sets out that, 'mariages contractit for certane yeiris' should be 'simpliciter dischairgit and the committaris thairof haldin, repute and punist as fornicatouris'.[35] Martin Martin's *Description of the Western Isles* preserves a memory of this older custom:

> It was an ancient custom in the islands that a man should take a maid to his wife, and keep her the space of a year without marrying her; and if she pleased him all the while, he married her at the end of the year, and legitimised these children; but if he did not love her, he returned her to her parents, and her portion also [that is, her 'tocher']; and if there happened to be any children, they were kept by the father: but this unreasonable custom was long ago brought into disuse.[36]

As we shall see, statements like this are partly responsible for the later confusion regarding 'handfast marriages'.

THE CANON LAW OF MARRIAGE: FORMATION

According to the developed classical canon law of the Middle Ages, enshrined in the *Corpus Iuris Canonici*, the one absolutely necessary requirement for a valid marriage was the willing consent of the parties. This was expressed in the maxim *consensus non concubitus facit matrimonium* [consent and not intercourse makes a marriage], a maxim later repeated by Lord Stair in his *Institutions of the Law of Scotland* published in 1681.[37] The age of consent was fourteen for men and twelve for women.[38] Despite the early age of capacity for marriage, parental consent was not required and parental disapproval was, strictly speaking, irrelevant in law. The Church encouraged everyone to marry in a regular fashion *in facie ecclesie* [in the face of the church] at a ceremony blessed by a priest after due and public proclamation of banns announcing the intention to marry. The Church also accepted some less formal or 'irregular' marriages as being equally valid, however, while strongly disapproving of them. A mere exchange of consents in the present tense was enough to constitute a valid marriage (marriage *per verba de presenti*). So, too, was an exchange of consents in the future tense (that is, an engagement to marry) if followed by intercourse (marriage *per verba de futuro subsequente copula*), the intercourse being presumed to have taken place on the faith of the promise. No public intimation of marriage or public ceremony was necessary, nor was the presence of a priest, although it was handy if there were witnesses who could speak to the exchange of consents.

There can be little doubt, however, that most medieval marriages continued to be arranged by the parents or kin of the parties. Given that marriage could be constituted at such an early age, and might indeed have been preceded by an even earlier betrothal, it may be questioned how real was the consent to marriage. There was certainly little room for romantic love and, in many cases, the prospective spouses may scarcely have met before their wedding day. The evidence of arranged marriages in other cultures, however, including at the present day, suggests that most parties were prepared to accept the arrangements made by their families and gave their consent readily enough whatever their private misgivings. There must, however, have been many cases in which considerable parental pressure was applied, both mental and physical. The Church's view on this was that, if the pressure exerted was such as to overcome the will of a reasonably constant man or woman, then that consent could not be regarded as genuine and the pretended marriage was consequently null and void. For example, not long before the Reformation, Matthew Kerr, commissary of St Andrews, declared null and invalid an alleged marriage between Edward Hering and Elizabeth Crichton on the grounds that Elizabeth had been seized by Edward and his accomplices and compelled to undergo a marriage ceremony 'by force, fear and violence enough to break the resolve of a constant woman'.[39]

It is often not possible to know what lies behind the bare words of a legal record. On 15 June 1494 an Edinburgh notary formally recorded that:

> In presence of me notary public and witnesses, a noble man William lord Ruthven and Isabel his spouse earnestly required and implored Margaret Ruthven their daughter to contract and complete marriage in face of the church with John Oliphant grandson and heir apparent of Laurence lord Oliphant, whereto the lord Ruthven and his said spouse stand obliged, as in Indentures [agreements] made thereupon is more fully contained, considering that he John and she Margaret are now of lawful age to contract and complete such marriage. Which Margaret

Ruthven in answer said that she would not complete nor contract marriage with the said John. And lord Ruthven asked her why she would not complete the said marriage. And she Margaret again answered and said because she had no carnal affection nor favour for him John, and that she declared this to her said father and mother a year ago and more . . . [40]

It is difficult to know what lies behind this record. Did Margaret's loving parents simply let her have her own way? Or did they beat her black and blue, yet still were unable to compel her agreement? Or did a richer and more acceptable suitor appear on the horizon? Without further information we cannot know.

THE CANON LAW OF MARRIAGE: IMPEDIMENTS

Then, as now, there was a number of possible impediments to marriage, such as bigamy and lack of capacity. But the most likely impediment to be raised in the Middle Ages was the claim that the parties stood in too close kinship to each other. Such impediments were remarkably extensive. Even after a relaxation of the rules in 1215, the canon law still prohibited marriage with a blood relative in the fourth degree: that is to say, within the fourth degree of descent from a common ancestor. To express it differently, parties who shared a common great-great-grandparent could not marry each other. Indeed, in the eyes of the canon law, if they married or had intercourse together, they committed the ecclesiastical offence of incest. This was the impediment of 'consanguinity'. There was also an impediment based on 'affinity' which arose, not from blood relationship, but from marriage or intercourse. It, too, extended to the fourth degree: for example, a marriage to someone related to a former spouse up to and including the fourth degree was prohibited. The prohibition of affinity applied not only to marriage but also to intercourse: thus, marriage to a second cousin once removed of a person one had slept with twenty-five years before was not permitted! There were further impediments of a 'spiritual' nature which arose from the bond created between godparent and godchild. As a result of these far-reaching prohibitions, there were many 'limping' marriages, valid on the face of it but liable to be declared null and void on the discovery of an impediment. The reason for these extensive prohibitions has been much debated by historians, lawyers and anthropologists, including Jack Goody, but, as yet, there is no consensus.[41] They caused great difficulty in Scotland as elsewhere.

THE DISSOLUTION OF MARRIAGE

Relationship within the forbidden degrees of kinship constituted the main ground for the dissolution or annulment of marriage in the later Middle Ages. Confusingly, the term used by canon lawyers to describe the annulment of marriage was 'divorce' (*divorcium*) granted on the ground that the marriage had been null and void from the beginning; in contrast to the modern use of the term 'divorce' to signify the end of a valid marriage. One Scottish example of a 'divorce' or annulment granted in 1522 because of a prior subsisting marriage is of particular interest because it gives the actual words in Scots spoken by the parties. William Preston, official of Lothian, declared that the pretended marriage between David Johnson and Margaret Elder was null and void because, four years previously, David had contracted marriage with Margaret Abernethy, 'as much by words about the future as the present' (*tam per verba de futuro quam de presenti*) with intercourse following, and this first Margaret was still alive. David is reported as having said to Margaret Abernethy, 'I promytt [promise] to yow Begis Abirnethy that I sall mary yow and that I sall nevere haiff ane uther wiff and therto I giff yow my fayth.'[42] This example illustrates just how difficult it could be to determine from the words spoken whether the promise given was in the present or the future tense although, in this case, the question did not arise as intercourse had in any event followed the promise.

DISPENSATION

In a small country like Scotland the problems created by the rules regarding the forbidden degrees were acute, particularly among the closely interrelated nobility. Although little evidence survives for the lower grades of society, there is no reason to believe that conscientious clergy did not apply the rules across the board. In the later Middle Ages, however, there was the possibility of obtaining a dispensation from some, at least, of the prohibited degrees. Here the rich and powerful were certainly at a considerable advantage because petitioning for a dispensation could be a very expensive process and might entail a supplication to Rome. The rules about the forbidden degrees and dispensation caused much cynicism: 'marry first and dispense later' became accepted wisdom. 'It were greit vexatioun to tarie upon dispensatioun,' wrote Sir David Lindsay of the Mount in *Squire Meldrum*; while, in 1554, the Archbishop of St Andrews wrote to the Pope complaining that it was hardly possible for two persons of good birth in Scotland to marry without transgressing the forbidden degrees. Many people, he said, married without a dispensation, promising to obtain one later but, afterwards, instead of doing so, they applied for an annulment.[43]

MARRIAGE AND DIVORCE AFTER THE REFORMATION

Irregular marriages began to be phased out within the Roman Catholic Communion following the encyclical *Ne Temere* in 1563. In Scotland, the new Church established after the Scottish Reformation of 1559–60, like the old, thoroughly disapproved of irregular or 'clandestine' marriages and, at first, seemed set to prohibit them. In 1562 the kirk session of Aberdeen fulminated against such relationships:

> Item, because syndrie and many within this town are *handfast*, as thai call it, and maid promeis of marriage a lang space bygane, sum sevin yeir, sum sex yeir, sum langer, sum schorter, and as yit will noch mary and compleit that honourable band, nother for fear of God nor luff of thair party, bot lyis and continewis in manifest fornicatioun and huirdom: Heirfor, it is statut and ordanit, that all sic personis as hes promeist marriage faithfully to compleit the samen.[44]

The use of the word 'handfast' here is significant as showing that the term was already associated with irregular marriage.

After a period of initial confusion, irregular marriages continued to be recognised in Scotland, though subject to heavy censure. In 1565 a report submitted to the General Assembly of the Church of Scotland recommended that those 'that ly in fornicatioun, under promise of marriage, whilk they deferre to solemnizt . . . Alsweill the man as the woman, sould publicklie in the place of repentance lykewayes satisfie on ane Sunday befor they be married.'[45] The Church's definition of fornication was not shared by all, as this example given by Michael Graham illustrates. In 1588,

> A woman stood up in the church of Clackmannan, before the entire congregation, and challenged James Anderson, commissioner from the Stirling Presbytery: 'I had ado with my awin husband undir promeis of marriage quhilk is na fornication. I will never confess fornication nor mak repentance for fornication.' The case was particularly sensitive because her husband was the parish minister, who challenged Anderson from the pulpit: 'Will ye tak it upon your conscience that it is fornication?'[46]

The matter was referred to the Synod which backed the view of the commissioner and directed the minister and his wife to make public repentance!

Despite this, marriages *per verba de presenti* and marriages *per verba de futuro subsequente copula* remained part of Scots law until they were abolished by the 1939 Marriage (S) Act, long after they had disappeared from England and the rest of Europe. Indeed, to these irregular marriages, surviving in Scotland, a third was sometimes added, marriage 'by cohabitation with habit and repute', though there was much confusion as to whether this was a separate way of constituting marriage or merely a method of proving the existence of a marriage. Although its exact status remained doubtful, marriage by cohabitation with habit and repute survived the 1939 Marriage Act, and was only finally abolished in 2006.[47] It has sometimes been suggested that, after the Scottish Reformation, there was one law of marriage recognised by the Church and another by the State.[48] It is suggested that this view is mistaken and that the evidence suggests that, as before the Reformation, so too afterwards, there was only one law of marriage in Scotland, recognised by both Church and State.

Divorce in the modern sense of the formal dissolution of a valid marriage was introduced shortly after the Reformation. There were two grounds: adultery, as was the case in most of the Protestant lands, and, less commonly, desertion. An early high-profile example of divorce for desertion was the action brought by Archibald Campbell, 5th Earl of Argyll, against his wife, Lady Jane Stewart, an illegitimate daughter of King James V. Jane Dawson has shown how, despite the best efforts of both Mary Queen of Scots and John Knox, acting as marriage brokers [!], the marriage eventually foundered, the parties making use of both the new Commissary Court, set up after the Reformation, and older Catholic procedures.[49] Adultery and desertion remained the sole grounds for divorce in Scotland until the twentieth century. In marked contrast to the position in England, divorce in Scotland was open to men and women equally, and to those of modest means as well as the rich.[50]

After the Reformation marriage to a known and named adulterer was a cause for nullity. In the case of *Whitlaw* v. *Ker* in 1598 it was argued that marriage was, 'ane blessing of God . . . quhilk aught not to be grantit and given to adulteriris, for the honorabil band of mariage ought not to be ane cloke to sic unlawful and dishonest copulation'.[51] In 1600 Parliament declared that a marriage contracted by the guilty party in a divorce for adultery with the person 'with quhome they are declarit be sentence of the ordinar judge to have committit the said crime and fact of adulterie' was null and void.[52] This Act was not formally repealed until 1964 by which time it long been the practice not to name the paramour in undefended actions of divorce for adultery.

MORALITY, SIN AND THE CRIMINAL LAW

After the Reformation in Scotland, there was a tendency, as in some other Protestant lands, to equate sin and crime.[53] What had previously been only an ecclesiastical offence became a crime. 'Notour' or notorious adultery was a crime punishable by death as were sodomy and bestiality. Other criminal offences included profaning the Sabbath and the cursing and beating of parents. This equation of sin and crime had truly horrendous consequences when it came to the prohibited degrees and the law of incest. In 1567 the Scots Parliament passed two Acts on the same day, the one regulating marriage, and the other criminalising incest. The Marriage Act allowed first cousins to marry for the first time, here following earlier English legislation: 'secundis in degrees of consanguinitie and affinitie and all degreis outwith the samin contenit in the word of the eternal God and that are not repugnant to the said word mycht and may lauchfullie marie'; while the Incest Act ordained that

Quhatsumever persoun or personis comitteris of the said abhominabill cryme of incest that is to say quhatsumever person or personis thay be that abuses thair body with sic personis in degree as Goddis word hes expreslie forbiddin in ony tyme cuming as is contenit in the xviii Cheptour of Leviticus salbe puneist to the deith.[54]

There was immediate uncertainty as to whether these Acts should be construed together or construed separately and also as to their proper interpretation. To the disgrace of Scottish jurisprudence, doubts remained until the 1567 Acts were eventually repealed in 1977 and 1986 respectively.[55] Part of the problem lay in the interpretation of the provisions of Leviticus. Were the words of Leviticus 18 to be interpreted literally or by analogy? Was the prohibition against intercourse between aunt and nephew, for example, to be taken to apply to uncle and niece as well? And should a prohibition framed in terms of consanguinity be taken to include also relationships by affinity?

Similar problems of interpretation arose elsewhere in Protestant lands, such as the Dutch Republic. They have been much discussed and commented on by Goody and others, but the Scottish story has largely escaped attention.[56] Despite the fact that incest, previously only an ecclesiastical offence, had become a crime punishable by death, Leviticus was interpreted very widely with quite appalling results. In 1569, only two years after the Acts of 1567, the Regent Moray put the following question to the General Assembly of the Church of Scotland. It concerned:

> Ane matter, that occurrit at our late being in Elgyn . . . Ane Nicol Sudderland [Sutherland] in Forres, was put to the knowledge of ane assise for incest, and with him the woman. The assyse hes convict him of the fault. But the question is, whither the same be incest or not; sa that we behoovit to delay the execution, quhill we behoovit to have your resolution at this Assemblie. The case is, that the woman was harlot of before to the said Nicoll's mother brother.[57]

It was answered that 'the kirk findeth it incest, and so hath resolved'. The subsequent fate of Nicoll Sutherland is unknown to the author but cases over the next hundred years or so make it clear that the reference to execution is to be taken quite literally. The death penalty in such cases of technical incest fell out of use towards the end of the seventeenth century but it remained on the statute book until repealed in 1887.[58]

The inquiries into moral weakness and backsliding conducted by the Kirk and its commissioners after the Reformation – an Inquisition under another name – must have been terrifying and deeply disruptive of family life. Such inquiries were by no means restricted to the nobility and gentry but touched everyman. As Henry Thomas Buckle commented:

> Enquiry into the conduct of individuals was carried on by the Church Courts with indecent eagerness, and faults and follies much fitter for private censures and admonition were brought forward in the face of the congregation. The hearers were charged every Sabbath-day that each individual should communicate to the kirk session . . . whatever matter of scandal or offence against religion and

morality should come to their ears, and thus an inquisitorial power was exercised by one half of the parish over the other.[59]

If Buckle had lived a hundred years later he would no doubt have compared the 'searching' and informing approved by the established Church in sixteenth- and seventeenth-century Scotland with that encouraged by totalitarian regimes in the twentieth.

'HANDFAST MARRIAGE'

The terms 'handfasting' and 'handfast marriage' have been the cause of much confusion. The use of the word 'handfast' by Aberdeen kirk session in the context of irregular marriage has already been noticed. It has, however, been asserted since at least the nineteenth century that there used to be an ancient custom of trial marriage in Scotland known as 'handfasting'. Such marriages, it was said, might last for a year and a day. As long ago as 1956, Alexander E. Anton, after acknowledging that this so-called custom of trial marriage in Scotland had entered into the annals of international jurisprudence, subjected the evidence for the existence of such a custom to rigorous examination.[60] He concluded that reports of the existence of such a custom were mistaken and rested on a misunderstanding of the medieval canon law and a misappropriation of the term 'handfast'. Anton's arguments on this score are convincing and have never been countered, though the existence of the so-called 'custom' is still widely credited both in Scotland and in the world of international ethnography.[61] In brief, Anton was able to show that many of the assertions about this custom of 'handfast' marriage could be traced back to the writings of two great nineteenth-century Highland historians, Donald Gregory and William Forbes Skene, who believed that they had identified peculiar marriage customs existing in Scots Gaelic society in the Middle Ages, 'peculiar' in the sense of not being canonical, and to which they attached the name 'handfasting'. Anton was able to show that Gregory and Skene's appropriation of the word 'handfasting' was inept and rested in part on a misunderstanding of the canon law doctrine of irregular marriage.[62]

It is, however, more difficult to agree with Anton's conclusion that 'there is no proof or approach to proof, that handfasting in Skene's sense or any other peculiar customs of marriage were recognised in medieval Scotland after the introduction of Christianity had given one rule of marriage to the whole Christian world'.[63] On the contrary, as has been seen, there is every reason to believe that 'peculiar' customs of marriage, similar if not identical to Celtic secular marriage as described by Irish historians, were recognised in Gaelic Scotland also. Much of the research on Celtic secular marriage was published after Anton wrote, and so was not available to him. Gregory and Skene, on the other hand, were correct in identifying peculiar customs of marriage in Gaelic society, which differed from those approved by canon law, but were mistaken in associating these customs with irregular marriage and 'handfasting'.

CONCLUSION

This chapter has concentrated on two areas fundamental to an understanding of the history of the family in Scotland before 1600: notions of clanship and kinship, and the law and practice of marriage. The role of the family in actions of assythment for slaughter and mutilation has also been touched on. There are other aspects of everyday family life which it has not been possible to examine: for example, the rules governing matrimonial property, the law of succession, the status of legitimacy and the custom of fosterage. Nor has it been possible to consider to what extent there may have been a preference for endogamous marriage within the kin. It is evident, however, that the story in Scotland does not correspond neatly to what might be termed the Western European norm. On the contrary, there are elements in the Scottish story which are reminiscent of Goody's 'eastern' or 'oriental' model, as well as much which conforms to his western bilineal model. The history of the family in Scotland, though tantalisingly poorly documented before 1600, would certainly repay further research.

Notes

1 Georges Duby, *The Knight, the Lady and the Priest: The Making of Modern Marriage in Medieval France*, trans. Barbara Bray (New York, 1985); Georges Duby, *Love and Marriage in the Middle Ages*, trans. Jane Dunnett (Cambridge, 1994); Jack Goody, *The Development of the Family and Marriage in Europe* (Cambridge, 1983). The many other books on the history of the family include Jean-Louis Flandrin, *Families in Former Times: Kinship, Household and Sexuality*, trans. Richard Southern (Cambridge, 1979) and David Herlihy, *Medieval Households* (Cambridge, MA and London, 1985).
2 Goody, *Family and Marriage*, pp. 10–12, following P. Guichard, *Structures Sociales 'orientales' et 'occidentales' dans l'Espagne Musulmane* (Paris, 1977).
3 Goody, *Family and Marriage*, p. 11, Table 1.
4 Goody, *Family and Marriage*, p. 11, Table 1.
5 Kenneth Nicholls, *Gaelic and Gaelicised Ireland in the Middle Ages*, 2nd edn (Dublin, [1972] 2003).
6 Nicholls, *Gaelic and Gaelicised Ireland*, pp. 11–13.
7 Edwin B. O'Neill and John D. McLaughlin, 'Insights into the O'Neills of Ireland from DNA Testing', in *Journal of Genetic Genealogy* 2 (2006), pp. 18–26.
8 Donncha Ó Corráin, *Ireland before the Normans* (Dublin, 1972), p. 38.
9 Nicholls, *Gaelic and Gaelicised Ireland*, p. 83. See also 'Celtic Secular Marriage' below. See also Margaret Mac Curtain and Donncha Ó Corráin (eds), *Women*

in *Irish Scociety: the Historical Dimension* (Dublin, 1978), and Art Cosgrove (ed.), *Marriage in Ireland* (Dublin, 1985).

10 T. C. Smout, *A History of the Scottish People 1560–1830* (London, 1969), p. 47.

11 The Hebrides did not become part of the Scottish kingdom until 1266; and Orkney and Shetland not until 1468 and 1469 respectively.

12 Margaret H. B. Sanderson, *Mary Stewart's People: Life in Mary Stewart's Scotland* (Edinburgh, 1987); Margaret H. B. Sanderson, *A Kindly Place? Living in Sixteenth-Century Scotland* (East Linton, 2002). See also, for example, Rosalind K. Marshall, *Virgins and Viragos: a History of Women in Scotland from 1080–1980* (London, 1983), Elizabeth Ewan and Maureen M. Meikle (eds), *Women in Scotland, c.1100–c.1750* (East Linton, 1999), and Elizabeth Ewan and Janay Nugent (eds), *Finding the Family in Medieval and Early Modern Scotland* (Aldershot, 2008).

13 David Sellar, 'Clans, origins of', in Derick S. Thomson (ed.), *Companion to Gaelic Scotland* (Oxford, 1983).

14 Kenneth Jackson, *The Gaelic Notes in the Book of Deer* (Cambridge, 1972). The word '*toisech*' signifies a leader, perhaps a 'chief'.

15 Hector L. MacQueen, 'The Kin of Kennedy: "kenkynnol" and the Common Law', in A. Grant and K. Stringer (eds), *Medieval Scotland: Crown, Lordship and Community* (Edinburgh, 1993). cf. *RMS*, i, app. ii, no. 913, the appointment of a captain of the kin of 'Clenconnon' by David II.

16 C. I. Fraser, *The Clan Fraser of Lovat*, 3rd edn (Edinburgh and London, 1979), p. 23.

17 B. Sykes, *Blood of the Isles: Exploring the Genetic Roots of our Tribal History* (London, 2006).

18 APS iii, 462, *Dictionary of the Older Scottish Tongue*.

19 Sir Norman Lamont of Knockdow (ed.), *An Inventory of Lamont Papers, 1291–1897* (Edinburgh, 1914), no. 24.

20 R. W. Munro, 'The Clan System – Fact or Fiction?', in Loraine Maclean of Dochgarroch (ed.), *The Middle Ages in the Highlands* (Inverness, 1981), pp. 117–29 at p. 119, quoting SRO [now NAS] Balnagown Papers, GD 297/164.

21 Jenny Wormald, *Lords and Men in Scotland: Bonds of Manrent 1442–1603* (Edinburgh, 1985), pp. 83–4 and App. B, nos 78 and 100.

22 Wormald, *Lords and Men*, App. B, no. 64.

23 See Charles Fraser-Macintosh, *An Account of the Confederation of Clan Chattan* (Glasgow, 1898), pp. 188–91. The Band was renewed on the 400th anniversary in August 2009 at Termit and Inverness.

24 *Spalding Club Miscellany*, ii, pp. 83–4; also in Gordon Donaldson, *Scottish Historical Documents* (Edinburgh and London, 1970), pp. 103–5.

25 W. R. Kermack, *The Clan MacGregor*, 2nd edn (Edinburgh, 1953).

26 P. G. B. McNeil (ed.), *The Practicks of Sir James Balfour of Pittendreich*, 2 vols (Edinburgh, 1962–3), 'Of assythment for slauchter', vol. 2, p. 516. This edition reprints the text of the first printed edition of 1754. For a history of the action of assythment in Scots law, see Robert Black, 'A Historical Survey of Delictual Liability in Scotland for Personal Injuries and Death', Part One, in *Comparative and International Law Journal of Southern Africa*, March 1975; also Jenny

Wormald, 'Bloodfeud, Kindred and Government in Early Modern Scotland', in *Past and Present* 87 (1980), pp. 54–97.

27 For a style of a Letter of Slains see Henry Hume, Lord Kames, *Historical Law Tracts*, 4th edn (Edinburgh, 1817), App. I.

28 McNeil, *Practicks of Sir James Balfour*, p. 517, c. 7.

29 McNeil, *Practicks of Sir James Balfour*, p. 516–17, cc. 2–3.

30 Nicholls, *Gaelic and Gaelicised Ireland*, p. 226: *Slainte*: also *slan*. The basic idea of this Irish word is that of 'guarantee' or 'indemnification'. See also Wormald, 'Bloodfeud', p. 62.

31 Peter Stein, *Legal Institutions: The Development of Dispute Settlement* (London, 1984), pp. 18–23 at 19.

32 Wormald, 'Bloodfeud', pp. 55 and 71. See also G. MacCormack, 'Revenge and Compensation in Early Law', in *Journal of Comparative Law* 21 (1973), p. 69. Surprisingly, MacCormack does not refer to Scots law.

33 The argument is set out in W. D. H. Sellar, 'Marriage, Divorce and Concubinage in Medieval Gaelic Society', in *Transactions of the Gaelic Society of Inverness* 51 (1979–80), pp. 464–93.

34 Sellar, 'Marriage, Divorce and Concubinage', pp. 485–7; and see R. Black, 'Colla Ciotach', in *TGSI* 48 (1972–4), pp. 215–19.

35 *Register of the Privy Council*, ix, pp. 26–30; and Donaldson, *Scottish Historical Documents*, pp. 171–5.

36 Martin Martin, *Description of the Western Isles of Scotland*, D. J. MacLeod (ed.) (Stirling, [1695] 1934), p. 175.

37 James Dalrymple, Viscount of Stair, *Institutions of the Law of Scotland*, I.4.6: *consensus non coitus facit matrimonium*. I have used D. M. Walker's edition of 1981, based on Stair's second edition of 1693. The literature on the canon law of marriage is vast and includes, in addition to the works of Duby and Goody cited in note 1, James A. Brundage, *Medieval Canon Law* (London, 1995); James A. Brundage, *Law, Sex and Christian Society in Medieval Europe* (Chicago, 1987); Christopher Brooke, *The Medieval Idea of Marriage* (Oxford, 1989); John C. Barry (ed.), *William Hay's Lectures on Marriage* (Edinburgh, 1967); *Liber Officialis Sancte Andree* (Edinburgh, 1845), introduction by Cosmo Innes; James D. Scanlon, 'Husband and Wife: Pre-Reformation Canon Law of Marriage of the Officials' Courts', in *An Introduction to Scottish Legal History* (Edinburgh, 1958), pp. 69–81. Ishbel C. M. Barnes, *Janet Kennedy, Royal Mistress* (Edinburgh, 2007) emphasises the cynicism in practice regarding the rules.

38 This was to remain true until the Marriage Act 1929.

39 *Liber Officialis*, p. 6, no. 6. The 'Official' and the commissary were the ordinary judges in the church courts: see Simon Ollivant, *The Court of the Official in Pre-Reformation Scotland* (Edinburgh, 1982).

40 J. Maitland Thomson, *The Public Records of Scotland* (Glasgow, 1922), pp. 92–3.

41 For these impediments see the sources listed at note 37; also Goody, *Family and Marriage*, pp. 48–59, and Sybil Wolfram, *In-Laws and Outlaws: Kinship and Marriage in England* (London, 1987).

42 *Liber Officialis*, p. 21, no. 33.

43 'Sir David Lyndsay's Works: The History of Squyer Meldrum' (London, 1865–71), lines 981–2, qtd in A. E. Anton, 'Handfasting in Scotland', in *Scottish Historical Review* 37 (1958), pp. 89–102; *Liber Officialis*, preface, pp. xxv–xxvi.

44 J. Stuart (ed.), *Selection from the Records of the Kirk Session, Presbytery and Synod of Aberdeen, 1562–1681* (Aberdeen, 1846), p. 11, qtd in Anton, 'Handfasting in Scotland', p. 99.

45 *Acts and Proceedings of the General Assemblies of the Kirk of Scotland from the year MDLX* [hereafter B. U. K.] (Edinburgh, 1839), vol. 1, p. 76.

46 Michael F. Graham, *Uses of Reform: 'Godly discipline' and Popular Behaviour in Scotland and France, 1560–1610* (Leiden, 1996), p. 282.

47 W. D. H. Sellar, 'Marriage by Cohabitation with Habit and Repute: Review and Requiem?', in D. L. Carey Miller and D. W. Meyers (eds), *Comparative and Historical Essays in Scots Law: A Tribute to Professor Sir Thomas Smith QC* (Edinburgh, 1992), pp. 117–36; Family Law (S) Act 2006 asp 2.

48 R. Mitchison and L. Leneman, *Sexuality and Social Control: Scotland 1660–1780* (Oxford, 1989), chapters 3 and 4.

49 Jane Dawson, 'The Noble and the Bastard: the earl of Argyll and the Law of Divorce in Reformation Scotland', in J. Goodare and A. A Macdonald (eds), *Sixteenth-Century Scotland: Essays in honour of Michael Lynch* (Leiden, 2008), pp. 147–68.

50 A. D. M. Forte, 'Some Aspects of the Law of Marriage in Scotland: 1500–1700', in Elizabeth M. Craik (ed.), *Marriage and Property* (Aberdeen, 1984); W. D. H. Sellar, 'Marriage, Divorce and the Forbidden Degrees: Canon Law and Scots Law', in W. N. Osborough (ed.), *Explorations in Law and History: Irish Legal History Society Discourses, 1988–1994* (Dublin, 1995). For an overview of the history of divorce in England after the Reformation see Sir John Baker, *An Introduction to English Legal History*, 4th edn (Edinburgh, 2002), chapter 28.

51 This curious case is discussed in John Riddell, *Inquiry into the Law and Practice in Scottish Peerages before, and after the Union*, 2 vols (Edinburgh, 1842), vol. 1, p. 397–9.

52 APS iv, 233, c. 29; repealed by the Statute Law Revision (S) Act 1964.

53 J. Irvine Smith, 'Criminal Law', in *Introduction to Scottish Legal History* (Edinburgh, 1958), pp. 280–301; R. H. Helmholz (ed.), *Canon Law in Protestant Lands* (Berlin, 1992).

54 In England the Marriage Act of 1540 had similarly permitted first cousins to marry, thus allowing King Henry VIII to marry as his fifth wife Katherine Howard, a first cousin of his second wife Anne Boleyn.

55 Marriage (S) Act 1977; Incest and Related Offences (S) Act 1986.

56 J. Witte, 'The Plight of the Canon Law in the Early Dutch Republic', in Helmholz, *Protestant Lands*; Goody, *Family and Marriage*, pp. 176–80; Sellar, 'Marriage, Divorce and the Forbidden Degrees', pp. 78–82.

57 B. U. K., vol. 1, pp. 151–2.

58 Criminal Procedure (S) Act 1887.

59 Henry Thomas Buckle, *On Scotland and the Scotch Intellect*, H. J. Hanham (ed. and

intro.) (Chicago, 1970), pp. 265–6. See also G. D. Henderson, *The Scottish Ruling Elder* (London, 1935), chapter 3, 'Kirk Session Discipline'.

60   Anton, 'Handfasting in Scotland', p. 99.
61   For example, Anton cites Westermarck, Jolovicz and Vinogradoff.
62   See Sellar, 'Marriage, Divorce and Concubinage', pp. 464–93; Donald Gregory, *History of the Western Highlands and Isles* (Edinburgh, 1836), p. 331; W. F. Skene, *The Highlanders of Scotland*, Alexander MacBain (ed.) (London, 1836), p. 108.
63   Anton, 'Handfasting', p. 102.

Chapter 5

'Hamperit in ane hony came': Sights, Sounds and Smells in the Medieval Town

Elizabeth Ewan

INTRODUCTION

Around 1500, the poet William Dunbar penned a description of Edinburgh, urging its merchants to emerge from the 'honeycomb' of small crowded booths in which their trade was confined and to take steps to make the town worthy of its status as the capital of Scotland.[1] Although his purpose was polemical, Dunbar, who knew the town well, provided a vivid portrait of a bustling, smelly, noisy town, where different social groups mixed, where trading, honest and dishonest, predominated, and where the authorities were less conscious of the reputation of their community than he thought that they should be. Edinburgh, by this time, was the largest town in Scotland but many of the features of the everyday lives of its inhabitants were found in other towns throughout the country. This chapter will explore the sights, sounds and smells of urban life and, through them, provide a glimpse of everyday urban life from the thirteenth to the sixteenth centuries.

Scottish towns were small, the population of most numbering in the hundreds rather than the thousands. Edinburgh, which benefited when Berwick was lost to England in the fourteenth century and became the capital from the late fifteenth century, probably had about 12,000 inhabitants in the mid-sixteenth century. The next largest towns in the late Middle Ages, including such places as Aberdeen, Perth, and Dundee, probably had between 10,000 and 5,000 inhabitants.[2] What these figures suggest is that, in most towns, few people would be complete strangers to each other. Urban society was characterised by the close proximity and interaction of people from all walks of life, both from within the town and beyond.

Towns were organised for trade. From the twelfth century onwards, charters were granted to the burghs by royal, aristocratic or ecclesiastical landlords, conferring certain trading privileges, often within a specified hinterland and, over time, granting increasing rights of self-government although the timing and extent varied from town to town. Urban society, like the rest of Scottish society, was hierarchical. Those who benefited most from such grants were the elite, the burgesses who were formally admitted to the 'freedom' or all the rights and privileges of the community, usually on payment of a certain sum, as heirs of burgess fathers or as husbands of burgess daughters. Occasionally, women were admitted to burgess-ship but this was the exception rather than the rule. The burgesses probably made up no more than one-third of the adult male population in most towns;[3] the majority of the inhabitants lived less privileged (and less recorded) lives.

With the growth of local government came an increasing number of written records about life in the town, mostly in the form of town council decisions or proceedings of the burgh courts before which many inhabitants found themselves during their lives. Unfortunately, however, these do not survive in any great number before about 1450 and, even then, are scarce until the sixteenth century. The earliest continuous run of town records comes from Aberdeen, beginning in 1398. As a result, written evidence for daily life in medieval towns is biased towards the end of the Middle Ages and towards those towns for which records survive. There are also other sources, however, which can provide glimpses of the lives of the inhabitants – archaeological evidence is especially helpful in revealing the lives of those who were not part of the elite; literary sources, though generally written from an elite perspective, can reveal many facets of everyday life; art historical and architectural sources can give insight into material culture and perspectives.

'ZOUR HIE CROCE, QUHAR GOLD AND SILK / SOULD BE': SIGHTS

Dunbar knew what a medieval town should be – a community with a bustling market, trading in luxury goods to the greater honour of the town. What did townspeople actually see when they walked around their community?

Few towns were walled, defences consisting mainly of natural features such as rivers or marshes, gates at the backs of individual properties, and ports on the main roads into town, the last functioning mainly to control traffic from the countryside. The lack of physical barriers contributed to the townspeople's physical integration with the population of the rest of the kingdom though, mentally, they considered themselves different in subtle ways from those beyond the town's limits. Some literary works speak contemptuously from an urban perspective of country people, while the insult 'carl' (peasant, churl) was frequently directed at opponents by townsmen and townswomen.[4] Such attitudes were most visible at times of crisis. In times of economic pressure, for example, distinctions were made between those poor who were born or had lived a long time in the town and those who came from elsewhere in determining to whom scarce resources would be made available.

Many towns had extensive arable and pastoral lands which were used to grow crops, graze livestock and otherwise harvest the natural resources of the countryside, such as wood and other building and heating materials, as well as wild berries and herbs for food and medicine. A common herd was appointed to look after the cattle during the daytime, herding them outside the town in the morning and back again at night.[5] Common lands were also used for other purposes, such as archery practice, games, and festivities, as well as such everyday activities as washing and bleaching linen, making them an integral part of most townspeople's experiences. Within the ports, the long narrow burgage rigs, which stretched back behind the buildings fronting the main streets, were often used for keeping livestock and cultivating vegetables as well as for waste disposal and for workshops and other buildings. Many properties included features such as gardens, stables, brewhouses, cowsheds, kilns, barns, granaries and even dovecots.[6] In 1518 John Boyman leased his garden and orchard in Ayr, along with the grass growing there, for two years, and agreed with the tenants that, if he should place any animals in the yard, he would pay them 4d a day for each large animal such as an ox or a horse.[7] From at least the fourteenth century, some well-off townspeople acquired their own separate rural properties which could supply them with food and other resources, purchased with the profits they had made from trade.[8] When the wealthy Edinburgh cloth merchant Francis Spottiswood died about 1540, among his possessions were a horse with a plough, a pair of harrows, a cart, a sledge and other agricultural implements.[9]

The industrial activities of towns could spill over beyond the bounds, as crafts such as skinning and tanning, pottery and tile-making, iron smithing, brewing, cloth dyeing and fulling, which required water and space or which were a fire risk, might be situated outside the ports. Even if people did not live in these areas (Perth seems to have been one of the few medieval towns with suburbs),[10] much of their day might be spent there. Stables for visitors' horses, religious houses and hospitals were also situated on the town's outskirts. The rhythms of the agricultural year determined urban industrial activities. Raw materials came seasonally from wetland, heathland, woodland, arable and seashore.[11] Scottish towns have been described as 'processing plants for the products of the countryside' and 'giant abattoirs, supporting a network of industries for the processing of hides, meats and bone'.[12] Even more important than such raw materials were people. Medieval towns were unable to sustain their size without immigration, and constant migration of new people from the hinterland ensured that links with the rural world were maintained.

Most Scottish towns had a single, long main street though some had more than one. Early high streets were often very wide. As towns grew, people with properties on the street frontages increasingly encroached upon the roads and lanes despite efforts by local and other authorities to prevent this. In October 1531, for example, James V ordered Dundee to reform its high street and to destroy shops and lean-tos which were built beyond the eavesdrop of the houses.[13] Along the street, there would be crowded houses and shops, as well as temporary booths and stalls on fair and market days, and chapmen and country people carrying their wares on horses or on their backs. Leading off the main street were narrower vennels or wynds, providing access to back roads and the inner parts of individual properties.

Properties and land use changed over time, with buildings being expanded, becoming derelict, being torn down and built anew, and with entire properties becoming waste or alternatively being increasingly built up. It has been estimated that many of the poorer houses in the towns had a lifespan of perhaps twenty to twenty-five years,[14] so repairs or rebuilding of dwellings would be a common experience for many townspeople.

Urban houses were constructed mainly of wood. In the early days of towns, most were probably built of wattle and daub, with flexible branches woven between upright posts and covered with a cladding of clay, mud or dung. Such use of wood left towns vulnerable to fire – seven towns burned in 1244 alone.[15] Some houses were built with wooden planks, and half-timbered buildings were also known though not as common as in England. Towards the end of the Middle Ages, stone was increasingly used; indeed, archaeological evidence suggests that stone houses may have been more common than previously thought though by no means the majority of urban buildings for this period.[16] Some buildings had stone undercrofts or first floors with wooden storeys above, served by forestairs. Jettied construction allowed upper storeys and wooden galleries to be built jutting over lower storeys, providing more accommodation space in the upper floors of a building but at the expense of cutting off light and warmth from the street and from neighbours in adjoining buildings.[17] Constricted space in some towns led to taller buildings as the population increased – for example, from about the mid-sixteenth century in Edinburgh, some dwellings began to reach five or six storeys in height. Often, such buildings were subdivided to provide living space for two or more households, some of which might be housed in a single room.[18] While most frontage properties probably belonged to wealthier inhabitants, with the housing of poorer families to the rear, not all prosperous families chose to live there. There is evidence of some wealthier properties in the Perth backlands, for example.[19] The burgages tended to have a mixture of social groups living side by side or above and below each other, and interacting during the course of each day.

In most houses, furnishings were basic – a trestle table and benches which could be stored against the wall, possibly some beds, and kists and other storage facilities. Tableware was mainly of wood and cookware of pottery though metal pots and pans etc were beginning to become more common in the later Middle Ages. Wealthier families had more elaborate furnishings, some of it possibly imported from overseas. Side tables where tableware and silverware could be displayed, elaborate aumbries or cupboards, and large carved and canopied beds are found in many merchants' houses, along with tapestry wall hangings and bed curtains, and an increasingly diverse assortment of cooking implements for the kitchen.[20] In the later sixteenth century, wealthy families might also adopt the latest trend of decorative ceilings, some of which still survive in buildings such as the one known as 'John Knox's House' in Edinburgh.[21] Although most urban households lived in homes of only one or two multi-purpose rooms, the elite, like their noble and royal counterparts, increasingly assigned specialised functions to different rooms. Late medieval property deeds speak of cellars, solars, lofts, galleries, and kitchens, as well as general chambers with unspecified functions. Heating came from hearths or, in elite houses in the later Middle Ages, from fireplaces.[22]

Clothing for most townsfolk was similar to that worn by countrypeople, of coarse woollen cloth.[23] Some, however, had access to finer fabrics from overseas which might make their way from the elite to those less well off, either as cast-offs given by employers to servants, apprentices and employees, or through the second-hand clothing markets. Sumptuary laws, passed from 1430 to 1701 to regulate the dress of various groups of subjects, imply that some townspeople dressed quite richly. In 1458 the law stipulated that burgess wives' and daughters' kerchiefs (head coverings) were to be homemade and short with little hoods, no long tails were to be worn except on holidays, and gowns were not to be of rich furs. Labouring men were to wear only grey and white on working days, though light blue, green and red were allowed on holidays.[24] Inhabitants of towns with royal courts or with many noble townhouses were the most likely to be in touch with the latest trends because they not only had the aristocratic examples before them but also access to the latest European fabrics and reports from merchants trading abroad. One Aberdeen townswoman of the fourteenth century, for example, dressed her hair with an Italian silk ribbon with delicate picoted edging.[25] Clothing spoke very visibly of social status and provided an effective way to distinguish the different social groups mingling on urban streets. In one of Dunbar's poems, the widow of a rich burgess commented that her husband had dressed her in rich clothes and jewels which 'hely raise my renovne amang the rude peple'.[26]

Shoes and boots of leather were intended to last a long time and many were patched over and over again. They might also be protected by wooden pattens designed to raise the foot above the dirt and mud of the urban street. Fashions changed, with late medieval Scots following the European trend in pointed shoes.[27] Leather was also used for belts and clothes fastenings. Women wore their household keys attached to their belts while men often kept their short knives there ready to use for eating or to settle a quarrel. Sometimes belts were made of silver or other precious metals and hung with purses of embossed leather or embroidered silk. Metal buckles and brooches were both functional and decorative.[28] Men and women, if they could afford it, wore rings of gold or silver, often with precious or semi-precious stones. Such valuable ornaments were useful not only as personal decoration but as objects which were easily pawned when ready cash or credit was needed.[29] For example, a silver belt with a red purse was pawned by William Afflek to Jonet Froster in Dundee.[30]

Clothing and jewellery were frequently passed on to the next generation, especially by women, as personal clothing and ornaments were among the few items over which they retained legal control once married.[31] Women's testaments often specified in great detail which clothes or jewellery should go to which beneficiary, suggesting that such legacies had importance both to the testator and to her legatees. For example, when Margaret Annand in Leith made her husband her executor shortly before she died in 1574, she trusted to his discretion to divide most of her goods between her three daughters but specified that her chain was to go to Margaret, her belt to Marion and her rings to Jane.[32]

Dunbar commented that the main goods for sale at the market cross were 'crudis [curds] and milk . . . cokill and wilk, Pansches [tripe], puddings of Iok and Iame [haggis of common people]'. Most townspeople had a grain-based diet, supplemented by seafood (important because of the many fish days required by the medieval Church), berries and nuts from local wood-lands and vegetables such as kale, turnips and beans, often grown in burgage gardens; for the elite there were imported luxuries such as figs, grapes and wine. Bread for most people was made of barley, oats or rye; the finer wheat bread was more common in the elite diet because wheat had often to be imported. Some families baked their own bread but many purchased their supplies from the town's baxters, the professional bakers. Oatcakes, por-ridge and bannocks were cheaper sources of grain. Barley was also consumed as ale which was safer to drink than water.[33] Meat was more available to urban folk than to their rural counterparts because livestock was brought to town for slaughter before woolfells and hides were exported overseas, and fleshers in every town cut up the carcasses for their customers. It is likely that the best cuts went to the wealthy, while poorer customers made do with tripe or haggis.

Much of the food was prepared locally.[34] The modern distinction between home and work is less clear-cut for the Middle Ages when the family formed an economic as well as a social unit and many buildings functioned as both domestic and working spaces. This was especially true for married women who fitted their money-earning activities around their domestic responsi-bilities. Wealthier families, with properties on the street frontages, might have shops or workshops on ground level and domestic rooms above or further back on their property. Workshops were also situated in the rear of burgages, sometimes with retail premises at the street front. Some craft activities took place in domestic contexts, especially those such as carding and spinning which tended to be carried out by married women fitting such tasks around household responsibilities.[35]

Towns were characterised by a greater variety of economic activities than the countryside. The wealthiest inhabitants were usually those who engaged in trade, such as merchants and master craftsmen. Wealthiest of all were the overseas merchants of the leading east coast towns, especially Edinburgh from the later fifteenth century. Scotland's export trade consisted largely of raw materials, especially wool, hides and fish, which were sent abroad in return for manufactured goods or luxury items such as wine and spices.[36] Some larger towns also had a concentration of professionals such as notaries, doctors and priests. The increasing importance of written records meant a growing demand for the services of scribes and others who could write. This was especially true in Edinburgh in the late Middle Ages with the growth of the law courts and institutions of central government there. Towns also provided the necessary size of clientele for doctors, apothecaries and surgeons.

In every town, the inhabitants depended on food producers to supply many of the necessities of life. Bread and ale were the staples of the urban diet and, as a result, the activities of baxters and brewsters were closely regulated from the very beginnings of a town's existence. Baking of bread was largely carried out by men, brewing by women, though there are examples of female bakers and male brewers.[37] Oatcakes, which formed a cheaper alternative to bread for the urban poor, were baked mainly by women.[38] Cookshops supplied meals for those without kitchens or hearths of their own.[39] Fleshers, fishwives, buttermen, fruitsellers and others, as well as overseas merchants supplying foreign imports, also supplied the town's dietary needs.

Many urban industries were based on the use of raw materials from the countryside. Wool which was not exported was used in the domestic cloth industry, providing work for carders, spinners, dyers, fullers, weavers and tailors. Hides from livestock provided leather that was processed by skinners and tanners and worked by shoemakers, belt-makers, armourers and others. Town woodlands were a renewable resource and were often managed by coppicing. Local clay was used by potters and iron smelted by smiths though better quality iron was also imported. Other artisans, such as the gold- and silversmiths found in a number of towns, relied more heavily on imported materials.[40]

Artisans employed labourers, apprentices and servants. Many urban boys were apprenticed to a craft in their early teens, with the hope of one day rising to the status of master craftsman though it is likely that many ended their days as journeymen in a master's shop. Girls were occasionally apprenticed, mainly in crafts such as the bonnetmakers of Edinburgh who included women among their members,[41] but were much more likely to enter domestic service, an occupation that trained them in the skills required for their expected future responsibilities as wives and mothers and also gave them the opportunity to earn some money for a dowry.[42] The towns also housed a large population of daily labourers and carriers, hucksters who sold foodstuffs in small quantities to the poor, and those who scraped a living from a variety of tasks such as selling second-hand goods and moneylending. In most towns, there was also a floating population of vagabonds as well as the native-born poor. During a typical day, the townsperson would see all of these people on the streets.

The high street usually broadened in the middle to accommodate public buildings and the marketplace, the heart of the town where the community's commerce and government were found as well as its spiritual life. The marketplace was generally the site of the town's tolbooth or town hall, the symbol of its self-government. A tolbooth was a sign of status, and erecting it was a communal effort. When Aberdeen's tolbooth was built in the early fifteenth century, each burgess had to contribute one day's work or 4d.[43] No expense was spared to erect a building befitting the town's honour and dignity – by the sixteenth century, many had towers or steeples, bells and clocks.[44] The tolbooth was the centre of civic life, not only the forum for government but also the local court where daily concerns, such as debts, disputes between neighbours, and property agreements, were heard and noted down by the town's common clerk. Many also functioned as jails, as well as centres of commerce, leasing out ground-floor booths to local townspeople. In 1457 Edinburgh had twenty-seven booths to lease out to townsmen and women though, in 1481, one was made into a prison.[45] Although only a minority of men would serve as town officials, in one way or another, the tolbooth figured in most townspeople's lives.

Presiding over the marketplace was the market cross, symbol of the king's peace and the central place of trade in the lives of the townspeople. The market cross was the site of public proclamations, punishments, celebrations, outlawings, legal proceedings and bargains and much else.[46] Here also was the tron or public weighbeam where goods were weighed and measured. Local authorities tried their best to regulate the commercial activities of those trading in the town, both in-dwellers and those from outside the town. Prices were set for staple goods, such as bread and ale; specific hours for selling were specified; all goods were to be brought to the marketplace where they were to be sold openly and under the supervision of the town authorities; the quality of goods was inspected by officials such as the ale tasters, flesh (meat) tasters and wine tasters; and the activities of unlicensed hucksters were strictly controlled. Town records are full of statutes concerning the regulation of trading activities, while the number of resulting prosecutions suggests that many people also found it possible to work around them. As towns grew and the volume of trade increased, separate places would be assigned for specific goods. In 1477 Edinburgh had over fifteen different locations for the wares sold there.[47] Smaller towns also experimented. In 1539 the officials at Haddington decided it would be better to have the salt market where the fish market had been.[48] Urban life was not static but adapted to changing conditions across the years.

Along with the tolbooth, the market served as the site of local justice. Most offences were punished with fines but, in some cases of verbal or physical assaults, a reconciliation ritual was imposed, with the offender publicly seeking the forgiveness of the victim. This ritual was often carried out in the kirk but could also be staged by the market cross. In what appears to have been a practice unique to Scotland, offenders were sometimes ordered to admonish their tongue for speaking false words, saying 'false tongue, you lied'.[49] Corporal punishments were also used. Offenders were placed in the stocks, the pillory or the jougs (an iron collar); these were usually located beside the cross where the offender was visible to the largest number of people. Some towns had their own punishments, intended to inflict humiliation. For example, in Dundee, some offenders had to wear the 'tolbooth beads',[50] while the Stirling records contain what may be the earliest surviving record of the branks or scold's bridle, described as 'the claspis and calvill of irne devisit of befoir . . . to be put and lokit on hir for xxiiij houris'. In the following years, the branks were used in several towns for offending men and women.[51] An Inverness man who threatened another with a knife, then insulted him and threw stones at him, was sentenced to pass through the four ports of the town and then to the tron wearing the branks; as if this were not enough publicity, his fault would also be published at the market cross.[52] Cuckstools were found in many towns. The cuckstool was usually a chair or seat set up in a prominent place, rather than the ducking stool found in some other countries. There was a cuckstool in Aberdeen from at least the fourteenth century; offenders placed here would be pelted with eggs, rotten vegetables and dung, all readily available in the marketplace. For more serious offences, such as theft, criminals might have their ear nailed to the tron or be branded on the face.[53] Such mutilations labelled the offender for life as a criminal. Banishment was also used as an effective sanction. It resulted not only in the practical problems of being cast out of the place where one made a living but also the psychological effect of being cut off from home and family and sent to what were seen as dangerous places beyond the bounds of the burgh.[54]

'FOR CRYIS OF CARLINGIS AND DEBAITTIS': SOUNDS

Marketplaces were the heart of town life. When townsfolk frequented them, all their senses were affected: the ears by the cries of market sellers and noisy debates between buyers and sellers; the eyes by the rich assortment of goods for sale and customers of all social stations; the nose by the stink of gutted fish and bleeding meat from livestock freshly slaughtered; touch by the jostling crowds and slippery road surfaces; and taste by the various foodstuffs on offer.

Like the marketplace, the medieval parish church provided a rich sensory (although perhaps less raucous) experience. It was often situated beside or near the marketplace. Here town dwellers marked the important stages of life, baptism, marriage and death, as well as at least yearly confession and taking of the Sacrament. The church was adorned with a profusion of images – mural paintings with stories from scripture and the lives of saints, carved statues of saints and evangelists at their altars, elaborate stone tombs of local families and nobles, stained-glass windows, embroidered hangings, flickering candles in many-branched chandeliers, precious gold and silver Communion vessels, richly bound psalters and mass books used by priests clothed in sumptuous vestments. There was the smell of incense and, above all, sound – chaplains saying masses at individual altars, the ringing of bells, the music of the choir at high mass, pilgrims crowding around relic shrines, and even the sound of commerce and law as debts were paid and lands redeemed at various places within the kirk and notaries conducted their legal business.[55]

Music and ceremonial became ever more elaborate in the late Middle Ages, the surroundings more magnificent. Several churches acquired organs while composers, such as Robert Carver, wrote beautiful music to enhance further the solemnity of religious services.[56] As urban craft guilds were established from the fifteenth century, each would establish its own altar to its patron saint.[57] Individuals also founded altars of their own where prayers were said for their souls and their memory was kept alive in the community or, if less wealthy, donated money and ornaments to already established altars. The personal connection might be stressed by marking the ornaments with the donor's name – the silver rood chalice in Haddington's parish church was inscribed 'John de Crumye and his spouse had me made'.[58]

There was a close connection between the churches and the town; many clergy came from local urban families, the town council acted as patron and employer of many more, and the upkeep and maintenance of the church was often paid for from town revenues. Such connections did not always guarantee the quality of the services. In 1530 the magistrates, deacons and community of Dundee swore in future not to present anyone to chaplainries in their gift unless he was an able cantor and, while they preferred to appoint the sons of burgesses, such men had to be as qualified as strangers for the position.[59] The parish church was where most townspeople were baptised, married and lay the night before burial when the Office of the Dead, known as dirige and placebo, was said over their bodies.[60] It was therefore the key to their spiritual salvation. Increasingly, masses for all the dead became part of the daily round of services; indeed, there were complaints from later medieval poets about the oversaying of diriges,[61] but perhaps those not wealthy enough to ensure individual masses for their souls might have disagreed.

Music was central to religious services, with boys trained in song-schools to sing the daily liturgy.[62] The church also provided a daily backdrop to everyday life through its bells, which punctuated the daily routine from waking in the morning to downing tools at night,[63] and the curfew when the town gates were closed. Bells were popular donations to the church, often being given personal names.[64] Bells announced the other major events which punctuated the life cycle, especially death. The Office for the Dead was 'preceded by a bell being rung through the town by a bellman, calling people to pray for the souls of the deceased'.[65] Bells also rang out to announce joyous occasions and celebrations, such as the birth of a prince.[66]

Bells were used by the town authorities to summon people to council meetings or important occasions. In late thirteenth-century Berwick, the brethren of the guild were to gather together before the ringing of the bell ceased.[67] Such bells also served as reminders to the rest of the townsfolk that their leaders were attending to town business and affairs. The day was begun and ended with bells. The 4 a.m. bell for Matins began the day, the curfew bell in the evening announced the time to retire to rest.[68] Towns also used other forms of music. Drums, trumpets, and pipes were played by minstrels hired by the town to attract the attention of the inhabitants. Occasionally nature could be put to use as well – the Selkirk watch was ordered to stay at their posts each night until the third crow of the cock.[69] Other means of keeping time (though not necessarily accurately) developed with the acquisition of town clocks from the fifteenth century. In 1454 John Cruikshank was paid 40s. for a year's service on the Aberdeen town clock and was 'to do his diligent business to the keeping of it', suggesting that this might not have been such a simple task. The Ayr town clock certainly required constant maintenance throughout the 1530s and 1540s.[70]

Music and bells also summoned townspeople to joyous occasions and organised recreational activities. Medieval people recognised the value of humour and laughter in promoting health.[71] In April 1518 Edinburgh attempted to elect Mr Francis Bothwell to the position of Little John, with responsibility 'to mak sportis and joscositeis' at the May festivities and games of the town. On the intervention of the Earl of Arran, who pointed out that Bothwell was a man 'usit to hiear and graver materis', he was – with reluctance – excused.[72] Despite Bothwell's apparent contempt, sports and play, as well as more solemn activities such as religious processions, weapon showings, and other communal gatherings, punctuated townspeople's daily working lives. Some activities were associated more with the town than with the countryside, perhaps because there were larger numbers of people in one place who could participate, but many were also open to those from outside the town and to the higher ranks of society. Historians need to be cautious about making too great a distinction between 'elite' and 'popular' culture – most leisure activities were not restricted to one social group.[73] Nor were most of the activities described below exclusively 'urban' but they formed an important part of town life.

Some of the more organised festive occasions, such as religious processions, plays, and Yule and Maytime drama, though staged in towns, were important in bringing in large crowds from the surrounding countryside and bringing together town and country folk as spectators. As James Henderson pointed out to the Edinburgh council in 1552, the lack of a playing field meant that there was no place 'to play interludes in to draw pepill till the toune nor pastime ground for the induellaris'. As a result, they were compelled at great expense (and also economic loss to Edinburgh) to seek their pleasures in other towns.[74] The mid-fifteenth-century poem, 'Peblis to the Play', describes the boisterous good times (and associated brawls and bruises) experienced on such occasions as countrypeople flocked to the town for Beltane festivities.[75]

The earliest references to such plays and activities are found in Aberdeen; in 1440 five merks were paid to stage 'ly Haliblude' play on Windmill Hill.[76] This may have been a standalone play. Loss of records makes it difficult to see the extent to which Scottish towns participated in the tradition of play cycles found in other towns in medieval Europe[77] although a list of props for a procession in Dundee, which included St Barbara's castle, six pairs of angel wings and twenty heads of hair, suggests a play cycle or at least a procession of tableaux, while the Aberdeen crafts in 1506 were ordered each to furnish their pageant.[78] Certainly there were religious processions from the mid-fifteenth century onwards on holy days such as Corpus Christi, Candlemas and various saints' days when the merchant and craft guilds accompanied the Sacrament and images of the saints through the town to the church.[79]

The extent to which such activities broke down class differences and united the elite groups in the procession and the other townspeople who were the witnesses has been much debated.[80] Even among those participating, such activities could foster enmity as much as unity. The processions tended to highlight differences in status rather than erase them, as fierce battles were fought between various crafts over precedence, the position near the host or sacred image being the most prestigious.[81] Some groups sought to undercut altogether some of the symbolism of such processions. For example, in 1524, many of the craftsmen of Aberdeen refused to carry the tokens of their crafts, apparently feeling that such tokens marked their status as inferior compared to that of the merchants. One of their number, the tailor John Pill, made this explicit by labelling the merchants as 'coffeis [tradesmen]' and indicating that the 'token' of their craft should be salt pork and herbs. He was forced to do penance with the token of his craft hung about his neck.[82]

Folk plays and activities were organised under a Lord of Misrule, usually known as the Abbot of Unreason or Bon-Accord, and increasingly by the early sixteenth century as Robin Hood, sometimes accompanied by Little John. Even such apparently 'popular' figures who were associated with a loosening of constraint at such times, however, were usually chosen from among the elite – some disorder may have been allowed but it was kept under strict control.[83] The attraction of Maytime drama and religious processions seems to have declined for at least some townspeople during the sixteenth century, with many men refusing the office to which they were elected, crafts resisting providing their stipulated pageants, and, after 1560, the opposition of the Reformed Church. Although such drama did not die out completely (there was even a short-lived attempt to revive it in Haddington in the 1570s), it may have become more typical of the countryside than the towns by the late sixteenth century.[84]

There were other processions for more secular activities. The common riding was undertaken to assert the town's control of its common lands. Haddington had a ceremony of 'Riding the Muir' around the common land of Gladsmuir. 'Drums were beaten, there was a muster of armed men, and the town ensign was carried in procession.'[85] Such activities were not without risk. Attempts by the town of Selkirk to deal with an encroachment on 25 July 1541 resulted in the death of the provost and a bailie.[86] In the late sixteenth century another form of secular procession was introduced by James VI – the riding of Parliament, a procession by Members of Parliament escorting the king up the High Street from Holyrood to the Edinburgh tolbooth.[87]

All male burgesses of a town were expected to be adequately equipped to defend the town and to serve the king in war if called for the forty days service he could demand of them. Parliament ordered annual wapinschaws (weapon showings), with the men of the town mustering on a nearby field. These may have involved archery contests and other demonstrations of skill. Wapinschaws did not always go as planned. In 1522, John Logy was accused of attacking Robert Mill on the head with an axe from behind at a Dundee wapinschaw.[88] On other occasions, the mustering was for very real warfare and involved elaborate planning. Ayr's preparations for joining in the wars with England in the early 1540s included making a town's pavilion out of canvas and other materials, a taffeta and silk standard and two banners of taffeta and red silk. The honour of the town was to be upheld in such affairs. There was also a proper send-off with a hogshead of wine drunk at the cross before the men went off to war in 1546–7.[89]

Another festive occasion experienced by a few towns was the royal entry or visit of the king or queen. Money was collected from citizens to present gifts, often of wine, to the sovereign.[90] Townspeople also shared in the bounty. At the 1503 entry of Margaret Tudor to Edinburgh, there were pageants, triumphal arches and, in the middle of the town beside the cross, 'a Fontayne, castynge forth of Wyn, and ychon drank that wold'. Margaret's visit to Aberdeen in May 1511 was commemorated by a poem by Dunbar who described the party of maidens dressed in green (a Maytime colour) and playing instruments who greeted her, the pageantry, the tapestry-decorated buildings, and the abundant wine flowing at the market cross.[91] The pageantry of royal entries became ever more elaborate in the sixteenth century, especially in the capital, where the high streets of Edinburgh and Canongate became a stage for royal pomp and display. Those who lived in towns beside royal courts also benefited from spectacles associated with other royal occasions – for example, tournaments or fireworks and music celebrating royal baptisms or weddings. Tournaments were often associated with Shrove Tuesday in early sixteenth-century Edinburgh, thus providing a royal counterpart to the more popular activities, such as football, which took place on that day.[92]

Other less formalised celebrations were common to town and country-side. Dancing and guising took place at Yule and other special times of the year. A dance called Gillatrypes, possibly of Highland origin, seems to have been popular among women, being danced not only by women in Elgin but also by the North Berwick women accused as witches in 1589.[93] Poems such as 'Peblis to the Play' describe boisterous dances which, though exaggerated for effect, probably reflect the dances of townspeople and those country folk who came to the town for fairs and other festive occasions such as Beltane. Singing was also popular. James IV was entertained by singing women in Canongate, Leith and Dumbarton.[94] Many songs have been lost but there are glimpses of this musical tradition. Some secular songs were preserved in altered form in the *Gude and Godlie Balladis* of 1542.[95] Song titles are mentioned in a number of poems; according to Dunbar, the low-skilled Edinburgh common minstrels knew only two, 'Now the day dawis' and 'Into Ioun', which they played over and over.[96]

Some towns appointed official minstrels; in others there seem to have been musicians hired by the town, craft guilds or individuals on specific occasions. They included drummers, pipers, harpists, fiddlers and trumpet-ers.[97] Meg of Abernethy, harpist in Aberdeen in 1398–1400, may have been one such musician.[98] Drummers and pipers were used for official proclama-tions, and sometimes to mark curfew. Sometimes, the occupation of town musician was a family affair. In Peebles in 1572 Robert Thomsoun, taber-nour, and his son were to strike the drum night and morning for the watch, while Edinburgh employed Jax Dow and his two sons in 1557.[99] Those who were not official minstrels often lived from hand to mouth, picking up employment where they could. An Edinburgh fifer, Patrick Caldwell who died in 1578, left a testament full of debts for the necessities of life, sug-gesting that he was barely making ends meet.[100] Such musicians were also vulnerable to periodic crackdowns from the mid-fifteenth century onwards; Dumfries outlawed all minstrels in 1548 except those who were appointed by the burgh. In 1574 Glasgow ordered the banishment of pipers, fiddlers and minstrels, lumping them together with other vagabonds, while Parliament included minstrels not in the service of a noble or a town with strong and idle beggars.[101] The authorities' concerns were not completely ill-founded. 'Minstrels showed a remarkable capacity to be seduced to the cause of unrighteousness or disorder, regardless of whether offence was to be given to the kirk or the burgh.'[102]

In 1427 Parliament ordered that hostelries for travellers, supplying food, drink and shelter, be provided in every burgh.[103] Alcohol was an important part of public festivities, sports days and other events such as guild feasts. Communal drinking was a force for conviviality – drinking parties, known as ale lawings, were often held once an agreement had been concluded.[104] Alehouses which sold ale, and taverns which sold wine, were often, like churches, the sites of business agreements such as the redemption of lands which took place in the Dundee tavern of Alexander Paterson in 1518,[105] so those involved did not have far to go. Drink might also be used to signal the end to disputes – in Stirling in 1549 two men who had assaulted each other were ordered to ask each other's forgiveness before the provost, then drink and be friends.[106] Drink money or ale was provided for workers in building and other contracts although certain tasks were not intended to be combined with alcohol. Facing the possibility of an English invasion in 1513, the Selkirk authorities ordered that anyone on the watch who went 'to potatioun and drink' while on duty would pay a 20 shilling fine.[107]

Drink was either purchased from brewers to be taken home in the customer's own containers or consumed in alehouses (or on the streets). The price of ale was chalked upon walls or doors by the town's official ale cunners or tasters. Christian Makzone of Elgin was incensed when the ale cunner undervalued her ale after tasting it, and made her displeasure known, calling him a 'reisky carll' and saying that she would live to see his bairns beg their meat, and that 'he could cun sowannis [a type of porridge] better than ale, fool swoin carle that he wes'. She was ordered to do penance in the parish kirk, ask his forgiveness and refrain from further brewing until she obtained a new licence from the town.[108] In January 1561 the Inverness authorities ordered that any free brewster, who 'rabuttis or reprewis' officers tasting the ale or contemptuously refused to sell the ale at the price set by the cunners, was to be discharged from brewing until Michaelmas.[109]

Alehouses and taverns were frequented by men and women although drunkenness appears to have been more associated with men than with women. The Dundee council recognised the possibility, however, adding at the end of its 1561 act against drunkards 'and the sam act to proceed upon Drunken Women'.[110] 'Drunk' was a term of abuse hurled against men but not apparently against women – Marion Murray of Elgin called Andrew Milln 'dovr drunkyn beist'. Women were certainly capable of tavern brawls, however. In Elgin in 1551 Jonet Maitland cast a stoup of ale in Isobel Douglas's face and then hit her on the head with the stoup, also hurling 'injurious evile' words for good measure. Isobel responded by hitting Jonet and then insulted the bailie who tried to stop the fight.[111]

Alehouses were usually open in the evening, although attempts were made to force them to close at curfew. In October 1513, in the aftermath of the battle of Flodden, the Selkirk authorities ordered that anyone on the watch who went to drink while on duty would pay a 20 shilling fine.[112] In 1559 the Dundee council ordered that no one should be found drinking in any alehouse or wine tavern after ten at night. Two years later, perhaps owing to the increasing influence of Reformed Church discipline, suppliers of drink were not allowed to sell their product after nine at night or in the morning until prayers and preaching were done, nor on Sunday afternoons in the time of preaching[113] – oddly, drink appears to have been more attractive than sermons to some Dundonians.

Other activities offering an alternative to preaching included sports which were played in urban and in rural communities but there seems to have been a greater variety of sports in urban centres. Organised sports contributed to a town's sense of self-worth. 'Having a horserace, or better still an ancient trophy, gave status to a burgh . . . The flood of visitors showed that the place was worth visiting, and everyone took trouble to dress well.'[114] Sports also brought town and country people together, as well as common people and the elite. Municipally organised horse races, archery and shooting contests especially tended to have extensive noble involvement.[115]

From the early fifteenth century archery was encouraged by the king and Parliament as a way to keep men ready for warfare, and each town was ordered to have its own butts for target practice. The Ayr burgh accounts show that preparing the butts could be quite an operation, involving many horses and men to carry the turfs and ready the site for an exercise which took place over five days.[116] Possibly archery became more of a recreation as developments in firearms began to render the bow less effective.[117] Municipally organised archery contests were found in some towns in the sixteenth century. The magistrates of Peebles asked John Whiteman to restore a silver arrow to the town, probably a prize in such a contest. Shooting competitions also developed in the later sixteenth century.[118]

Horse racing may have developed from the earlier tournaments hosted by kings and nobles. The earliest record of formal town races comes from Haddington in 1552 and from Peebles in 1569 where a silver bell was offered for a prize. Horse racing may have compensated for the late sixteenth-century decline in traditional drama. Several such contests involved a procession with the secular symbol of the horse race or other contest prize, perhaps replacing older medieval religious processions.[119]

Other organised sports were often associated with particular times of the year. For example, football was played on Christmas Day in many communities in north-east Scotland. Such games involved large numbers of men and could be played over many miles in the fields and moors outside the town.[120] There was a variety of other ball games, including bowling games such as lang bowlis, pennystanes, and kyles or skittles. Disorder associated with such games lay behind statutes such as that of Dundee in 1558 which complained about bowls and pennystanes.[121] The number of people injured or killed by golf clubs suggests that golf may have been a more violent game than it is today (or its players marginally less restrained). 'Sport was neither polite nor viewed from a distance . . . It was often raw, rambunctious, intemperate and immediate.'[122]

One ball game which was largely urban by the Late Middle Ages was caich which was played by two individuals or teams striking a ball against a wall. This game required more-specialised equipment, including a ball which would bounce, a flat wall of finished masonry or plaster, and a flat patch of ground beside it of beaten earth or stone flags.[123] The latter two might be more easily found in towns than in rural settlements. Catchpoles existed in many towns. In 1548 Jonet Turing of Edinburgh had a catchpole in her property in Bishop of Murray's Close. Her neighbours were ordered to let her use the close and to gather up any balls 'striking forth' of the catchpole when anyone happened to play therein.[124] Church walls were sometimes used and it may have been this secular use of the kirkyard which led Aberdeen's council in 1547 to warn fathers and masters that they would be held responsible for any young men, servants, bairns or craftsmen breaking the glass windows of the kirk or the slates of the lodge. The Haddington minister complained about Sabbath breakers playing against the kirk wall[125] – it is not clear if the practice would have been more permissible on other days of the week.

Hawking and hunting were probably restricted to the wealthiest inhabitants but other animal sports involved a larger crowd. There is little documentary evidence for such sports, although bull-baiting is mentioned in Stirling in 1529 and in Edinburgh in the 1550s.[126] Archaeological evidence hints at the possibility of cockfighting and dogfighting in Perth as well as bear-baiting in Dunbar.[127] The students of St Andrews enjoyed cockfighting just before Lent in 1415, to the disapproval of the college authorities.[128]

One feature of many sports was gambling; David Hume of Wedderburn, a frequent competitor in the Peebles horse races, would bet on himself. Money was also gambled on cards and dice. Peebles enacted a statute in 1468 against anyone receiving in his house players at dice, either of hazard or raffle.[129] Sometimes individuals were offered inducements to stop gambling. On 14 December 1519 Henry Halis received a worset doublet from James Wedderburn of Dundee and in return promised not to play at dice after Christmas Day (he seems to have been given a short grace period in which to adjust). If he did play again, he would immediately owe Wedderburn twenty merks for the doublet.[130] In a comment which might be of interest to modern demographic historians, the author of *The Thre Prestis of Peblis* (c.1484–9) commented that third-generation burgess sons often gambled hard and were easily enticed to the tavern, and this was why burgess families did not prosper into the third generation.[131]

Leisure time was also spent in telling stories and in reading. Although only a minority of the population was literate, the percentage may have been higher in the towns than in the countryside. The growth of professional groups, such as lawyers and notaries, the provision of schools and universities, the establishment of the printing press in Edinburgh and other towns in the sixteenth century, and the Education Act of 1496 all contributed to the development of literacy as a desirable skill and a growing urban rendership for literary works.[132] One feature of urban literacy was the development of networks of literate townsmen and townswomen who shared manuscripts and books, the best-known example being that centred around George Bannatyne, compiler of the Bannatyne Manuscript of 1568.[133] The lending of books was not without risk. In a practice which might serve as a model to modern teachers lending their books to students, John Steinson, a notary and rector of Glasgow University inscribed one book, 'So oft my bukis beris my name / becauss oft sundry fra me tane / be fraud or stoulth, god thaim haf the sayme / yat haldis my buikis and seis my name.'[134]

Literacy among urban men and women was helped by the provision of schools, usually associated with parish churches and religious houses, but also maintained by the town. It is likely that urban children had more access to such institutions than rural ones although, even in towns, the majority of children probably would not have attended school. Much of the education was found in song-schools that aimed at providing men who would enter the clergy and staff the churches but, by the later fifteenth century, many graduates also entered secular careers. There was some schooling for girls though the focus was more on practical skills, such as sewing and possibly reading.[135] Further education was provided for some boys by the establishment of universities at St Andrews, Glasgow, Aberdeen and Edinburgh in the fifteenth and sixteenth centuries although many students continued to travel to Europe for their university studies. Most students would have been between fourteen and eighteen though some might stay at university for longer.[136]

The enjoyment of written works was not limited to those who could read, as books and manuscripts as well as shorter prints and broadsides[137] could be read aloud, and poems and stories recited from memory. Townspeople participated in a lively oral culture. Some traces of this can be found in folktales and ballads, many of them passed on orally through the centuries and later recorded by collectors. Popular stories of Little John, Robin Hood and Wallace circulated widely. Occasionally, traditional rhymes and proverbs were written down; some are found in the commonplace book of John Maxwell, assembled in 1584–9, as well as in a late sixteenth-century collection of proverbs.[138] One particularly vivid tradition which appeared in both elite and popular culture was flyting, the ritualised exchange of insults. This highly oral form which could be heard in the streets of the towns was also produced in written form by court poets. Indeed, writers such as William Stewart played with the form by composing flytings ostensibly taking place 'between two lowly artisans rather than between proud, self-consciously literary poets'.[139]

'STINK OF HADDOCKIS AND OF SCAITTIS': SMELLS

Stewart's poem about the flyting between a tailor and soutar (cobbler) involved a great deal of flinging of dirt, both literally and metaphorically. Medieval towns were not pleasant smelling, even to contemporaries. Dunbar complained about the reek of haddock and scaits (fish), while a treatise on plague in the later sixteenth century advised the Edinburgh authorities to take preventive measures through cleaning up the foul air which haunted the town from the 'grait reik of colis without vinde to dispache the same, corruptioun of Herbis, sic as Caill and growand Treis, Moist heveie sauer [smell] of Lint [flax], Hempe & Hedder [heather] steipit in Vater'. Other causes of corrupt air included standing water, earth, dung, stinking privies, and dead unburied corpses, especially human ones.[140] Residents complained as well – when Walter Car rented a workshop in Dundee, he soon protested to his landlord about the reek from the adjacent house and asked to be moved somewhere else if the situation could not be improved.[141] Many townspeople suffered from chronic sinusitis, a condition probably caused by dust and smoke polluting the air.[142]

The records tend to be more articulate about smells and hygiene during outbreaks of disease because of the belief that foul air spread infection. But glimpses of common practices can be found in statutes directed at market sellers. Livestock was slaughtered in the town and fleshers often slung carcasses on to any convenient surface. In Selkirk the tolbooth provided a convenient place. Edinburgh furriers and skinners were in the habit of hanging their skins on the forestairs of houses. Fish were gutted on the street. Edinburgh fish sellers were taxed to pay for the cleansing of the High Street from the dirt which they had created.[143]

Much filth deposited in the marketplace and in the streets would be cleared by scavenging animals but they themselves contributed to the noise and smell. Even domestic animals would be expected to earn their keep, cats through hunting mice and rats, dogs through hunting, guarding houses and herding livestock. Feral dogs and cats roamed the streets and dumps; the poet Montgomerie refers to such dogs as 'midden dogs'.[144] Sometimes scavenging went too far. In October 1566 the Edinburgh council ordered a door made for the Boroughmuir gallows so that dogs could no longer drag off the bodies.[145]

The towns were home to many other animals. As well as the cattle kept in some backlands, pigs were frequently found in the streets, feeding off scraps in the road and out of troughs placed by their owners at doors, under stairs or even in open windows. Pigs were useful for 'the conversion of food scraps such as waste from milling into a source of meat for human consumption', but they caused their own problems. Long legged, speedy and bristle backed, they had a bad reputation. Various laws were enacted to try to keep them under control, off the streets and out of other people's crops and gardens.[146] It was not just crops which were damaged. One fuller in Dundee, who laid out a piece of black cloth to dry, had it torn apart by swine.[147] Nor were animals always kept outside. Jonet Anderson kept geese in her chambers in the upper part of an Edinburgh house, thereby rotting the floorboards, and was ordered by the authorities in 1540 to desist.[148]

The authorities were mainly concerned with middens and filth in public places. The market area was particularly vulnerable to such dirt. Selkirk tried to keep an area of 40 feet (12 m) around the cross clean by regularly ordering people to remove middens.[149] Towns had to deal with fleshers who cut up flesh on their boards or hung carcasses on the tolbooth, letting blood run onto the road, hucksters selling fish and tying them in bundles or gutting them on the street, fish sellers bringing fish and oysters to town, and other sellers bringing their goods by horse and then allowing the horse to stand in the street 'eiting and fouling of the same'.[150] Individual household-ers were periodically warned to clean up the middens lying in front of their houses.[151] Many towns employed official cleansers. In Berwick the town took on responsibility for cleaning the streets from at least the early four-teenth century.[152] In Perth the pynours (labourers) cleaned the streets and the markets from at least 1511, disposing of the waste and rubbish in the Tay.[153] There was cleansing on special occasions – in Ayr in 1536, the cause-way was cleaned on the eve of the Corpus Christi procession 'for honour of the sacrament'.[154] There was also involuntary cleansing, as a number of contemporaries pointed out, by the long trains of women's dresses which were favoured in the sixteenth century. As one disapproving poet put it, such fashions caused women with 'sic fowl taills / To sweep the calsay clene / the dust vpskailllis [disperses into the air]'.[155]

Fouling of water sources, such as streams and lochs, was a major problem, polluting the water supply for everyone else. Industries were often the worst offenders. In 1521 Will Wilson of Dundee promised that neither he nor his servants would in future cast 'wad paist' (waste from dyeing) in the burn or dam of the town.[156] Many of the more noxious crafts, such as dyeing and tanning, were situated on the outskirts of the town. This meant that the worst of the smells might not penetrate the town but, as they were heavy users of water in their production processes, it also meant that it was more likely that the water sources would be polluted.

Much garbage was disposed of in the backlands, sometimes spread over one or more adjoining properties, especially if some were waste or aban-doned. As well as waste from food and industrial production, floors of soiled straw and roofs of smoke-blackened thatch might be dumped in the backlands if not taken out to the fields. The backlands also had dung and straw from the homes of livestock, poultry and domestic animals. Rubbish pits were dug, middens were heaped up and periodically cleared or buried with layers of sand to decrease the smell and increase the stability of the land.[157] Human waste was disposed of in cesspits in backyards, although earth closets were sometimes attached to houses, and some wealthier fami-lies had internal latrines. Indeed, such latrines may have been more common than excavation suggests, as generally the wealthier urban buildings have not been as subject to investigation as poorer dwellings.[158] Moss was often used for 'toilet paper'.[159] The street, ditches or streams also provided toilet facili-ties although David Lindsay advised female playgoers, who had failed 'to teme your bleddir' before attending his long play, to lift up their skirts and 'plat [throw down] in ane disch' or shove in a wisp of straw.[160] Not everyone was so fastidious. After various groups used the Selkirk tolbooth in the

1530s, the town had to order that its use be restricted to the council and visiting officials, as when it was not, 'benkins, stulis [benches and stools] wer distoit and fillit with fylth of men and bestis, quhilk was schaime to sie'.[161]

Some attempt was made to channel waste away from living areas through ditches and gutters. Boundaries between properties were often marked by gullies or ditches which also helped to drain water and sewage from the yard. Some householders illegally constructed drains into the streets; others joined with neighbours to create common gutters. Co-operation was needed to maintain these; disputes arose when building operations by one person disrupted the functioning of the gutters of another, for example, by constructing a forestair which jutted out into the close and impeded the flow of water.[162]

DISEASE AND DEATH

The unhygienic conditions of urban life meant that disease and death of family members, friends and neighbours were very much a part of everyday experience. Acute infection seems to have been a very common cause of death.[163] Infant and childhood mortality was high. Childhood diseases and infections, such as measles, whooping cough and diphtheria, would be fatal to many. Although burial evidence has to be treated cautiously because we do not know the reasons why particular groups were buried at any one site, high sub-adult death rates are common in urban cemeteries. In one Aberdeen burial ground, 53 per cent of the males and females interred had died before the age of six while, in a Linlithgow cemetery, the figure was 58 per cent. Of those, about a quarter had died before the age of two. In a Holyrood cemetery, which was probably the parish cemetery for the inhabitants of the Canongate, nearly 50 per cent of the burials were of sub-adults.[164] Iron-deficiency anaemia seems to have been common among children, perhaps caused partly by prolonged breastfeeding by mothers who were themselves deficient in iron.[165] Death in childbed was an ever-present danger for women. The evidence of some cemeteries suggests that many women died in young adulthood while men's deaths were more evenly spread over the adult years.[166]

Parasites were common in children and adults. Tapeworm, for example, could be contracted from dogs and pigs which wandered through the town, as well as from eating undercooked pork and fish. Grain might be contaminated by plants such as corn-cockle while ergot of rye produced the disease known as St Anthony's Fire which, at its worst, produced 'severe convulsions, mental confusion and gangrene'.[167] The coarse grain-based diet wore down surfaces on the teeth, causing dental problems although it offered some protection from plaque.[168] Indeed, those with the more refined diet associated with higher social status often had more caries in their teeth than their less well-off neighbours.[169] Hard physical labour put stresses on the bodies of men and of women although there is evidence that the gendering of tasks often resulted in stress on different parts of the bodies of men than those of women.[170] For those who lived into old age, osteoarthritis was common.[171]

Many types of illnesses appear in the miracle stories of cures associated with various Scottish saints such as Margaret, Aebbe, Ninian and Machar. These stories often involved townspeople, either those living locally or those who had travelled from further away. Among the ailments suffered were blindness, palsy, crippled limbs, dropsy, insanity, and deafness.[172] What this could mean for daily life is seen in one such man from Whithorn who had a 'robust torso, but withered lower limbs with bony growths on his hands: the interpretation being that he was crippled and had to propel himself along with his hands'.[173] Sometimes people with disabilities made an effort to carry out the responsibilities of citizenship. In 1531 the Selkirk authorities had to order that no deaf man should take part in the town watch.[174]

There are occasional glimpses of mental illness. In 1561 John Henderson, a burgess of Auchterarder, stole a pocket knife in Stirling and, when he was caught, cried out 'in maner of frannessy or desperation . . . Put me doun, put me doun I set nocht by quhidder I gang to God or the dewill.' The bailie, taking pity on his condition, released him to the care of a fellow burgess of Auchterarder and ordered him to look after him until such time as God would by his grace bring him to his right wits.[175] Sometimes temporary insanity might be feigned by people to get out of awkward situations. Hector Mechelson of Dundee decided he did not like the marriage contract he had agreed to for his daughter Elizabeth in February 1530 and repudiated it a few days later, claiming that he had not been in his right mind when it was made. The diarist James Melville recounted an occasion in St Andrews in 1580 where a man used his apparent madness to convey a political warning to the Earl of Morton.[176]

Diseases such as plague, leprosy, and syphilis were dealt with by the authorities by isolation and exclusion. Leprosy appears in Scottish records from the twelfth century. In 1178 the occupants of the hospital of St Nicholas beside St Andrews were referred to as the 'leprous sick'.[177] Parliament seems to have associated leprosy largely with towns, partly because lepers from the countryside went there to beg, and attempted to isolate lepers from healthy townspeople because of concerns about infection.[178] The town authorities followed suit. In 1450 the Ayr burgh court ordered that lepers were not to have dealings with others without carrying a cup as a symbol of their condition.[179] Once a townsperson was identified as a leper, this was announced publicly to the community. He or she was then excluded from urban society and had to move to the leper hospital, situated beyond the town limits, to join others in begging alms from passers-by while perhaps producing some of their own food on the lepers' croft.[180] By the sixteenth century there was a leper hospital on the outskirts of every major burgh although some of the inmates may not have been lepers but sufferers from other disfiguring diseases.[181] Despite the authorities' concerns, however, not all lepers were completely cut off from former friends and families. Some Glasgow lepers in 1582 were reported to have special friends within the town who received them in their houses. The town responded with a compromise, ordering that in future they were to come in the town only two days in the week, and 'in quiet and secreit manner'.[182] It is not clear if the isolation of lepers continued after their death. At least some lepers were buried in the cemetery in St Giles', Edinburgh, although there may have been a hospital near the church which cared for them during life.[183]

In the Middle Ages leprosy had the added stigma of being associated with sexual promiscuity, contributing to an attitude that lepers were the authors of their own misfortune, expressed most famously in the poet Robert Henryson's description of the leprous Cresseid in his 'Testament of Cresseid'. The term 'lipper' was often thrown at opponents as an insult, as when William Paterson of Inverness called Margaret Waus 'blay lipper hwyr' in December 1565.[184] More directly associated with sexual behaviour was syphilis or, as it was known, 'grandgore' although it is not clear to what extent the exact connection was recognised at the time. It was first identified in Aberdeen in 1497, and was dealt with by ordering prostitutes to desist from their occupation or be banished. When it reached Edinburgh, the authorities ordered the segregation of victims on Inchkeith in the Forth.[185] Despite these measures, grandgore was in Scotland to stay and became common enough to become a useful term to hurl at opponents, especially because of the disfiguring scabs associated with the disease. An Elgin woman called two other women 'schabbit clangoris carlis birdis' and they responded that she was a 'schabit, blerit, clangorit carling'.[186] At least three of the people buried in St Giles' in Edinburgh had signs of syphilis.[187]

Plague (or at least a disease which contemporaries labelled as pestilence) hit Scotland during almost every decade between 1349 and 1600.[188] Both the bubonic and pneumonic forms of the disease ravaged the country, the pneumonic plague perhaps flourishing especially well in the damp and cold climates of the Forth and Clyde valleys.[189] It has been argued that plague was largely an urban disease, perhaps because rats flourished in the crowded towns, although recent research has emphasised that it also affected rural areas. It is, however, more visible as an urban problem because of the better survival of urban than rural records for the Middle Ages.[190]

When plague raged in an area, the response of individual urban authorities from at least the fifteenth century onwards was to cut off all contact with the world outside, even when this was to the economic detriment of the community. Visitors from affected areas were denied access, and the local inhabitants were forbidden to travel to such places. In 1530, for example, the inhabitants of Haddington were forbidden to travel to Edinburgh or Leith which had been hit by plagues, and no traders from those places were allowed into the town.[191] It was believed that disease was carried by people, clothes and foodstuffs, especially grain, although infected air was blamed by some.[192] Such measures also affected life by disrupting towns' 'annual traditions, and those occasions on which people congregated and involved themselves in plays and pastimes'.[193]

If plague did enter the town despite such precautions (and it usually did), attempts were made to isolate affected individuals and goods. Suspected victims were either quarantined within their houses for a set period or sent to areas outside the town, such as the Burgh Muir of Edinburgh or the Foul Muir of Ayr.[194] Houses of plague victims were 'cleansed', often by burning bunches of aromatic herbs or branches of trees such as juniper to disinfect the air although this carried with it the risk of fire. Dry powders might also be sprinkled among clothing and on tapestry hangings before the house was fumigated.[195]

The problems that quarantine could cause individuals were shown when two Edinburgh women, confined to their house because of plague, were convicted of persuading Bessie Anderson to sell the feathers from their bed, presumably in an effort to get money for food, and were banished for life (Bessie was apparently regarded as less at fault and was banished during the provost's will).[196] The three women were fortunate. Many infractions of plague regulations were dealt with harshly. Andrew Clune of Stirling was charged with deliberately infecting the town in 1545 by sending infected gear to his wife who subsequently died. It did not help his case that he was reported as saying that he 'had put ane blok [amount] in Striveling of the pest that suld nevir gang furth of it'. He was sentenced to death.[197]

Mortality could also come from harvest failure and dearth. Moreover, famine weakened people's resistance to disease. Towns tried to safeguard their inhabitants by imposing fixed prices on foodstuffs in times of shortage so that the poor could still eat. In his sixteenth-century treatise, Dr Gilbert Skeyne connected famine and plague because famine forced people to eat evil and corrupt meat which was one of the ways in which he believed plague was spread.[198]

Illness, from epidemics or more everyday diseases or accidents, was endured by most medieval people. Some townsfolk had more resources than those living in the countryside, as hospitals (though intended for the poor as much as the sick) were often established in or beside towns.[199] Professional medical men tended to practise in urban areas. Apothecaries could be consulted for medicinal herbs while barbers might set broken bones and leeches provided the medieval cure-all of bloodletting.[200] Opinions about the effectiveness of the medical men varied. A certain scepticism is evinced in the late thirteenth-century miracle stories of St Margaret when the writer describes a wealthy woman who sought help from the saint after spending all her money on doctors, believing their promises that they would make her well.[201] On the other hand, town courts had some faith in their local practitioners. In assault cases, doctors were often called in to determine the severity of the physical injury suffered by the victim, and attackers were ordered to pay medical men to heal the wounds they had caused.[202] The fact that many townspeople survived, despite chronic childhood illnesses, suggests that there was some form of medical care available.[203]

Doctors cost money; most people probably relied on traditional medical lore to treat themselves. Skeyne had advice for the poor 'quha may not spend large on medicine'.[204] Opium and deadly nightshade were used to relieve pain; tormentil in small amounts was recommended for worms in children while, for the wealthy, imported figs could be used as purgatives. Mosses were used for the packing of wounds.[205] People also relied on local healers. Alison Peirson, executed as a witch in 1588, had gone often to St Andrews to heal people in the previous sixteen years. Medical knowledge was often passed from one generation to the next although, in the case of Christian Livingston of Leith who claimed that her ability to heal with the help of the fairies came from her daughter who had met them,[206] the usual pattern of generational transmission was reversed.

Magical practices were also tried. Euphamia MacCalzeane of Edinburgh placed a bored stone under her pillow during childbirth.[207] Preventive charms were used by many. Rings and other ornaments might bear the word or abbreviation for ananizapta (may the antidote of Jesus avert death by poisoning and the Holy Trinity sanctify my food and drink), a popular medieval charm to ward off falling sickness and sudden or violent death.[208] Such appeals for good health were found throughout all levels of society – the formula 'In my defence god me defende / And bring my saull to ane guide ende', which combined prayer with a good-luck charm, appears in Scottish manuscripts from the sixteenth to eighteenth centuries.[209]

Saints were another source of healing, and many townspeople made pilgrimages to Scottish or foreign shrines in the hope of a physical cure as well as for their spiritual health. St Triduana, whose shrine was at Restalrig just outside Edinburgh, was credited with curing eye ailments.[210] Alexander Stephenson from Aberdeen, who suffered from crippled feet and worms, tried the local shrines but, when these did not heal him, he took a ship to Kent in 1445 and dragged himself to Canterbury on his knees. This had better results – he celebrated his cure by dancing non-stop for three days and, having apparently acquired a taste for foreign pilgrimage, went on to the shrine at Wilsnack in Saxony.[211] Such trips did not always work out as planned. William, a thirteenth-century baker from Perth, was murdered in Rochester on his way to Canterbury and, as a result, became a local saint in England.[212]

From a medieval perspective, perhaps such a fate was preferable to a physical cure; William earned a lasting reputation denied to most of the townsfolk discussed here, even if that reputation was confined to England. For most Scottish townspeople, life ended in their own homes, with burial following shortly afterwards in the cemetery of their parish church or favoured religious house. Medieval preachers may have argued that death was the great leveller but, in reality, status distinctions continued after death, even if sometimes on the surface only. Most people were buried in a simple shroud but wooden coffins became more common, at least for the elite, in the later Middle Ages. Such coffins were often of fairly cheap construction but served the purpose of holding the body under a richly embroidered mortcloth, often provided by a guild, during the funerary ceremonies.[213] Status was also indicated by place of burial, with the wealthier townspeople paying for lairs within the church, and the richest benefactors requesting burial before the altars which they had founded.[214] Even in the crowded urban cemeteries, where graves were intercut and bones intermingled over time, there could be divisions. Four people with signs of leprosy, buried before the fourteenth century in St Giles', were buried close to one another, perhaps in a 'designated area for marginal members of society'.[215]

The medieval dead remained a part of the living urban community. Prayers were said for their souls by their families and by the local priests and chaplains, and these acted as a reminder that those still in this world could help the departed in Purgatory.[216] Prayers for the dead punctuated the daily round of services in the church, and acted rather as modern memorial brasses and stained-glass windows do today, perpetuating the memory of those who could afford to endow them.[217] For the vast majority of ordinary townsfolk, there were no such permanent memorials but the work of historians in volumes such as this may go a little way to perpetuate their memory as well.

Notes

1 'Quhy will ze, merchantis of renoun' (also known as 'To the Merchants of Edinburgh') in Priscilla Bawcutt (ed.), *The Poems of William Dunbar*, 2 vols (Glasgow, 1998), Poem 55. All references in the text are to this edition. The quote in the title is from line 39.

2 Elizabeth Gemmill and Nicholas Mayhew, *Changing Values in Medieval Scotland* (Cambridge, 1995), pp. 9–10.

3 David Ditchburn and A. J. MacDonald, 'Medieval Scotland, 1100–1560', in R. A. Houston and W. W. J. Knox (eds), *The New Penguin History of Scotland* (London, 2001), p. 145.

4 Priscilla J. Bawcutt, *Dunbar the Makar* (Oxford, 1992), p. 43; 'Peblis to the Play', in Allan. H. MacLaine (ed.), *The Christis Kirk Tradition: Scots Poems of Folk Festivity* (Glasgow, 1996), pp. 85–6; William Mackay and Herbert C. Boyd (eds), *Records of Inverness*, 2 vols (Aberdeen, 1911–24), vol. 1, p. 14. Of course, there was also a class dimension to this insult.

5 Peter Yeoman, *Medieval Scotland: An Archaeological Perspective* (London, 1995), p. 66.

6 James Beveridge and James Russell (eds), *Protocol Books of James Foulis, 1546–1553 and Nicol Thounis, 1559–1564* (Edinburgh, 1927), *passim*.

7 John Anderson and Francis J. Grant (eds), *Protocol Book of Gavin Ros NP 1512–1532* (Edinburgh, 1908), no. 252.

8 For examples see maps of 'Burgesses' landed interest', in Peter G. B. McNeill and Hector L. MacQueen (eds), *Atlas of Scottish History to 1707* (Edinburgh, 1996), p. 236.

9 John Warrack, *Domestic Life in Scotland, 1488–1688* (London, 1920), p. 67.

10 Russel Coleman, 'The Archaeology of Burgage Plots in Scottish Medieval Towns: A Review', *PSAS* 134 (2004), p. 290.

11 Yeoman, *Medieval Scotland*, pp. 66–8, 72; Margaret Sanderson, *A Kindly Place? Living in Sixteenth-Century Scotland* (East Linton, 2002), pp. 60–1.

12 Yeoman, *Medieval Scotland*, pp. 68, 72.

13 Dundee City Archives, Dundee Protocol Book 1520–34, f.213r; Yeoman, *Medieval Scotland*, p. 55.

14 H. Murray, 'Medieval Wooden and Wattle Buildings Excavated in Perth and Aberdeen', in Anne T. Simpson and Sylvia Stevenson (eds), *Town Houses and Structures in Medieval Scotland: A Seminar* (Glasgow, 1980), pp. 39–43.

15 Elizabeth Ewan, *Townlife in Fourteenth-Century Scotland* (Edinburgh, 1990), p. 15.

16 Coleman, 'Burgage Plots', p. 296; Yeoman, *Medieval Scotland*, p. 69; Derek Hall, *Burgess, Merchant and Priest: Burgh Life in the Scottish Medieval Town* (Edinburgh, 2002), pp. 17–19, 34.

17 Michael Asselmeyer, 'Medieval Architecture', in Bob Harris and Alan R. MacDonald (eds), *Scotland: The Making and Unmaking of the Nation*, 5 vols (Dundee, 2006), vol. 1, p. 190 and Fig. 8; Sanderson, *Kindly Place*, pp. 78–9.

18 Sanderson, *Kindly Place*, pp. 71,76.

19 Derek Hall and Catherine Smith, 'Medieval Archaeology', in Harris and MacDonald, *Scotland: Making and Unmaking*, vol. 1, p. 141; Coleman, 'Burgage Plots', pp. 293–4.

20 Warrack, *Domestic Life in Scotland*, pp. 65–74; Alexander Maxwell, *Old Dundee* (Edinburgh, 1891), pp. 234–46, 367–70; Sanderson, *Kindly Place*, pp. 82–98.

21 For discussion and illustrations of such ceilings, see Michael Bath, *Renaissance Decorative Painting in Scotland* (Edinburgh, 2003).

22 Sanderson, *Kindly Place*, pp. 69–71, 75–84.

23 Hall and Smith, 'Medieval Archaeology', p. 140.

24 F. J. Shaw, 'Sumptuary Legislation in Scotland', in *Juridical Review* (1979), pp. 81–90, 104–7; Maxwell, *Old Dundee*, pp. 248–53, 375–7; G. DesBrisay, E. Ewan and L. Diack, 'Life in the Two Towns', in E. Patricia Dennison, David Ditchburn and Michael Lynch (eds), *Aberdeen Before 1800: A New History* (East Linton, 2002), pp. 62–3.

25 J. A. Stones, D. H. Evans and J. C. Murray (eds), *A Tale of Two Burghs: The Archaeology of Old and New Aberdeen* (Aberdeen, 1987), pp. 32, 33, illustration 63.

26 William Dunbar, 'The Tretis of the Tua Mariit Wemen and the Wedo', in Bawcutt, *Poems of William Dunbar*, line 368. For an example of the symbolic nature of clothing see John J. McGavin, *Theatricality and Narrative in Medieval and Early Modern Scotland* (Aldershot, 2007), pp. 18–19.

27 Yeoman, *Medieval Scotland*, p. 81; DesBrisay et al., 'Life in the Two Towns', p. 63.

28 Stones, *Two Burghs*, pp. 32, 33, illustrations 60, 62. See also National Museum of Scotland, *Angels, Nobles and Unicorns: Art and Patronage in Medieval Scotland* (Edinburgh, 1982), p. 40.

29 For example, Aberdeen City Archives, Aberdeen Council Register, iv, pp. 373, 406; Dundee City Archives, Dundee Book of Church, ff 77r, 77v, 78v; Maxwell, *Old Dundee*, pp. 253–7.

30 Dundee Book of Church, f 69v. (13 December 1521).

31 A. D. M. Forte, 'Some Aspects of the Law of Marriage in Scotland: 1500–1700', in Elizabeth Craik (ed.), *Marriage and Property: Women and Marital Customs in History* (Aberdeen, 1984), p. 111.

32 NAS, CC8/3/3 – partial transcript at www.scotlandspeople.gov.uk/content/Images/FamousScots/example-trans. This testament is also discussed in C. Spence, 'Women and Business in Sixteenth-Century Edinburgh: Evidence from the Testaments', *Journal of Scottish Historical Studies* 28:1 (May 2008), p. 9.

33 Hall and Smith, 'Medieval Archaeology', pp. 148–9, 151; Catherine Smith, 'The Environmental Evidence', in Coleman, 'Burgage Plots', pp. 309–11.

34 For the gendered aspects of food preparation see Janay Nugent and Megan Butler, 'A Loaded Plate: Food Symbolism and the Early Modern Scottish Household', in *Journal of Scottish Historical Studies* 30.1 (2010), pp. 43–63.

35 Elizabeth Ewan, 'Mons Meg and Merchant Meg: Women in Late Medieval Edinburgh', in Terry Brotherstone and David Ditchburn (eds), *Freedom and Authority: Scotland c.1050–c.1650* (East Linton, 2000), pp. 132–4.

36 David Ditchburn, 'Scotland and Europe', in Harris and MacDonald, *Scotland: Making and Unmaking*, vol. 1, pp. 114–16.

37 Ewan, 'Mons Meg', pp. 136–9.

38 Gemmill and Mayhew, *Changing Values in Medieval Scotland*, pp. 41–2.

39 Sanderson, *Kindly Place*, pp. 60–1.

40 Hall and Smith, 'Medieval Archaeology', pp. 153–5, 149.

41 J. D. Marwick et al. (eds), *Extracts from the Records of the Burgh of Edinburgh*, [Hereafter *Edin Recs*] 5 vols (Edinburgh, 1869–92), vol. 1, pp. 199–200.

42 Elizabeth Ewan, 'Mistresses of Themselves? Female Domestic Servants and By-Employments in Sixteenth-Century Towns', in A. Fauve-Chamoux (ed.), *Domestic Service and the Formation of European Identity* (Bern, 2004), p. 412.

43 W. C. Dickinson (ed.), *Early Records of the Burgh of Aberdeen* (Edinburgh, 1957), p. 238.

44 G. Stell, 'The Earliest Tolbooths: A Preliminary Survey', in *PSAS* 111 (1981), pp. 445–53. See Alan R. MacDonald, *The Burghs and Parliament in Scotland, c.1550–1651* (Aldershot, 2007), pp. 140–2, for a detailed discussion of the Edinburgh tolbooth.

45 George S. Pryde (ed.), *Ayr Burgh Accounts 1534–1624* (Edinburgh, 1937), p. 113; R. Adam and T. Hunter (eds), *Edinburgh Records. The Burgh Accounts* (Edinburgh, 1899), vol. 1, p. 110. Booths are listed in *Edin Recs*, vol. 1, pp. 16–18, 39.

46 For a bargain 'beside the mercat cross', see A. H. Millar (ed.), *The Compt Buik of David Wedderburne, merchant of Dundee 1587–1630* (Edinburgh, 1898), pp. 45–6 (1596).

47 *Edin Recs*, vol. 1, pp. 34–6.

48 NAS, Haddington Burgh Records, B30/9/2 f.98v (14 February 1538/9).

49 Elizabeth Ewan, '"Many Injurious Words": Defamation and Gender in Late Medieval Scotland', in R. Andrew McDonald (ed.), *History, Literature, and Music in Scotland, 700–1560* (Toronto, 2002), pp. 173–6.

50 Dundee Book of Church, ff 37r44r (1521).

51 *Extracts from the Records of the Royal Burgh of Stirling* [hereafter *Stirling Recs*] 2 vols (Glasgow, 1887–9), vol. 1, p. 43 (13 August 1546).

52 Mackay and Boyd, *Records of Inverness*, p. 59.

53 Mackay and Boyd, *Records of Inverness*, pp. 31, 33; Adam and Hunter, *Edinburgh Records. The Burgh Accounts*, vol. 1, pp. 208, 279.

54 Ewan, *Townlife*, p. 57; Mackay and Boyd, *Records of Inverness*, pp. 31, 33; Lizanne Henderson and Edward J. Cowan, *Scottish Fairy Belief: A History* (East Linton, 2001), p. 44.

55 *Angels, Nobles and Unicorns*, p. 103; Margo Todd, 'Church and Religion', in Harris and MacDonald, *Scotland: Making and Unmaking*, vol. 2, p. 107; Margaret Sanderson, *Ayrshire and the Reformation: People and Change, 1490–1600* (East Linton, 1997), pp. 21–2.

56 John Purser, *Scotland's Music: A History of the Traditional and Classical Music of Scotland from Earliest Times to the Present Day* (Edinburgh, [1992] 2007), pp. 58–9, 97–106, 108; J. Cooper (ed.), *Cartularium Ecclesie Sancti Nicholai Aberdonensis*, 2 vols (Aberdeen, 1888–92), vol. 2, p. 326; Pryde, *Ayr Burgh Accounts*, p. 20, 75.

57 *Edin Recs*, vol. 1, pp. 9–11; Todd, 'Church and Religion', p. 108.

58 W. W. Hay Newton, 'Altar-Plate of the Collegiate Church, Haddington', in *PSAS* I (1851–4), p. 57.

59 Dundee City Archives, Protocol Book, f 154v. The Haddington Council kept a similar watchful eye over its clergy, Thomas Thomson, 'A Description of the Oldest Council Books and Other Records of the Town of Haddington' (Edinburgh, 1859), pp. 397–8. See also Mairi Cowan, 'The Spiritual Ties of Kinship in Pre-Reformation Scotland', in Elizabeth Ewan and Janay Nugent (eds), *Finding the Family in Medieval and Early Modern Scotland* (Aldershot, 2008), pp. 119–20.

60 Janet Foggie, 'The Medieval Church', in Harris and MacDonald, *Scotland: Making and Unmaking*, vol. 1, p. 101.

61 Bawcutt, *Dunbar the Makar*, pp. 199–203.

62 Purser, *Scotland's Music*, pp. 75, 109, 117.

63 John Stuart (ed.), *Extracts from the Council Register of the Burgh of Aberdeen*, 2 vols (Aberdeen, 1844–8), vol. 2, p. 366.

64 Cooper, *Cart. Sancti Nicholai*, vol. 2, p. 13. A 1351 donation of bells called Lawrence and Mary to the parish church of Aberdeen.

65 Foggie, 'The Medieval Church', p. 101; Maxwell, *Old Dundee*, pp. 41–2.

66 Pryde, *Ayr Burgh Accounts*, pp. 82, 85. On the significance and meaning of bells, see Purser, *Scotland's Music*, pp. 42–3.

67 'Statuta Gilde', in Cosmo Innes (ed.), *Ancient Laws and Customs of the Burghs of Scotland*, 23 vols (Edinburgh, 1868–1910), vol. 1, pp. 64–88.

68 Maxwell, *Old Dundee*, p. 379.

69 J. Imrie, et al. (eds), *Burgh Court Book of Selkirk, 1503–45* (Edinburgh, 1960), pp. 93,102.

70 Elizabeth Gemmill (ed.) *Aberdeen Guild Court Records, 1437–1468* (Edinburgh, 2005), p. 150. For the Ayr town clock see Pryde, *Ayr Burgh Accounts, passim*.

71 D. Parkinson, 'Prescriptions for Laughter in some Middle Scots Poems', in Steven R. McKenna (ed.), *Selected Essays on Scottish Language and Literature* (Lewiston, NY, 1992), pp. 27–8; Bawcutt, *Dunbar the Makar*, p. 191; Priscilla Bawcutt, 'Poets "of this Natioun"', in Priscilla Bawcutt and Janet Hadley Williams (eds), *A Companion to Medieval Scottish Poetry* (Woodbridge, 2006), pp. 14–16.

72 *Edin Recs*, vol. 1, p. 176.

73 See discussion in Henderson and Cowan, *Scottish Fairy Belief*, pp. 10–11, for references to this debate.

74 Anna J. Mill, *Mediaeval Plays in Scotland* (New York and London, [1924] 1969), p. 351.

75 A. M. Kinghorn (ed.), *Peblis, to the Play* (London, 1974), pp. 2–9. Discussed in Eila Williamson, 'Drama and Entertainment in Peebles in the Fifteenth and Sixteenth Centuries', in *Medieval English Theatre* 22 (2000), pp. 131–3.

76 Mill, *Mediaeval Plays*, p. 61.

77 Eila Williamson and John J. McGavin, 'Crossing the Border: The Provincial Records of Southeast Scotland', in Audrey Douglas and Sally-Beth MacLean (eds), *REED in Review* (Toronto, 2006), p. 163.

78 Mill, *Mediaeval Plays*, pp. 119–20.

79 Mill, *Mediaeval Plays*, pp. 177–8 (Edinburgh), 247–9 (Haddington), 261 (Lanark), 272 (Perth).

80 Williamson, 'Drama and Entertainment in Peebles', pp. 128–30, 135, 138.

81 MacDonald, *Burghs and Parliament in Scotland*, pp. 160–1. For example, Edinburgh websters and the walkers, shearers and bonnetmakers in 1531, *Edin Recs*, vol. 2, pp. 48–50.

82 Stuart, *Extracts . . . Aberdeen*, vol. 1, p. 445. Discussed in detail in McGavin, *Theatricality*, pp. 19–20.

83 Mill, *Mediaeval Plays*, pp. 21–35; Williamson, 'Drama and Entertainment in Peebles', pp. 127–31, 135, 138.

84 John McGavin, 'Drama in Sixteenth-Century Haddington', in *European Medieval Drama* 1 (1997), pp. 147–59.

85 McGavin, 'Drama in Sixteenth-Century Haddington', p. 146. See also the Selkirk common riding, Peter Symms, 'Selkirk at the Time of Flodden and the Charter', in John M. Gilbert (ed.), *Flower of the Forest. Selkirk: A New History* (Galashiels, 1985), pp. 44–5.

86 The Selkirk burgh court entry is transcribed in Symms, 'Selkirk at the Time of Flodden', pp. 44–5.

87 MacDonald, *Burghs and Parliament in Scotland*, pp. 157–66.

88 Dundee Book of Church, f 89v (May 1522).

89 Pryde, *Ayr Burgh Accounts*, pp. 89, 96, 100, 125. For wapinschawings in Dundee, see Maxwell, *Old Dundee*, pp. 265–8.

90 Gemmill, *Aberdeen Guild Court Records*, pp. 118, 156.

91 John Yonge, cited in Ian Campbell, 'James IV and Edinburgh's First Triumphal Arches', in D. Mays (ed.), *The Architecture of Scottish Cities* (East Linton, 1997), pp. 26–7. See also Mill, *Mediaeval Plays*, pp. 78–85; Dunbar, 'Blyth Aberdeane, thow beriall of all tounis', in Bawcutt, *Poems of Dunbar*, line 58.

92 MacDonald, *Burghs and Parliament in Scotland*, chapters 5, 6; K. Stevenson, *Chivalry and Knighthood in Scotland, 1424–1513* (Woodbridge, 2006), pp. 63–102. For popular celebrations see Mill, *Mediaeval Plays*, p. 10 and note 7.

93 Mill, *Mediaeval Plays*, p. 15; Henderson and Cowan, *Scottish Fairy Belief*, p. 134.

94 Thomas Dickson (ed.), *Accounts of the Lord High Treasurer of Scotland*, 8 vols (Edinburgh, 1877–1978), vol. 2, pp. 132, 428, vol. 3, pp. 197, 198.

95 Kinghorn, '*Peblis to the Play*', ll. 191–240; Allan H. MacLaine, Introduction, in *Christis Kirk Tradition*, pp. v–vi, xviii; Purser, *Scotland's Music*, pp. 120, 274.

96 One is also mentioned in 'Colkelbie Sow'. There are lists of songs in 'Colkelbie Sow' and 'The Complaynt of Scotland' although it is not always clear if these represent real songs or titles made up by the author. See discussion in Gregory Kratzmann (ed.), *Colkelbie Sow and the Talis of the Fyve Bestes* (New York, 1983), p. 9.

97 John McGavin, 'Secular Music in the Burgh of Haddington, 1530–1640', in Fiona Kisby (ed.), *Music and Musicians in Renaissance Cities and Towns* (Cambridge, 2001), pp. 47–9, 54, 55; Mill, *Mediaeval Plays*, pp. 37–41.

98 'Meg of Abernethy', in Elizabeth Ewan et al. (eds), *The Biographical Dictionary of Scottish Women* (Edinburgh, 2007), p. 262.

99 Williamson, 'Drama in Peebles', p. 136; *Edin Accounts*, vol. 1, p. 204. See also McGavin, 'Secular Music', pp. 49, 55.

100 Sanderson, *Kindly Place*, p. 66.

101 Mill, *Mediaeval Plays*, pp. 37, 40, 41; J. D. Marwick and R. Renwick (eds), *Extracts from the Records of the Burgh of Glasgow* 28 vols (Glasgow, 1876–1916), vol. 1, pp. 28–9.

102 McGavin, 'Secular Music', p. 53.

103 T. Thomson and C. Innes (eds), *Acts of the Parliaments of Scotland*, 11 vols (Edinburgh, 1844–75), vol. 2, p. 14; Ewan, *Townlife*, pp. 12–13.

104 Sanderson, *Kindly Place*, p. 110.

105 Dundee Protocol Book, p. 4; Sanderson, *Kindly Place*, pp. 109–11.

106 Stirling Council Archives, B66/15/2 f 109r (25 February 1549).

107 Imrie, *Burgh Court Book of Selkirk*, p. 25. For contracts, see Elizabeth Ewan, 'For Whatever Ales Ye', in Elizabeth Ewan and Maureen Meikle (eds), *Women in Scotland c.1100–c.1750* (East Linton, 1999), p. 131.

108 William Cramond (ed.), *The Records of Elgin*, 2 vols (Aberdeen, 1903–8), vol. 1, pp. 167–8.

109 Highland Regional Archives, Inverness Burgh Court, I, f 135v. The fine was imposed a week later, Mackay and Boyd, *Records of Inverness*, pp. 50–1.
110 A. J. Warden, *Burgh Laws of Dundee* (London, 1872), p. 25.
111 Cramond, *Records of Elgin*, vol. 1, pp. 68, 107–8.
112 Imrie, *Burgh Court Book of Selkirk*, p. 25; Symms, 'Selkirk at the time of Flodden', pp. 51–2.
113 Warden, *Burgh Laws of Dundee*, pp. 18, 26.
114 John Burnett, *Riot, Revelry and Rout. Sport in Lowland Scotland before 1860* (East Linton, 2000), pp. 170, 29.
115 Burnett, *Riot, Revelry and Rout*, pp. 31, 169–70; Williamson and McGavin, 'Crossing the Border', p. 160.
116 Pryde, *Ayr Burgh Accounts*, pp. 18–19.
117 Burnett, *Riot, Revelry and Rout*, pp. 12, 156.
118 Eila Williamson, 'Horse-Racing in Scotland in the Sixteenth and Seventeenth Centuries: Peebles and Beyond', in ROSC 14 (2001–2), p. 31; Burnett, *Riot, Revelry and Rout*, pp. 142–3.
119 Williamson, 'Horse-Racing in Scotland', pp. 31, 35; Williamson and McGavin, 'Crossing the Border', pp. 159–60.
120 Burnett, *Riot, Revelry and Rout*, pp. 20, 81.
121 Maxwell, *Old Dundee*, p. 387; Burnett, *Riot, Revelry and Rout*, pp. 20, 32–40.
122 Burnett, *Riot, Revelry and Rout*, pp. 4–5, 16.
123 Burnett, *Riot, Revelry and Rout*, pp. 19–20, 45–8.
124 Edinburgh City Archives, Neighbourhood Book, f. 23r; Burnett, *Riot, Revelry and Rout*, pp. 45–8.
125 Stuart, *Extracts . . . Aberdeen*, vol. 1, p. 249; John McGavin, 'The Kirk, the Burgh and Fun', in *Early Theatre* 1 (1998), p. 22.
126 *Stirling Recs*, p. 27; Robert Adam (ed.), *Edinburgh Records. The Burgh Accounts: Vol 1* (Edinburgh, 1899), pp. 110, 209, 241. My thanks to Dr Mairi Cowan for the Edinburgh reference.
127 Williamson and McGavin, 'Crossing the Border', p. 164; Catherine Smith, 'Dogs, Cats and Horses in the Scottish Medieval Town', in *PSAS* 128 (1998), pp. 880–1.
128 Maxwell, *Old Dundee*, pp. 387–8; A. I. Dunlop (ed.), *Acta Facultatis Artium Universitatis Sanctiandree, 1413–1588*, 2 vols (Edinburgh, 1964), vol. 1, pp. clxxiv, 4; Bawcutt, *Dunbar the Makar*, p. 70.
129 Williamson, 'Horse-Racing', p. 38; Williamson, 'Drama in Peebles', p. 134.
130 Dundee Protocol Book, p. 13.
131 Williamson, 'Drama in Peebles', pp. 133–4.
132 T. van Heijnsbergen, 'Early Modern Literature', in Harris and MacDonald, *Scotland: Making and Unmaking*, vol. 2, p. 236; Bawcutt, 'Poets', pp. 3–4.
133 Van Heijnsbergen, 'Early Modern Literature', p. 233; T. van Heijnsbergen and Nicola Royan (eds), *Literature, Letters and the Canonical in Early Modern Scotland* (East Linton, 2002), Introduction pp. xvii–xix. For women book owners, see Priscilla Bawcutt, 'My Bright Buke: Women and their Books in Medieval and Renaissance Scotland', in J. Wogan-Browne et al. (eds), *Medieval Women: Texts and Contexts in Late Medieval Britain* (Turnhout, 2000), pp. 18–34.

134 John Durkan and Anthony Ross, *Early Scottish Libraries* (Glasgow, 1961), p. 145. Discussed in van Heijnsbergen and Royan, *Literature, Letters and the Canonical*, p. xviii.

135 *Edin Recs*, vol. 1, p. 76; Dundee City Archives, Dundee Council Records 1562–3, 23 December 1562; Murray Pittock, 'Contrasting Cultures: Town and Country', in Ditchburn and Lynch, *Aberdeen Before 1800*, p. 358.

136 Foggie, 'Medieval Church', pp. 96–7.

137 Bawcutt, *Dunbar the Makar*, p. 15; Bawcutt, 'Poets', pp. 17–18.

138 Priscilla Bawcutt, 'The Commonplace Book of John Maxwell', in A. Gardner-Medwin and J. Hadley Williams (eds), *A Day Estivall* (Aberdeen, 1990), pp. 59–68; Erskine Beveridge (ed.), *Fergusson's Scottish Proverbs from the Original Print of 1641* (Edinburgh, 1924).

139 Keely Fisher, 'The Contemporary Humour in William Stewart's *The Flytting betuix the Sowtar and the Tailzour*', in van Heijnsbergen and Royan, *Literature, Letters and the Canonical*, pp. 7, xvi. For stories of Wallace etc. see 'Sym and His Broder', in MacLaine, *Christis Kirk Tradition*, pp. 1–3.

140 Gilbert Skeyne, *Ane Breve Descriptiovn of the Pest Quhair In the Cavsis, Signis and sum Special Preservatioun and Cure thairof ar Contenit in Tracts by Dr Gilbert Skeyne* (Edinburgh, [1568] 1860); also discussed in T. C. Smout, 'Coping with Plague in Sixteenth and Seventeenth Century Scotland', in *Scotia* 2 (1978).

141 Maxwell, *Old Dundee*, p. 247.

142 David Henderson, 'The Human Bones', in *Archaeological Excavations in St Giles' Cathedral, Edinburgh 1981–93*, Scottish Archaeological Internet Report 22 (2006), p. 35, www.sair.org.uk

143 Imrie, *Burgh Court Book of Selkirk*, p. 174; *Edin Recs*, vol. 1, pp. 105, 124.

144 Smith, 'Dogs, Cats and Horses in the Scottish Medieval Town', pp. 869, 873–5.

145 *Edin Recs*, vol. 2, p. 121; discussed in Fisher, 'Contemporary Humour', p. 13.

146 Catherine Smith, 'A grumphie in the sty: An Archaeological View of Pigs in Scotland from their Earliest Domestication to the Agricultural Revolution', in *PSAS* 130 (2000), pp. 713–14; Dundee Book of Church, f 50v (1521); Maxwell, *Old Dundee*, p. 103.

147 *Edin Recs*, vol. 1, p. 12; Maxwell, *Old Dundee*, p. 199.

148 Edinburgh City Archives, Neighbourhood Book, 13r.

149 Imrie, *Burgh Court Book of Selkirk*, pp. 143, 198, 221; Symms, 'Selkirk in the Time of Flodden', pp. 59–60.

150 Dundee Book of Church, f. 47v; Imrie, *Burgh Court Book of Selkirk*, p. 74; *Edin Recs*, vol. 1, pp. 105–6, 124.

151 *Edin Recs*, vol. 1, pp. 177–8 (1518).

152 Ewan, *Townlife*, p. 23.

153 Marion L. Stavert (ed.), *The Perth Guildry Book, 1452–1601* (Edinburgh, 1993), pp. 458–9.

154 Pryde, *Ayr Burgh Accounts*, p. 20.

155 Dunbar, 'Doveritt with Dreme', in Bawcutt, *Poems of Dunbar*, vol. 2, ll. 73–4. See also Sir David Lyndsay, 'Ane supplication . . . in contemptioun of side

taillis', in Douglas Hamer (ed.), *The Works of Sir David Lindsay of the Mount* (Edinburgh, 1931–6), pp. 118–22.

156   Dundee Book of Church, 41r; Maxwell, *Old Dundee*, pp. 195–6; Coleman, 'Burgage Plots', p. 308.

157   Coleman, 'Burgage Plots', pp. 299, 300, 302.

158   Yeoman, *Medieval Scotland*, pp. 59–60, 62.

159   Hall, *Burgess, Merchant and Priest*, p. 13.

160   G. Walker, '"Faill Nocht to Teme Your Bleddir": Passing Time in Sir David Lindsay's *Ane Satyre of the Thrie Estaitis*', in *Medieval English Theatre* 22 (2000), pp. 53–4.

161   Imrie, *Burgh Court Book of Selkirk*, p. 213.

162   Edinburgh City Archives, Neighbourhood Book, 4v, 8r, 9v; Dundee Book of Church, 39r; Sanderson, *Kindly Place*, pp. 79–80, 107.

163   J. F. Cross and M. F. Bruce, 'The Skeleton Remains', in J. A. Stones (ed.), *Three Scottish Carmelite Friaries. Excavations at Aberdeen, Linlithgow and Perth 1980–83* (Edinburgh, 1989) p. 141.

164   Cross and Bruce, 'Skeleton Remains', p. 121; C. Hazel, 'Human Bones', in Susan Bain, 'Excavation of a Medieval Cemetery at Holyrood Abbey, Edinburgh', *PSAS* 128 (1998), p. 1072.

165   Cross and Bruce, 'Skeleton Remains', pp. 135–6; Henderson, 'Human Bones', p. 38.

166   Cross and Bruce, 'Skeleton Remains', p. 122.

167   Hall and Smith, 'Medieval Archaeology', p. 151.

168   M. J. Rains and D. W. Hall (eds), *Excavations in St Andrews 1980–89* (Glasgow, 1997), pp. 125, 133, 136–7; Cross and Bruce, 'Skeleton Remains', p. 139.

169   Henderson, 'Human Bones', p. 37.

170   Hall and Smith, 'Medieval Archaeology', pp. 150–1; Rains and Hall, *Excavations in St Andrews*, pp. 122–5; Yeoman, *Medieval Scotland*, p. 85.

171   Henderson, 'Human Bones', pp. 30–2.

172   Robert Bartlett (ed.), *The Miracles of Saint Aebbe of Coldingham and Saint Margaret of Scotland* (Oxford, 2003), pp. xxiii, xxxviii–xxxix; W. M. Metcalfe (ed.), *Legends of SS Ninian and Machor* (Paisley, 1904), 'St Machar' lines 1587–1600.

173   Yeoman, *Medieval Scotland*, p. 85.

174   Imrie, *Burgh Court Book of Selkirk*, p. 111. See also the Aberdeen sailor who ran wild in Dunfermline, Bartlett, *Miracles of Aebbe and Margaret*, p. xliii.

175   *Extracts from the Records of the Royal Burgh of Stirling*, 2 vols (Glasgow, 1887–9), vol. 1, p. 79.

176   Protocol Book of Dundee, f 160v; McGavin, *Theatricality*, pp. 85–108.

177   Derek W. Hall, 'Archaeological Excavations at St Nicholas Farm, St Andrews, 1986–87', in *Tayside and Fife Archaeological Journal* I (1995), p. 48.

178   *Records of the Parliaments of Scotland to 1707* (www.rps.ac.uk) 9 March 1428, 10 June 1429.

179   NAS, Ayr Burgh Records, B6/12/1, 13 April 1450.

180   *Extracts . . . Stirling*, vol. 1, pp. 3, 5, 27; J. D. Marwick (ed.), *Extracts From the*

Records of the Burgh of Glasgow A.D. *1573–1642* (Glasgow, 1876), vol. 1, p. 1; Cosmo Innes (ed.), *Registrum Episcopatus Aberdonensis* (Aberdeen, 1845), pp. ii, iii, 283–4.

181 Hall and Smith, 'Medieval Archaeology', p. 153.
182 Marwick, *Extracts . . . Glasgow*, vol. 1, p. 93.
183 Henderson, 'Human Bones', pp. 34, 68; Mark Collard and John A. Lawson, 'Discussion', in *Excavations in St Giles'*, p. 68.
184 Mackay and Boyd, *Records of Inverness*, p. 128. 'Blay' means livid or blue in the skin. For leprosy and sexual misbehaviour, see Felicity Riddy, '"Abject and Odious": Masculine and Feminine in Henryson's Testament of Cresseid', in Helen Cooper and Sally Mapstone (eds), *The Long Fifteenth Century* (Oxford, 1997), pp. 229–48.
185 Stuart, *Extracts . . . Aberdeen*, vol. 1, p. 425; *Edin Recs*, vol. 1, pp. 71–2.
186 Cramond, *Records of Elgin*, vol. 1, p. 72.
187 Henderson, 'Human Bones', p. 33.
188 Richard Oram, '"It cannot be decernit quha are clean and quha are foulle": Epidemic Disease in 16th- and 17th-century Scotland: Problems and Responses', in *Renaissance and Reformation* 30.4 (2006–7), pp. 13–39. See also discussion of 1530 Edinburgh outbreak, Fisher, 'Contemporary Humour', pp. 13–17.
189 Audrey-Beth Fitch, 'Assumptions about Plague in Late Medieval Scotland', in *Scotia* 11 (1987), pp. 32–3, 37.
190 Fitch, 'Plague', pp. 33–5; Oram, 'Epidemic Disease', pp. 17–20.
191 For measures taken in Haddington during plague outbreaks, see Thomas Thomson, 'A Description of the Oldest Council Books and Other Records of the Town of Haddington, with Copious Extracts', in *PSAS* 2 (1854–7), pp. 393–5. For other examples, see Oram, 'Epidemic Disease', pp. 22–9.
192 Smout, 'Coping with Plague', p. 23; Oram, 'Epidemic Disease', p. 24.
193 McGavin, 'Drama in Haddington', p. 146.
194 McGavin, 'Drama in Haddington', pp. 146, 150; Smout, 'Coping with Plague', pp. 23, 26; Oram, 'Epidemic Disease', pp. 25–6.
195 Smout, 'Coping with Plague', pp. 26–7; Oram, 'Epidemic Disease', pp. 28–9.
196 *Edin Recs*, vol. 2, p. 42.
197 *Stirling Recs*, p. 44.
198 Skeyne, *Ane Breve Descriptioun*, pp. 6–7.
199 John Durkan, 'Care of the Poor: Pre-Reformation Hospitals', in David McRoberts (ed.), *Essays on the Scottish Reformation* (Glasgow, 1962), pp. 268–80.
200 Cramond, *Records of Elgin*, vol. 1, 61–2; Dundee Book of Church, ff 14r, 17r, 37r; Stuart, *Extracts . . . Aberdeen*, vol. 1, pp. 352–3.
201 Bartlett, *Miracles of SS Aebbe and Margaret*, p. 111.
202 Edinburgh City Archives, SL150/1/3, 7–8; Dundee City Archives, Dundee Town Council Books, vol. 4, 105v (19 March 1556/7).
203 Hazel, 'Human Bones', p. 1073.
204 Skeyne, *Ane Breve Descriptioun*, p. 29.
205 Hall and Smith, 'Medieval Archaeology', p. 150. See Skeyne, *Ane Breve Descriptioun*, for use of tormentil.

206 Henderson and Cowan, *Scottish Fairy Belief*, pp. 85, 86; Joyce Miller, 'Devices and Directions: Folk Healing Aspects as Witchcraft Practice in Seventeenth-Century Scotland', in Julian Goodare (ed.), *The Scottish Witch-hunt in Context* (Manchester, 2002), pp. 95–6; Owen Davies, 'A Comparative Perspective on Scottish Cunning-Folk and Charmers', in J. Goodare et al. (eds), *Witchcraft and Belief in Early Modern Scotland* (Basingstoke, 2008), pp. 198–9. Davies tentatively suggests that women may have made up a larger proportion of local healers in Scotland than in England.

207 Henderson and Cowan, *Scottish Fairy Belief*, pp. 87–8, 93, 100; Miller, 'Devices', pp. 95–105; Davies, 'Comparative Perspective', pp. 187–8. For a possible witch's stone from Dumbarton, see R. Coleman, 'Three Excavations in Medieval Dumbarton', in *PSAS* 134 (2004), p. 345. But see Hugh Cheape's comments about modern interpretations of such objects in '"Charms against Witchcraft:" Magic and Mischief in Museum Collections', in Goodare, *Witchcraft and Belief*, pp. 227–48.

208 Virginia Glenn, *Romanesque and Gothic Decorative Metalwork and Ivory Carvings in the Museum of Scotland* (Edinburgh, 2002), pp. 44, 72–3, 76.

209 Bawcutt, 'Maxwell', pp. 64–5.

210 'Triduana', in Ewan et al., *Biographical Dictionary of Scottish Women*, p. 357. See also Peter A. Yeoman, 'Saint Margaret's Shrine at Dunfermline Abbey', in Richard Fawcett (ed.), *Royal Dunfermline* (Edinburgh, 2005), pp. 79–88, and Audrey-Beth Fitch in the present volume.

211 Peter Yeoman, *Pilgrimage in Medieval Scotland* (London, 1999), p. 114; Ditchburn, 'Scotland and Europe', p. 59.

212 Yeoman, *Pilgrimage in Medieval Scotland*, p. 114.

213 *Excavations in St Giles'*, pp. 19–21; Stavert, *Perth Guildry Book*, pp. 135–6.

214 Dundee Book of Church, ff 163v–168v; Maxwell, *Old Dundee*, pp. 119–21; Cowan, 'Spiritual Ties of Kinship', pp. 119–21; Sanderson, *Ayrshire and the Reformation*, pp. 15–17. Desire for burial in the church remained powerful after the Reformation, Margo Todd, *The Culture of Protestantism in Early Modern Scotland* (New Haven, 2002), pp. 333–7.

215 Henderson, 'Human Bones', p. 38.

216 Cowan, 'Spiritual Ties of Kinship', pp. 115, 118–25.

217 Sanderson, *Ayrshire and the Reformation*, p. 17.

Chapter 6

Playtime Everyday: The Material Culture of Medieval Gaming

Mark A. Hall

The ball is round. The game lasts 90 minutes
That's a fact. Everything else is pure theory.
Here we go![1]

RULES OF THE GAME

This chapter[2] offers the reader an exploratory analysis of the everyday experience of gaming in medieval Scotland. The chronological focus is post-AD 1200 medieval Scotland but its wider range encompasses the first millennium AD. By gaming, what is meant is board and dice games. The original intent, had space permitted, was to also pursue sports – principally hunting (a key example of play as both life and escape from life), tournaments, archery, curling, ball games (including football) and bat and ball games (including golf, cricket and tennis). They require and need their own study, not least for the opportunity they offer to get to grips with the everyday in localised contexts.[3] Nevertheless, such games are an aspect of play, and the broader analysis of play outlined here applies to sports as much as to the gaming activity that is the focus of this chapter. Let us look briefly then at play. The analysis begins with a brief examination of the wider contexts of both play and the everyday before outlining the evidence from Scotland and its nuanced understanding set within a European context.

OPENING GAMBIT

Play is primarily a free activity that creates an area of its own in space and time where it can unfold its own inner order. There are two key, contrasting approaches to the cultural phenomenon of play. One argues that play prefigured culture and civilisation, characterising it as the archetypal opposite of that which is rational, controlled and systematised. It is a view that remains useful in some of its detail but that has been for many superseded by a more functional approach which sees forms of play as embedded and interwoven with social structures.[4] It thus has a greater concern with particular forms of play and their social contexts. Board and dice games, for example, are clear cases of play forms with cultural and cross-cultural contexts. Games playing

informs many other areas of social practice: gambling was, and is, a root
cause of disorder, crime and ill health; games form a key aspect of twentieth-
century culture (particularly in their IT dimension);[5] games can be part of the
treatment as well as the cause of illness; games employ most, if not all, the
senses; they are a form of communication and they can be indulged in on the
move either for their own pleasure or to make travel bearable. According
to Suetonius, the Emperor Claudius' addiction to board games was such
that, 'he . . . used to play while out driving, on a special board fitted to his
carriage which prevented the game from upsetting' (presumably a reference
to a pegged board).[6] It is this wide relevance of gaming that so readily suggested the chapter title's allusion to Jacques Tati's film masterpiece, *Playtime*,
in which Tati structures his acute and hilarious observations of life in one
Parisian day as a game.[7]

Even when played in very restricted social circles, as was the case with
the medieval game of *Rithmimachia*, the 'Battle of Numbers', later known as
'The Philosopher's Game',[8] such pursuits still qualify as an everyday, if not
an everyone, experience. Every life is lived through everyday experiences –
the usual, commonplace things of every day – which, varying from context
to context, cannot be avoided by anyone. The everyday as commonplace
has long been a concern of archaeology-inflected material culture studies, as
observed by Cecil Curwen (following General Pitt Rivers), it is 'the common
objects that are often more important than the rare ones, just because they
are common and it is surely one of the prime objects of excavation to obtain
data for the study of the evolution not only of pottery but all common
objects'.[9] This comment was made in the context of a study of quern stones,
primarily as chronological markers in the archaeological record, and so
appropriate in the interwar development of archaeological practice. A more
nuanced approach today, combining 'common' and 'rare' objects for a fuller
grasp of everyday life, was skilfully demonstrated by the 2006–7 Victoria
and Albert Museum exhibition *At Home in Renaissance Italy* which explored
the domestic sphere of Italian life so as to chart its impact and influence on
the Renaissance, particularly bringing out the contemporary everyday experience of it.[10] The everyday experiences in this domestic sphere included a
variety of board and gambling games, part of a wider leisure theme, which
revealed much about interpersonal relationships and gender roles as well as
the social spread of art.[11] Games and play, then, have a complex role in the
everyday for they are, as enacted or performed, or even manufactured, part
of the everyday but in their purpose are meant to enable an escape from the
everyday. Play can be viewed as a performed metaphor of the human condition, both mirroring specific situations in life (as between competing ethnic
and national groups, for example) and the broader structures of human
existence – the struggle to know what is coming.[12]

GAME ON

Let us now examine some of the key pieces of evidence for the pursuit of board games and dicing. I shall adopt the convenience of chronology and begin with the Picts and their contemporaries. There is no decisive, direct evidence that Roman board games, which were certainly being played on and around Hadrian's and the Antonine Walls, were adopted by the Picts (though the evidence certainly and persuasively bears that interpretation) but it is worth noting – as an example of how gaming can tell us about wider societal issues – that one of the earliest epigraphic references to the Picts is made in a gaming context. In 1983 a copper alloy *pyragus* or dicing cup was found near Froitzheim, Germany, bearing a hexagram inscription – the style typical of those used in the Roman game *alea* (a precursor of backgammon) – PICTOS/VICTOS/HOSTIS/DELETEA/LUDITE/SECURI, which can be translated as 'The Picts defeated, the enemy wiped out, play without fear!'

The cup may date to the early fourth century and refer to the Roman campaigning in Britain in the late third and early fourth centuries.[13] I have recently considered this evidence and that more generally for first millennium AD Scotland in more detail elsewhere,[14] and here I will confine my comments on the games played by the Picts and their neighbours, to the *tafl* group, of which the commonest form appears to have been *hnefatafl*, or king's table.[15] This was (and remains) a contest between two unequal forces. The king piece of the defending side occupies the central cell or intersection, surrounded by his defenders. The aim is to get the king to one of the four corner cells and so secure victory. The usually larger attacking force is arranged along the edges of the board and has to try to capture the king piece by surrounding it on four sides. All the pieces move orthogonally as the rook does in chess.

The game is generally held to be of Scandinavian origin, with the earliest board fragment dated to the fifth century AD, from a grave at Wimose, Funen, and it seems to have been carried by the Vikings to all the counties they raided or settled (Figure 6.1). There is, though, a number of boards from Scottish sites that suggest that the game was known prior to the arrival of the Vikings. Pictish phases at Buckquoy, Howe and Birsay, Orkney have produced *hnefatafl* boards incised on stone. And there is a surface find of a stone board from Dun Chonallaich, near Kilmartin, Argyll, which is presumed to be Dalriadic.[16] The broch site at Scalloway, Shetland, has also produced gaming pieces that could have been used in a *tafl*-type game, notably one that could readily be a *hnefi* or, if from a very elaborate set, even a pawn (Figure 6.2).[17] The excavators are reluctant to accept a *tafl* identification because of their early and pre-Viking dating. Certainly the identification is not absolute because we do not know when the *tafl* games began to be played nor, at this early pre-Viking date, do we know what, if any, other games were played alongside them. Comparison with other later Iron Age figurines suggests

Figure 6.1 *Set of pieces for 'hnefatafl' from Viking ship burial excavated in Westness, Orkney.* © *Trustees of the National Museums Scotland.*

that these pieces may also have had a ritual function, possibly as part of the toolkit of a shaman or druid, which does not rule out use as gaming pieces as there is a reinforcing cross over between games play and fortune prediction or divination and magic.

Evidence from pre-Viking Anglo-Saxon England (including Sutton Hoo) includes a large number of playing pieces, some of which were undoubtedly for *tafl* games.[18] There developed an Anglo-Irish connection for, by the early tenth century, it was known in elite Christian circles of both countries. The cornerstone of the evidence is a folio from an eleventh-century copy of a tenth-century Irish Gospel Book (Corpus Christi College, Oxon 122g). This illumination shows the layout for *hnefatafl* in the shape of an allegorical game on the harmony of the Gospels, known as *Alea Evangeli* – 'the Game of the Gospels' or 'Evangelists'. Its title caption notes that the game was brought to Ireland by Dubinsi, Bishop of Bangor (d.953), from the court of King Athelstan (r.925–40).[19]

Perhaps then we should not be surprised to find assemblages of incised board games from ecclesiastical sites (including Raholp and Downpatrick, County Down, Tintagel, Cornwall and Whithorn, Galloway) and particularly notable in this regard are the *hnefatafl* boards from Inchmarnock, Bute. Excavation by Headland Archaeology at Inchmarnock in recent years has recovered thirty-five gaming boards (plus additional fragments and an unfinished board) along with a number of other slates with graffiti designs and

Figure 6.2 The figurative cone playing piece from Scalloway Broch, Shetland. © Crown copyright reproduced courtesy of Historic Scotland.

inscriptions and lettering, clear indications of a monastic school function. The majority of the boards appear to be for *hnefatafl* (and probably of ninth to tenth-century date) though both alquerque and merelles are represented in significant numbers.[20] The excavation report seems tacitly to suggest a pre-twelfth-century date for these but, from a site with a difficult-to-cope-with, unclear stratigraphy, there is no good evidence to support this inference. Without such evidence, it is perhaps wiser to hold with twelfth-century and later dating of British examples of merelles and alquerque. Indeed, the presence of these two essentially twelfth-century and later games (as evidenced from Britain) suggests that the balance for gaming-board execution and usage at Inchmarnock is fairly evenly poised between early and later medieval times.

As should be clear from the foregoing discussion, the nature of any other insular games certainly being played remains rather opaque. There are names known – including *brandubh* ('black raven') and *fidcheall* ('wood sense') – but, though they are admirably poetic, they do not tell us very much. As far as the evidence allows, it seems most likely that *fidcheall* and *brandubh* were variants of the *tafl* type of game, using Gaelic nomenclature and cultural references. If so, the principles of play could be conjectured to be basically those of *hnefatafl*. Given the meaning of *fidcheall*, 'wood sense', it could have referred to any board game that was played and certainly within later medieval texts (*circa* post-AD 1200) it is equated to chess, just as chess becomes *tawlbwrdd* (a form of *hnefatafl*) in some late medieval Welsh translations of French Romance texts.[21] The textual references certainly indicate that such board games were an essential aspect of court or elite lifestyles. In the Old Irish tale (*Scela Cano meic Gartnain*), describing Cano's departure for Ireland with the people of Skye in 688, we learn of 'a royal retinue sailing in currachs, complete with fifty well-armed warriors, fifty well-dressed ladies and fifty liveried gillies each with the silver leads of two greyhounds in his right hand, a musical instrument in his left and the board of a fidchell game on his back, along with gold and silver playing men'.[22] Similarly, we can quote verse 2 of the mid-thirteenth century 'Poem of Aenghus Mor Mac Domhnaill, King of the Isles', translated by Thomas Clancy as: 'To you he left his position, yours each breastplate, each treasure, his hats, his stores, his slender swords, yours, his brown ivory chessmen'.[23] Both *fidcheall* and *brandubh* are listed in Irish law texts of the seventh and eighth centuries as games to be taught to boys of noble birth – along with how to swim, ride a horse and throw a spear, part of their training for a life of leisure, hunting and warfare.[24] Though not necessarily all of the slates found at Inchmarnock were used in a teaching context, still the quantity and focus of the material may suggest secular elite pupils being taught the everyday business of an elite lifestyle. Of course, the ecclesiastics on site may also have been learning and playing the game. Parallel but later evidence suggestive of this idea takes the shape of a fourteenth-century misericord from Montbenoit, France.[25] This can be read as both a reference to Dominican anti-gaming tracts and sermons but also as indicative of the monastic pursuit of these games.

The board shown in the misericord is probably for chess. Finds of chess pieces are rare in Scotland but, with the exception of one, they are all from the west coast. The best-known pieces come from the Uig Bay area of the Isle of Lewis. The recent re-examination of the Lewis chess pieces, or rather the Lewis hoard of gaming pieces, takes the view that their presence on Lewis is less the result of an accident (with the implication of geographic irrelevance) and more because they were meant to be there, their cultural significance fully in tune with the politics, religion and culture of the Western Isles and their position along the sea lanes connecting the Scandinavian and Irish Sea worlds. While the hoard certainly includes chess pieces, its smaller number of disc pieces or tablemen have received less attention, and some of the geometric pawns in particular could have as equally have been used for *hne-fatafl* as for chess, and probably interchangeably.[26] The Lewis pieces aside, chess pieces from Scotland are few and known only as single finds. There is a figurative walrus ivory knight, possibly from Skye but certainly from the Western Isles, and an abstract bone/walrus ivory knight from Rothesay Castle, Bute (on display in Bute Museum, Rothesay, Figure 6.3). In addition, Wilson describes an elaborate walrus ivory figurative queen piece in the collection at Penicuik House, and supposedly collected in the north of Scotland in 1682,[27] and possibly no longer extant is a piece from Dunstaffnage Castle, a walrus ivory king piece. This is described by Pennant as an 'ivory image' or 'inauguration sculpture', made in memory of the Stone of Destiny.[28] The exception from the east of Scotland is an abstract jet bishop piece from the Meal Vennel site in Perth (Figure 6.4).[29] The geographical focus of these finds and their quality are sufficient to indicate the importance of high-status gaming in this region of Scotland. The chess pieces listed above are generally dated to the eleventh to thirteenth centuries; chess pieces from the end of the medieval period are much rarer finds (I know of none from Scotland). That the status of the game was maintained, though, is indicated by the variety of text references, often to royal possessions. These include inventories, Romance tales and moral treatises, a number of which are quoted in the *Dictionary of the Older Scottish Tongue* and the *Etymological Dictionary of the Scottish Language*.[30] That rather abbreviated discussion of chess has carried us into the later medieval period where there are several other games to take note of. I will begin with the finds from the excavations at Finlaggan, Islay,[31] which help to make the case that such pastimes were not confined to the amusements of the elite but were more widely played.

The Finlaggan evidence includes a single fragment of a graffiti gaming board (Figure 6.5), incised on a slate. Its use as a gaming board presumably predates any use as a building slate, possibly having been scratched out to pass the time during construction work. It is probably a fragment from an *alquerque* board. This is a war, or leaping-capture, game widely played in

Figure 6.3 *Bone chess knight from Rothesay Castle, Bute. © The Bute Museum, Rothesay, Isle of Bute.*

Mediterranean and Asian cultures. It is probably of pre-medieval origin. It seems to have entered Europe via Spain. A tenth-century Arabic manuscript mentions a game called '*Quirkat*', and the game of '*El-Quirkat*' was introduced to Spain via the Islamic conquest. Once played in Spain it became known as *Alquerque*. It is a game for two players, each with twelve pieces arranged on a board of twenty-five points. Through alternate moves, each player tries to capture the other player's pieces by jumping over them.[32] Incised or graffiti *alquerque* boards are comparatively rare in Britain. Examples have been recorded from the cloisters of Norwich Cathedral, from Norwich Castle and from St Mary's Church, Cavendish, Suffolk.[33] There are at least three other

Figure 6.4 *Jet chess bishop from excavations in Perth. © Perth Museum & Art Gallery, Perth & Kinross Council, Scotland.*

Scottish sites that have produced evidence for this game: single, slate-incised examples come from Dundonald Castle, Ayrshire and from Ballumbie Church, Angus (excavated in 2006), while Inchmarnock has a clutch of one complete board and ten fragments of other boards.[34] There may also

Figure 6.5 *Fragment of a slate gaming board from excavations in Finlaggan, Islay.*
© *Trustees of the National Museums Scotland.*

be a variant or incomplete example from Carrick Castle which survives
as a slate-incised fragment.[35] The Spanish *Alfonso Codex* of 1283 (a gaming
compendium compiled for King Alfonso X of León and Castile) describes
three variations of *alquerque*, for three, nine and twelve pieces per player, of
whom there were usually two but sometimes four. It also has parallels with
the chase game of *fox and geese* (sometimes referred to as *tod and lambs* in
Scotland). The Spanish variant of this, *catch the hare*, is also recorded in the
Alfonso manuscript as being played on the *alquerque* board.[36] It is worth a
passing speculation that a copy of this manuscript could have spent time in
Scotland. King Edward I, a known ardent player of chess (the main subject of
the Codex) was also married to Eleanor of Castile, Alfonso's sister. Recently
one of the Codex miniatures has been suggested to depict Edward playing
against his then fiancée, Eleanor.[37] Alfonso's book would surely have been
an eminently suitable gift to a brother monarch (and we might note that
Edward's gifts to Eleanor included a chess set). To pile speculation upon
speculation, it seems conceivable that Edward would have taken any copy of
the book with him during his visits to Scotland.[38]

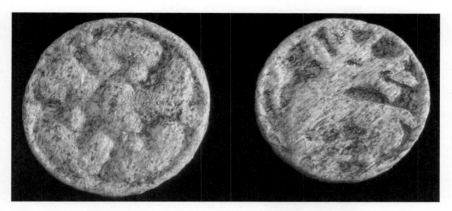

Figure 6.6   *Two bone, decorated tablesmen from excavations in Finlaggan, Islay.*
© *Trustees of the National Museums Scotland.*

The Finlaggan excavations also recovered three bone playing pieces, readily identifiable as tablesmen. Tables were really a family of games.[39] The medieval variations probably derived from the Roman game of *tabula*, surviving today as backgammon. Popular throughout the medieval period from at least the eleventh century onwards, their popularity is demon-strated by the finds of pieces and boards notably, for example, the set from Gloucester,[40] and by the medieval depictions of the game (for example, the misericords in St George's Chapel, Windsor and in Manchester, both late fifteenth century).[41] The two smaller, well-decorated, Finlaggan pieces were found together (Figure 6.6). Though one is zoomorphic (possibly depicting a unicorn) and the other of interlace design, this does not argue against a close association because they may well represent opposing sides of the same set of pieces (the one side fabulous beasts and the other of geometric or abstract forms). We cannot rule out the pieces representing two sets, with each side in each set being of similar design but distinguished by colour. Sets may also have been of mixed media. Egan, in his discussion of the London pieces,[42] suggested that black stained wooden discs could have been opposed by bone or ivory pieces rather than by pale wooden ones. In contrast, the third piece, is about a third as big again as the other two and more simply decorated. Both 'groups' fit into recognised series. If the combined weight of evidence for both pieces suggests a pre-fifteenth-century date, what does the wider picture of such playing pieces suggest? From Scotland there is a small tally of figurative bone gaming pieces, including from Iona Abbey; the Bishop's Palace, Kirkwall, Orkney; Dalcross Castle, Inverness-shire; Stonehaven, Aberdeenshire; Urquhart Castle and Melrose Abbey.[43] The animals and monsters depicted include mermaids, rabbits, a grotesque, a horseman, a centaur and an eagle. None of these pieces has a fully secure archaeological context and, on artistic grounds, have been dated to the eleventh to twelfth

Figure 6.7 *Improvised, reused pottery gaming pieces from excavations in Perth.* © *Perth Museum & Art Gallery, Perth & Kinross Council, Scotland.*

centuries and so considered to be Romanesque. Recently, however, the pieces from Iona, and also a large interlace disc from Rum, have been redated to the fifteenth to sixteenth centuries in line with the West Highland art tradition.[44] Other related material includes the Rum disc just mentioned and also the blank ivory discs found with the Lewis chess pieces, possibly unfinished tablesmen. From Rothesay Castle, Bute comes a bone tablesman decorated with a floral motif within concentric circles, comparable to wooden examples from Threave and Perth.[45] Also of note for this discussion is a stone disc from Carrick Castle, Argyll which is crudely decorated with the head of a queen.[46] This could be imitating the more elaborate bone tablesmen described above, though it is also possible that this represents an improvised queen piece for a low-status chess set.

The larger piece from Finlaggan has its upper surface incised with two concentric circles just inside the rim and a central compass point within a small circle. The simpler geometric style of decoration on this piece distinguishes it from the other two bone playing pieces and again is consistent with a wider series of such pieces. These simpler forms of tablesmen come in a variety of materials – skeletal, stone, reused pottery and wood – with a variety of ring and dot and/or concentric circle decoration. Examples across these various media include pieces from Perth High Street, Urquhart Castle and Aberdeen.[47] They range in date from the twelfth to the fifteenth centuries. Outside Scotland the picture is similar, and a brief list could cite Goltho in Lincolnshire, Loughor Castle in Glamorgan, London, York and Trondheim,

Norway.[48] Figure 6.7 shows some of the cruder pottery counters/playing pieces from Perth, demonstrative of the wider range of gaming pieces used (not necessarily exclusively for one type of game). The larger piece from Finlaggan is less accomplished than the two smaller pieces and may, like the series of stone discs from the site, indicate gaming practised across all social levels at Finlaggan. The Lord of the Isles and his elite companions were peripatetic in their occupation of Finlaggan and so it would have been for their prized sets of chess and tables. What was not peripatetic was the poorer quality material culture of the permanent occupants who kept the site maintained and ticking over in readiness for the return of their lord.

I noted above the merelles boards from Inchmarnock. Merelles (Figure 6.8), particularly its variant, nine men's morris, was one of the most popular medieval board games. In terms of archaeological evidence, the boards most often survive as graffiti-incised designs on stone. The evidence has been reviewed several times, including for Scotland by Robertson in the 1960s.[49] His paper dealt with later medieval examples primarily from monastic sites, notably Arbroath and Dryburgh. More recent finds – including St Magnus Cathedral, Kirkwall, Jedburgh Abbey and Inchmarnock[50] – maintain this predominantly monastic distribution. The game was played by Romans and by Vikings but the known British examples date from the later medieval period, with no boards dating with any certainty earlier than the eleventh or twelfth centuries. It was certainly a game known to the Vikings – they introduced it to the Faroes, for example, where there is a tenth-century board from Toftanes.[51] The accepted convention is that the game was a Norman introduction to mainland Britain. The Normans played the game presumably because their Viking forebears did. The evidence for the game in pre-eleventh-century Normandy/Brittany is, however, opaque. I know of no surviving boards for merelles. There is gaming evidence, mostly in the form of dice and playing pieces (for example, from the tenth-century ship burial from the Ile de Croix[52]) though the latter are generally of the type associated with the game *hnefatafl*. By the later medieval period various satires portray merelles as the game of the peasantry and urban poor, in contrast with backgammon as the game of the urban rich, and chess as the game of the aristocratic and church elites.[53] This was not an absolute hierarchy; archaeological evidence (including a number of lead badges and toys depicting chess boards from the Netherlands[54]) indicates that chess was popular at all levels of society.

The overwhelming majority of the gaming material culture from late medieval Scotland (in contrast with the first millennium AD) is related to urban or proto-urban sites, leaving a want of evidence from rural, peasant sites. When such sites are excavated, they are notoriously lacking in almost any material culture, and it is tempting to see the lack of gaming evidence likewise as a symptom of material poverty. One way to test this and to explore the question more fully would be to identify and excavate rural set-tlement sites in proximity to, or dependent upon, some of the towns, castles

Figure 6.8 *Slate incised nine men's morris board from Inchmarnock, off Bute.*
© *Headland Archaeology (UK) Ltd and with thanks to the Society of Antiquaries*
of Scotland for permission to reproduce.

and churches discussed in this paper as producing gaming evidence (that is,
more hinterland studies at various scales). This has been done, for example,
and albeit on a very small scale, in Sweden. There is a notable contrast
between the royal castle of Edsholm and the neighbouring farms of Skramle

and Djupsundet, in the bailiwick of Värmland.[55] One of the contrasts between the materially impoverished farms and the castle was thrown up by the gaming evidence from the castle. This comprises at least two chess pieces and a die (all of horn). Their presence in the castle and absence from the two farms were interpreted as being less likely to mean that farm-dwellers had no, nor needed no, leisure time than that they chose not to indulge in such pursuits. The evidence from the castle also supports nuances of interpretation beyond thrift versus luxury. In one of the castle buildings, interpreted as a possible tavern or barracks, were found together a coin, a pair of dice and a third of a wine mug – eloquent testimony to the boredom-defeating life of the soldiers stationed there.

'GOD DOES NOT PLAY DICE'[56]

I want to bring things to a close by looking at one final aspect of gaming, namely, the medieval concern with dicing, a classic example of a cultural pursuit that attracted both praise and condemnation (Figure 6.9). Concern over their criminal context was part of a wider European pattern where the repression of three offensive behaviours was particularly targeted: prostitution, gambling and blasphemy.[57] Games and gambling were widely perceived as having a strong link to violence and, to varying degrees, most forms of games were the subject of legal attention because they were amenable to gambling, and it was gambling (and the violence it could lead to) that was the real concern. Gambling was most readily associated with dice, and was seen to

Figure 6.9 *A selection of bone dice from excavations in Perth. © Perth Museum & Art Gallery, Perth & Kinross Council, Scotland.*

lead to theft, brawling and murder. The East Window of St Peter Mancroft, Norwich, includes a scene of two dice players with daggers drawn. Gambling also disturbed divine order through blasphemy. Gambling was perceived as an attack on sustenance and sociability: on production, commerce and the family. These problems are neatly summarised in Chaucer's word picture of tavern life and gambling in *The Pardoner's Tale*, 'the very mother of lying, of deceit and cursed swearing, of blasphemy and manslaughter'.[58] The fight was still being fought by the Reformed Church. An entry for 11 November 1611 in the kirk session register of St John's Perth records the account of an informer recounting his Sunday time spent gambling with dice and drinking in the house of Walter Young who was a deacon of the kirk. He blamed his wife but would not let her be questioned and so threatened the beadle of the kirk that he was warded.[59]

In some respects the link to blasphemy promoted greater concern than gambling because it was a direct sin against God. In Florence in 1501, a gambler was hanged for the sacrilegious act of defacing with horsedung an image of the Virgin Mary.[60] This recalls a much earlier incident of the late twelfth century recorded (and derived from an earlier French source) in Walter Bower's early fifteenth-century *Scotichronicon*.[61] During the siege of Châteauroux by Philip of France, mercenaries were playing dice in front of the church of the Blessed Virgin Mary: one of them, frustrated at loosing his winnings, blasphemed and then broke off an arm from a nearby statue of the Virgin; blood was seen to pour from the arm and it was treated as a miraculous relic. Bower notes 'the wretched mercenary was that very day snatched away by the Devil to that place to which he was already leading him and ended his life in a most miserable fashion'. This destination, Hell, is graphically indicated by Bruegel's magnificent painting, *Triumph of Death*, which includes, bottom right, cards, money and a backgammon board all overturned in the face of the advancing army of Death. It was painted in c.1562 when gaming was still seen as an example of the general folly and wickedness of humankind, rather in the tradition of Hieronymus Bosch and his contemporaries, which also developed from earlier outlooks (as evidenced, for example, by the stained-glass windows in Norwich – showing a bishop being taken away by Death against the background of a chess board – and Chartres – where the Prodigal Son window includes a gaming scene).[62]

The connection between gambling and dice also has other reflexes for not only were dice frequently used as tools of divination and fortune-telling, itself a root of gambling, but they had a role in so-doing in the life of Christ: dice were used at the crucifixion to cast lots to gamble for Christ's clothing, thus making his clothing subject to fate. This made dice doubly open to clerical condemnation. It also meant that dice were frequently depicted in a wide range of artistic media as *Arma Christi* or instruments of Christ's passion. A probably early sixteenth-century bench end from the Cathedral of St Magnus, Kirkwall, Orkney, includes three dice in its depiction.[63] In

Norwich Cathedral a fifteenth-century nave roof boss shows three dice being cast for Christ's garments, with violence about to erupt.[64] A fifteenth-century octagonal font in Meigle parish church, Perthshire, shows them beside Christ's clothing.[65] Many illuminated manuscripts and printed books also show the Passion dice (for example, the mid-fourteenth-century ivory devotional book now in the Victoria and Albert Museum)[66] and often this is in connection with the Mass of St Gregory. Examples include, on a chantry chapel reredos at Hexham Abbey, Robert Campin's c.1430 painting of the Mass and a 1539 feathers-on-panel depiction from Mexico (school of Peter of Ghent).[67] Gambling and dicing, then, could be seen as immoral and socially disturbing acts requiring the attentions of the Church and secular legal authorities. There were, though, in the medieval period, variant views. Even divination was not universally frowned upon, as some thought that casting lots, for example, was a way to divine the will of God (something Augustine of Hippo approved of in his commentary on Psalm 30). There are several biblical precedents for the use of lots, and the *Lex Frisionum* indicates that in Frisia lots were kept in a reliquary on the altar, one of them marked with a cross and used to determine guilt or innocence. More broadly on gaming, during the canonisation enquiry into St Thomas Cantilupe, Bishop of Hereford, evidence was taken from Hugh le Barber, one of Cantilupe's servants. Part of his evidence recounts how he, Hugh, became blind. He prayed for recovery, hoping that he could at least see sufficiently again to see the host being raised, to move around and 'to play at chess and dice'.[68] That he could make such a statement in the context of the proposed canonisation of a venerable ecclesiastic shows that such games were not entirely frowned upon by the Church. Indeed, there is further evidence of their incorporation in the cult of saints. The museum collections in Aschaffenburg, Bavaria include a double-sided gaming board from the church of Sts Peter and Alexander. The edges of the boards have glass compartments for keeping relics. This board, which dates to c.1300, probably arrived in Aschaffenburg in the sixteenth century when Cardinal Albrecht of Brandenburg fled the Reformation in the Halle area. Contemporary documentation of 1531, listing the relics that the cardinal brought with him, includes the gaming board (for both chess and backgammon) of St Rupert.[69] This more inclusive view of games is one that chimes well with the admittedly slight and almost casual remarks of St Thomas Aquinas. In his *Summa Theologica*, he expressed approval of women's hairstyles and of games and diversions, including verbal play and dramatic representations: 'It is good that women should adorn themselves in order to cultivate the love of their husbands and games give delight in that they lighten the fatigue of our labours.'[70] There was, of course, a clear distinction between frivolous and useful games (though equally some games can be found in both of these camps), which Rabelais's *Litany of Games*, satirises. Smith, in his discussion of this list contrasts it with John of Salisbury's comments on frivolous and useful games, in *Policraticus*.[71] This apparent contradiction between seeing gaming as both evil and good should occasion no surprise, being yet another everyday manifestation of the thread of contradictory opposites that runs through medieval culture.

CHECKMATE

We have now reached endgame and the pieces must go back in their box. This chapter has, I hope, introduced the reader to the broad range of evidence for board and dice games in medieval Scotland. Such a review of the evidence enables us to see that we can go beyond simply saying that our medieval forebears' experiences encompassed the playing of games. The diversity of the surviving evidence and the diversity of the board and dice games played (and we by no means know the whole range played) eloquently speak of everyday experiences in a variety of social contexts – urban, rural, ecclesiastical, domestic and lordly residence (and each by no means limited to a single social class) – by people with nested identities and in varied positions on the moral spectrum. The pursuit of games was morally contested and this opened it up to a rich vein of metaphorical interpretations. Not least the Scottish evidence makes a significant case study to the regional diversity of the everyday European experience.

Notes

1 The quote is the conclusion to the opening narration (that asks why we are here and how we know what we know and why questions lead to more questions) of the innovative German film *Run Lola Run* (1998, D. Tom Tykwer).
2 I am grateful for Ted Cowan's encouragement to pursue this chapter and to the organisers and audiences of three conferences – *The Scottish Folk: Ordinary People and Everyday Life* (The Scottish Medievalists, Pitlochry, January 2006), *Everyday Life* (Dundee University, September 2006) and the *13th Annual Meeting of the European Association of Archaeologists* (Zadar, Croatia, 18–23 September 2007) – at which variant versions of this chapter were presented. Attendance of the last named was made possible by a travel grant from the British Academy and a grant from the Scottish Museums Federation.
3 See, for example, C. Reeves, *Pleasures and Pastimes in Medieval England* (Stroud, 1995), a comprehensive overview that provides a useful comparison for the Scottish evidence. For a Scottish-accented history of tennis see L. St J. Butler and P. J. Wordie, *The Royal Game* (Stirling, 1989). The local variations in football and handball are effectively demonstrated by the post-medieval account of the game at Scone. This was played annually on Shrove Tuesday from 2 p.m. to sunset, the teams composed of married men against bachelors. No kicking was allowed, in contrast to Inverness where a game on the same day was played by married women against spinsters, kicking allowed. It was said at the time to be of

medieval origin, introduced by a wandering Italian, T. Robert 'Parish of Scone', in J. Sinclair (ed.), *The Statistical Account of Scotland 1791–1799* (Wakefield, [1791] 1976), pp. 585–6. A second notable instance of handball in Perthshire is the game formerly played in Rattray, of which a silver ball trophy of c.1600 survives in the collections of Perth Museum & Art Gallery; see R. Rodger, 'The Silver Ball of Rattray: A Unique Scottish Sporting Trophy', in *Proc. Soc. Antiq. Scot.* 122 (1992), pp. 403–11; P. Baxter, *Football in Perthshire: Past and Present* (Perth, 1898), pp. 149–52 and J. Burnett 'A Note on the Silver Ball of Rattray', in *Proc. Soc. Antiq. Scot.* 128 (1998), pp. 1101–4. For curling see D. B. Smith, *Curling: An Illustrated History* (Edinburgh, 1981).

4   The archetypal, 'non-rational' approach is typified by J. Huizinga, *Homo Ludens A Study of the Play Element in Culture* (Boston, 1950). The embedded view is typified by R. Callois *Les jeux et les hommes* (Paris, 1958), translated as *Man, Play and Games* by M. Barosh (1961, reprinted Urbana and Chicago, 2001). An insightful case study of the medieval context is provided by A. Borst, *Medieval Worlds: Barbarians, Heretics and Artists* (Cambridge and Oxford, 1991), pp. 195–214.

5   For example see L. King (ed.), *Game On, the History and Culture of Videogames* (London, 2002). The twentieth century witnessed the invention, by John van Neumann, of game theory, an analysis of economic, military and policy planning and strategies – J. A. Paulos, *Beyond Numeracy* (London, 1991), pp. 91–4.

6   The Suetonius quote appears in D. Parlett, *The Oxford History of Board Games* (Oxford, 1991), p. 72, and is discussed in M. A. Hall, *Playtime in Pictland: The Material Culture of Gaming in First Millennium AD Scotland* (Rosemarkie, 2007).

7   The film was released in 1967, directed, co-written and starring Jacques Tati. For a discussion of it see J. Harding, *Jacques Tati, Frame-by-Frame* (London, 1984), pp. 117–37.

8   This medieval game was played primarily in universities across Europe as a teaching aid in exploring the power and beauty of numbers. The most useful discussions are in Borst, *Medieval Worlds*, pp. 203–6, and A. S. Moyer, *The Philosopher's Game: Rithmomachia in Medieval and Renaissance Europe* (Ann Arbor, 2001), but see also J. Stigter 'Rithmomachia, the Philosopher's Game An Introduction to its History and Rules', in I. Finkel (ed.), *Ancient Board Games in Perspective Papers from the 1990 British Museum colloquium with added contributions* (London, 2007), pp. 263–9.

9   E. C. Curwen, 'Querns', in *Antiquity* 11.2 (1937), pp. 133–51.

10 The exhibition ran from 5 October 2006 to 7 January 2007 and was accompanied by the excellent catalogue: M. Ajmar-Wollheim and F. Dennis (eds), *At Home in Renaissance Italy* (London, 2006).

11 Wollheim and Dennis, *At Home in Renaissance Italy*, pp. 216–19, 327–30, for a discussion of the various games at a time when cards began to supersede chess and the pursuit of illegal gambling in the domestic environment.

12 The performed metaphor argument is my summary of the philosophical discussion in J. Gray, *Straw Dogs: Thoughts on Humans and Other Animals* (London, 2002), pp. 182–7. Later, at p. 196, Gray astutely observes that 'the point of playing is that play has no point'.

13 For full details of the excavation see H. G. Horn, 'Si per misit, nil nisi vota feret', in 'Ein römischer Spielturm aus Froitzheim', in *Bonner Jahrbucher* 185 (1985), pp. 139–60. For an up-to-date account in English see E. Hartley, J. Hawkes, M. Henig and F. Mee, *Constantine the Great York's Roman Emperor* (York, 2006). Its relevance to the Pictish gaming context is more fully discussed in Hall, *Playtime in Pictland*, pp. 3–4.

14 Hall, *Playtime in Pictland*, is also relevant to notes 15–24 following.

15 For a fuller examination of the *tafl* group see H. J. R. Murray, *A History of Board Games Other than Chess* (Oxford, 1952), pp. 55–64, and Parlett, *Oxford History of Board Games*, pp. 196–204. For a fresh examination of the documentary evidence for *hnefatafl* in early medieval England see I. Payne, 'Did the Anglo-Saxons play Games of Chance? Some thoughts on Old English Board Games', in *The Antiquaries Journal* 86 (2006), pp. 330–44.

16 For the boards from Buckquoy, Howe, Birsay and Dun Chonallaich see Hall, *Playtime in Pictland*, pp. 12–13, which includes further references.

17 Hall, *Playtime in Pictland*, for details and further references. A paper in preparation will revisit the question of the *tafl* variants, particularly *hnefatafl*, *fidcheall* and *gwyddbwyll*, in the context of Roman board-game influence in Britain and Ireland: M. A. Hall and K. Forsyth, 'On the Compatibility of Gaelic "fidchell" and its P-Celtic cognates with the Roman introduction of tafl-like games to Britain and Ireland'.

18 S. Youngs, 'The Gaming Pieces', in R. B. Mitford and A. Care-Evans (eds), *The Sutton Hoo Ship Burial*, vol. 3, II (London, 1983), pp. 853–74.

19 J. A. Robinson, *The Times of St Dunstan* (Oxford, 1923), pp. 69–71; and Murray, *History of Board Games Other than Chess*, pp. 61–2.

20 C. Lowe (ed.), *Inchmarnock. An Early Historic Island Monastery and its archaeological landscape* (Edinburgh, 2008), esp. pp. 116–28 and 191–2. One gameboard design that may have been missed is IS 71 (p. 173), paralleled by a similar example from St Blane's Church, Bute (J. Anderson. 'Description of a Collection of Objects found in excavations at St Blane's church, Bute, Exhibited by the Marquis of Bute', in *Proc. Soc. Antiq. Scot.* 34 (1899–1900), pp. 307–25, at 313) both of which may be practice attempts at circular variants of chess, merelles or the Astronomical Game.

21 For more details and references see Hall, *Playtime in Pictland*, pp. 11–12.

22 D. MacLean, 'Maelrubai, Applecross and the late Pictish contribution west of Druimalban', in D. Henry (ed.), *The Worm, the Germ and the Thorn: Pictish and related studies presented to Isabel Henderson* (Balgavies, 1997), pp. 173–87, at 174.

23 T. O. Clancy, *The Triumph Tree: Scotland's Earliest Poetry AD 550–1350* (Edinburgh, 1998), pp. 288–94.

24 F. Kelly, *Early Irish Farming – A Study Based Mainly On The Law Texts Of The 7th and 8th Centuries AD* (Dublin, 1997), p. 452.

25 S. Béthmont-Gallerand 'La joute à cheval-bâton, un jeu et une image de l'enfance à la fin du Moyen Age', in *The Profane Arts of the Middle Ages*, vol. IX (2001) nos 1 and 2, pp. 186–96, esp. 183 and fig. 1.

26 The earliest published account, still important, is F. Madden, 'Historical remarks

on the introduction of chess into Europe and on the ancient chess-men discovered in the Isle of Lewis', *Archaeologia* XXIV (1832), pp. 203–91. The majority of the pieces are in the British Museum whose most recent account is J. Robinson, *The Lewis Chessmen* (London, 2004). The most recent in-depth analysis is D. Caldwell, M. A. Hall and C. Wilkinson, 'The Lewis Hoard of Gaming Pieces: A Re-Examination of their Context, Meaning, Discovery and Manufacture', in *Medieval Archaeology* 53 (2009), pp. 155–203.

27 D. Wilson, *Prehistoric Annals of Scotland* (London and Cambridge, 1863), pp. 357–8.

28 T. Pennant, *A Tour in Scotland and a Voyage to the Hebrides 1772* Part 1 (London, [1772] 1776), p. 409.

29 Mark A. Hall, 'Cultural Interaction on the Medieval Burgh of Perth, Scotland 1200–1600', in G. Helmig, B. Scholkman and M. Untermann (eds), *Medieval Europe Basel 2002, Pre-printed Papers*, vol. 1 (Hertingen, 2002), pp. 290–301, at 298. For its excavation see A. Cox (ed.), 'Backland activities in medieval Perth: excavations at Meal Vennel and Scott Street', *Proc. Soc. Antiq. Scot.* 126 (1996), pp. 733–821, at 182.

30 For chess see W. A. Craigie, *A Dictionary of the Older Scottish Tongue from the Twelfth Century to the End of the Seventeenth*, vol. 1, A–C (Chicago and London, 1937), p. 513. For tables see J. Jamieson, *An Etymological Dictionary of the Scottish Language*, vol. IV (Paisley, 1882), p. 490.

31 For a full account of the Finlaggan material see M. A. Hall, 'Finlaggan at Play: the Gaming Equipment', in D. Caldwell, *Excavations at Finlaggan, Islay* (Edinburgh, forthcoming).

32 Murray, *History of Board Games Other than Chess*, pp. 65–71, and Parlett, *Oxford History of Board Games*, pp. 243–7.

33 Both are recorded in Murray, *History of Board Games Other than Chess*, p. 66.

34 D. Caldwell, 'Incised and Engraved Slates', in G. Ewart and D. Pringle 'Dundonald Castle Excavations 1986–93', in *Scottish Archaeological Journal* 26.1–2 (2004), pp. 107–9; for a note by M. A. Hall on the incised slate from Ballumbie see the excavation report in preparation by SUAT Ltd; A. Ritchie, 'Gaming boards', in Lowe, *Inchmarnock*, pp. 116–28, esp. 126–7.

35 G. Ewart and F. Baker, 'Carrick castle: symbol and source of Campbell power in south Argyll from the 14th to the 17th century', in *Proc. Soc. Antiq. Scot.* 128 (1998), pp. 937–1016, at 975 and illus. 23.

36 There is no accessible edition of the Alfonso Codex in English (to my knowledge) but an excellent introduction to it, with all the illuminations reproduced, can be found at www.historicgames.com/alphonso/index.html. For useful discussions of the manuscript see O. R. Constable, 'Class and Courtly Culture in Medieval Castille: The *Libro de ajedrez* of Alfonso X, el Sabio', in *Speculum* 82.2 (2007), pp. 301–47 and D. E. Carpenter, '"Alea jacta est": At the Gaming Table with Alfonso the Learned', in *Journal of Medieval History* 24.4 (1998), pp. 333–45. For a new German translation, with detailed commentary, see Ulrich Schädler and Ricardo Calvo (eds), *Alfons X. 'der Weise': Das Buch der Spiele* (Berlin and Zurich, 2009).

37   M. Yalom, *Birth of the Chess Queen* (London, 2004), p. 61.

38   Olivia Constable, pers. comm., disagrees with me here suggesting a copy of such
     a luxurious manuscript so late in Alfonso's life would seem unlikely.

39   H. J. R. Murray, 'The Medieval Games of Tables', in *Medium Aevum* 10.2 (1942),
     pp. 57–69.

40   M. Watkins, *Gloucester, the Normans and Domesday, Exhibition Catalogue and
     Guide* (Gloucester, 1985) and I. J. Stewart and M. Watkins, 'An eleventh century
     bone tabula set from Gloucester', in *Medieval Archaeology* 28 (1984), pp. 185–90.

41   Mark A. Hall, 'Where the Abbot Carries Dice: Gaming-Board Misericords in
     Context', in E. C. Block and M. Jones (eds), *Profane Imagery in Marginal Arts of
     the Middle Ages* (Turnhout, 2009).

42   G. Egan, *Medieval Finds from Excavations in London: 6, The Medieval Household –
     Daily Living c. 1150–1450* (London, 1998), p. 294.

43   V. Glenn, *Romanesque and Gothic Decorative Metalwork and Ivory Carvings in
     the Museum of Scotland* (Edinburgh, 2003), pp. 184 (Iona), 182–3 (Kirkwall),
     183 (Urquhart); A. Kluge-Pinsker, *Schachspiel und Trictrac Zeugnisse mittelalter-
     erlicher spielfreude in salischer zeit* (Sigmaringen, 1991) pp. cat. B59 (Iona), cat.
     B60 (Kirkwall), cat. B57 (Dalcross), cat. B58 (Stonehaven), cat. B56 (Urquhart);
     cat. B55 (Melrose); and see Hall, 'Finlaggan at Play: The Gaming Equipment'
     (forthcoming).

44   Glenn, *Romanesque and Gothic Decorative Metalwork and Ivory Carvings in the
     Museum of Scotland*, pp. 184–5.

45   The piece from Bute Castle is on display in Bute Museum, Rothesay (but has
     not so far been published). For Threave see G. L. Good and C. J. Tabraham,
     'Excavations at Threave Castle, Galloway', in *Medieval Archaeology* 25 (1981),
     pp. 90–140, at 119. For Perth, see N. Q. Bogdan (ed.), *Perth High Street
     Excavations 1975–77* (forthcoming).

46   See note 36 above.

47   For Perth, see Bogdan, *Perth High Street Excavations*. For Urquhart see R.
     Samson, 'Finds from Urquhart Castle in the National Museum, Edinburgh',
     Proc. Soc. Antiq. Scot. 112 (1982), pp. 465–76, at 475. For Aberdeen see A.
     MacGregor, 'Bone Antler and Ivory Objects', in J. C. Murray (ed.), *Excavations
     in the Medieval Burgh of Aberdeen 1973–81* (Edinburgh, 1982), pp. 180–2.

48   For a discussion and references to these pieces see Hall, 'Finlaggan at Play: The
     Gaming Equipment'.

49   W. N. Robertson, 'The Game of Merelles in Scotland', *Proc. Soc. Antiq. Scot.* 98
     (1967), pp. 321–3.

50   For St Magnus see 'Nine Men's Morris Board', in *New Orkney Antiquarian
     Journal* 2 (2002), p. 44. For Jedburgh see J. H. Lewis and J. G. Ewart, *Jedburgh
     Abbey, the Archaeology and Architecture of a Border Abbey* (Edinburgh, 1995),
     pp. 105–10. For Inchmarnock see Lowe, *Inchmarnock*.

51   S. S. Hansen, 'The Norse Landnam in the Faroe Islands in the light of recent
     excavations at Toftanes, Leirvík', *Northern Studies* 25 (1998), pp. 58–64, esp. fig.
     11b.

52   N. S. Price, *The Vikings in Brittany* (London, 1989), fig. 30 and p. 97/415.

53 M. A. Hall, 'Gaming Board Badges', in H. J. E. van Beuningen, A. M. Koldeweij and D. Kicken (eds), *Heilig en Profaan 2 – 1200 Laatmiddeleuse Insignes uit openbare en particuliere collecties*, pp. 173–8 (Cothen, 2001; Rotterdam Papers 12).

54 Hall, 'Gaming Board Badges'.

55 The evidence summarised here is fully discussed in E. Svensson, 'Life in the Bailiffs Castle of Edsholm', in L. Ersgård (ed.), *Thirteen Essays on Medieval Artefacts – Papers of the Archaeological Institute University of Lund 1993–1994*, New Series, vol. 10, pp. 159–66.

56 Albert Einstein's frequently uttered scoff on quantum theory as recorded, for example, by his biographer, B. Hoffman. See *The Concise Oxford Dictionary of Quotations*, 2nd edn (Oxford, 1981), p. 92:14.

57 T. Dean, *Crime in Medieval Europe 1200–1500* (London, 2001), esp. pp. 52–7 and M. K. McIntosh, *Controlling Misbehaviour in England 1370–1600* (Cambridge, 1998), esp. pp. 70, 77–8, 90, 96–107.

58 N. Coghill, *Geoffrey Chaucer, The Canterbury Tales, translated into modern English* (London, 1952), *The Pardoner's Tale* is at pp. 151–60, with quote at p. 155.

59 From the extract of the Kirk Session Register that appears in J. P. Lawson, *The Book of Perth* (Edinburgh, 1847), pp. 266–7 (note also the details of prohibitions by the Kirk on golf, football and ninepins, pp. 188, 200 and 242).

60 Dean, *Crime in Medieval Europe*, p. 57.

61 D. E. R. Watt (gen. ed.), *Scotichronicon by Walter Bower*, vol. 4, Books VII and VIII (Aberdeen, 1994), Bk VIII, p. 375.

62 The bench end is in the collections of the National Museums of Scotland and see D. Caldwell, *Angels, Nobles and Unicorns, Art and Patronage in Medieval Scotland* (Edinburgh, 1984), pp. 107–8 no. F7.

63 M. Rose and J. Hedgecoe, *Stories in Stone, the Medieval Roof Carvings of Norwich Cathedral* (Norwich, 1997), pl. p. 108.

64 RCAHMS *South-East Perth, an archaeological landscape* (Edinburgh, 1994), p. 24 and fig. c.

65 N. MacGregor and E. Langmuir, *Seeing Salvation, Images of Christ in Art* (London, 2000), pl. 48.

66 The St Gregory's mass theme is discussed in M. A. Hall, 'Where the Abbot Carries Dice: Gaming-Board Misericords in Context', in E. C. Block and M. Jones (eds), *Profane Imagery in Marginal Arts of the Middle Ages* (Turnhout, 2009).

67 Hall, 'Where the Abbot Carries Dice: Gaming-Board Misericords in Context'.

68 M. Jancey 'A Servant Speaks of his Master, Hugh Le Barber's evidence in 1307', in M. Jancey (ed.), *St. Thomas Cantilupe Bishop of Hereford, Essays in his Honour* (Hereford, 1982), pp. 199–201, quote at p. 200. Barber goes on to name Dom Philip Walense rector of the church at Stretton, as someone Hugh used to play chess and dice with, both at his home and when they were in London.

69 I. Jenderko-Sichelscmidt, M. Marquart and G. Ermischer, *Stiftsmuseum der Stadt Aschaffenburg* (Munich, 1994), pp. 84–6 (cat. 70). This case also indicates the Church divisions on how much the pursuit of games should be tolerated or condemned. There are several fifteenth- to sixteenth-century examples of such

boards, as well as dice and cards, being burnt as part of back-to-basics, fire-and-brimstone campaigns to force people to give up perceived decadent pursuits. See, for example, ibid., cat. 71 (Bamberg, Germany) and M. G. Muzzarelli, 'Sumptuous Shoes, Making and Wearing in Medieval Italy', in G. Riello and P. McNeil (eds), *Shoes: A History from Sandals to Sneakers* (Oxford and New York, 2006), pp. 50–75, fig. 2.12 (an Italian woodcut, as the bonfire burns a pope looks on and hair and long-toed shoes are cut). At a more personal level of reforming zeal, it is worth noting the suggestion that the circumstances of the disposal of the Gloucester tabulae set in the early twelfth century may be associated with Walter of Gloucester retiring to Llanthony Priory – I. J. Stewart, 'The Gloucester tabulae set: a unique insight into the Norman aristocracy', in *Medieval Europe 1992 Art and Symbolism Pre-printed Papers*, vol. 7 (York, 1992), pp. 29–34.

70   St Thomas Aquinas *Summa Theologica I and II* (1266–7), pp. 32, 1 and 13, quoted in U. Eco *Art and Beauty in the Middle Ages* (London and New York, 1986), pp. 98–9.

71   W. F. Smith (ed. and trans.) *Rabelais: The Five Books and Minor Writings together with Letters and Documents Illustrating His Life*, vol. 1, *Gargantua* (Cambridge, 1934), chapter xxii (The Games of Gargantua) and p. 112ff. (John of Salisbury).

Chapter 7

Women of Independence in Barbour's Bruce *and* Blind Harry's *Wallace*

Rebecca Boorsma

INTRODUCTION

Women are obviously crucial to any exploration of everyday life but uncovering the Scottish evidence for the investigation of their roles is often much more difficult than might be imagined. A perusal of the major literary sources for the Wars of Independence suggests that this defining period in the establishment of Scottish identity also raised interesting questions about the part played by women in the conflict and thus their changing place in everyday life during the fourteenth and fifteenth centuries when John Barbour's *Bruce* and Blind Harry's *Wallace* were produced. In his edition of Barbour's *Bruce*, A. A. M. Duncan asserts that many people despise, as some still fear, the study of the literature and history of Scotland.[1] Using literature to study history is taboo. An exception is when there are so few sources that a piece of literature 'becomes the only, or the main source for historians almost by default, obscuring the boundaries between faithful chronicling and literary invention'.[2] Such is commonly the case with Blind Harry's *Wallace*; so few primary sources focusing on the hero exist that many look to Harry's epic to fill in the gaps. A problem arises when such a source, despite the author's protestations, is historically inaccurate. Cowan and Gifford suggest that literature has 'too long and too often been ignored or neglected by mainstream or "establishment" authorities', as a suspicious medium that historians 'do not care to comprehend'. They further argue that 'historians delude themselves into thinking that while they deal in facts, creative writers deal in fiction'.[3] Distortion of historical 'facts' arises from different interpretations of sources, making interpretations of historical events as fluid as conclusions about symbolism in poetry.

Given the similarities between the disciplines of history and literary criticism, it is odd that so few historians make use of literature. Yet, if one is to investigate the past in the hope of discovering meaning within the present, literature can prove particularly effective, notably when dealing with subjects overlooked by commonly employed documents.[4] For example, until recently, historians have tended to ignore medieval women between the twelfth and sixteenth centuries unless they were notorious wives, witches or women of substance. As Marshall asserts in her analysis of medieval marriage, 'chroniclers concern themselves with deeds of kings and men of war' to the detriment of potential sources for the study of women and their consequent disregard,[5] further compounded by historians' lack of interest in scrutinising past gender roles. Two epic poems that do well in presenting the lives of women are Barbour's *Bruce* (c.1375) and Blind Harry's *Wallace* (late 1470s). Both feature women's participation in medieval Scottish society and their roles during the Wars of Independence.

IMAGES OF WOMEN

Barbour's *Bruce* and Harry's *Wallace* can potentially prove useful in the study of Scottish medieval women because poetry, and literature in general, are the products of the 'cultural matrix' in which the poem was derived. According to Newlyn, late medieval poetry reflects and 'helps to create images of women' which, in turn, 'support and continue the culture's existing social and political arrangements', displaying how literature is not written in an isolated space but grows from, and contributes to, communities.[6]

During the period under discussion, the fourteenth and fifteenth centuries, male and female physical characteristics equated with corresponding socially constructed roles of gender.[7] For example, there was not a divide between a woman's physical and moral strength, as medieval assumptions presented women, because of their sex, to be morally and physically weak. Lacquer implies that this stereotype arose from what he calls the 'one-sex' model – a concept developed by the Greeks which remained prevalent until the eighteenth century.[8] The general consensus of the 'one-sex' model argued that men and women possessed the same biological components yet female reproductive organs existed 'inside rather than outside' becoming the 'lesser' physiological structure.[9] Thus began the long tradition of defining femininity by comparison between the female reproductive system and the male form. A woman was unable to exude male gender traits, such as virtue, or physical qualities, such as strength.

SUTHFASTNESS

A point of contention for historians considering the use of *The Bruce* and *Wallace* as investigative tools is their lack of historical accuracy, though Barbour is generally regarded more favourably, his reputation as an authority deriving from his position as a public and church official, his listening to first-hand accounts of witnesses to the events he describes, and his use of legitimate written documents to complete his storyline.[10] Some historians utilise these qualities to enhance the belief that the '*Bruce* is mostly historical fact, while *Wallace* is mostly fiction'.[11] This is understandable because Barbour claimed to be aiming for truthfulness – 'suthfastnes that schawys the thing rycht as it wes'.[12] Critics have asserted that the historical inaccuracies in *Wallace* were due to Harry's blindness limiting his education.[13] In reality, it seems unlikely that Harry was blind from birth as he provides abundant detail when describing the Scottish landscape and was well versed in medieval romance literature including those texts written in Latin.[14] He was possibly at least partially sighted.[15]

Even though the texts were meant to provide some historical commentary, Barbour and Harry were writing in a tradition where 'literary flavour' was 'found in even unimaginative works such as king lists' or other official documents,[16] to detrimental effect. A common example is the manner in which Barbour confuses King Robert with his grandfather, for example, by having him refuse to swear fealty to Edward I. Browne finds such an error immensely strange because Barbour 'lived in the next generation [to Bruce], and who, as he tells us, had obtained information from men who had borne a part in the events he narrates'.[17] The poet's purpose is to portray Bruce as a man who stood against Balliol and Edward I from the onset of the Wars of Independence.[18] Consequently, Barbour's claim of presenting a true account of the king's conquests appears to be nothing more than a common medieval literary topos.[19]

Wallace is similar to *The Bruce* in that it claims to be a true history of events yet, when historians research it, they find a history 'that never was',[20] an apt description as the battles portrayed in the poem, the chronological sequence of the events, and the general outline of Harry's text do not particularly correspond with the known occurrences of Wallace's lifetime.[21] When fact does arise within the poem, it 'sometimes puzzles as much as surprises'.[22] Gaigie expresses the common belief that Harry's creative licence blended with his distancing from the historical events to create a fully fictional poem: 'the further back in time the scene is laid the more license will the poet be allowed, and his audience will not permit want of historic accuracy to detract from their appreciation of the work as a literary product'.[23] He also asserts, more contentiously, that *The Bruce* and *Wallace* were originally intended for entertainment and the lack of fact is of no concern to anyone except Scottish historians. The presence of fiction over fact therefore meant little to the medieval authors because their primary intent was to create a narrative emphasising the roles of their respective heroes through the medium of iconic literary pieces rather than by detailed histories.

Despite the amount of fiction in *The Bruce* and *Wallace*, some historians have been bold enough to scrutinise the poems. When using the texts for historical analyses, scholars investigate 'the works' connection with larger historical processes' and have 'tended to reduce ideologies to a significant theme or idea': nationalism.[24] It has been claimed that it was not until Wallace and Bruce that the Scottish people were bound 'securely into a nation'.[25] The inspiring language, imagery of freedom and goals of the heroes in the poems, combined with the language and imagery of the Declaration of Arbroath imply an element of nationalism during the medieval era. The precise meaning of nationalism in a fourteenth-century context has long been debated yet one investigator asserts 'that late medieval Scotland recognised itself as a nation' since 'many of the Scottish people identified themselves with the land and its inhabitants'.[26] Harry, in particular, depicts recognition of Scotland as a nation in his descriptions of English deaths by utilising a 'narrative distance' to control the 'emotional response of his audience'. Harry supplies various details of Wallace's constant slaying of the English yet his descriptions evoke little emotional response in the reader. In contrast, he limits the details of the Scottish deaths by claiming such illustrations would be too powerful for the readers to endure.[27] Harry used such phrases as 'all off a nacioun' and 'trew Scottis' to display how Scotland could 'overcome the ethnic, linguistic, and political differences which had the potential to divide Scotland and make it vulnerable to English aggression'.[28]

When reviewing *The Bruce* and nationalism, the matter is more complicated than that of *Wallace* because Barbour's elements of chivalry often overshadow elements of national identity. The conventions of medieval chivalric romance guide The *Bruce* as seen through Barbour's emphasis on heroic deeds of the honourable knights, James Douglas and Robert Bruce,[29] who maintained the balance between prudence and vanity by fighting vigorously for their cause while resisting the allure of greed. Robert Bruce, for example, allowed the people of Rathlin to maintain their possessions 'free from all his men' upon their naming himself as their lord,[30] resulting in the loyalty of the islanders and reflecting the noble character of the king. Douglas was similarly noble, refusing to seek 'personal glory through individual feats of arms', displaying his strength of character and his total allegiance to Bruce.[31] Chivalry and selflessness appear to be Barbour's main message though it has been suggested that the knightly virtues of prowess and loyalty 'are of no account unless they are supported by the ideas of "fredome" and "richt"' indicating that national identity is as much the concern of *Bruce* as it is of *Wallace*.[32] The elements of freedom and the rights of the Scottish people are the driving forces behind Robert's and Douglas's fervent fighting; 'A noble heart will have no ease / Nor aught else that pleases him / If freedom fails, for free decision / Is longed above all else.'[33] Robert and Douglas therefore do not fight because they are gallant warriors; they fight because they have lost their freedom and, in turn, become gallant warriors. Their national identity therefore overshadows their chivalry.

FREEDOM AND THE FEMALE ROLE

The validity of literature as an historical source is also of great importance in examining the notion of 'freedom' in *The Bruce* and *Wallace*.[34] Given Barbour's elitist ties, however, one must wonder whether he meant 'fredome is a noble thing' literally.[35] Barbour and Harry do not pursue the rights of the lower classes when describing the fight for freedom but rather focus on the oppression of the ruling ranks. The nobility has more to lose than the peasants, and their loss of freedom particularly 'offends because men of property are oppressed, treated as serfs, [and] afflicted with the most wicked injustice to which a bad ruler can descend – disinheritance'.[36] The literature of the *Bruce* and the *Wallace* therefore do not present a rose-coloured history of Scotland's past but one that was somewhat uncaring of those outside the nobility. Although the poems often deal with peasants, such as Barbour's focus on the farmer from Linlithgow or the women willing to give everything they owned to help Wallace's cause, the poems' main concentration is on noble heroes, their successes and the meaning of their victories.

The poems offer more insight into the period, however, than the presence of a patriotic nationalism.[37] Because of its very nature, literature is not created within an isolated space 'but grows out of the life of the community' from which it originates, thus providing an avenue to study other aspects of contemporary society, such as gender relations.[38] Yet *The Bruce* and *Wallace* are generally studied with reference to nationalism with little attention, if any, paid to gender, a subject thus marginalised.

The Wars of Independence comprise a period in Scottish history that rarely involves looking into the female experience. Goldstein argues that, although the participation of women in the wars is occasionally discussed, few have 'systematically examined the variety of ways in which women experienced a conflict that was in a large part imposed on them by their husbands, brothers and sons, lords, bishops and priests'.[39] The historical discipline therefore appears to be thinking in male terms as few concentrate on the female role in the national struggle. Even Goldstein is guilty of claiming that it was a man's war with women feeling the effects of it as opposed to being active participants or promoters of the fighting. The overlooking of women during the Wars of Independence is perhaps the result of the manner in which the chronicles present women as innocent casualties.[40] Truth in these descriptions may have been lacking as it is likely that the chronicles were following the codes of chivalric conduct in presenting the grisly casualties of war brought on by the enemy. Edward, for example, received an unfavourable reputation in 1306 for abandoning chivalric conventions by punishing in a manner 'intended to be commensurate with their spouses' perfidy' the wives and widows of 'those who, in the king's opinion, had offended him most grievously'.[41] Presenting the women as casualties in the chronicles may therefore not have been because of the women's innocence but rather because of the propaganda the authors wished to promote. Yet the chronicle stereotype limited the role of Scottish women for generations to come. Ewan, in her discussion on the progress of women's history, claims that this stereotype has stunted the perception of women, resulting in 'few strong female figures' comparable to Wallace or Bruce.[42] Women have thus become unworthy of attention because of their passive, docile natures, leaving the position of active historical players to the men of Scotland.

A common manner in which to explore historically women's lives is through their oppression as daughters, wives or widows who enjoyed little legal independence. Ewan explores the ways in which women could have gained independence and potentially power within such a system. She ultimately concludes that widows were the only women able to enjoy any form of freedom to control their lives.[43] If women were, indeed, seeking a degree of independence for themselves, it is odd that no one has suggested a parallel to Scottish male freedom fighters seeking independence from England.

A possible female desire for autonomy may be reflected in the levels of social control, a matter of great concern within the period. Ewan focuses on how effective insults were in promoting such control. 'Priest's whore' (whore meaning fornicator rather than prostitute), was one of the more insulting phrases as it rendered women sleeping with men who had sworn a vow of chastity worse than average adulterers.[44] In fact, in Scotland, as well as elsewhere, 'whore' was the most frequently recorded term of abuse against women.[45] The purpose behind calling women such names was in the hope of controlling those who stepped outside their defined roles as wife and mother. Gossip, too, was a very powerful and informal way to keep social control.[46] It was broadly understood that sexual insults were an effective weapon against women, even those engaged in quarrels concerning the everyday or the mundane.[47] This meant that, if women overstepped their boundaries in bartering, brewing or any other work activities, they ran the risk of damaged reputations or worse. The problem with the study of gossip and insults is that the focus is on the breaking of elements of social control as opposed to the true female experience. Rather than discussing the oppression of women, one longs for analysis on how women lived, worked and prayed, irrespective of societal restraints. Without studies of that type, the question remains whether there are female histories or if women simply are case studies for the history of social control and conformity.

The attempt to contain women was not the only element of restriction because both sexes felt the pressure for compliance. Contemporary sources reflect that 'sensuality, cruelty and sexual lust, like piety, asceticism and voluntary poverty, existed in medieval society among both sexes'.[48] Studies completed on the medieval male perception of reputation prove that taunts of 'whoremonger' or 'whoremaster' were 'almost as damaging to men as "whore" was to women', implying that gossip informally controlled men as well as women.[49] The difference between the social control felt by men and that felt by women, however, was that punishments for women who transgressed exceeded those of the men. If they committed adultery, women tarnished their grace and, in one act, 'defiled their body, damned their soul, robbed their husband of "his right" and potentially imposed an illegitimate line upon his posterity'.[50] Historical perceptions such as this make it nearly impossible to present women of the past as anything other than meek and passive.

The courtly literature from the period unfortunately furthers the passive perception of women. When delving into romantic poems, the women are presented 'only as passive onlookers, figures whose main function is to inspire their heroes to great deeds'.[51] Furthermore, when scrutinising the female character in the texts, one sees a docile and submissive figure fulfilling the role of an 'ideal woman'.[52] On the other hand, The Bruce and Wallace, which represent women as active participants, modify the view of the weak female character. Ultimately the goal is to understand the true history of women, making both genres of literature indispensable because comparison between the two provides a well-rounded perception of the past.

The costume of women's history shrouds the diversity of female experience because women are lumped together without reverence for class or race, generalising the female experience to conditions of either passivity or punishment. Without taking into account the various types of female and those omitted from court transcripts, chronicles or law books, the history of women is not complete. In comparison to the nobility, few secondary sources explore townswomen and peasants.[53] There is a consensus about their careers and lifestyle but little about their personalities, unlike elevated characters such as Mary Queen of Scots. In the introduction of The Edinburgh History of Scottish Literature, the editors make note of how 'more writing by women is discussed here than in any previous history of Scottish literature' yet only point to two chapters in the second volume which, within a three-volume series, hardly seems vast.[54] If the history of women is incomplete, and even overshadowed by the history of national identity, then the history of Scotland is incomplete as well. In the words of the philosopher John Macmurray, 'things have too long been seen from a man's, rather than a human, point of view'.[55]

Bruce and Wallace are helpful in the investigation of fourteenth- and fifteenth-century women. Although only four women are named in the Bruce, Dame Marjory, Joan, and the two Isabellas, other unnamed women grace the pages of the poem.[56] For instance, in Book 16, King Robert paused his troops to assist a woman in labour and, in Book 19, a nameless 'lady' thwarted the plans of the Soulis Conspiracy so saving King Robert. The prevalence of women in Wallace is similar to that of Bruce, with interactions between Wallace and his female companions in the forms of trysts and secret meetings.[57] Few women in Wallace have names but their role is more likely to portray female reality than do more prominent characters because 'there is less need to shape them and they may appear in a way that more closely approximates social reality'.[58] Anonymous women were not of royal blood and therefore did not have to abide by the rules of courtly conduct. It was essential for women of the court to give 'at least the appearance of living a virtuous life and not do anything that might give rise to rumour and speculation', thus restricting their actions much more than those of their less distinguished sisters. Any comments on women in these texts are likely to be reliable because women are not the main concern of the poems; instead, the focus is on the respective heroes and presenting them in the best light.[59]

Bruce and *Wallace* reflect the amount of female participation in the societies which produced the poems, as well as the roles women played during the Wars of Independence, while illuminating gender issues and the gender variances in the period. While women obviously possessed a large amount of control within the domestic arena, they also played a role within the political and martial realms in which they were 'viewed in a generally positive and active light, not negatively as temptresses or passively as ideals'.[60] Women were active social participants, and were not outsiders who failed to do more than feel the effects of male actions.

MOTHERS AND WIDOWS

In the poems the common roles of women appear to be minding children, providing food and warmth and attending to the production or upkeep of clothing. When Barbour discusses the Black Douglas's fearful reputation, he portrays him as 'more dreadful than was any devil in hell'.[61] Moreover, he relates how when women 'wanted to scold their children, they would consign them with a very angry face to the Black Douglas'.[62] Thus was reputation exploited to reprimand and regulate children.

The role of mother, then as now, appears to have been for life. When Wallace's mother learned that he had killed young Selbie, son of the constable of Dundee, she wept and cried that, unless he ceased such activity, he would surely be killed. Her maternal resourcefulness disguised him as a pilgrim in order to smuggle him into Dunfermline and then across the Forth to Linlithgow.[63] Mothers in the texts are revered as the saviours of heroes and promoters of legends, their roles as dramatic as they are domestic.

The perceptions of domesticity continue with the women of the *Wallace* who provide the hero with comfort and sustenance. At Dunnipace a widow provided food, refreshment and shelter.[64] When travelling through Dumbarton, Wallace called at a widow's house who offered rest in her nearby barn; 'baith meit and drynk scho brocht in gret plente'. The widow then marked the doors of houses which sheltered Englishmen so that Wallace could target them.[65] She was thus something more than a nurturer, a role frequently assigned to women in the poem. Harry seems to wish to stress that women are completely behind their men in the fight for freedom. Women, and widows in particular, in *Wallace* therefore fulfil the role 'centered around the home and the family with responsibility for providing food, raising children, and all the other tasks associated with keeping a home'.[66] It is noteworthy that almost all the women Wallace encounters are widows with little explanation as to how they acquired their widowhood. Perhaps it was down to the war but may also have been due to natural causes. Because the women have apparently chosen not to remarry, they are exhibiting some of the independent qualities discussed by Shahar and Ewan. By choosing not to remarry during the Wars of Independence, widows could support the cause of their choice rather than subscribing to the side favoured by their husbands. Numerous women, the majority of them widows, assist Wallace in his fight, so reflecting the effects of war; women are left alone to care for their children, becoming innocent survivors. What is not in doubt is that women dominated the domestic realm by providing comfort through shelter and food.

Another element of domesticity exhibited within *Bruce* and *Wallace* is the attention to the production and maintenance of clothing. As Bruce led his procession from Limerick, he heard a woman cry and 'quickly asked what that was. "It's a laundry-woman, Sir", someone said, "who is taken in childbirth now".'[67] Robert decides that the army should stay and wait for the child to be born rather than leave the woman behind, so suggesting that the laundry woman was a part of the 'small folk' who followed the soldiers. The laundry woman, by travelling with King Robert, indicates that women were as much a part of the campaign in Ireland as the men. *Bruce* also indicates what the women would provide, such as the replenishment and washing of clothing, while travelling with the Scottish army. The domestic realm, even though it has moved outside the private domain, therefore remains the responsibility of women. *Wallace* presents a similar scene concerning clothing. In the hope of helping Wallace flee the scene of slaughter, a 'gude wyff' dressed Wallace in a 'russet gown' of her own which he put on over his clothes. A neat touch was to provide a 'soudly courche', a dirty kerchief – for a clean one would have attracted attention – which was placed over his head and neck, topped off with a woven white hat. As a finishing touch, she gave him 'a rok, syn set him doun to spin', the very epitome of female domesticity.[68] For several centuries to come, women would congregate to exchange news and gossip while spinning with their portable stones. The misdirection worked well, leaving Wallace out of the grips of the enemy. Ewan claims that the spinning ruse may have worked on the English because, as males, they failed to realise Wallace was spinning incorrectly.[69] Women are thus the spinners in medieval society and, accordingly, the main manufacturers of clothing. They are full participants in the Scottish community through motherhood and by providing food, shelter and clothing. *Bruce* and *Wallace* consequently illustrate how women contribute to the social order through the functioning of their domestic roles but they are also major players in the calamitous events then engulfing the nation.

Bruce and *Wallace* indicate that women participated beyond the domestic level through involvement, albeit limited, with the political issues of the period. Women's responsibilities included the provision of male heirs and advice, if sought. In the opening section of his poem, Barbour, discussing royal succession, states that 'no female could succeed as long a male could be found, descended, no matter how, in a direct line',[70] indicating that it was possible for women to succeed but that a greater preference was given to male succession.

Women often used their domestic abilities within the political realm, as seen with the queen of England's (completely fictitious) attempt to visit William Wallace in order to secure peace. In justifying her efforts to the English king, the queen states that 'Perchance he will erar on wemen rew [sooner have pity] / Than on your men; yhe haiff don him sic der [harm].' She added philosophically that 'It ma nocht scaith suppos it do na vaill' [It may do no harm suppose it does no good]. Edward I uncharacteristically conceded, the unlikely implication being that he was finding the Scots too tough an enemy. Thus, the female disposition could be of service as a political weapon.[71]

WOMEN AT WAR

Some said the queen loved Wallace but, says Harry, that would not be surprising, for such a high-minded individual as the hero, of such repute, so well made, will always have good fortune where women are concerned, though he did not go so far as to claim that the queen of England undertook her strenuous embassy purely out of love. When the queen meets Wallace, Harry comments on her superior advisers, including fifty ladies, distinguished and renowned, some of whom were widows and others nuns, accompanied by seven old priests.[72] The queen understood the nature of politics, its importance, and her role therein. Whether the meeting between the queen and Wallace occurred historically is of no concern but the event does demonstrate that women, in some manner, could be involved with the political decisions of the period by offering advice. Confirmation of such political involvement is indicated by the Ragman Roll which 'records the fealty and homage of some two thousand Scottish freeholders, great and small, male and female' with 'the names of some seventy women'.[73] Thus, some women clearly moved beyond their domestic roles by acting as political participants.

Women in *Bruce* and *Wallace* were martially active by travelling with the troops and bringing them comfort or by promoting the Scottish cause through song; they also retrieved arrows to help further the fighting. No matter the manner in which women participated, either directly or indirectly, by actually contributing to war, medieval women showed that they were more than innocent casualties. Until the nineteenth century, armies 'were accompanied by large numbers of civilians', a majority of whom were women 'who provided services for the soldiers, including laundering, clothes-mending, and selling goods'.[74] Barbour acknowledges that women offer comfort to men at war, making women crucial to Bruce's progress.[75] Early in Barbour's *Bruce*, for example, the queen and other 'fair and comely ladies' stayed with the king and his troop, 'each for love of their husbands, a true love and loyalty wanting to share their sufferings' and pain, rather than be apart from them.[76] Such women inspired their warrior husbands, 'for love is of such great strength that it makes light of all suffering, and often gives such strength and such power to easy-going men that they can endure great tribulations'.[77]

Women were entrusted with the celebration of military achievement through song. Barbour directed those interested in the story of how Sir John de Soulis captured Sir Andrew Harclay of Cumberland to 'hear young women, when they are at play', since they 'sing [of] it among themselves everyday'.[78] The astonishing nature of John's feats led Barbour to believe that they 'will be prized for evermore, as long as men can remember them',[79] thus the women promote pride and patriotism.

Goldstein asserts that 'Barbour's women consistently find themselves acting as political subjects who contribute in several ways to the national cause.'[80] Women used their domestic roles to contribute to the cause but also moved beyond the realm of domesticity by embracing military opportunities. One example in *Bruce* is the assistance women provided the troops in the scene of the steward's defence at Mary-Gate. On the day the Scots 'were most [heavily] attacked and the shot was thickest, women with child and small children gathered up arrows in armfuls, carrying them to those who were on the wall'.[81] The scene could be propaganda with Barbour desiring to show how passionate the people of Scotland were for the independence of their country but, on a simpler level, Barbour could be illustrating women's positive role. The proximity to fighting, whether travelling with, or supporting the troops, allowed women to understand the costs of war. Wallace's wife, for example, pays the supreme price at the hands of Hasilrig, leaving Wallace suffering as a widower. Her understanding of the cruelty of war implies that women of the period were as acquainted with conflict as the men. Hendry recognises 'that the "woman's sphere" is as big as the men's sphere, their world as much as a universe', giving women ample opportunity to leave home and experience what men were experiencing.[82] Rather than being withdrawn from their communities, women were active domestically, politically and militarily. The stereotype of the docile and passive female therefore seems entirely unsuitable for women of the Wars of Independence.

The political and military contributions women made were indispensable as they helped advance the Scottish cause. Their actions directly altered the progression of the war to a more positive outcome. At a very basic level, women offered supplies and troops to the warriors. As already mentioned, one of the main female roles was as providers of food; in addition, however, women offered fiscal assistance and their sons. En route to Dundaff, for example, a widow presented Wallace with some silver and two of her sons 'that worthi war and wycht', retaining her third son until he was old enough to learn the arts of war.[83] In providing her sons, the widow elevated Wallace from a man on the run hiding in forests to a traveller with guards at his disposal. In this manner, the widow, who set aside her motherly instincts, transformed a difficult situation for Wallace. Similarly, early in Harry's text was an incident that almost ended Wallace's expedition and career through a near-death experience. A woman again came to the rescue, this time in the shape of Wallace's nurse. After being jailed in Ayr, Wallace became gravely ill and, when the jailer visited him, thinking the hero had paid his debt to Nature, he threw the body over the prison wall. Wallace's nurse went to retrieve the corpse but, upon bringing Wallace home and discovering that he was still alive, the nurse's daughter suckled him with her breast milk to bring him back to health.[84] Without the actions of the nurse, the Wallace campaign would have perished along with him as well as the freedom of the Scottish nation. A woman also saved King Robert but in a completely different manner. The plans of a 'wicked conspiracy against Robert, the brave king'[85] were 'exposed by a lady . . . before [the conspirators] could carry out their intentions'.[86] After putting down the Soulis Conspiracy, Bruce was able to maintain control over his domain, rendering the woman saviour of king and kingdom. Factual content in these events may be elusive but the point remains that Harry and Barbour believed that women could do more than inspire men to arms by directly assisting in their struggle.

The success of Wallace's campaign is commonly attributed to Wallace's wife, Marion Braidfute, as her murder inspired him to fight fervently against the English. When Wallace learns of her death, he vows that 'for hir saik thar sall ten thousand dee' and 'by the end of the poem, he must have achieved that aim, although the reader loses count of the dead'.[87] Wallace, however, seems to need very little inspiration for the slaughter which begins well before his meeting with Marion. In Book II, for instance, Wallace smites Lord Percy's steward when he attempts to apprehend Wallace's freshly caught fish. The motive behind the killing is allegedly to teach the steward manners yet, as the text progresses, it seems that Wallace needs very little motivation to kill, leading Goldstein to label Harry's text as 'a brutal narrative'.[88] Marion therefore plays little role in the development of the Wars of Independence as Wallace eradicated the English, and would continue to slaughter them, with little thought of her existence beyond Book VI.

CONCLUSION

Given that Barbour's *Bruce* and Harry's *Wallace* are the products of the 'cultural matrix' from which the poems derived, they help 'create images of women' which, in turn, 'support and continue the culture's existing social and political arrangements', displaying how literature can be used to study gender variances within the period.[89] The portrayal of men and women in literature is therefore representative of the roles the sexes maintained in Scottish society. As previously seen, men and women each participated in the Wars of Independence leaving the characters to appear 'idealised, contributing their part either for or against the great goal of independence'.[90] Beyond such participation, the characters also expressed a degree of equality between men and women. The characteristics of men like Douglas, for example, appear to differ very little from women like Wallace's nurse, rendering the virtues demonstrated by women almost equivalent to those of men. Bravery, for instance, was a quality possessed by all loyal knights in *Bruce* but Lady Joan of the Tower, 'who was . . . of great bravery', also exhibited such traits.[91] Despite such similarities between the sexes, *Bruce* and *Wallace* do expose gender differences. The characteristic emotion of weeping belonged solely to women, supposedly leaving little to be done by men. An exception is Robert's reconnection with the Earl of Lennox, causing the king and his men to weep 'out of compassion'.[92] After stating that a group of soldiers wept, Barbour quickly corrects himself and claims that they were not truly crying since 'weeping comes to men with misgiving, and no-one can cry without grief, except women who can wet their cheeks with tears whenever they like, even though very often nothing is hurting them'.[93] The implication is that men who cry without reason lose their masculinity while, in women, weeping is a sign of femininity. Through time such facets became everyday assumptions about gender.

Literature thus has much more to reveal about everyday attitudes and actions than more conventional sources can ever be expected to communicate. To the great deeds of the heroes of Scotland's most famous series of wars we can now add, it is to be hoped, women of independence.

Notes

1 A. A. M. Duncan (ed.), *The Bruce* (Edinburgh, 1997), 'Introduction', p. vii.
2 Sonja Cameron, 'Keeping the Customer Satisfied: Barbour's *Bruce* and a Phantom Division at Bannockburn', in Edward J. Cowan and Douglas Gifford (eds), *The Polar Twins* (Edinburgh, 1999), p. 61.
3 Edward J. Cowan and Douglas Gifford, 'Introduction: Adopting and Adapting the Polar Twins', in Cowan and Gifford, *The Polar Twins*, pp. 9–10.
4 Graeme Morton, *William Wallace: Man and Myth* (Thrupp, 2004), p. 6.
5 Rosalind K. Marshall, *Virgins and Viragos: A History of Women in Scotland from 1080–1980* (London, 1983), p. 17.
6 Evelyn S. Newlyn, 'Images of Women in Sixteenth-Century Scottish Literary Manuscripts', in Elizabeth Ewan and Maureen M. Meikle (eds), *Women in Scotland c.1100–c.1750* (East Linton, 1999), p. 56.
7 Siân Reynolds, 'Historiography and Gender: Scottish and International Dimensions', in Terry Brotherstone, Deborah Simonton, and Oonagh Walsh (eds), *Gendering Scottish History: An International Approach* (Glasgow, 2000), p. 5.
8 Susan Dwyer Amussen, review of Thomas Laqueur, *Making Sex: Body and Gender from the Greeks to Freud*, in *Journal of the Interdisciplinary History* 24.3 (winter 1994), p. 521.
9 Amussen, review, p. 521.

10 R. James Goldstein, *The Matter of Scotland: Historical Narrative in Medieval Scotland* (Lincoln, 1993), p. 142.

11 Grace C. Wilson, 'Barbour's *Bruce* and Harry's *Wallace*: Complements, Compensations, and Conventions', in *Studies of Scottish Literature* xxv (1990), p. 193.

12 Duncan, *The Bruce*, pp. 1, 7–8.

13 Morton, *William Wallace*, p. 38.

14 W. Hand Browne, review of J. T. T. Brown, *The Wallace and The Bruce Restudied*, in *Modern Language Notes* 16.1 (January 1901), pp. 25–6.

15 W. A. Gaigie, 'Barbour and Blind Harry as Literature', in *Scottish Review* 22.43 (July 1893), p. 201.

16 Benjamin T. Hudson, 'The Scottish Gaze', in R. Andrew McDonald (ed.), *History, Literature, and Music in Scotland, 700–1560* (Toronto, 2002), p. 29.

17 Browne, review, p. 26.

18 A. M. Kinghorn, 'Scottish Historiography in the Fourteenth Century: A New Introduction to Barbour's *Bruce*', in *Studies in Scottish Literature* 6 (July 1968–April 1969), p. 141.

19 Cameron, 'Keeping the Customer Satisfied', p. 68.

20 Cowan and Gifford, 'Introduction: Adopting and Adapting the Polar Twins', p. 4.

21 For a discussion of the historical Wallace see Edward J. Cowan (ed.), *The Wallace Book* (Edinburgh, 2007).

22 George Neilson, 'Blind Harry's *Wallace*', in *Essay and Studies By Members of the English Associations* (Oxford, 1910), p. 87.

23 Gaigie, 'Barbour and Blind Harry as Literature', p. 173.

24 Goldstein, *The Matter of Scotland*, p. 151.

25 Douglas Gifford and Alan Riach, *Scotlands: Poets and the Nation* (Manchester, 2004), p. xix.

26 Richard J. Moll, '"Off Quhat Nacion Art Thow?" National Identity in Blind Harry's *Wallace*', in MacDonald, *History, Literature, and Music in Scotland*, p. 121.

27 Goldstein, *The Matter of Scotland*, pp. 224, 228.

28 Moll, 'National Identity in Blind Harry's *Wallace*', p. 134.

29 Margaret McIntyre, review of R. James Goldstein, *The Matter of Scotland: Historical Narrative in Medieval Scotland*, in *Speculum* 69.4 (October 1994), p. 1177.

30 Duncan, *The Bruce*, p. 148.

31 Anne M. McKim, 'James Douglas and Barbour's Idea of Knighthood', in W. H. Jackson (ed.), *Knighthood in Medieval Literature* (Suffolk, 1981), pp. 78–9.

32 Kurt Wittig, *The Scottish Tradition in Literature* (Westport, CT, 1958), p. 13.

33 Duncan, *The Bruce*, p. 56.

34 See Edward J. Cowan, *'For Freedom Alone': The Declaration of Arbroath 1320* (Edinburgh, [2003] 2008).

35 Goldstein, *The Matter of Scotland*, p. 163.

36 Duncan, *The Bruce*, p. 10.

37 R. James Goldstein, 'Freedom is a Noble Thing! The Ideological Project of John

Barbour's *Bruce*', in Dietrach Strauss and Horst W. Drescher (eds), *Scottish Language and Literature, Medieval and Renaissance* (Frankfurt, 1984), p. 196.

38 Wittig, *The Scottish Tradition in Literature*, p. 3.

39 R. James Goldstein, 'The Women of the Wars of Independence in Literature and History', in *Studies in Scottish Literature* xxvi (1991), p. 272.

40 Goldstein, 'The Women of the Wars of Independence', p. 277.

41 Cynthia Neville, 'Widows of the War: Edward I and the Women of Scotland During the War of Independence', in Sue Sheridan Walker (ed.), *Wife and Widow in Medieval England* (Ann Arbor, 1993), p. 122.

42 Elizabeth Ewan, 'A Realm of One's Own? The Place of Medieval and Early Modern Women in Scottish History', in Brotherstone et al., *Gendering Scottish History*, p. 27.

43 Elizabeth Ewan, 'The Female Character: Early and Middle Scots Literature as a Source for the History of Women in Late Medieval Scotland', in *ACTA: Celtic Connections* xvi (1993), p. 33.

44 Elizabeth Ewan, '"Many Injurious Words": Defamation and Gender in Later Medieval Scotland', in MacDonald, *History, Literature, and Music in Scotland*, p. 168.

45 Ewan, 'Many Injurious Words', p. 167.

46 Elizabeth Ewan, 'Crime or Culture? Women and Daily Life in Late-Medieval Scotland', in Yvonne G. Brown and Rona Ferguson (eds), *Twisted Sisters: Women, Crime and Deviance in Scotland Since 1400* (East Linton, 2002), p. 130.

47 Bernard Capp, 'The Double Standard Revisited: Plebian Women and Male Sexual Reputation in Early Modern England', in *Past and Present* 162 (February 1999), p. 70.

48 Shulamith Shahar, *The Fourth Estate: A History of Women in the Middle Ages*, trans. Chaya Galai (London, 1996), p. 172.

49 Capp, 'The Double Standard Revisited', p. 72.

50 Barry Reay, *Popular Cultures in England 1550–1750* (London and New York, 1998), pp. 15–16.

51 Ewan, 'The Female Character', p. 29.

52 Ewan, 'The Female Character', p. 29.

53 Shahar, *Fourth Estate*, p. 219.

54 Ian Brown, Thomas Clancy, Susan Manning and Murray Pittock, 'Scottish Literature: Criticism and the Canon', in Ian Brown (ed.), *The Edinburgh History of Scottish Literature*, vol. 1, *One From Columba to the Union* (Edinburgh, 2007), p. 7.

55 Joy Hendry, 'Snug in the Asylum of Taciturnity: Women's History in Scotland', in Ian Donnachie and Christopher Whatley (eds), *The Manufacture of Scottish History* (Edinburgh, 1992), p. 128.

56 Duncan, *The Bruce*, p. 12.

57 Goldstein, *The Matter of Scotland*, p. 254.

58 Ewan, 'The Female Character', p. 29.

59 Ewan, 'The Female Character', p. 30.

60 Ewan, 'The Female Character', p. 33.

61 Duncan, *The Bruce*, p. 578.

62 Duncan, *The Bruce*, p. 578.

63 Anne McKim (ed.), *The Wallace* (Edinburgh, 2003), pp. 260–90.

64 McKim, *The Wallace*, Book Ten, p. 624.

65 McKim, *The Wallace*, Book Ten, pp. 690–708.

66 Ewan, 'The Female Character', p. 30.

67 Duncan, *The Bruce*, p. 592.

68 McKim, *The Wallace*, Book One, p. 8.

69 Ewan, 'The Female Character', p. 32.

70 Duncan, *The Bruce*, p. 48.

71 McKim, *The Wallace*, Book Eight, pp. 1113–30.

72 McKim, *The Wallace*, Book Eight, pp. 1218–21.

73 Neville, 'Widows of the War', pp. 114–15.

74 Ewan, 'The Female Character', p. 31.

75 Bernice W. Kilman, 'The Idea of Chivalry in John Barbour's *Bruce*', in *Mediaeval Studies* 35 (1973), p. 480.

76 Duncan, *The Bruce*, p. 106.

77 Duncan, *The Bruce*, p. 106.

78 Duncan, *The Bruce*, p. 606.

79 Duncan, *The Bruce*, p. 606.

80 Goldstein, *The Matter of Scotland*, p. 191.

81 Duncan, *The Bruce*, p. 656.

82 Hendry, 'Snug in the Asylum of Taciturnity', p. 142.

83 McKim, *The Wallace*, Book Five, pp. 429–34.

84 McKim, *The Wallace*, Book Two, pp. 258–75.

85 Duncan, *The Bruce*, p. 698.

86 Duncan, *The Bruce*, p. 698.

87 Felicity Riddy, 'Unmapping the Territory: Blind Harry's *Wallace*', in Cowan, *The Wallace Book*, p. 109; Duncan, *The Wallace*, Book Six, p. 222.

88 Goldstein, 'The Women of the Wars of Independence', p. 280.

89 Newlyn, 'Images of Women', p. 56.

90 Ewan, 'The Female Character', p. 36.

91 Duncan, *The Bruce*, p. 745.

92 Duncan, *The Bruce*, p. 136.

93 Duncan, *The Bruce*, p. 136.

Chapter 8

Everyday Life in the Histories of Scotland from Walter Bower to George Buchanan

Nicola Royan

INTRODUCTION

Fundamentally, everyday life is not the concern of medieval and early modern writers of history. Their primary interest is in the extraordinary: whether that means people, such as kings, nobles and bishops, or whether that means events or deeds, natural or artificial, such as famines, comets, battles, and martyrdoms. The Scots are no exception to this. In the most significant kind of history writing at this period, the grand history of the Scots from their origins, the writers rarely stray from the doings of kings and magnates. The prevalence of these attitudes to historical narrative owes much to the view of history as exemplary, where deeds are described in order to be emulated or avoided by those in government. This use is demonstrated quite clearly in *The Testament of the Papyngo* by Sir David Lyndsay, where he specifically refers to past kings as a warning to James V. The duty of the governed is, by and large, to be docile, hard working and invisible, unless required to deliver an appropriate and limited rebuke to their governors. Even the most radical of these texts, such as those by George Buchanan and John Mair, tend to see political action by the commons as the work of the mob, rather than considered and legitimate intervention in government. Yet these narratives reflect the experience of living in Scotland in the fourteenth, fifteenth and sixteenth centuries; the everyday may only be a backdrop to what they describe but it is still necessarily there.

In this chapter, I consider only a small selection of possible texts, some originally written in Latin (although I quote translations) and some in the vernacular. I refer primarily to: Walter Bower's *Scotichronicon* (c.1449), the major medieval chronicle; John Mair's *Historia Maioris Britanniae* (1521) and Hector Boece's *Scotorum historia a prima gentis origine* (1527) both printed by the same printer in Paris but remarkably different in style; John Bellenden's *Chronicles of Scotland* (c.1540) at base a translation of Boece's text but with various revisions (the version cited here is the print, probably the final revision); and George Buchanan's *Historia rerum Scoticarum* (1582) and its first translation into English in 1690. My study is therefore by no means exhaustive but designed to give a flavour of the material to be found, its strengths and its limitations. All the narratives of this period, those discussed and also those omitted, are primarily composed of a series of episodes involving individuals. In the case of the great chronicles and histories, these individuals are kings, magnates and bishops, often playing against anonymous figures from further down the social scale; in the deliberately partisan *Historie of the Reformation*, the individual who gets most attention is John Knox himself, which serves to emphasise the extraordinary events he describes. To see daily life in the main narratives, we have to read through the stories to the assumptions behind the events. That, in itself, brings its own difficulties. Often the glimpse we get is partial: when Bower, for instance, refers to a woman dressed in bridal clothes (as an act of defiance), it is clear that he shares an understanding of what that looks like with his first audience, but naturally enough, he does not include the specifics for his twenty-first century readership. In other cases, reading through the described event only provides the material from which the everyday might be constructed: to make sense of several striking episodes in various narratives, for instance, John McGavin considers what the expectations of the ordinary event would be, whether that is a public trial or a royal departure.[1] To do this effectively requires the support of documentary material and wider record, as well as reading between the lines. Moreover, the events which attract narration cannot be entirely ordinary: McGavin is concerned with those regular enough for particular variations to be worth recording in the eyes of the chronicler but special enough to attract that kind of variation. To find far more mundane details of food, clothing and daily habits, we have to look elsewhere in the accounts.

IN SEARCH OF THE EVERYDAY

Fortunately, most of these chronicles include descriptions of the realm, usually placed at the very beginning of the great histories. These sections are primarily geographical but also anthropological, often designed to present the realm and its inhabitants to those living outside it, as well as those within. In short, they are designed to give a sense of place and people – precisely the everyday that is required. Andrew of Wyntoun offers a neatly concise one:

> Blessit Brettane beylde sulde be   *shelter*
> Off al þe ilis in þe se,
> Qwhar flouris ar feil on feyldis fayr,   *pleasant*
> Hail of hew, haylssum of ayre.
> Off al corn þar is copy gret,
> Pes and atis, bere and qwhet;
> Bath froyt on tre and fische in flude,
> And til catel pasture gude.[2]

In writing his *Original Chronicle* (*c.*1424) in St Serf's Priory in Loch Leven, Wyntoun attempts to situate Scottish history into a universal context, from

Figure 8.1 *The slaughter of a cow, fifteenth century, Iona Abbey. © Royal Commission on the Ancient and Historical Monuments of Scotland. Licensor www.scran.ac.uk.*

the beginning of the world (hence its title 'Original'). This accounts for the brevity of this description because he has a good deal of material to include; short though they are, however, these lines include the main features of these kinds of accounts. The stress is on what the land produces and its benefit to humanity, mostly in the form of food; it is positive, not to say enthusiastic, and, in consequence, marks out the realm as particularly blessed. The limitations of this are clearly evident, however. Firstly, accentuated here by Wyntoun's brevity, the description is so general that it is hard to get a specific image of the territory: the only distinguishing features here are the types of corn, peas, oats, barley and wheat, a grouping not necessarily found universally. Secondly, Wyntoun is working to particular literary expectations of what should be included. The more extensive ones follow a recognisable pattern, shared with historical accounts written across Europe: they usually begin with locating the realm geographically with reference to other realms, and discuss and describe the various regions before describing the people. Sometimes these descriptions are simply borrowed from a source or a previous model. For instance, in *Scotichronicon*, Bower repeats Fordun's description of the Scottish realm from the *Chronica Gentis Scotorum*, already forty years old when Bower starts reworking the material;[3] he also includes a few lines of his own (marked *scriptor* in the chief manuscript) but is otherwise happy to accept an earlier authority. To a modern reader, this seems all the more surprising when much older writers, such as Isidore of Seville, describing Scotland at a great distance of space and, indeed, time, are quoted with equal authority to personal and contemporary observation. This pattern, however, is not unusual; this means of authenticating the description, ensuring that it looks familiar to the readership, recurs well into the sixteenth century.

In addition, these descriptions are designed – quite reasonably – to show the particular realm in question in its best light, and the Scots are no exception. As Wyntoun suggests, the Britons, and more specifically the Scots, are blessed by heaven. Obviously partisan in one way, they may also be intended to make other political and moral points. In *Scotorum Historia*, Boece, especially, uses his description to contrast the moral virtue of the ancient Scots with his contemporary society. As principal of King's College, Aberdeen, and an exponent of humanist ideas, Boece may have been drawing on personal observation, on the Scots' tradition of historiography, or directly on classical models, such as Tacitus' *Germania*, then recently rediscovered. How much we can trust his account, therefore, is open to question and needs careful handling. By this point, it should be clear that any depiction or reading of the everyday in the Scottish histories needs a considerable amount of unpicking and sifting to be useful. Nevertheless, some useful information can be gleaned, though it may not be quite what is expected.

Taking the descriptions of the realm as its base, this chapter picks out aspects of the description which relate to the everyday. The nature of the sources means that this discussion in no way covers all aspects of everyday life, and thus these notes cannot replace archaeological or documentary study; instead, they can merely supplement it. So, we learn that Fife is a source of coal, and we might surmise that coal therefore is a major form of fuel at least around the point of production, particularly 'profittable for operation of smithis';[4] we learn elsewhere that heather is used as an alternative fuel, which is regarded as excellent.[5] These details are recorded because they are not common practice on the Continent where many writers sought a readership, not with a view to a complete image of Scottish life. We cannot determine from these narratives, though, what the precise geographical range was of these different practices, nor whether they applied equally to the highest and lowest in society. Similarly, though Bellenden records that various animals are trapped for their fur beside Loch Ness, and that those furs 'ar coft with gret price amang uncouth marchandis',[6] no detail is provided of method or economic turnover. Its purpose is to illustrate the unconventional wealth of the area, rather than to explore systematically the economic arrangements of the realm. We are told, therefore, about practices, habits and features that are different or distinctive, and those which might be considered essential to the character of the realm.

FEEDING THE FOLK

As is clear from Wyntoun's description, one of the dominant features of these descriptions is what the land produces. Naturally, food is the most important resource. All the chronicles discuss the plenitude of fish in Scotland's rivers and seas, and in many cases, the particular habits of the salmon which seems to be considered something of a national fish. Only Boece and Bellenden consider how it might be fished, however, following a method described as 'uncouth' in Bellenden, *novus* [new] in Boece:

> For the peple makis ane lang mand (wicker basket), narow halsit, and wyid mouthit, with mony stobis inouth, maid with sik craft, that the fische thrawis thameself in it, and can nocht get furth agane; and als sone as the see ebbis, the fische ar tane dry in the crelis.[7]

This may well derive from local knowledge: Boece spent much of his life at King's College, Aberdeen, and is also known to have visited Pluscarden

Abbey, just outside Elgin, so may well have seen fishing on the Spey, as well as on the Dee and the Don. Bellenden was Archdeacon of Moray in the 1530s so he also had northerly connections (though how much time he spent there is unclear) and he was also not adverse to revising Boece's accounts in his translations of *Scotorum Historia*; here, however, the *Chronicles of Scotland* (c.1540) stay close to their source text. What happens to the fish so caught is not specified: some, at least, were presumably consumed locally and perhaps others went to market but the extent of the industry is not described. The same is true of the description of fishing for freshwater pearls; the manner is presented but no economic summary is offered. Bellenden's assertion, that Scots shellfish are generally 'mair profitable to the mouth than any procreatioun of perlis',[8] may suggest as much disapproval of personal adornment over sustenance as dissatisfaction with the quality of the pearls.

In *History of Greater Britain*, John Mair similarly records particular methods of fishing from his locality, where people go 'in Lent and in summer, at the winter and summer solstice' to the coast and hook out lobster and crab in quantity.[9] Mair's reference to specific seasons may relate both to religious practice (fasting in Lent and also in Advent, around the winter solstice), as well as to seasonal variations in the availability of the fish and alternative foodstuffs. The placing of these events in Mair's home locality suggests that his account is based on personal observation; this impression is confirmed by other aspects of his description where he describes tasting or discussing a particular product. Mair's approach to writing historiography is slightly different from the other writers here for, although his history is still concerned with the deeds of the great and the good and still largely reliant on the authority of written narrative, he is more likely to question his sources and to include signalled personal knowledge. This might in part be attributed to his more familiar role as a theologian and philosopher which had different rhetorical expectations; it also in part resulted from his desire to bring together Scottish and English historiography to create a unified narrative, supporting an act of political union between the realms and requiring Mair to negotiate between wildly discrepant sources. For readers in quest of the everyday, this is a gift, since Mair appears as a more trustworthy and direct witness than his contemporaries. It is rare, however, for Mair's descriptions to contrast radically with the more traditional material; instead, his apparently personal observations provide a gloss to the standard account. In the case of fishing, for instance, Mair's discussion confirms the regular descriptions of the wealth of Scotland's freshwater fishing, accompanied by lists of names; in all these texts, these detailed descriptions allow us to infer the significance of fish, both freshwater and marine, in the diets of Scots.

Animal husbandry is also important. Following Fordun, Bower records that mountainous regions of Scotland are 'full of pasture for animal fodder' (*pascuosa . . . armentorum herbagiis*).[10] This provides for sheep, cattle and horses although the sheep here are designated as wool producing and the cattle as dairy, rather than as meat animals. While Fordun appears to echo Herodotus in this account, Mair again appears more reliant on his own experience. He comments on the quantities of sheep and cattle held by men in the Highlands; he also notes that British beef is better than French beef while the reverse is true of mutton, something he ascribes to the nature of the pasture.[11] Bellenden, following Boece, is also concerned with the eating of beasts. While describing the south-west of Scotland, Bellenden's account notes that in Carrick, Kyle and Cunningham 'ar mony fair ky and oxin, of quhilk the flesche is richt delicius and tender; the talloun of their wambis is sa sappy, that it fresis nevir, . . . in the maner of oulie [oil]';[12] no other region seems to produce quite the same, as the only other notice of sheep is the peculiarity of those that pasture on Dundore in Garioch, whose flesh is red and fleece yellow.[13] Even in this description, therefore, the role of which is to describe the actuality of the realm, variety overcomes repetition, just as in the main narrative.

Fowl are also a source of food and other goods. Their farming is rarely described: we might speculate that keeping hens was simply too common and domestic to be worthy of attention. Bellenden does make one reference, again to a particular practice in Glenmore in keeping away foxes:

> Ilk hous of this cuntre, nurisis ane young tod [fox] certane dayis, and mengis [mixes] the flesche thairof, eftir that it be slane, with sic meit as thay gif to thair fowlis, or uthir smal beistis; and sa mony as etis of this meit ar preservit twa monethis eftir fra ony dammage of toddis: for toddis will eit na flesche that gustis [tastes] of thair awin kind.[14]

It is recorded as a piece of pure observation, and although it is described as successful, there is no suggestion that it might be repeated elsewhere. It is merely held as an example of practice particular to this area. It is, thus, an example of the everyday – a method of pest control – yet it is also unusual enough to merit inclusion in this account. This is the balance necessary in these texts so, although only ever partial, they can sometimes contain unexpected snippets of new material.

Occasionally, knowledge appears both to be widespread and also more specific than the generalities of the classical writers. For instance, both Mair and Bellenden discuss the use made of solan geese (gannets). Bellenden records that 'within the bowellis of thir geis, is ane fatnes of singular medicine; for it helis mony infirmiteis, speciallie sik as cumis be gut and cater disceding in the hanches and lethes of men and wemen'.[15] In this Bellenden is translating Boece for Boece, too, comments on the particular use of this fat in the treatment of hips. Boece was trained in medicine, which might give his account special weight; he seems to have practised rarely because the combination of priest and doctor was not generally permitted. Mair also notes this use of the solan geese although his perception is slightly different:

he says that 'these birds are extremely fat, and the fat skilfully extracted is very serviceable in the preparation of drugs'.[16] This suggests perhaps more of an ointment although, in fact, none of the writers actually specifies the form of application. Mair also notes that the birds are good to eat: Boece and Bellenden austerely concentrate on the medical and natural historical attractions of the bird.

In their pursuit of the geographical, Boece, Bellenden and Buchanan note areas of the realm suitable for different crops but do not describe the husbandry or the experience of farming. As just one example, Bellenden describes Moray as having 'gret aboundance and fouth of quheit, beir, aitis, and siclik cornis, with gret plente of nutis and appilis',[17] but human participation in bringing these fruits forth is not described. Mair again provides most information regarding the staple grains, oats and barley for, although the other writers are clear about the importance of grain to the economy, they do not specify how it is used nor how it is grown. In *Historia*, Mair asserts, on the basis of his own experience, that oat bread is common throughout Britain, particularly Wales, northern England and, of course, among the 'Scottish peasantry'.[18] He provides detail on its preparation and its milling, and then the preparation of Scottish oatcakes – 'bannoka' is the vernacular name he gives. He narrows his focus to the Scots to refute French accusations of Scottish barbarism in eating such bread; however, his refutation was also directed towards Scottish townspeople (and thereby indirectly towards English readers as well). Mair does draw on authorities in this section, noting Froissart, Pliny and the Bible, but these are clearly supportive rather than primary evidence.[19] He demonstrates the same approach when discussing the brewing of ale. Again he refers to his own experience, this time with regard to the second boiling required for a particularly fine brew. He notes the place of women as brewsters but their gender is secondary to the recipe. Again there is a patriotic tinge to his presentation: ale is good for its drinkers ('it keeps the bowels open, it is nourishing and it quenches thirst'),[20] and thus he does not feel the lack of wine, whether in consumption or in culture, whatever the French might imply.

Rather than ale or beer, Boece mentions a Highland brew which appears to a modern reader to approximate to whisky: called *aqua viva*, 'live water', its significance lies not only in its ability *animos exhilarare* to 'gladden the spirits' but also in its entirely local origin, for Boece is keen to stress that it is not brewed from exotic spices but rather from humble domestic herbs.[21] In general, and in contrast to Mair's enthusiastic personal consumption of local food and produce, Boece generally expresses disapproval of anything that might incline towards self-indulgence; most strikingly, he attributes some decline in Scots morale and strength to the introduction of lunch by Malcolm Canmore and his (Anglo-Saxon) wife Margaret.[22] *Aqua viva*, however, escapes such condemnation, presumably because it is indigenous rather than imported. What might therefore appear straightforward description of common practice, in fact is part of a complex negotiation of competing moral and political desires.

THE AULD SCOTS

This is further reflected in a general celebration of the simple across all writers of all periods. Sometimes this appears to be a straightforward reflection of personal taste and experience, as with Mair and oat bread. In other places, particularly Boece and Buchanan, simplicity becomes associated with the remote and, indeed, with the Highland. Buchanan focuses on those far removed from his everyday life, those on the island of Rona:

> So that these in my Judgement, are the only persons in the whole world, who want nothing, but have all things to Satiety, and besides being ignorant of Luxury and Covetousness they enjoy that Innocency and Tranquillity, which others take great pains to obtain from the Precepts and Institutions of Wise men.[23]

Such a statement is clearly reminiscent of classical models of the noble savage, such as the *Germania*, whereby the remote serves as a judgement on the present existence of the writer and his circle. Boece, of course, attributes austere virtue to the ancient people of Scotland in his account at the end of the description of the realm;[24] he also praises the contemporary Highlander, however, comments extended by Bellenden:

> For the peple thairof (the Highlands) hes na repair with marchandis of uncouth realmes; and, because thay ar nocht corruppit, nor mingit with uncouth blude, thay ar the more strang and rude, and may suffir mair hungir, walking, and distres, than ony uthir peple of Albion; maist hardy at jeoperdyis; richt agill and deliver of bodyis; richt ingenius to every new inventioun; maist sichty in craft of chevalrie; and kepis thair faith and promes with maist severite and constance.[25]

Here Boece's quest for the exemplary is married with the need for distinctiveness in the description. Indeed, of all the peoples of Scotland, those inhabiting the north, often defined as Gaelic speakers, receive more space than the Lowlanders by whom and among whom (Buchanan excepted) these histories were written. This is in part powered by the literary quest for difference: there is, for example, far more comment about Highland dress than about its Lowland equivalent. The garment – some version of the plaid – is described reasonably consistently but the interpretation depends on the perspective of the writer. In his discussion of early customs, Boece alone mentions a fabric patterned like roads or squared pavement; for him (and here Bellenden repeats his view) the garment is distinguished by its simplicity and practicality rather than by its elegance.[26] Mair asserts that 'From the mid-leg to the foot they go uncovered; their dress is for an over garment, a loose plaid and a shirt saffron-dyed'[27] and, though he specifies that the common Lowland soldier fights in a woollen garment instead of the Highland pitch-covered

linen, he does not describe the ordinary dress of his neighbours. Both Boece
and Mair must derive their knowledge from some observation: Bower, following Fordun, merely describes their dress as unsightly.[28] Bower's dismissal
(supported by quotations from Isidore and Solinus) reflects his sense of
threat posed by the Highlands and he differentiates strongly between the two
peoples:

> The coastal people are docile and civilised, trustworthy, long-suffering and cour-
> teous, decent in their dress, polite and peaceable, devout in worship, but always
> ready to resist injuries threatened by their enemies. The island or highland people
> however are fierce and untameable, uncouth and unpleasant, much given to theft,
> fond of doing nothing, but their minds are quick to learn and they are cunning . . .
> They are however loyal and obedient to the king and the kingdom, and they are
> easily made to submit to the laws, if rule is exerted over them.[29]

Mair is also sceptical about the two peoples, replicating a similar division to
Bower's, though rather than use the terms 'coastal' and 'highland', he uses
montani and *domestici*, those of the mountains and those who are civilised.[30]
Bower's anxiety is straightforwardly about internal disruption while Mair's
is a little more complex for he is keen to assert the similarities between the
Scots and the English, thereby easing the path to union, but he is also aware
that the people of the north undermine that similarity. Boece, in contrast,
uses Gaelic life as a model of earlier simplicity, and locates disruptive elements instead in the Borders, using similar markers of rebellion and harm.
Bellenden translates the passage like this:

> For nocht allanerlie in Annandail, bot in all the dalis afore rehersit, ar mony strang
> and wekit thevis, invading the cuntre with perpetuall thift, reif and slauchter,
> quhen thay se ony trublus time.[31]

Such wider and polemic concerns might be seen to detract from the quest
for everyday life but we can derive useful information nevertheless. Firstly,
that describing the Highlander is so important and that their way of life and
dress are evidently markedly different suggest strongly that most of Scottish
daily life was fairly similar to the experience of other northern Europeans
and certainly to that of the English. Readerships for these histories include
the local, such as Bower's patron, but they also clearly address readers on
the Continent and south of the border; the writers were also reasonably well
travelled and were able to compare, however implicitly, their experience of
other places with their homes. So the evidence that Boece, Mair, Bellenden,
and Buchanan saw geographical features and their impact on human life as
most significant suggests a parity of general diet, dress and organisation.

Simultaneously, we are reminded of the perspective and intent of the
writer. While reading *The History of Greater Britain*, for instance, it is possible to be so charmed by the apparently personal insights into Scottish life
as to forget the work's purpose, to argue for British union, and also to grant

Mair more knowledge than he might have had, particularly outside his home area and Fife. While this does not detract from the anecdotes and the link to personal experience, it might also indicate areas of weakness. Boece and Buchanan might appear as useful correctives to that stance: both writers have their own agendas, however, Boece to effect some form of moral regeneration in line with familiar literary patterns, Buchanan to justify himself in a series of political and scholarly arguments. That Buchanan's scholarly combat is in part constructed on a very early analysis of the relationship between Welsh and Gaelic cannot obliterate his aggressive positioning.

Of course, the focus on the distinctive has an ironic result. The 'domestic Scot' fades from view in comparison to his exotic northern brother; the characteristics and style of existence attributed to the Highlander in these texts, in social order, in dress, in food and drink, surely lie behind the Tartanry of Scott so that the problematic and unincorporated figure comes to stand for some image of Scottishness from the eighteenth century onwards. This is perhaps the most striking influence of these generally unsurprising, if interesting, accounts of the Scots realm. What we are told about the southern Scots is confirmed both in modern experience, since the geography of rural Scotland is still recognisable in these descriptions, and also in other material; moreover it blends – at least in these literary accounts – with our understanding of other regions of Britain. The image of the Highlander, however, is distinct, and remains so, and yet it comes about more or less by accident. The survival and promulgation of this image, taken as a type of the Scots, would probably appal some of the writers; it might just have pleased them to have written something so durable. It reminds us, as modern readers, that whatever we seek in these accounts to enrich our understanding of daily life in the fifteenth and sixteenth centuries, we need to read carefully.

Notes

1 John McGavin, *Theatricality and Narrative in Medieval and Early Modern Scotland* (Aldershot, 2007).

2 Andrew of Wyntoun, *Original Chronicle*, F. J. Amours (ed.) 6 vols, Scottish Text Society First Ser. 50, 53, 54, 56, 57, 63 (Edinburgh and London, 1903–14), vol. 2, p. 109.

3 Walter Bower, *Scotichronicon*, D. E. R. Watt (gen. ed.), 9 vols (Aberdeen and Edinburgh, 1987–98), vol. I, Books 1–2, J. and W. MacQueen (ed. and trans.) (Aberdeen, 1993), vol. 1, p. 181.

4 John Bellenden, *The Chronicles of Scotland c.1540* (Edinburgh, 1821), p. xxxvi; Hector Boece, *Scotorum Historiae a prima gentis origin xix libri* (Paris, 1527), fol. 10.

5 John Mair, *Historia Maioris Britanniae* (Paris, 1521), John Mair, *History of Greater Britain*, A. Constable (trans. and ed.) Scottish History Society 10 (Edinburgh, 1892), pp. 39–40.

6 Bellenden, *Chronicles of Scotland*, p. xxxiii.

7 Bellenden, *Chronicles of Scotland*, pp. xxxiii–xxxiv; Boece, *Scotorum Historiae*, fol. ix.

8 Bellenden, *Chronicles of Scotland*, p. xlv.

9 Mair, *History of Greater Britain*, pp. 33–4.

10 Bower, *Scotichronicon*, pp. 182–3.

11 Mair, *History of Greater Britain*, p. 38.

12 Bellenden, *Chronicles of Scotland*, p. xxix.

13 Bellenden, *Chronicles of Scotland*, p. xl.

14 Bellenden, *Chronicles of Scotland*, p. xli.

15 Bellenden, *Chronicles of Scotland*, p. xxxvii.

16 Mair, *History of Greater Britain*, pp. 34–5.

17 Bellenden, *Chronicles of Scotland*, p. xxxiii.

18 Mair, *History of Greater Britain*, pp. 8–12.

19 Mair, *History of Greater Britain*, pp. 8, 11.

20 Mair, *History of Greater Britain*, p. 14.

21 Boece, *Scotorum Historiae*, fol. 18.

22 Boece, *Scotorum Historiae*, p. 268.

23 George Buchanan, *Rerum Scoticarum Historia* (Edinburgh, 1582), George Buchanan, *The History of Scotland written in Latin by George Buchanan; faithfully rendered into English*, J. Fraser (trans.) (London, 1690), p. 32.

24 Boece, *Scotorum Historiae*, fols 5v, 17v–20.

25 Bellenden, *Chronicles of Scotland*, p. xxvi.

26 Bellenden, *Chronicles of Scotland*, p. lvi.

27 Mair, *History of Greater Britain*, p. 49.

28 Bower, *Scotichronicon*, p. 185.

29 Bower, *Scotichronicon*, p. 185.

30 Mair, *History of Greater Britain*, pp. 48–50.

31 Bellenden, *Chronicles of Scotland*, p. xxvii.

Chapter 9

Disease, Death and the Hereafter in Medieval Scotland

Richard D. Oram

I that in heill wes and gladness
Am trublit now with gret seiknes
And feblit with infermite:
Timor mortis conturbat me.[1]

INTRODUCTION

The first stanza of William Dunbar's *Lament for the Makaris*, probably composed in the decades either side of 1500, encapsulates what were probably three of the pressing concerns of the general populace of medieval Scotland: illness, death, and the uncertainty of the afterlife. The link between these three subjects was made all the closer by the regular medieval Christian association of disease with sin, whereby the former was a consequence of, if not punishment for, the latter. One major tension produced by this belief in a spiritual origin of disease was profound distrust of secular medicine among the clergy who were instructed that there was only one sure remedy for illness, a pure and unquestioning Christian existence.[2] This tension made itself manifest in a number of ways at different levels, from the scornful dismissal by the clergy of the supposed skills and effectiveness of professional mediciners to the persecution as witches of the non-professional practitioners of herbal or folk medicine. But what clerics like Bernard of Clairvaux thundered from their pulpits or in their writings and ordinary people chose to believe or disregard were clearly two wholly different things. The evidence from Scotland suggests that the lay populace and clergy pursued all the options available to them in their hunt for physical and spiritual well-being, despite the deep suspicions harboured towards some of the groups who claimed to offer cures. Their efforts have left us with a richly textured record of the diseases which afflicted the medieval population and the physical and spiritual remedies sought by sufferers and their kin to secure release from illness in this world and salvation in the next.

THE EVERYDAY OF DISEASE AND DEATH

Most of our knowledge of the diseases which afflicted medieval Scots survives either in the physical evidence to be obtained from excavated skeletal remains or in the written accounts of miraculous cures obtained by individuals at the shrines of certain saints. The former brings us into a form of direct contact with the individual, and forensic analysis of their remains can tell us much about their quality of life and, possibly, manner of death. Bones provide us with a record of a variety of diseases and afflictions, usually relating to dietary deficiencies affecting growth or chronic infections leaving distinctive signatures on bone surfaces or in bone structures – for example tuberculosis, leprosy and syphilis – in addition to the obvious record of bone trauma – breaks and other damage – which can provide clues as to the work pattern and lifestyle of the individual. In most cases, however, diseases affect the organs, soft tissues and flesh of the body rather than the bones and, consequently, leave no trace of their effects and no indication of the cause of death of the victim. To an extent, records of miraculous cures or, occasionally, spectacular deaths chronicled by contemporaries can provide a glimpse of these kinds of disease but, generally, they lack the precision in recording of symptoms that would enable precise diagnosis to be made. There are, however, many more positive aspects of both forensic examination of skeletal evidence and analysis of the documentary record than these limitations might suggest. Unusually, indeed uniquely, for sources of information relating to medieval Scotland, both of these forms of evidence illustrate the lives and deaths of the populace in general, of both the sexes, all ages and every social grade. For an era of Scottish history when most women, all children and the majority of the rural peasantry and urban poor are little more than silent shadows in the record, the data relating to health, disease and death provide them with at least a whispered postscript to their unreported lives.

Of all these sources of evidence, it is the large-scale excavation of major medieval cemeteries that has been the most productive. Such excavations provide an adequate sample of the population from which to identify significant physical indicators relating to disease, diet, work regime and even local genetic traits manifest in physical characteristics. The biggest of these excavations to date has been the programme of work at Whithorn in Galloway between 1984 and 1991 where over 1,600 individuals were identified in the late medieval cemetery on the slopes south of the cathedral priory ruins.[3] Smaller cemeteries, containing what are probably representative samples of the local population, have been excavated around a number of parish church sites, such as Cairston near Stromness in Orkney, Holy Trinity St Andrews, St Mary's Dundee and St Giles' Elgin.[4] Less representative in terms of evidence for general health are the excavations of burials from within churches for these are more probably interments of relatively high-status individuals or families who could afford to secure themselves a prestigious grave close to an altar or other devotional focus. While family groups can provide good evidence for possible genetic disorders and the like, they do not offer the same demographic spread as the large external cemeteries. Good examples of church burials have been identified in the recent major excavation within the parish church of St Nicholas at Aberdeen, where 924 burials were discovered; the parish church at Cockpen in Lothian where burials were identified but not excavated; Glasgow Cathedral where eighty-four interments were revealed; and what appear to be local lay burials in the churches of the Carmelite convents at Linlithgow and Perth.[5] A final class of burial where significant numbers of individuals have now been excavated is from purely monastic contexts, most notably from the excavations at Jedburgh Abbey, but these by their very nature tend to comprise very distinctive and essentially atypical populations.[6]

As well as the obvious evidence for healed or unhealed bone trauma and other non-infection-associated damage to bony tissues, skeletons have provided abundant evidence for a broad range of diseases which affected the children and adults of medieval Scotland. Among the most obvious are those which leave traces of 'metabolic insult', childhood illnesses which produced sufficient stress in the sufferer to affect the normal growth pattern of the child and leave distinctive signatures in the child's bones. Analysis of teeth from adult skeletons, for example, can show evidence of such stress in the tooth enamel which is laid down during childhood and not developed subsequently with the growth of the rest of the body. Defects, known as enamel hypoplasia, reveal that many individuals became exposed to hazards during infancy and up to around age four which resulted in significant 'metabolic insults'. Two main causes of this trend are suggested: increased exposure to infections as a consequence of loss of antibody protection from the mother's milk following weaning, and greater exposure to hard-and soft-tissue trauma, and subsequent infection, among crawling and toddling infants. There is a growing body of evidence to suggest that individuals with the most pronounced hypoplasia rarely lived into young adulthood, that is, beyond age twenty-five.[7] At Glasgow Cathedral, 17 per cent of burials with surviving teeth were identified as having enamel hypoplasia which might suggest that the kind of metabolic shocks which produced the effect were not simply indicators of poverty, for the burials within the building probably come from the more affluent segments of medieval Glaswegian society.[8] A second major marker of traumatic growth disturbance is the presence of so-called Harris lines in the long bones of the body, such as the major leg bones. These show up as horizontal plates of denser material within the bone structure. In the excavations at the Carmelite friary in Aberdeen, eighteen out of twenty-three adult skeletons and sixteen child skeletons were found to have Harris lines. Taken together, such physical evidence indicates that childhood for a significant number of individuals in the urban population of medieval Scotland was scarred by recurring episodes of extreme illness which affected

Figure 9.1 *Medieval cemetery at Whithorn, Galloway, which contained individuals of all ages and revealed evidence for levels of nutrition and physical deterioration owing to the rigours of hard work and the consequences of infection, as well as the risks of pregnancy and childbirth. R. Oram.*

their physical growth and future life expectancy. For many, it seems, life quite literally fitted Thomas Hobbes's 'nasty, brutish and short' definition.

Dietary deficiencies cause a range of metabolic diseases whose presence has been identified among the medieval population. Pitting of the surface of the upper part of the eye sockets, referred to as *cribra orbitalia*, is associated particularly with iron-deficiency anaemia. This development was for long thought to indicate anaemia occurring shortly before, and current at, the time of death but more recent research has suggested that the presence of *cribra orbitalia* in adult skeletons was a result of childhood anaemia. It is also associated with vitamin C deficiency manifest as scurvy. The cemetery populations at the Carmelite friaries at Aberdeen and Linlithgow revealed eight child and adolescent examples at the former but no adult cases while, at the latter, there were twenty instances, ten adult (seven female and three male) and ten child (five to eight years old), and at Stromness two child skulls displaying symptoms were identified.[9] These differences in victim profile suggest that not only gender-specific physiological factors were at work but possibly also gender- and age-related differences in diet. There may also be evidence for regional variation in diet, with some medieval Aberdonians apparently enjoying a more iron- and vitamin-rich eating regime than their Linlithgow contemporaries.

Although most infectious diseases affect the soft tissues and will leave little or no trace on bone, some and especially long-lasting or chronic infections will result in bone lesions. The pathology can rarely allow identification of a specific variety of illness but the nature and location of the bone damage can often give an indication of the likely appearance and symptoms of the disease. Lesions around the external ear openings and sinus and palatal areas in the skull, for example, point to severe ear and sinus infections which probably entailed chronic pressure pain and nasal and aural discharges. Several cases of both types were identified at the Aberdeen, Linlithgow and Perth friary excavations.[10] Osteomyelitis, an inflammation of the bone and marrow which is caused by pus-producing bacteria in which the pus drains to the bone surface through channels, evident in major lesions in the form of irregular eruptions from the surface of the affected bone, was identified in one burial from Stromness, two individuals at Linlithgow and one at Perth, and in sixteen cases at Whithorn.[11] Most occurred in lower limb bones, especially the tibia, where the bone is covered only by a shallow layer of soft tissue on the shin and where injuries to the soft tissue can be long lasting, difficult to treat hygienically and easy to aggravate or repeat, which can allow infections to penetrate to the bone and become established. The most traumatic bone damage, other than as a consequence of leprosy or syphilis (see below), is associated with tuberculosis. At Aberdeen, several vertebrae in one child had collapsed as a consequence of tuberculosis infection resulting in massive distortion of the spine, while lesions on the inner faces of some ribs from a young adult at Linlithgow and the vertebrae of two other adults may be evidence of tuberculosis, the Linlithgow case possibly representing an example of the pulmonary variety of the disease.[12] There may be up to five cases of tuberculosis-related bone degeneration at Whithorn.[13] Taken together, the data from these excavations provide tangible evidence for a broad range of acute diseases active within the human population of medieval Scotland. It must be remembered, however, that these cases represent what is probably only the tip of an iceberg in terms of the prevalence and impact of disease, for pathological evidence for infection is likely to occur only where it was chronic and advanced. Many infectious diseases which we know were present in medieval Scotland – such as typhus – either kill the host before pathological bone changes occur or the sufferer recovers in a period again shorter than that in which the infection can leave a distinctive signature in the hard tissue of the body. For such illnesses it is often the documentary record, rather than the physical evidence of the skeleton, that provides the most information.

Incidental references in chroniclers' accounts of events occasionally provide insights into medical conditions affecting individuals. One of the most informative is that provided by the English cleric, William of Newburgh, of the symptoms suffered by King Malcolm IV of Scotland (1153–65).[14] His account of the king's severe head and foot pains, coupled with the soubriquet of 'big-head' applied to him in the notice of his death in the Annals of Ulster, has led to the identification of Malcolm's illness as Paget's disease, or *osteatis deformans*, a condition which involves 'excessive and disorganised resorption and formation of bone', mainly in the lower legs and cranium with the latter becoming enlarged and expanding down over the ears.[15] More contentious is the identification of the illness which afflicted Robert Bruce for the last two decades of his life. For English chroniclers this was certainly leprosy, its visitation on the king being a sign of God's judgement on him for his manifold and manifestly mortal sins, while for less hostile reporters it was an unnamed disease which signified nothing.[16] Modern opinion remains sharply divided.

Among the richest documentary evidence for disease and the quest for a cure is the wealth of material relating to miracles worked at shrines. It has been estimated that 90 per cent of miracles recorded in English and Continental sources for the period 1100 to 1400 involved healing of what we would probably consider physiological or psychological illnesses.[17] The reports of miracles often include details of the symptoms of the ailment experienced by the individual seeking the cure and, while some are clearly generic and lacking in specific detail, others allow for conjecture as to the identity of the disease. Analysis of the forty-two individuals 'cured' by the miraculous intervention of St Æbbe of Coldingham, described in the late twelfth century *Vita et Miracula S Æbbe Virginis*, has shown that thirty-seven suffered from physical maladies ranging from paralysis to swellings and four were afflicted with what appear to have been mental illnesses.[18] Of these

forty-two people, the majority (twenty-six) were female at a ratio of nearly
two to one over males. This ratio is striking in that it is the reverse of that
recorded in respect of most other cults, where males were almost invariably
in the majority. It is also apparent in the case of Coldingham that most of
those seeking a cure were young and from relatively poor backgrounds.
Similar analysis of the forty-two miraculous cures worked at the shrine of St
Margaret at Dunfermline, described in the mid-thirteenth century *Miracula
S Margarite Scotorum Regine*, shows that thirty-six were in respect of what
can be described as physical maladies and six in respect of mental illnesses.[19]
At Dunfermline, however, the ratio was roughly two to one male over
female and from a more widely spread social range than was evident in the
Coldingham miracles. Some cults clearly attracted a better class of devotee
and had greater drawing power from around the country, which is reflected
in the selection of stories for the *Miracula* collections, but it is equally clear
that certain saints were regarded as having particular efficacy in respect of
certain types of malady.

One striking aspect of the various illnesses described in these miracle
stories is the number attributed to some form or other of demonic possession or attack. Both the Æbbe and the Margaret stories give accounts of maladies that appeared after encounters with other-worldly entities – spirits of
the dead, creatures more readily identifiable as the 'bad fairies' of folktales,
Christian demons – who took malevolent pleasure from gratuitously tor-
menting the living.[20] The torments took physical manifestations, such as the
sudden striking dumb of a victim, paralysis of limbs, grossly swollen bodies,
as well as mental derangement caused by demonic possession. We can see in
these explanations an attempt to rationalise the seemingly irrational appearance of illness in individuals who had apparently enjoyed good health up
to the sudden onset of their affliction. How else could such a person have
succumbed to such an ailment if not as a consequence of an encounter with
a malevolent entity? The stories, too, reveal a world fraught with dangers,
especially supernatural dangers, located in places remote from the safer environments of the community and home. There is as much in the *Miracula*
collections that speak of the psychological neuroses of medieval Scotland as
of the physical maladies which afflicted its people.

The fundamental medieval belief in the moral or spiritual nature of
disease – and of the cures which could be effected through spiritual means –
can be seen in a number of Scottish examples of efforts to obtain miraculous
cures for more clearly recognisable physical conditions through penitential
pilgrimages and vigils at altars and shrines. Most of these cases involve what
can be described as 'ordinary people', peasants and townsmen rather than
members of the top strata in the social hierarchy, and consequently their
attitudes and beliefs, and indeed their ailments, can be seen as a reflection of
those of Scottish society in general. The maladies which affected these individuals ranged from the banal to the extraordinary, physical and, clearly,

mental illnesses. At one extreme, we encounter what may have been vari-
cose ulcers on the leg as the subject of one of the cures worked by St Ninian
of Whithorn in a late fourteenth-century Scots *Life* of the saint.[21] This
describes how an Elgin burgess, John Balormy, suffered for three years from
what the author of the text described as 'ye worme' in one leg and knee,
resulting in 'rynnand' or suppurating 'holis'. Neither charms nor the use
of 'stane', probably a stone like a bloodstone, which was believed to stop
bleeding, could end his suffering and it appeared likely that he would lose
the leg. Balormy travelled to Whithorn, crawled into the cathedral church
on his hands and one good knee to the high altar, made offerings there
before having a bed set up in the church where he was visited in a dream by
the saint and a miraculous cure effected overnight. At the opposite extreme
are cases of what the miracle stories present as instances of demonic possession, many of which appear to a modern reader to record neurological
or psychological/psychiatric disorders rather than physiological illnesses.
Individuals struck dumb, blind or left paralysed after some extremely traumatic episode are represented in a number of the miracles but, as revealing,
is the evidence within these accounts of contemporary attitudes towards,
and treatment of, sufferers. Most disturbing, perhaps, is the story of the
young man who had lost his powers of speech in childhood and who for
eighteen years was disbelieved by family and friends who tested his silence
by stabbing his legs with forks, hanging him up by his thumbs or suspending
him by his feet.[22]

THE THREE GREAT SCOURGES: LEPROSY

Graphic though such accounts are, the most detailed illustrations of the
impact of disease on Scotland's medieval population are found where
various forms of documentary record can be combined with the physical
evidence. This position is particularly true of the three great scourges of the
medieval world: leprosy, plague and syphilis. Before the first onslaught of
the plague in the mid-fourteenth century, the disease probably most feared
by the people of medieval Scotland was lepromatous leprosy, referred to
medically today as Hansen's disease, caused by the bacterium *Mycobacterium
leprae*. Medieval attitudes towards leprosy were complex and should not
be caricatured by more modern visions of the outcast leper wandering the
roads on the margins of society, shunned by the 'clean', warning others of
their presence with handbell or clappers, and living off the pittances thrown
to them by the fearful populace. Of all diseases, leprosy was regarded most
widely as a consequence of moral and spiritual corruption, the external
decay of the body mirroring the internal decay of the soul.[23] The slow degen-
erative nature of the illness and its shocking, highly visual symptoms fixed
it in popular belief as a judgement inflicted by God on the sufferer for their
sins.[24] Nevertheless, it was regarded as a treatable malady and not simply

by exclusion of sufferers from the rest of society but by a combination of physical and spiritual cures.

Evidence for the presence of leprosy in Scotland since at least the earlier Middle Ages has been identified in skeletal remains from the Hallow Hill long-cist cemetery in St Andrews. One female skeleton from the cemetery was found to have extreme bone resorption in the upper jaw and nasal region, diagnostic as an advanced state of infection.[25] Evidence from southern Britain indicates that leprosy was well established in these islands by the tenth century but that incidences of the disease increased markedly down to the fourteenth century, when it was probably at its height. It is possible that this rise was linked to the increased level of communication between Britain, including Scotland, and the Mediterranean world as a consequence of crusade and pilgrimage in the late eleventh century.[26] Individual burials of later medieval date displaying evidence of leprosy have also been found spread widely over Scotland. At Newark Bay in Orkney, a thirteenth- or fourteenth-century late-adolescent male skeleton recovered from a sea-eroded section of medieval cemetery was identified as displaying advanced bone deterioration typical of lepromatous leprosy: resorption of the nasal bones and anterior alveolar bone (front upper jaw) with associated loss of the teeth, unfused metopic suture on the cranium, and a large lytic lesion (hole caused by advanced infection) in the hard palate of the mouth.[27] The advanced state of bone resorption in the youth from Newark Bay suggests that he had been exposed to infection from an early age and that leprosy may have been quite common in the Northern Isles at this date. Some support is lent to this view by reports of miracles worked by the relics of St Magnus at Kirkwall soon after 1137, where two Shetlanders stricken with leprosy were cured by the saint's intervention.[28] At the opposite end of the country, one burial displaying physical changes to the bones of the toes, lower legs and spine associated with leprosy and tuberculosis was identified in the fifteenth-century cemetery at Whithorn.[29]

While these isolated burials provide us with a graphic image of how individuals are affected by leprosy, they do not provide any indication of the scale of infection within the Scottish population. Most lepers in medieval Scotland were probably inmates of one of the numerous hospitals that were scattered around the kingdom but, though burials have been unearthed at some of these sites, no leper hospital cemetery has been the target of modern excavation.[30] Strict segregation of lepers from the healthy population was enforced in Scotland in common with procedure in England and on the Continent.[31] In the 'Laws of the Four Burghs', which originated in a late twelfth-century compendium of customary law, clause 58 set out the procedure for dealing with lepers in royal burghs.[32] This clause stipulated that, if the individual had personal property from which he might be clothed and maintained, he was to be put in the burgh hospital but, if he had insufficient resources, the other burgesses would arrange a collection to the amount of 20 shillings for his support. The law also placed restrictions on lepers begging for alms, prohibiting them from going from door to door through the town but to keep to the highway and only to sit at the town gates and seek alms from travellers entering or leaving the burgh. The final part of the clause prohibited any townsman to shelter a leper in their house on pain of forfeiture of all their goods and property. This probably late twelfth-century law illustrates well the mixture of fear and compassion which characterised medieval attitudes to those afflicted with the disease. It reveals, interestingly, the existence in the twelfth century of sick hospitals, as opposed to simply almshouses, in the burghs and the means by which individual inhabitants of those hospitals were expected to be provided for. Conversely, however, it also highlights the attempts at segregation of the infected from the rest of society and the harsh penalties imposed on other townsmen who were found to have, as the enactors saw it, endangered their fellows through sheltering lepers in their midst. Clause 58 of the 'Laws of the Four Burghs' continued to form the basis of official policy towards lepers in Scotland throughout the Middle Ages, and the Chamberlain on his eyre (circuit) round the burghs was expected to enquire of the burgh authorities if they were making the required four-monthly inspections for identifying and expelling lepers from their midst and, if any lepers had been received secretly into the town,[33] but individual burghs enacted further regulations for local application. At Berwick in the late thirteenth century, the Gild Statutes contained an ordinance that no leper, later defined as a non-native of the burgh, was to enter the bounds of the burgh ports and, if any made casual entry to the burgh, they were to be thrown out. If any leper breached this statute, their clothing was to be seized and burned and they were to be ejected naked from the town.[34] This statute emphasises two particular dimensions of attitudes to the sick and the poor prevalent in medieval society: a willingness to look after the needs of their own but not outsiders, and a deep-seated fear of contagion through physical contact with the poor, the sick and their filth.

Refinements of the original 'Laws of the Four Burghs' clause were enacted in the fifteenth century. Parliamentary legislation of March 1428 decreed that no leper was to enter any burgh except at prescribed times – Monday, Wednesday and Friday for four hours between 10 a.m. and 2 p.m. – but not if these hours coincided with markets or fairs. They were prohibited from begging anywhere other than at their own hospital or at the burgh gate and outside the towns. Clergy, too, were charged with identifying lepers, an extension of their spiritual responsibility for the cure of souls, and to denounce them (with the intention that the leper be separated from the rest of society and enter a hospital). Town officials were bound to observe this statute and to act against any leper who breached its provisions, requiring the perpetual banishment of the perpetrator from the burgh.[35] It is implicit within this legislation that the lepers were a recognised element within the community and had their expected place, that is, in the leper hospital. As the twelfth-century 'Laws of the Four Burghs' and the Berwick Gild Statutes emphasise, lepers had their place in society and were not simply outcasts expelled from communities to roam aimlessly in search of alms.

The implication from the Berwick ordinance is that there were also indigent lepers moving as beggars between burghs but that most lepers were housed in hospitals where provision could be made for them. Some pieces of legislation, coupled with the evidence of grants of property for the support of leper hospitals, underscore the 'good works' dimension of alms-giving to those stricken with the disease but also reveal tellingly particular beliefs concerning the nature of the disease and the diseased. In the late twelfth-century 'Laws of the Forests' attributed to King William, for example, it is decreed that the flesh of any wild game found dead or wounded in a hunting forest was to be given to a house or hospital of lepers, if there was one nearby, and then, if there was none, it was to be given to the poor and sick.[36] Lepers, clearly, were regarded as a priority case among those whom it was the spiritual duty of the king to support but the generosity of the gift is tempered when the medical opinion prevailing at the time, based as it was on the ancient Greek Hippocratic tradition of physical and mental condition being dictated by the balance of substances known as 'humours' within the body, is considered. Game meat was regarded as having a heavy, melancholic quality which was considered dangerous for those medically vulnerable, but capable of recovery, to ingest. Lepers, however, were viewed as already beyond hope of physical recovery so it was acceptable to feed them such dangerous meat.[37] Even less acceptable to modern eyes was the injunction that if any pork or salmon offered for sale at a burgh market was found to be rotten, it was to be seized by the baillies and sent at once to the lepers. If there were no lepers at the burgh it was to be destroyed immediately.[38] As with the venison and other game, there was no perceived problem with giving foodstuffs that had been deemed unfit for public consumption to lepers for, as has been said of the practice in England, as they were already riddled with disease, they could eat the rotten meat with impunity.[39]

Leper hospitals were founded in Scotland from the twelfth century, and eventually represented about one-fifth of all hospital establishments in the kingdom, a proportion broadly equivalent to that in England.[40] One of the earliest was St Nicholas's, founded before 1127, which lay close to the shore near the East Sands at St Andrews.[41] The hospital attracted gifts from various benefactors for the support of 'the infirm lepers', their gifts constituting works of Christian charity which would both benefit the inmates of the hospital and help secure the salvation of the donors' souls.[42] There have been several small-scale excavations and watching briefs at the site, and sections of the precinct walls, which enclosed an area at least 100 metres by 70 metres (330 feet by 230 feet), and ancillary buildings of the complex have been exposed but the remains have been robbed for stonework in the past and heavily disturbed by ploughing. What seems to have been an extensive area of burials was found during agricultural operations in the 1960s but all the bone was reburied without archaeological recording.[43] No trace of a chapel was identified but a large building measuring 26 metres by 15 metres (85 feet by 50 feet) may have been the main infirmary hall.[44] The soil structure of the site indicated that much of the large area enclosed by the precinct wall may have been given over to agriculture or garden cultivation, which would accord well with the aim to have self-sufficiency in food production and also to have physical labour by the inmates as part of the regimen of spiritual cleansing that accompanied the effort to provide a bodily cure.

Among the Scottish burghs, there were certainly leper hospitals at Aberdeen, Dundee, Edinburgh, Elgin, Glasgow, Haddington, Montrose and St Andrews, and it is likely that there were similar hospitals at other major burghs such as Berwick, Inverness, Perth and Roxburgh.[45] It was not, however, simply an urban disease, and there were also numerous hospitals in rural locations, such as Aldcambus, Kincase near Ayr, Legerwood, and Rulemouth.[46] Beyond the one hospital at Glasgow and that at Kincase, it is striking that there are no known leper hospitals in south-west Scotland nor are any known for definite in the Highlands, Hebrides and Northern Isles. While there are traditions of segregation of lepers from the rest of the community in these regions, especially in the Northern Isles, the presence of a leper in the burials at Newark Bay in Orkney could point to a less rigorously enforced separation, possibly owing more to the fact that Orkney and Shetland lay under Danish rather than Scottish rule until the late 1460s than to any significant culture difference in attitudes to the disease.

THE THREE GREAT SCOURGES: PLAGUE

The link made in the Middle Ages between divine retribution for the sins of humanity and disease can be seen clearest in perceptions of what has been described as 'the worst disaster suffered by the people of Scotland in recorded history', the first epidemic of plague which swept through the country in 1349 to 1351.[47] In contrast to the rest of the British Isles and most of mainland Europe, where the progress and impact of the epidemic were recorded in a host of chronicles, memoirs and letters, there are few records of the Scottish experience in the Great Mortality as it was known, nor do records of subsequent epidemics survive in significant quantity before the 1500s. Many of the English or Continental records convey a heightened sense of what might be described as spiritual anxiety: fear, disbelief (or perhaps more correctly a questioning of belief) and resignation, coupled with shock and, in many cases, an outpouring of violence directed against minorities – racial, cultural and socio-economic.[48] Most of the few Scottish references are distinctly more prosaic and matter of fact than such foreign accounts. The nearest contemporary account of the Scottish experience occurs in the so-called *Gesta Annalia II* portion of the work attributed traditionally to John of Fordun. The account is straightforward in its reporting of the scale of the epidemic and the mortality: 'nearly a third of mankind were thereby made to pay the debt of nature'.[49] The cause and nature of the disease, however, needed no rationalisation: it was 'by God's will' that humanity had been afflicted in this way. In the early fifteenth century, Abbot Walter Bower of Inchcolm expanded upon the *Gesta Annalia II* report, commenting that such plagues 'occurred from time to time because of the sins of mankind'.[50] Later that century, the link between human sinfulness and divinely inflicted punishments was still being made explicitly in literary works connected to the plague, like Robert Henrysson's 'Prayer for the Pest', a prayer poem written in the 1480s.[51] For Henrysson, the visitation of plague was God's judgement on a sinful society: 'our syn is all the cause of this'.

The *Gesta Annalia II* and Bower accounts provide some additional information on the physical impact of the plague. According to the *Gesta Annalia* text, the symptoms were marked by a 'strange and unwonted kind of death' where 'the flesh of the sick was somehow puffed out and swollen' with death occurring within two days. The chronicler added that it was mainly the 'meaner sort and common people' who were afflicted and that the nobles were rarely touched.[52] There is a number of possible reasons for this apparent class division in the victims, with the better general health and lifestyle of the nobility as opposed to the overcrowded and insanitary living conditions of the general populace perhaps being an important factor. But the opportunity and ability of nobles to quit plague-stricken areas are perhaps the most important considerations. In 1362, King David II certainly took himself and his household into the country between Aberdeen and Inverness partly in an effort to avoid the epidemic which was raging that year in the southern part of his kingdom.[53] Bower's account of the impact of the plague is mostly a direct repetition of the earlier text but he added that twenty-four canons of the cathedral priory at St Andrews perished in the epidemic, with all but three of them being priests. The deaths of so many clergy clearly troubled Bower who knew the victims as 'men of ample education, circumspect in spiritual and in temporal matters, and upright and honourable in their way of life'.[54] Shock at the deaths of such individuals, whose Christian lifestyle was surely beyond reproach, was a common reaction among commentators on the plague, most of whom were at a loss to explain why the godly suffered the same fate as the sinful. It also posed a more direct problem in that there was an extreme shortage of qualified clergy in some areas, which meant that more people were dying without the benefits of confession and absolution and, consequently, falling into perdition.[55] For some observers, the mortality among the clergy was clearly a sign of the corruption of the Church and God's displeasure with its state while, for others, it was a sign of how diabolical forces were seeking to overturn the principal bulwark on earth against the forces of evil. From a modern epidemiological perspective, some answers can be offered to the question of why so many clerics may have died. In the case of the deaths at St Andrews, the canons lived in close proximity to one another in the dormitory, ate together in the refectory and prayed together in the chancel of the cathedral church. Close contact seems here to be a likely mechanism for the spread of an evidently highly infectious disease. Bower also identified twenty-one of the victims among the canons at St Andrews as priests, and it is likely that these men would have had a role outside their convent as chaplains and confessors to townsfolk. Such roles would have brought them into close physical contact with their charges and could well have rendered them particularly exposed to infection from the dying to whom they would have been giving spiritual comfort and administering last rites.

Widespread mortality returned to Scotland in 1362, with the epidemic raging from February to December.[56] According to the chroniclers, the level of mortality in this second visitation was as severe as in the first, with Bower commenting that it seemed that nearly a third of those who had survived the first mortality perished in the second.[57] Bower also noted that its victims on this occasion came from all ranks, magnate and peasant alike, whereas in the first epidemic the upper levels of the social hierarchy appear to have avoided infection more successfully. English accounts of the epidemic, however, throw up some interesting observations. Like Bower, most noted that nobles as well as commoners perished on this occasion. Unlike him, however, there was widespread agreement among the English chroniclers that more men than women perished in the outbreak and that the heaviest toll was of younger men and boys.[58] This information could be interpreted as showing that there had been a certain amount of acquired immunity to the disease in the adult population, the nobles perhaps suffering disproportionately on this occasion owing to their earlier avoidance of infection, but the difference between the genders is more difficult to explain and may point to an altogether different disease from that which had ravaged the country in the late 1340s.[59] In common with the rest of Europe, further epidemics ravaged Scotland periodically for the remainder of the Middle Ages, each time with steadily diminishing levels of mortality. The English 'third pestilence' of 1369 passed unrecorded in Scottish sources and may not have reached the kingdom, for Bower referred to the epidemic which spread to Scotland from England in 1380 as the 'Third Plague' and claimed that it, like those before it, had caused the death of about one-third of the population.[60] Subsequent outbreaks, from the recorded English 'fifth pestilence' of 1390–3, passed without comment in Scottish sources, despite the fact that the two main chroniclers of the period, Andrew of Wyntoun and Walter Bower, were contemporaries. As the ending of the tradition of numbering the epidemics in England also occurred around this date – the 'fifth pestilence' was the last labelled in this way – it is possible that folk had begun to accept that, horrific though the very thought was, the plague had become simply another fact of life and death to be added to the catalogue of ills which afflicted them. As legislation from the later fifteenth century and more substantial record evidence from the 1500s demonstrate, plague had not disappeared but had merely ceased to command the headlines that it had won in fourteenth-century chronicles. Although it has been said that these later episodes saw plague become a mainly urban phenomenon, epidemics still struck rural areas as well as the more densely populated towns.[61] The low level of record evidence for the impact of the plague in the first epidemic in the mid-fourteenth century and the consistently understated accounts given of later epidemics have probably led us significantly to underestimate the effects of the disease on, not only the population levels and economic well-being of the kingdom, but also the consequences of these national traumas in terms of public and private religious devotions and individuals' preparations for death.

For many people of all degrees, heavenly protection and forgiveness were the only sure safeguards against the scourge of plague. One consequence of this belief was the development in the later medieval period of cults of saints who were regarded as having particular value as intercessors and protectors in times of epidemic. At the forefront of these saints stood the Blessed Virgin Mary whose cult attained new levels of popularity all across Europe in the wake of the first epidemic in the mid-fourteenth century. She was invoked in numerous prayers and sermons with the request for her intercession with Christ to secure the lifting of the scourge of plague.[62] It is, however, difficult to separate general devotion to the Virgin as the principal intercessor on behalf of humanity from devotion to her as protectress against plague. After Mary, the two most popular 'plague saints' were Sebastian and Roch. Bower's account of the 1349 epidemic in Scotland includes a story of how St Sebastian had been responsible for ending an episode of plague in Würzburg in Germany where death had been visited on the city by one 'good' and one 'evil' angel but where their onslaught had been stopped once relics of the saint had been brought from Rome and an altar to him built.[63] In Scotland, there was apparently particular devotion to the cult of St Sebastian in Aberdeen, where various gifts and offerings were made to his altar in the parish church of St Nicholas. In comparison with England, where his intercession was invoked in prayers,[64] his cult was significantly less widespread than that of St Roch. Chapels dedicated to St Roch, who was promoted from the late fourteenth century as patron of the plague stricken,[65] were located close to several major Scottish burghs. Those at Edinburgh, Stirling, Glasgow and Dundee were sited at the places where the temporary booths to house the infected, who were required to remove themselves from the towns, were erected. The provision of chapels at the plague booth sites dedicated to this saint underscores the belief in the divine origin of the disease and the best source of its cure.

Although a religious view of plague as a heaven-sent scourge for humanity dominated popular perceptions of the disease into the seventeenth century, and most efforts to control or contain its spread involved communal penances, prayers and moral restraint,[66] from the time of the first epidemic in the mid-fourteenth century, physicians were attempting to find a medicinal solution. One of the earliest medical treatises on plague prevention and cure to reach Scotland was Sir John Mandeville or John of Bordeaux/ Burgundy's later fourteenth-century Latin text which appears to have been in circulation in Scotland by the early fifteenth century and, as surviving manuscripts from the monastic libraries of Kelso and Paisley abbeys demonstrate, had been translated into Scots as 'A nobyl tretyse agayne ye Pestilens'.[67] The treatise specifies a series of measures to be followed, chiefly dietary regimes and bloodletting, but still finishes with the request that those who have recovered from or avoided the disease should thank the Grace of God and remember the author in their prayers.[68] The tension between the quest for a physical remedy for what was widely regarded as a spiritual malady, articulated in the twelfth century by Bernard of Clairvaux, was still very much in evidence in the texts of medical treatises copied in Scottish monastic libraries in the fifteenth century.

Scotland's close academic and cultural contacts with mainland Europe, both before and after the foundation of the University of St Andrews in 1412, may have provided an important medium for the northward transmission of Continental ideas on plague control over six decades in advance of the adoption of similar ideas in England. The earliest surviving record of official measures intended to control the spread of plague in Scotland dates from October 1456.[69] Epidemiological observation by physicians and civil authorities in the northern Italian city states had led, in the late fourteenth century, to the issuing of public orders for control of the infected and regulation of communication with them.[70] Such measures revolved around prevention, containment and survival rather than remedy: it would be a further five centuries before medicine was sufficiently advanced effectively to combat bacteria and bacilli. The 1456 legislation provided the basis for all Scotland's epidemic control measures for the next two centuries, setting out basic rules on quarantine, regulations for the movement of people and goods, fumigation and burning of infected properties. How these basic rules were interpreted and implemented was largely at the discretion of the local administrations in burghs, regalities and baronies but there is no doubt that they were enforced, albeit with varying degrees of success.

One aspect of popular perceptions of plague and its means of transmission, common throughout much of Europe as early as the 1346–53 epidemic, was probably present in Scotland from the same time but first becomes evident in records of official anti-plague measures only at the end of the fifteenth century: fear of the poor and their squalor and suspicion that they were spreading the disease deliberately.[71] Society's underclasses, especially beggars and vagrants, who were already subject to strictly enforced laws on their activities, faced even harsher controls which involved the branding and expulsion of all who could not prove that they were natives of the burgh, with potential execution of those who repeatedly breached the rules and attempted to gain unlawful entry to a town. Native beggars were issued with a token to display clearly.[72] Those on the margins of society were useful to employ as gravediggers, collectors of the dead, cleansers of infected properties, and nurses for the dying, for they were considered otherwise to be of little value to their communities. From the initial phases of plague's course through Europe, there was also a suspicion that these groups deliberately spread the disease both as a means of prolonging their economic betterment through the fulfilment of these unattractive but necessary tasks but also out of class hatred for their social superiors.[73] The most draconian actions against the poor in respect of the plague fears of richer citizens, however, occurred in the sixteenth century, and were probably a sign of wider social tensions in a century of protracted religious and political upheaval.

Fear of contagion by human and material carriers of plague drove much of the late medieval legislation. In 1499, the burgh council in Edinburgh promulgated a series of Acts which centred on prohibition of movement of people and goods, modelled on measures adopted in northern Italian cities in the 1450s which had quite effectively quarantined entire communities. The Edinburgh legislation was radical for a community which survived effectively on handling trade, for it suspended all communication and traffic of goods to and from towns and districts where infection was suspected. Furthermore, it suspended Edinburgh's own markets and effectively closed down trade within the burgh. With contagion regarded as the chief means of transmitting the disease, the council also closed all the schools, where children – who were themselves regarded as dangerous, uncontrollable and potentially dirty – could come into contact with sources of plague and pass it on to other family members. All children under fifteen were ordered to be kept off the streets, along with dogs and pigs, three groups who were regarded as the most likely vectors of transmission. All importers of goods, but especially of wool, hides or textiles, had to have a licence to conduct trade and had to be able to be able to provide testimonials that it came from uninfected areas. Failure to produce such licences resulted in the burning of the goods and the possible forfeiture and banishment from the burgh for life of the transgressor.[74] For townsmen harbouring refugees or concealing infection within their households, or visitors who entered the burgh without proof of 'cleanness', the punishments were even more draconian: execution for the former and at least branding and expulsion for the latter.

While there is little evidence of punishments being applied, the few instances that are recorded demonstrate clearly that the regulations were enforced. At Edinburgh, the best-known example was of a tailor who, in August 1530, concealed the death from plague of his wife and attended mass while her corpse lay in their house. On the discovery of this situation and on account of what was regarded as reckless endangerment of his fellow burgesses through coming to church, he was sentenced to be hanged outside

his house door but escaped with his life when the rope's breaking was interpreted as a sign of God's will on the matter: he was instead banished for life
with his children.[75] Two women convicted of likewise endangering their
fellows were less fortunate, suffering execution by drowning in the burgh's
flooded quarry pits.[76] Such rigorousness possibly helped increase the effectiveness of quarantine and reporting mechanisms, which were themselves
becoming more responsive and carefully managed in the early 1500s.[77] There
were, nevertheless, individuals who regarded the measures designed to
protect them and their fellows from risk of disease as oppressive and intrusive and sought to escape from their controls. One prominent case is that of
Adam Multrar, an Irvine merchant, who in June 1500 publicly denounced
the burgh council and advertised that he was quitting the town on account
of what he considered to be wholly unnecessary restrictions placed on the
movement of goods and people, which were hindering his ability to carry on
his business.[78] For many others through the sixteenth century, the response
was much less public and more direct, involving surreptitious movement
of people and goods, and concealment of places of origin. As the growing
body of local and national legislation through the 1500s and down to the
1640s demonstrates, people found ingenious ways to circumvent restrictions
and, as individual cases make clear, many of those breaching the laws were
members of the same classes who clamoured for their imposition or were
active in their enforcement.

Among medieval Scots, as deeply rooted as plague in popular belief in
divinely ordained punishments for society's sinfulness was venereal infection.
Gonorrhoea was probably the only significant venereal disease present in
medieval Scotland until the appearance of syphilis on an epidemic scale in the
mid 1490s and, if the references to it which occur across Western Europe from
late antiquity onwards are a reflection of its apparent ubiquity, it was probably already endemic in Scotland before the Middle Ages. There is no known
equivalent in Scotland of the English legislation of the 1160s which attempted
to control the spread of what was referred to as 'the perilous infirmity of
burning', an allusion to the burning sensation in the urethra which is one
symptom of infection with gonorrhoea, and subsequent measures designed
to ensure the clean sexual health of prostitutes in major English towns.[79]
Documented instances of this disease from elsewhere in medieval Britain and
Europe, however, make it unlikely that it was not also present in Scotland.

THE THREE GREAT SCOURGES: SYPHILIS

Syphilis has left a clear imprint in Scotland's historical and archaeological
record. There is evidence for the presence of some form of syphilis in Europe
long before the traditional timing of its arrival from the New World in 1493
but there is, as yet, no agreement as to whether this was a venereal or non-
venereal variety. Debate has raged for decades over the possible presence

of *Treponema pallida*, the syphilis bacterium, in the medieval European population but excavated skeletal evidence for congenital syphilitic infection of individuals has been identified at cemetery sites dating from the twelfth to mid-fifteenth centuries from western Turkey to Britain.[80] In Scotland, evidence of syphilitic infection has been identified in pre-1493 burials from the major cemetery site adjacent to the cathedral priory at Whithorn and of apparently congenital syphilis in one late twelfth- or thirteenth-century child burial from Kintradwell in Sutherland.[81] This, however, is a mere handful of evidence in comparison with the volume of record evidence for syphilis in the post-1493 period when, if the term 'cunt-bitten' which appears in William Dunbar's poetry by the early 1500s can be taken as a measure of its commonality, the disease and its consequences had embedded themselves firmly in the Scottish social and cultural consciousness.

Regardless of debates over the origins of the disease, it is in the later 1490s and early 1500s that syphilis clearly emerged as a widespread problem in Scotland. Legislation was enacted by burgh councils intended to rid their communities of what was evidently considered to be a new scourge, referred to as 'grandgore'. In April 1497 in Aberdeen, the council ordained that, for the avoidance of 'the infirmitey cummout of Franche and strang partis', all prostitutes should cease their trade, quit their booths and brothels, and engage in honest work for their support under threat of branding and banishment.[82] In September of the same year, the burgh council of Edinburgh took the even more radical step of requiring 'all maner of personis [. . .in the burgh], quhilkis ar infectit or hes bene infectit vncurit with this said contagius plage callit the grandgor', to quit the burgh and assemble at Leith for shipment to the island of Inchkeith in the Firth of Forth 'and thair remane quhill [until] God prouyde for thair health'.[83] Again, anyone ignoring the order was to be branded and banished from the town. It is, however, nowhere recorded how many individuals presented themselves to the authorities at Leith. The disease was clearly already widespread within the kingdom by that date, the Treasurer's Accounts for September 1497 recording a gift of three shillings and sixpence made by King James IV at St John's Town of Dalry in northern Galloway 'to ane woman with the grantgore thare'.[84] The king was passing through the village on his pilgrimage to the shrine of St Ninian at Whithorn, a place with an established reputation of curative powers, and it is possible that the woman was also heading there. Others, however, sought more earthly cures for their infection. In 1509, Thomas Lyn, burgess of Edinburgh, received a respite for causing the death of the chaplain, Lancelot Patonsoun, whom he had undertaken to cure of syphilis.[85] Details of the treatment which may have killed Patonsoun are, sadly, not recorded. That a priest should die in the course of treatment for a sexually transmitted disease, however, returns us neatly to the question of the medieval cultural linkage between physical and moral corruption, the spiritual origin – and cure – of illnesses, and the supposed post-mortem consequences for the deceased.

THE ART OF DYING

One central concern of the medieval population was to have a 'good death', a condition for which they were provided with manuals of behaviour for the dying typified by the *Ars moriendi*.[86] It was important to die fully confessed and absolved, with one's spirit reinforced with the knowledge that you had done good works in life for which the reward would be received in death and the judgement to come. Heaven or, at worst, a season in Purgatory, awaited those who died fortified in the Lord and who had made provision for the hereafter. For those who died unconfessed and otherwise unprepared, Hell's jaws gaped, as illustrated by the English poet Geoffrey Chaucer in the *Pardoner's Tale* in his *Canterbury Tales*, while the fate of particular types of sinner formed the graphic subject matter of poems such as John Gower's *Vox Clamantis*.[87] Chaucer and Gower were highly influential in Scottish literary circles in the fifteenth century, and their views on death can be seen in the works of Henryson and Dunbar. The terror of damnation haunts the anguished language of Henryson's prayer for the removal from over the heads of humanity of the sudden and foul manner of death brought by the plague. Horror at the consequences of the 'bad death', whose victim had not even had the opportunity to repent for past sins, saturates its verses:

> [. . .] that we sowld thus be haistely put doun,
> And dye as beistis without confessioun

Use of famine or some lingering form of sickness, which would at least allow the victim to prepare for the end, was Henryson's plea, not the lifting of the threat of death which the plague presented. Henryson was in no doubt that this unheard of mortality among humans was part of a divinely ordained plan and, consequently, it was in itself sinful to seek to avoid the death which God had appointed for you, but surely God could be persuaded to give the faithful a chance to prepare themselves better for the inevitable end? In the aftermath of the first epidemics of plague in the fourteenth century, the Church had found it necessary to find ways of reassuring the surviving members of families that the souls of their loved ones, who had died so suddenly, were not languishing in eternal damnation but still had a chance of rescue from that fate through the actions of their living relatives. Alongside this reassurance, however, there was still an ingrained Christian tradition of unquestioned acceptance of the individual's unavoidable fate as ordained by God. This fatalism, and a fear of sudden, unprepared-for death, are common motifs in much of Henryson's work and, indeed, are common in much fifteenth-century quasi-religious poetry, such as the English poet John Lydgate's prayers which accept the inevitability of death but seek release from the threat of a bad end.[88]

Migration of the soul at the point of death is a concept that is not unique to Christianity, nor is the belief that the actions of the living can determine the destination of their souls after death. Belief that the living can have some influence over the future fate of the souls of the dead, generally, and concern for an individual's soul's residence and welfare, however, are particular elements of medieval Christianity that did not end at the point of death but actually intensified thereafter. There was through the twelfth and thirteenth centuries a growing emphasis on the ability of the living to affect the spiritual welfare of the dead, to ensure the salvation of their souls and limit their suffering in Purgatory through the offering of prayers and the saying of masses. The clearest manifestation of this phenomenon is the increasing provision made in grants of property or rental income by laymen and clergy to the Church for masses specifically for the welfare of the souls of the dead, marked out by the clause *pro anima defunctorum*. The intention of these grants was that the beneficiaries who were specifically named by the granters should be formally commemorated in the mass ceremonies and prayers of the recipients, either daily or at designated anniversaries. There are hundreds of such grants surviving, typified by this example from shortly before 1248 in which Isabella Bruce, daughter of Earl David of Huntingdon, gave the monks of Lindores Abbey the whole of her property at Craigie (now a suburb of Dundee) specifically to support one monk who, in return, would celebrate masses for the welfare of her soul and the souls of all her ancestors and successors in perpetuity.[89] There was an obligation on donors and their heirs to ensure that the grant was put into effect, failure to do so jeopardising the mortal souls of all involved. Such a situation occurred in the late twelfth century in connection with a deathbed bequest *pro anima* made by William de Morville, Lord of Lauderdale and Cunninghame, to the monks of Melrose. William's heirs, his sister Helen and her husband, Roland of Galloway, failed to honour the bequest and, following Roland's death in 1200, the monks of Melrose clearly pursued their right to the property and raised the spectre of damnation over the souls of the dead men. Eventually, Roland's son, Alan, together with his mother, Helen, substituted property in Peebles-shire for the land William had bequeathed and, in return, the monks absolved William and Roland's souls of their respective sins.[90] The Christian obligation to ensure that a soul had not been consigned to perdition through the omission of others remained a powerful force throughout the medieval period and, in Scotland, impelled men who might be no relation of the original donors to enact bequests that had been made *pro anima*, in some cases decades after the original but inactive gift.[91] This obligation possibly became stronger in the later medieval period when greater numbers of individuals set out their wishes for post-mortem spiritual arrangements in wills and testaments, but particularly after the demographic crisis of the mid-fourteenth century which had raised the horror of sudden and unconfessed death, perhaps of entire families, possible hasty disposal of the dead, and, with no close heirs surviving, consignment of the dead to oblivion from memory and the removal of any lingering chance of salvation.

Very few wills survive in Scotland from before the middle decades of the sixteenth century. Elsewhere in Britain and in Europe, significant numbers of wills from the late thirteenth century onwards are preserved and supply one of the major sources of evidence for the dying or deceased's efforts to provide for their spiritual welfare in the hereafter and, especially, to secure their place in the memories of succeeding generations.[92] The earliest existing example from Scotland appears to be that of Sir James Douglas of Dalkeith, dating from September 1390.[93] This document comprises a long and detailed account of arrangements for his place of burial, curation of the estate on behalf of his potentially underage heirs, disposal of his very personal property – clothing, armour, horses, jewels and plate – around family, friends and loyal servants, and a series of gifts to ecclesiastical establishments, not just for the saying of masses and prayers on his behalf but also to provide altar cloths, mass vestments and other paraphernalia which would ensure his remembrance during the celebration of divine offices. In the absence of wills, there are other forms of indirect evidence of post-mortem intentions. Confirmations of grants of property in mortmain, for example, provide some indication of will arrangements but, like Sir James Douglas's testament, they deal almost exclusively with provision made by the propertied classes for endowment of a chaplainry or other religious institution with income from which to pay for masses and prayers for the deceased in perpetuity. An illustration of such confirmations is that by James IV in 1504 of a grant by Walter Tyrie of Lownie who appears to have been heir and executor of his late uncle, Master Gilbert Tyrie, which bequeathed rents worth £10 per annum from land in Lownie for the support of a chaplain at the altar of St Peter the Apostle in the parish kirk of Meigle in Perthshire.[94] For folk of lesser means, alternative paths to secure remembrance had to be found.

There is a reasonable body of evidence for Scottish burgesses' efforts to secure the eternal remembrance and, consequently, salvation. At the church of St Nicholas in Aberdeen, the gifts of twenty-one burgesses, burgess families and partnerships made between 1340 and 1362 are recorded.[95] These gifts ranged from foundation of new altars and chaplainries (with stipulation that the donor was to be buried before that altar), laying of decorated pavements, painting of murals, gifts of bells for the tower, and provision of images, mass books, vestments, altar cloths and chalices for specific altars. For those who could afford it, a burial place was secured in front of the altar of a particular chapel, where the donor would secure maximum spiritual benefits from all services conducted there. Most, however, sought remembrance and inclusion in services by having their names enrolled as donors or by having their gifts bear their names or coats of arms if they had them. At St Nicholas, Aberdeen, there is a noticeable increase in the numbers of such grants made in the decade immediately following the first plague epidemic. There is a similar burst of endowment at St Giles', Edinburgh,[96] but it cannot be determined clearly whether these two churches experienced an upsurge in bequests as a consequence of any plague fears which permeated contemporary Scottish society. Much more research is needed to determine the chronology, pattern and nature of endowments made to parish churches in Scotland in the post-1350 period before commentary on changes in religious attitudes in Scotland consequent on plague can be made with the same confidence as in respect of England and mainland Europe.[97]

Some of the changes, which seem to be reflected in the increasingly detailed *pro anima* charters and testaments, relate specifically to arrangements for interment. As those in St Nicholas, Aberdeen demonstrate, the intention of some benefactors was for their burial to occur in marked graves close to altars or images. These kinds of provision reveal evidence for devotion to particular saints, strong personal attachment to locations, and close bonds of affection between individuals. They also signal the creation of collective family burial places, the lairs of modern Scottish burial tradition, which both established an individual's place within a lineage but also ensured that all those buried in that place benefited from the spiritual provision made by successive generations of the family. This seems to be one key factor in the desire for remembrance, and inclusion in the thoughts and prayers of the living, that became more pronounced throughout most of Western Christendom in the aftermath of the Great Mortality in the mid-fourteenth century. While there is little evidence from the pre-plague era for individuals – other, perhaps, than kings and bishops – specifying chosen places of burial, such a concern becomes increasingly common thereafter for nobles and even the wealthier townsmen. In Sir James Douglas's will of 1390, for example, he directed that his body was to be buried alongside the corpse of his first wife in the church of Newbattle Abbey.[98] Part of this process, too, appears to have been a progressive development in the use of decorated slabs to cover graves of lesser nobles, burgesses and clergy, several of which by the later fourteenth century in Scotland had begun to bear inscriptions naming the deceased and often giving dates. One of the finest surviving is from the site of the parish church of St James at Roxburgh, now preserved at Kelso Abbey, which bears the inscription HIC JACET IOHANNA BVLLOC / QVE OBIT / ANNO DNI MCCCLXXI ORATE P[RO] A[N]I[M]A EIVS [Here lies Joanna Bullock, who died in the year of the Lord 1371. Pray for her soul].[99] Actual burials in the twelfth and thirteenth centuries, however, tended to be straightforwardly in mass and undifferentiated graves in cemeteries for the bulk of laity and clergy although some individuals may have enjoyed the placing of a small, decorated headstone to mark them out.[100] Interment in graves marked by elaborate tomb structures or in prominent, individual locations within church buildings tended to be the preserve of secular and religious elites. This social differentiation in death was exposed clearly in the great medieval lay cemetery at Whithorn, where the 1,605 late thirteenth- to mid-fifteenth-century burials unearthed in the 1984–91 excavations had been placed in graves which were either unmarked or which may have had temporary, perishable markers, possibly of wood.[101] By way of contrast, the contemporary bishops of Whithorn and some of the major lay lords of western Galloway were buried in graves within the cathedral church, either beneath the pavement in front of the high altar or in richly decorated tomb recesses in the walls of the nave of the church.[102] Research on burial practice in central Italy and Flanders in the fourteenth and fifteenth centuries has indicated that this dichotomy became more blurred in the aftermath of the plague epidemics of the time, with individuals who stood much lower in the lay socio-economic hierarchy, as well as those in its upper echelons, displaying much greater concern over the location of their graves, the form of their funeral service – and post-mortem provision of masses – and the long-term distinguishing of their burial place by the construction of some form of monument.[103]

For the richest members of later medieval Scottish society, foundation and construction of a collegiate church represented the acme of provision for the afterlife. Colleges of priests and chaplains, supported on rich endowments which provided income for their prebends, were employed to say masses and prayers for eternity for the founder, his ancestors and his descendants. Analysis of this development in fourteenth- to sixteenth-century Scotland – the last collegiate establishment, Biggar, was founded by Lord Fleming in 1546 – is curiously lacking, as is study of the alternative form of large-scale provision, chantries within existing churches. In England, recent research has shown the complex decisions which governed the establishment of such institutions and the factors which influenced choices of location within a church.[104] Siting was not random but was selected to maximise whenever possible the spiritual benefits of the wider physical setting of the structure. One of the finest surviving examples of a chantry chapel within a larger church in Scotland is that constructed by Bishop Robert de Cardeny for himself in the two eastern bays of the south aisle of the nave of Dunkeld Cathedral. He first endowed a perpetual vicarage to celebrate mass at the altar of St Ninian located in the chapel which he probably began to have built around 1406, when work started on the cathedral's new nave, within which he was eventually buried in 1436/7 in a splendid tomb decorated with his effigy dressed in full pontifical vestments and with angels bearing armorial devices on the front panels of the tomb chest.[105] The chapel and tomb were separated from the nave by wooden screens in the arcades, the slots which held their fixings can be seen clearly in the piers. As the evidence from England indicates, Cardeny specifically selected the location of his chantry and tomb and provided it not only with an altar as the immediate focus for devotions, from which his soul would benefit, but sited it immediately adjacent to the main altar in the nave of his cathedral, services at which would have been directly observable through the screens from his chantry.

By the late Middle Ages, relatively minor local lairds were also investing

substantially in provision for their post-mortem spiritual welfare. At Clunie
in Perthshire, for example, the Scrimgeours established both a chantry
chapel on their lands as well as paying for a weekly mass in the parish church
where they were obliged to be buried. In March 1529, a Great Seal mortmain confirmation was given to a charter of Mr John Scrimgeour, precentor
of Brechin and lord of the lands of Fardle in the parish of Clunie, dated
27 October 1528.[106] John's charter narrated how his late brother, David
Scrimgeour, had established a chaplainry in the chapel of the Holy Spirit
on his manor of Little Gourdie, which he had also built. The chaplain was
to say daily masses at Little Gourdie and one mass weekly at Clunie where
David was buried. Commemoration, however, continued to be achieved
through other means for those who lacked the resources to do more, following the patterns recognisable at Aberdeen in the mid-fourteenth century.
At Dunkeld the dean, Donald McNaughton (1420–40), was responsible for
the decoration of the chapel of the Virgin Mary in the nave opposite the
chantry chapel of his uncle, Bishop Robert de Cardeny. Among his endowments was the glazing of the large, traceried window which lit the altar, with
his personal arms being depicted on the glass.[107] For as long as that window
remained intact – which McNaughton had no reason to believe would not be
for eternity – the dean could literally rest assured that his soul was receiving
benefit from the prayers and devotions of all who saw his work.

CONCLUSION

As with so much of the evidence for the life of the people of medieval
Scotland, the bulk of that reviewed in this overview of disease, death and the
hereafter remains focused on the upper ranks of society, and perhaps leaves
the silent majority of medieval Scots under-represented. Although their
physical remains have provided us with previously unimaginable insights
into the diseases which tormented them in life, and the concerns of their
socio-economic superiors perhaps point towards the fears which tormented
their thoughts of death and the afterlife, we lack genuinely direct evidence
for, and understanding of, the experience of the bulk of the Scottish population in these areas. That is not to say that they were consigned to oblivion
and perdition by their better-off fellows. Medieval Christianity was inclusive in death as well as in life and, to make a bequest simply for the benefit
of your soul alone, was a selfish act which threatened the efficacy of the
endowment. A donor might name themselves and their families specifically
as the intended beneficiaries but they also extended the intended spiritual
benefits to *omnium fidelium defunctorum* – all the faithful dead. You may not
have possessed the means personally to save yourself or your family from
poverty, sickness and premature death but, provided you died a good death,
confessed and absolved, your nameless soul was guaranteed inclusion in the
collective prayers of all who remembered the Christian departed.

Notes

1 William Dunbar, *Lament for the Makaris* (Edinburgh, 1508), stanza 1.

2 P. L. Allen, *The Wages of Sin* (Chicago, 2000), p. 9.

3 P. H. Hill, *Whithorn and St Ninian: The Excavation of a Monastic Town 1984–91* (Stroud, 1997), chapter 11.

4 T. Stevens, M. Melikian and S. J. Grieve, 'Excavations at an early medieval cemetery at Stromness, Orkney', *PSAS* 135 (2005), pp. 371–93; J. R. Mackenzie and C. Moloney, 'Medieval development and the cemetery of the church of the Holy Trinity, Logies Lane, St Andrews', *TAFAJ* 3 (1997), pp. 143–60; G. Brown and J. A. Roberts, 'Archaeological excavations in the medieval cemetery at the City Churches, Dundee', *TAFAJ* 6 (2000), pp. 32–69; D. W. Hall, A. D. S. MacDonald, D. R. Perry and J. Terry and others, 'The archaeology of Elgin: excavations on Ladyhill and in the High Street, with an overview of the archaeology of the burgh', *PSAS* 128 (1998), pp. 753–829 at 801–4.

5 J. Stones (ed.), *The East Kirk of St Nicholas Project 2006: Initial Report* (Aberdeen, 2008); J. O'Sullivan and N. M. M. Holmes, 'Archaeological Excavations at Cockpen Medieval Parish Church, Midlothian, 1993', *PSAS* 125 (1995), pp. 881–900 at 896–7; S. T. Driscoll (ed.), *Excavations at Glasgow Cathedral 1988–1997* (Leeds, 2002), chapter 4; J. A. Stones, 'The Burials', in J. A. Stones (ed.), *Three Scottish Carmelite Friaries: Excavations at Aberdeen, Linlithgow and Perth 1980–86* (Edinburgh, 1989), pp. 111–42 at 112–13.

6 R. Grove, 'The Human Burials', in J. Lewis and G. Ewart (eds), *Jedburgh Abbey: the Archaeology and Architecture of a Borders Abbey* (Edinburgh, 1995), pp. 117–30.

7 Stones, 'The Burials', p. 134.

8 Driscoll, *Glasgow Cathedral*, pp. 139–40.

9 Stones, 'The Burials', pp. 135, 137; Stevens, 'Stromness medieval cemetery', p. 390.

10 Stones, 'The Burials', p. 137.

11 Stevens, 'Stromness medieval cemetery', p. 389; Stones, 'The Burials', pp. 137 and illust. 78; A. Cardy, 'The Human Bones', in Hill, *Whithorn and St Ninian*, p. 540.

12 Stones, 'The Burials', pp. 137 and illust. 79.

13 Cardy, 'The Human Bones', pp. 541–2.

14 William of Newburgh, *Historia Rerum Anglicarum*, in R. Howlett (ed.) *Chronicles of the Reigns of Stephen, Henry II and Richard I* (London, 1884), pp. 147–8.

15 A. A. M. Duncan, *The Kingship of the Scots 842–1292* (Edinburgh, 2002), pp. 74–5 and note 96.

16 G. W. S. Barrow, *Robert Bruce and the community of the Realm of Scotland*, 3rd edn (Edinburgh, [1965] 1988), pp. 322–3.

17 Allen, *Wages of Sin*, 9.

18 R. Bartlett (ed. and trans.), *The Miracles of St Æbbe of Coldingham and St Margaret of Scotland* (Oxford, 2003), pp. xxiii–xxiv.

19 Bartlett, *Miracles of St Æbbe and St Margaret*, pp. xxxviii–xl.

20 Bartlett, *Miracles of St Æbbe and St Margaret*, pp. l–liv.

21 W. M. Metcalfe (ed.), *Legends of the Saints*, 2 vols (Edinburgh, 1896), vol. 2, pp. 304–45 at 343–5.
22 Bartlett, *Miracles of St Æbbe and St Margaret*, p. 45.
23 C. Rawcliffe, *Leprosy in Medieval England* (Woodbridge, 2006), chapter 2.
24 Rawcliffe, *Leprosy*, pp. 48–55.
25 E. Proudfoot and others, 'Excavations at the long cist cemetery on the Hallow Hill, St Andrews, Fife, 1975–7', *PSAS* 126 (1996), pp. 387–454 at 411, 429.
26 P. Yeoman, *Medieval Scotland: an Archaeological Perspective* (London, 1995), p. 67.
27 G. M. Taylor, S. Widdison, I. N. Brown and D. Young, 'A medieval case of lepromatous leprosy from 13th–14th century Orkney, Scotland', *Journal of Archaeological Science* 27 (2000), pp. 1133–8.
28 *Orkneyinga Saga*, H. Pálsson and P. Edwards (trans.) (Harmondsworth, 1978), p. 105.
29 Cardy, 'The Human Bones', p. 543.
30 Yeoman, *Medieval Scotland*, p. 85.
31 Rawcliffe, *Leprosy*, p. 182.
32 *APS*, i, 'Leges Quatuor Burgorum', p. 32.
33 *APS*, i, pp. 316, 317.
34 *APS*, i, p. 92*, clause xviii.
35 *RPS*, 1428/3/9. Accessed 31 January 2009.
36 *APS*, i, p. 328.
37 Rawcliffe, *Leprosy*, p. 80.
38 *APS*, i, p. 365, clause 48.
39 Rawcliffe, *Leprosy*, pp. 80–1.
40 Rawcliffe, *Leprosy*, pp. 107–8; D. Hall, '"Unto yone hospital at the tounis end": The Scottish Medieval Hospital', in *Tayside and Fife Archaeological Journal* 12 (2006), pp. 89–105; Hall, MacDonald, Perry et al., 'Archaeology of Elgin', p. 818.
41 D. E. Easson, *Medieval Religious Houses: Scotland* (London, 1957), p. 154.
42 *RRS*, ii, nos 202, 385.
43 For summaries of the archaeological work at St Nicholas Farm see the Canmore and SCRAN entries at: www.rcahms.gov.uk/pls/portal/canmore.newcandig_details_gis?inumlink=34312 and http://www.scran.ac.uk/database/record.php?usi=000-000-109-008-C
44 Yeoman, *Medieval Scotland*, p. 67.
45 Easson, *Medieval Religious Houses*, pp. 135, 139, 141, 144, 145, 150, 154; *Medieval Hospitals Gazetteer*, Perth Leper Hospital (unpublished report, SUAT, Perth, no date).
46 Easson, *Medieval Religious Houses*, pp. 135, 148, 149, 154; *RRS*, ii, no. 470.
47 A. Grant, *Independence and Nationhood: Scotland 1306–1469* (London, 1984), p. 75.
48 See, for example, P. Zeigler, *The Black Death*, rev. edn (Stroud, [1969] 2003), especially chapter 5, Germany: The Flagellants and Persecution of the Jews. For contemporary documents illustrating such attitudes, see R. Horrox (ed.), *The Black Death* (Manchester, 1994), chapter V: Human Agency.

49 W. F. Skene (ed.), *John of Fordun's Chronicle of the Scottish Nation*, 2 vols (Edinburgh, 1872), vol. 2, p. 359.
50 Walter Bower, *Scotichronicon*, D. E. R. Watt (gen. ed.), 7 vols (Edinburgh, 1996), vol. 7, p. 273.
51 G. Gregory Smith (ed.), *The Poems of Robert Henryson*, 3 vols (Edinburgh, 1908), vol. 3, pp. 162–8.
52 *Chron. Fordun*, vol. 2, p. 359.
53 Bower, *Scotichronicon*, vol. 7, p. 319.
54 Bower, *Scotichronicon*, vol. 7, p. 273.
55 K. Jillings, *Scotland's Black Death: the Foul Death of the English* (Stroud, 2003), p. 95; Ziegler, *Black Death*, pp. 194–5 and chapter 17; C. Harper-Bill, 'The English Church and Religion after the Black Death', in M. Ormrod and P. Lindley (eds), *The Black Death in England* (Donington, 1996), pp. 79–123.
56 *Chron. Fordun*, vol. 2, p. 369.
57 Bower, *Scotichronicon*, vol. 7, p. 319.
58 Horrox, *The Black Death*, pp. 85–8.
59 J. F. D. Shrewsbury, *A History of Bubonic Plague in the British Isles* (Cambridge, 1971), pp. 127–8.
60 Bower, *Scotichronicon*, vol. 7, p. 381. He reported that it entered Scotland in plunder seized by a Scottish raiding party in northern England in October 1380. An epidemic, the so-called 'Fourth Pestilence', had been raging in England between 1374 and 1379.
61 R. D. Oram, '"It cannot be decernit quha are clean and quha are foulle": Responses to Epidemic Disease in Sixteenth- and Seventeenth-Century Scotland', in *Renaissance and Reformation* 30.4 (2007), pp. 13–39 at 17–20.
62 Horrox, *Black Death*, pp. 123–5.
63 Bower, *Scotichronicon*, vol. 7, p. 275.
64 Horrox, *Black Death*, pp. 125–6.
65 D. Farmer (ed.), *Oxford Dictionary of Saints*, 4th edn (Oxford, 1997), pp. 430–1.
66 Oram, 'Responses to epidemic disease', pp. 13–39.
67 J. Comrie, *A History of Scottish Medicine*, 2 vols (London, 1932), vol. 1, p. 147; *Liber S Marie de Calchou*, 2 vols (Edinburgh, 1846), vol. 2, pp. 448–51. For John, his identity and the treatise, see Shrewsbury, *History of Bubonic Plague*, pp. 139–41.
68 A modern English translation of John's text can be found in Horrox, *Black Death*, pp. 184–93.
69 *RPS* 1456/7 accessed 6 February 2009.
70 W. Naphy and A. Spicer, *The Black Death: A History of Plagues 1345–1730* (Stroud, 2001), pp. 75–80.
71 Oram, 'Responses to epidemic disease', pp. 23–4.
72 Oram, 'Responses to epidemic disease', pp. 23–4.
73 Horrox, *Black Death*, pp. 222–6.
74 J. D. Marwick (ed.), *Extracts from the Records of the Royal Burgh of Edinburgh*, AD *1403–1528* (Edinburgh, 1869), pp. 72, 74–6.
75 J. D. Marwick (ed.), *Extracts from the Records of the Royal Burgh of Edinburgh*, AD *1528–1557* (Edinburgh, 1871), pp. 35–7.

76   Marwick, *Edinburgh Records, 1528–1557*, pp. 42, 43.
77   Marwick, *Edinburgh Records, 1403–1528*, p. 105.
78   J. Bain and C. Rogers (eds), *Liber Protocollorum M Cuthberti Simonis* AD *1499–1513 and Rental Book of the Diocese of Glasgow*, 2 vols (London, 1875), vol. 2, pp. 6–7.
79   M. J. O'Dowd and E. E. Philipp, *The History of Obstetrics and Gynaecology*, 2nd edn (London, [1994] 2000), p. 226.
80   Y. S. Erdal, 'A pre-Columbian case of congenital syphilis from Anatolia (Nicaea, 13th century AD)', *International Journal of Osteoarchaeology* 16:1 (2005), pp. 16–33; S. Connor, 'Medieval Essex girl makes medical history', *The Independent*, Sunday, 27 May 2001.
81   Cardy, 'The Human Bones', and D. A. Lunt and M. E. Watts, 'The Human Dentitions', in Hill, *Whithorn and St Ninian*, pp. 542–3, 592, 598; O. Lelong and J. A. Roberts, 'St Trolla's Chapel, Kintradwell, Sutherland: The Occupants of the Medieval Burial Ground and their Patron Saint', in *Scottish Archaeological Journal* 25:2 (2003), pp. 147–63 at 153, 156.
82   J. Stuart (ed.), *Extracts from the Council Register of the Burgh of Aberdeen, 1398–1570* (Aberdeen, 1844), p. 425.
83   Marwick, *Edinburgh Records, 1403–1528*, 7, pp. 1–2.
84   T. Dickson (ed.) *Accounts of the Lord High Treasurer of Scotland*, 13 vols (Edinburgh, 1877), vol. 1, p. 356.
85   R. Pitcairn (ed.), *Criminal Trials in Scotland*, 3 vols (Edinburgh, 1833), vol. 1, p. 110.
86   Horrox, *Black Death*, pp. 344–6.
87   Horrox, *Black Death*, pp. 342–4, 347–51.
88   R. Watson, *The Literature of Scotland* (London, 1984), pp. 35–8; Horrox, *Black Death*, pp. 124–5.
89   J. Dowden (ed.), *Chartulary of the Abbey of Lindores 1195–1479* (Edinburgh, 1903), no. XL.
90   *Liber S Marie de Melros* (Edinburgh, 1837), nos 83–5; K. J. Stringer, 'Reform monasticism in Celtic Scotland: Galloway, c.1140–c.1240', in E. J. Cowan and R. A. McDonald (eds), *Alba: Celtic Scotland in the Medieval Era* (East Linton, 2000), pp. 127–65 at 144.
91   For discussion of this behaviour see R. D. Oram, 'Lay religiosity, piety and devotion in Scotland c.1300–c.1450', *Florilegium* 25 (2008), pp. 95–126.
92   S. K. Cohn, 'Place of the dead in Flanders and Tuscany: Towards a Comparative History of the Black Death', in B. Gordon and P. Marshall (eds), *The Place of the Dead: Death and Remembrance in Late Medieval and Early Modern Europe* (Cambridge, 2000) pp. 17–43.
93   *Registrum Honoris de Morton*, 2 vols (Edinburgh, 1853), vol 2, no. 193.
94   *RMS*, ii, no. 2797.
95   J. Cooper (ed.), *Cartularium Ecclesiae Sancti Nicholai Aberdonensis*, 2 vols (Aberdeen, 1888), vol. 1, no. IX.
96   *Registrum Cartarum Ecclesie Sancti Egidii de Edinburgh* (Edinburgh, 1859), nos 2–12.

97 For example, C. Burgess, '"Longing to be prayed for": Death and Commemoration in an English Parish Church in the Later Middle Ages', in Gordon and Marshall (eds), *Place of the Dead*, pp. 44–65.

98 *Morton Registrum*, vol. 2, p. 170.

99 C. Martin and R. D. Oram, 'Medieval Roxburgh: A Preliminary Assessment of the Burgh and its Locality', *PSAS* 137 (2007), pp. 357–404 at 396 and illust. 29.

100 For an example of such a headstone see Martin and Oram, 'Medieval Roxburgh', p. 396 no. 3 and illust. 30.

101 P. Hill, D. Pollock, D. Ronan, and A. Nicholson, 'Period V: Priory and Town (*c.*1250 x 1300–1600 AD) in Hill, *Whithorn*, pp. 253, 255–60

102 C. A. Ralegh Radford and G. Donaldson, *Whithorn and Kirkmadrine* (Edinburgh, 1953), p. 31.

103 Cohn, 'The Place of the Dead in Flanders and Tuscany', pp. 17–43.

104 S. Roffey, *Chantry Chapels and Medieval Strategies for the Afterlife* (Stroud, 2008).

105 A. Myln, *Vitae Dunkeldensis Ecclesiae Episcoporum* (Edinburgh, 1831), pp. 16–17; R. Fawcett, *Scottish Medieval Churches: Architecture and Furnishings* (Stroud, 2002), p. 313.

106 *RMS*, iii, no. 759.

107 Myln, *Vitae*, p. 18.

Chapter 10

'Detestable Slaves of the Devil': Changing Ideas about Witchcraft in Sixteenth-Century Scotland

Lizanne Henderson

> . . . that witchcraft, and Witches have bene, and are, the former part is clearelie
> proved by the Scriptures, and the last by dailie experience and confessions.[1]

INTRODUCTION

There was nothing everyday about witchcraft. It was, by definition, an exceptional crime. People could have easily lived out their days without ever knowing a witch or experiencing the trauma of a witch-hunt in their community. The possibility of witchcraft was, however, ever present. The knowledge that magical and supernatural forces were part of the natural world was something that most of society shared, including those who were sceptical about witchcraft. Even the staunchest of critics would have acknowledged the reality of the Devil and his potential influence on everyone, regardless of age, sex, or social standing. For most people, though they may have never personally been affected by a witch's curse, they knew it could happen, anytime, anywhere, any way.

Witchcraft trials can be used as a key to unlocking the everyday experiences, attitudes, beliefs and customs of ordinary people. The confession of a witch by the name of Bessie Dunlop in 1576 revealed information not only about her life and experiences but also of those of the people she knew and lived among. A laird's wife paid a peck of meal and some cheese for a potion of ginger, cloves, aniseed and liquorice mixed with strong ale to be given to a young woman suffering from dwams (faintings). A chamberlain enquired about stolen barley, two blacksmiths were accused of thieving plough irons, a woman was accused of stealing a cloak, and servants were beaten for the theft of various items of clothing and linen from their mistress. Gypsies were denounced as idle vagabonds, leading wicked and mischievous lives, committing murders and theft. A man was advised to cancel his daughter's forthcoming marriage because it would end in her shameful death; she would commit suicide by throwing herself off a cliff. Instead the bride's youngest sister was wedded to the would-be groom. Bessie's own knowledge of charming and witchcraft was acquired from the spirit world, a relationship that began while she was in a state of anxiety, having recently given birth to a baby who was seriously ill and would later die. Infant mortality was high in the sixteenth century, and the loss of a child an all too familiar experience. Her husband was also very unwell at the time, and her cows and sheep were fairing badly. Bessie lived at a time when famine and disease were rife in Scotland.[2]

In 1590, Bessie Roy was out gathering flax in the fields, in the company of other women, when they drew a 'compass' in the ground out of which were conjured 'worms' that told them of future events. A fellow wet-nurse accused Roy of stealing her breast milk, an act, it would seem, of jealousy and, perhaps, a fear of competition that might threaten her livelihood. She was also accused of enchanting a plaid which caused a woman's death, of being an expert thief, and of bewitching domestic animals.[3]

The Aberdeenshire trials of 1596 contain a wealth of information on everything from calendar customs to attitudes towards sex. Folk were chastised for dancing at Halloween. Spells were bought for a variety of purposes, such as for success at fishing, for a happy marriage, to prolong life, to raise and lay the wind, or to cause harm or mischief towards others; for instance, a woman purchased a spell against her mother-in-law. One man could tell his lover that she was pregnant, stating the exact time when the child was conceived. He knew the child's sex and when it would be born. Margaret Bain, a midwife, was able to transfer all the pains and torments of childbirth to a woman's spouse. Another woman bewitched a man to switch his affections from his wife to his harlot. Helen Gray cast a spell on a man giving him a permanent erection that eventually killed him: 'his wand lay never doun'.[4] One woman caused a cow to give blood instead of milk while, yet another, produced a suspiciously large number of cheeses. Crops were blasted in the fields for no good reason and blights affected livestock. The bewitching of draught oxen was greatly feared. People were accused of poisoning food and causing animals to languish through starvation. Mills were attacked by witches, threatening food production, and several individuals were blamed with causing fevers, madness, drownings and death. Some were experts in charming or healing animals or in predicting their deaths.[5]

When misfortunes occurred, witchcraft was considered by many to be a plausible explanation, in much the same way that others might have believed that God was punishing them for misdeeds or for a weakness of faith. While the source of the witch's power was extraordinary and unnatural, the effects were almost always directed towards disrupting ordinary, natural and everyday events. The witch figure, in other words, represented disharmony, imbalance and chaos in people's everyday existence. What made witchcraft potentially even more sinister was that the witch operated from within society, a known member of the community, and was not some unseen, external force but a living, breathing person. For many people living in the sixteenth century, the witch was a tangible reality and witchcraft a continual and ubiquitous threat.

DISCOVERING DEMONS

By the time King James penned his tract *Daemonologie* (1597) Scotland had experienced its first large-scale witch-hunt (1590–1) and was about to embark upon a second major purge. The writing of *Daemonologie* was inspired, at least in part, by James's conviction that the threat posed by witchcraft, to the good and godly citizens of Scotland, was a clear and present danger. Witchcraft had always been in existence – scriptural proof substantiated that – but James was convinced, as were many of his contemporaries, that the 'fearefull aboundinge at this time in this countrie, of these detestable slaves of the Devill, the Witches or enchaunters',[6] were on the increase; 'I pray God to purge this Cuntrie of these divellische practices: for they were never so rife in these partes, as they are now.'[7] And no one was entirely safe from succumbing to the Devil's temptations to join his ever-growing army. God permitted three kinds of people to be so tempted:

> the wicked for their horrible sinnes, to punish them in the like measure; the godly that are sleeping in anie great sinnes or infirmities and weaknesse in faith, to waken them up the faster by such an uncout forme: and, third, even some of the best of subjects, that their patience may bee tried before the world, as Job's was.[8]

James's overall argument seems to rest upon the assumption that, although magic and general superstitious practice had been more a part of the everyday experience of people living in pre-Reformation Scotland, witchcraft and demonic interference were not only on the rise post-1560 but were of a more heinous variety, a product of 'the greate wickednesse of the people'. God was essentially punishing them for failing to adhere sufficiently to the true Protestant faith. In other words, it was the sins of the people at large that allowed witchcraft and magic to flourish. Witches and devils were breeding, it would seem, in the fertile seedbed of community wickedness. In the writings of demonologists, however, this concept was not particularly new, nor was it the preserve of Protestant thinking. For instance, in the late fifteenth century, the authors of the *Malleus Maleficarum* (1486) described witches as apostates, and witchcraft as the worst form of heresy; 'of all superstition it is essentially the vilest, the most evil and the worst, wherefore it derives its name from doing evil, and from blaspheming the true faith'. As for why witchcraft was on the increase, three things had to concur – the Devil, the witch and the permission of God – therefore, 'the origin and the increase of this heresy arises from this foul connexion' between humankind and the Devil.[9] The shared preoccupation of Roman Catholic and of Protestant reformers with purity of faith goes some way to explain the widespread intolerance of witchcraft both in Scotland and continental Europe.

Magic and supernatural beliefs and practices had always played an important part in the everyday experience and worldview of the majority of people living in medieval Scotland. The preternatural world was, at times,

DAEMONOLO-
GIE, IN FORME
of a Dialogue,
Diuided into three Bookes.

EDINBVRGH
Printed by Robert Walde-graue
Printer to the Kings Majeftie. An.1597.
Cum Privilegio Regio.

Figure 10.1 *Front page of James VI's treatise Daemonologie, 1597. Licensor www. scran.ac.uk.*

seamlessly joined to the natural world and could, potentially, be experienced by young and old, rich and poor, male and female; there were few barriers to the supernatural world, or at least to certain aspects of it. What is less certain is how and why the function, understanding and interpretation of such magical beliefs underwent such profound change during the course of the sixteenth century if, indeed, they did. On the surface, it would undoubtedly appear that radical reinterpretation, with regard to supernatural belief systems, was afoot, particularly in the post-Reformation period. But one does not have to scratch the surface too deeply to detect evidence of what might be supposed to be centuries-old folk belief and practice, continuing unabated, despite the intense pressure of religious, social, economic and political change. As Michael Bailey has argued, the post-1500 period is 'most well known not for new systems of magic, but for new levels of legal condemnation and prosecution of magical crimes'.[10]

Among one of the most odious indicators of a detectable shift in attitudes towards the supernatural was the widespread persecution of persons suspected of witchcraft throughout much of Europe, a phenomenon which, on the Continent, has its roots in the early fifteenth century. At the same time, the stereotype of the diabolical witch was beginning to take shape and would, by century's end, be widespread among demonologists and prosecuting authorities,[11] though there was still much scope for debate as to what constituted witchcraft. With regard to witch-hunting, in relative terms, Scotland was among one of the worst affected European nations. In the years between the ratification of the Witchcraft Act in 1563 and the repeal of that same Act in 1736, at least 3,837 known individuals were officially accused of witchcraft, with around half of that number being legally executed.[12] There is a handful of cases dealing with witchcraft, before and after the period when it was considered a punishable offence in Scotland, and there is substantial evidence that witch belief continued to exert a powerful influence over the minds of some well into the eighteenth century.[13] It is, however, with the sixteenth century that this chapter is concerned; the century that spawned the first large-scale witch-hunts on Scottish soil and, it is argued, was witness to a perceivable escalation in fears and anxieties about the power of the Devil and his minions in the world. What I have referred to elsewhere as the 'rise of the demonic' in sixteenth-century Scotland led directly to an increase in witchcraft accusations and persecutions and, more importantly, the need felt by the authorities to introduce tougher legislation – most notably the Witchcraft Act – to combat the growing presence of evil. Alleged practitioners of witchcraft were, perhaps, the most obvious targets but the demonisation process also had an impact upon related supernatural beliefs, folk customs and traditions, notably, in a Scottish context, upon charming and fairy belief. As the fear of witches, and their master the Devil, spread like an epidemic across the land, 'the fairies swiftly became so enmeshed with witchcraft that it is often difficult to distinguish them from Satan's unholy

regiments'.[14] The prominent role given to fairies in Scottish witchcraft confessions and accusations is also discussed, with particular reference to the
widespread demonisation of popular folk beliefs by the authorities, as is the
attack on charmers and traditional healers. Several individuals are investigated, though prominence will be given to the trial of Jonet Boyman (1572)
– a previously unstudied witch trial. The wealth of information contained
in this confession reveals much about sixteenth-century customary practice
and provides a glimpse into the mental world of a convicted witch, and by
extension, the mentalities of her friends, family and associates. The changing
attitude towards the fairies, as evidenced in the Boyman trial, among others,
can be a useful indicator of the changes that learned ideas towards witchcraft were undergoing in Scotland; the beginnings of this transformation
can be traced to the second half of the sixteenth century. King James VI of
Scotland (later, in 1603, to become James I of England) was very much part
of this ideological turn, and his role, with specific reference to his short but
nonetheless influential tract, *Daemonologie* (1597) is discussed, as is the claim
made by Christina Larner, among others, that James imported 'educated
witch theory' from the Continent and, in the process, essentially introduced
large-scale witch-hunting to Scotland.[15]

THE DEVIL

All societies must confront the existence of evil and attempt to solve or, at
the very least, explain the dilemma. In the Western world, the Devil emerged
as the ultimate personification of evil, though the scope and nature of his
powers and influence have waxed and waned over the centuries. In the first
millennium of the Christian era, while present, the figure of the Devil was
relatively unobtrusive, of concern mainly to theologians and philosophers
rather than to ordinary people. The image of Satan the destroyer, however,
began to take firm shape across Europe in the twelfth and thirteenth centuries. In parallel development with shifts taking place in religious doctrine,
as well as a proliferation of demonic imagery in Romanesque art, the Devil
was, quite literally, becoming a more visible presence in the world. Jeffrey
B. Russell has demonstrated that the Christian concept of the Devil drew
heavily from folkloric elements and borrowings of characteristics from
earlier traditions, such as those associated with Cernunnos, the Celtic god
of hunting, fertility and the underworld.[16] Robert Muchembled has noted
that, before the end of the fifteenth century, the Devil was 'remarkable for
his variety'. In Christianity's long-standing battle against paganism 'certain
hard cores resisted total destruction but were nevertheless gradually assimilated, cloaked in a new veil, reoriented in a different context, while retaining
a peculiar evocative power'. Fragments of belief, from various 'demonic
cultures' were submerged within a 'rising tide of theological Satanism' but
were not fully destroyed. Thus, the Evil One took numerous forms.[17] By the

fourteenth century, the negative features of the Devil were greatly accentuated, and his frightening presence was moving out of the ecclesiastical realm
and into the lay world. No longer a metaphorical concept, artistic representations of the Devil and the Kingdom of Hell quite deliberately stressed 'the
notion of sin' to provoke confession. The depiction of Satan and the 'related
pastoral message encouraged not only religious obedience, but recognition
of the power of Church and State, cementing the social order by recourse
to a strict moral code'. Demonology, a 'science of demons', was slowly
becoming defined in the fifteenth century, which obscured but in no way
obliterated folk beliefs about the Devil.[18]

Early Scottish literature stressed the monstrous qualities of demons. The
poem known as *Rowll's Cursing* (c.1500), for instance, described long-tailed,
dragon-headed 'vgly devillis' with glowing eyes and 'warwolf nalis', while
William Dunbar wrote of 'devillis als blak as pik [pitch]'.[19] Eldrich poetry,
which emerged at this time, is full of deformed and animalistic demons, with
horns, hooves, feathers and wings, who fly through the air breathing down
poison on the earth. Curiously, such exotic and grotesque physical characteristics are not particularly acute in the witch-trial evidence where demons,
and even the Devil himself, can be somewhat mundane by comparison. At
least two areas where learned and folk tradition seem to agree is that the
Devil is a black man – though it remains unclear if this is always a reference
to the colour of his skin, his hair, his clothing or something else entirely –
and that the Devil is a shape-shifter, able to take the form of a human or an
animal. Thomas Leys (1597) from Aberdeen, for instance, saw the Devil in
the form of a magpie and jackdaw but there are reports of him assuming the
form of a dog, cat, rat, horse and so on.[20]

The confessions often contain instances where learned and popular ideas
and imagery of the Devil can be separated out as demonstrably distinct from
one another. For instance, while learned tradition perpetuated an image of
the Devil as a cloven-hoofed male with horns and a pointed tail, the folk
tradition was more likely to describe the Devil as quite ordinary in appearance often, but not necessarily, dressed in black with a hint of the trickster
about him. At other times, it is more certain that folk interpretations of the
Devil or related supernatural beings, such as fairies and ghosts, have been
twisted or altered to fit elite stereotypes. There are several examples where
the combination of leading questions and the use of torture forced people to
recount experiences and encounters with the Devil that they would not have
otherwise confessed. The portrayal of the Devil in *Daemonologie* is closer to
medieval and biblical notions of a fallen angel, able to assume the form of a
man or transform into a goat at witches' sabbats. James also classified other
spirits, such as ghosts, fairies and brownies, as nothing more than a guise
adopted by demons. The folk, on the other hand, seem to have regarded all
such manifestations as distinct entities, at least throughout most of the sixteenth century and, arguably, beyond though, by the 1590s, the stereotype

of the Devil was starting to come together. Information about learned ideas of what the Devil was and what he was capable of would have been gathered from the pulpit and probably disseminated quite quickly among the populace. What they did with that knowledge, or how it was incorporated within existing folk traditions, are impossible to gauge.

The role of the Devil in Scotland is a complex one. Descriptions of his, and sometimes her, physical appearance are inconsistent and highly variable. This may have been in part for the simple reason that the Devil was a shape-shifter and a master of disguise. Jonet Boyman (1572) met the fairies; Bessie Dunlop (1576) and Alison Peirson (1588) communicated with ghosts; and Christian Reid (1597) and Andrew Man (1598) claimed to have met an angel. Their prosecutors, however, told them they had met demons. There was further ambiguity about the extent of the Devil's powers – a topic that fascinated and obsessed many demonologists on points of theory though it may also have been an issue for the unlettered peasant on more pragmatic points of everyday reality.

It might be possible to state confidently that the demonic elements, including the Demonic Pact and the corporal presence of the Devil, were of more concern to the prosecutors of witchcraft than to the accused themselves. Even then, he was not particularly well defined until post-1590 and appeared more frequently in cases conducted by the higher courts. At lower levels of authority, including some kirk sessions, anxieties about the Devil, concentrating more on harms done between neighbours, were not as pronounced as those found higher up the legal food chain. For instance, the vast majority of trials from the court of justiciary and the privy council are notable for their concern with the witch's relationship with her Satanic master, reflecting central authority's worries about the diabolical threat that witches posed. What is harder to account for is that, in many trials, the Devil is conspicuous by his absence. Stuart MacDonald's concentrated local study revealed that the Devil rarely made an appearance in Fife, while Joyce Miller has counted only 392 mentions of the Devil in the surviving trial records.[21] The incomplete nature of the records might account for the distortion in the figures, as might regional particularism, or possibly the Devil's presence was so much assumed and taken for granted as to need no further elaboration. He was forever there behind the scenes but not always cast in the starring role. Regardless of whether or not the Devil was featured in the witch trials as a concrete entity, walking among us here on earth, or merely an abstract concept leading the people into sin, both Church and State were ultimately concerned with wider issues of moral and social behaviour. Indeed, the witch-hunts as a whole should be seen as part of a broader programme of reform and spiritual rehabilitation.

It is extremely difficult to measure the level of impact that changes in demonological theory had on the everyday cultural activities and social lives of ordinary people though it can be assumed that the swing towards more radical ideas of individual guilt, morality, and the punishment of sin influenced many to alter their attitudes and behaviour. As an instrument of social control and religious conformity, the ever-present threat of Hell and Satanic invasion was a powerful, if somewhat repressive, tool. In the sixteenth century, as 'Satan became an increasingly insistent presence in European culture',[22] this tool was sharpened by another wave of religious and political reform.

THE REFORMATION

Scotland underwent significant religious change and conflict during the sixteenth century. A Protestant establishment was set up in August 1560, some forty-three years after Martin Luther nailed his ninety-five theses on the church door at Wittenberg in 1517, though Lutheran ideas had migrated to Scotland by 1525. The first martyr to the Protestant cause was Patrick Hamilton who was burned at the stake in St Andrews in 1528. Reformation was eventually achieved under the watchful eye of John Knox (1510–72) who was originally motivated by Luther but, while in Geneva, he was influenced by the awe-inspiring John Calvin (1509–64). Both Luther and Calvin spoke out against witchcraft and endorsed the use of capital punishment against witches, while John Knox most likely had a hand in drafting the Scottish Witchcraft Act.[23]

Encouraged by Calvin's *Institutes of the Christian Religion* (1536; 1559), Knox and his cohorts produced for Scotland a programme for reform, never fully implemented, in their *Book of Discipline* (1560). This work would be continued by Andrew Melville who returned to Scotland from Geneva in 1574 and set down a new system of Presbyterianism in a second *Book of Discipline* (1578) which advocated the setting up of a full system of church courts – kirk session, presbytery, synod and general assembly. The kirk session, in particular, operated as a 'new intermediary organ of control in the social structure' which would have powerful ramifications for the behavioural and social life of people living within reach of the session.[24] Melville and his followers preached that there was no scriptural authority for a distinction between bishop and priest, *episcopus* and *presbyter*, hence Presbyterian. This attack upon the hierarchies of the Church caused some considerable alarm, not least for the young James VI who shrewdly anticipated the dangerous precedent this might set for the hierarchies of State, hence 'No bishop, no King!'[25] And so the Scottish witch-hunts were born during a period of momentous religious change and social reform, and grew to adulthood against a backdrop of political tension, warfare and Protestant extremism.

There has been an assumption that the suppression of popular culture began with the Reformation but there is ample evidence to suggest that the medieval Church also took a dim view of folk practices and belief systems.

Popular plays, carnivals and processions, for instance, had come under criticism by the Church well before 1560, while witchcraft and sorcery had been condemned by the Scottish Church since at least the thirteenth century, excommunication being the favoured punishment for 'witches and all who countenance and protect and support them in their evil doings as well as those who are parties with them in their misdeeds'. The statutes of the Scottish Church insisted upon excommunication for male and for female witches as well as for fortune-tellers and violators of the kirk.[26] That said, the subsequent attack on 'superstition' and popular culture in the years post-1560 greatly intensified as the Church regarded its position as increasingly more besieged.[27] Furthermore, throughout the sixteenth century and into the seventeenth, clear distinctions were being drawn by the elite, including the clergy, between the sacred and secular worlds and many began to distance themselves from any involvement that they may have had with folk culture.[28]

Of even greater significance was the apocalyptic message of Calvinism that folk were living in the Last Days and that the world as they knew it was coming to an end. The cosmic struggle between God and the Devil was growing ever more intense, and signs of the encroaching doomsday, as predicted by the book of Revelation, were detectable on a daily basis, not least the threat of witchcraft. It is a theme which lies at the heart of *Daemonologie*; witches and demonic interference spring from two sources, human sin and the impending end of the world. As King James explained, 'the consummation of the worlde, and our deliverance drawing neare, makes Sathan to rage the more in his instruments, knowing his kingdome to be so neare an ende'.[29] In this climate, anything considered magical or superstitious had to be rooted out and destroyed in preparation for the second coming of Jesus Christ. In fairness, this plan of attack was not originally initiated by the Calvinists but, rather, they refined an agenda that had been in existence for over a century.[30]

It has been observed worldwide that, to legitimise themselves, new regimes impose strict social controls over their subjects. The Calvinist ascendancy in Scotland, however, should not be regarded as a catalyst in the suppression of folk custom and tradition but, rather, as part of an ongoing process. 'What it represented was a period of heightened social control which, in turn, led the Church and State to demand a higher level of conformity in folk belief and culture.'[31] It was the emergence of this new system of social control, in conjunction with changes taking place within the legal system and central administration, that escalated the attack on folk customs and beliefs. In this context, witchcraft can be seen to be just another item on the list that the Protestants sought to extinguish. Witchcraft was, as Stuart Clark pointed out, 'at the very heart of the reforming process'.[32] During the years when witch persecutions peaked – roughly between 1590 and 1662 – witchcraft represented chaos, disorder and evil, and followers of the Devil were the consummate social and religious deviants. Witches posed a threat not only to the individual but to the very fabric of society, to the security of the State and to the harmony of the Church.

The Protestant reinvention of a world in which there could be only the forces of good and evil, while undoubtedly well intended, effectively shat-tered the grey area once inhabited by witches, charmers and a host of magical beings, consigning them all to the ranks of the Devil whose power appeared to be growing stronger than ever. In the late sixteenth century, we can trace the beginnings of a debate over the issue of exactly what powers witches could or could not possess and of what the Devil was truly capable; it was a debate that would rage on until the early eighteenth century, and arguably beyond. What is less clear is the level of influence the academic arguments and musings of scholars, demonologists and clerics had on the beliefs and opinions of ordinary folk and what possible impact it may have had on their daily lives. Did magic even have a reformation?[33] James VI may have insisted that no quarter was to be given to witches, charmers or magical practition-ers, that any kind of supernatural visitation could come only from the Devil and that, 'since the comming of Christ in the flesh . . . all miracles, visions, prophecies, and appearances of angels or good spirites are ceased',[34] but was his viewpoint widely shared by his subjects?

SCOTTISH WITCH-HUNTING

The Scottish witch-hunts were initially inspired by the ruling classes, by ministers and by lay judges who became sincerely convinced that they were engaged in a spiritual and, at times, bloody war between the forces of good and evil. As both Church and State became deeply worried about the levels of non-conformity within Scotland, repressive measures were undertaken to discourage and destroy any unofficial source of empowerment, including witchcraft, that might be recognised by the people. At village level, the need to purge one's community of the destructive threats of heresy, deviance and demon worship took on greater meaning. It was a battle that had been brewing for several generations before the first witch was sacrificed to the cause but, once it began, it hit Scotland like a series of earthquakes – some places were situated at the epicentre of a quake, many communities lay on the fractured fault lines they created, while others were spared entirely from the aftershocks and were relatively unaffected. The first tremors were felt in the mid-sixteenth century and gained in momentum by the last decade of the century. Scaremongering about the dangers posed by witchcraft, as exemplified in James VI's treatise *Daemonologie*, was unleashed, feeding upon the fears and conflicts that frequently impinged upon everyday life. The disappointments, frustrations, jealousies and rivalries of daily existence are often manifested in the evidence.[35]

What was understood by witch, witchcraft or sorcery in a sixteenth century Scottish context can be remarkably challenging to pin down.

Potentially, these terms could mean different things to different people and, of course, their meanings were subjected to alteration as the century progressed. As Stuart Clark has pointed out, witchcraft was 'a set of cultural practices' as opposed to a fixed set of beliefs.[36] Belief is, naturally, an area of historical investigation that is much harder to access than cultural practice. While we might say that believing in witches is, arguably, 'normal', the need to punish witches is 'abnormal'. In the bigger scheme of things, variations of witch belief have always been, and continue to be, around. But intensive witch-hunting, in terms of what might be labelled 'super-hunts', was restricted to a period lasting no more than a century, from the mid-1500s to the mid-1600s, a pattern that fits Scotland as well as most other European nations. The conclusion that magical beliefs in the sixteenth and seventeenth centuries were not drastically different from those of the fourteenth or fifteenth century is compelling. Rather, the 'points of focus shifted and certain pre-existing elements intensified while others declined'.[37]

Richard Kieckhefer has argued for a broad 'common tradition' of magic that permeated every level of medieval society, around which a variety of particular beliefs and traditions gathered.[38] Across the social spectrum, though there were some profound differences in understanding and conceptualising of what a witch actually was, there was not a strict dichotomy between elite and popular belief in magic; such models have proven insufficient.

William Dunbar was not in doubt about the nature of a witch. His poem *The Birth of Antichrist* (c.1507) describes, in the form of a prophetic dream, that on the day of ascension of the Antichrist, he will be greeted by all manner of 'terribill monsturis', dragons and griffins, and the air will be infected with their poison. Also there to meet him are the magicians Simon Magus and Merlin, the prophet Muhammad, as well as a retinue of witches; 'Jonet the wedo on a bwsum hame rydand, / Off wytchis with ane windir garesoun' ['Jonet the widow on a broom home riding, of witches with a strange/marvellous troop/company']. Together the unholy legion will descend from the sky 'with reik and fyre' and 'preiche in eird the Antechristis impyre [reign], And than it salbe neir the warldis end.' The reference to 'Jonet the wedo' is obscure, though Priscilla Bawcutt suggests that it might have been a type-name for a witch.[39] The stereotype of the witch was that she was unmarried or widowed, a reinforcement of the dangers of uncontrolled and unsupervised women. In Scotland, however, the existing evidence on marital status of accused witches points to a majority of 78 per cent married, 20 per cent widowed, and a tiny 2 per cent single.[40] The literary construct of the witch was therefore at odds with the reality of witchcraft accusations. The apocalyptic message of the poem takes it for granted that sorcerers and broomstick-riding witches will be among the Devil's advocates on earth, suggesting that, as early as the first decade of the sixteenth century, the close relationship between the witch, the Devil and the End of Days was well understood, at least in literary circles.

One might expect to find a definition of what a witch is in the wording of the Witchcraft Act. No explicit definition of witchcraft is forthcoming, however, and the word 'witch' does not even occur. One possible reason for this omission might have been that 'the crime envisaged by the legislators was not the thought-crime of being a witch, but the practice of specific acts of witchcraft'.[41] There are, of course, indications of what witchcraft was thought to entail, such as 'abominabill' and 'vane superstitioun' which carried the meaning of dangerous or false belief and, as Julian Goodare has argued, hints at the anti-Catholic subtext of the document.[42] The Act makes clear that no person, regardless of their station or condition in life, should use any manner of witchcraft, sorcery or necromancy, 'nor gif thame selfis furth to have ony sic craft or knawlege thairof, thairthrow abusand the pepill'. The implication here is that magical practitioners were actively soliciting clients and making claims to knowledge that was expressly forbidden by God. The phrase 'abusing the people' suggested that witches, sorcerers and necromancers were, in effect, tricking people into believing that their skills were desirable, even beneficial, but in reality the people were being misled as all such power was demonic in origin. The category of people this most closely fits was the charmers, many of whom provided a range of services including healing, love magic, divination and counter-magical spells. People would not, as a general rule, have sought out the company or assistance of maleficent witches, nor were witches known for seeking out clients. The suggestion put forth by Goodare is that, in placing so much emphasis upon the 'beneficent' charmers, the legislation of 1563 'did not directly intend to punish the witches who were actually convicted during the following century and a half of witch-hunting'.[43] At this stage, the drafters of the Witchcraft Act were perhaps more concerned with what they saw as overt signs of non-conformity and the illegal use of magic, and were not yet fully aware of the lurking menace of the demonic witch. Once the Protestant regime had time to bed in, and as more demonological texts went into print, it would not be long before the focus shifted on to the more terrifying vision of a diabolical witch.

While it is a fact that many charmers and folk healers were caught up in the general panic of the witch-hunts, it should be pointed out that, in practice, they were often shown more leniency than accused witches, primarily because their crimes were of a less serious nature. Although the Witchcraft Act had stipulated the death penalty, the punishments typically meted out were comparable to punishments inflicted on those charged with adultery, abuse of the Sabbath, observance of 'superstitious' days and so on. While the practice of folk medicine was never condoned by the authorities, some level of toleration may have extended to healers for the simple reason that they performed a much needed and highly necessary service in communities devoid of alternative medical assistance. If the source of a healer's powers was thought to be dubious, however, such as through the conjuration of spirits, or deemed to be demonically inspired, such as by the fairies, the consequences could prove fatal. In the sixteenth century, the potential for confusion between the activities of charmers, healers and witches was, arguably, more pronounced among the learned and the literate classes than among the folk at large who may have had a much clearer idea of the distinctions. As Joyce Miller has pointed out, 'unlike witches, who were labelled by others, charmers knew who they were and would label themselves as such'.[44] A witch could be a charmer and might have had an ability to heal as well as commit murder and cause illness but a charmer or a folk healer, though in possession of the same ability to hurt as well as to cure, would not necessarily be called a witch. Furthermore, anyone, from any walk of life, could make use of charms, amulets and traditional medicine without ever being called either a charmer or a witch.[45]

Whatever the potential shortcomings of the 1563 Witchcraft Act, further legislative Acts followed. In 1573 the privy council took the bold step of declaring that witchcraft was to be treated as a *crimen exceptum*, or exceptional crime, and in 1575 the general assembly set out articles that claimed 'the Kirk hath power to cognosce and decerne upon heresies, blasphemie, witchcraft, and violation of the Sabbath day without prejudice always of the civill punishment'. In 1583 it would appear that the general assembly did not consider that enough was yet being done for it issued a complaint to the king 'that there is no punishment for incest, adulterie, witchcraft, murthers, abominable and horrible oaths, in such sort that daylie sinne inreaseth, and provoketh the wrath of God against the whole countrie'.[46]

THE WITCHES

It is exceptionally difficult to obtain evidence of the nature of witch belief, and related supernatural phenomena, in the period before witchcraft was criminalised. There are few traces of the crime in the Scottish records before 1563. It is an historical irony that so often the best sources of information on folk belief and popular culture arise at the very time when such beliefs and activities were under pressure to reform, or when attempts were being made to bring about their outright eradication. There are, however, snippets of random evidence that might allow us at least to conjecture what witchcraft meant to people living in the era before the widespread persecution of witches.

Among the aristocracy, witchcraft could be closely aligned to treason. An alleged conspiracy to kill the king, James III, and his brother, the Earl of Mar, led to the execution of 'several witches' in 1479, a case that bears striking similarities to the North Berwick trials of 1590–1 in that its focus was on treason against the king. In 1510, the Justice Ayre at Jedburgh enquired 'gif thair be ony witchecraft or sossary wsyt in the realme', indicating that there was some concern about this issue, at least in some localities.[47] In 1536,

Lanie Scot was convicted '*de magica arte vulgo* witchcraft' in Aberdeen.[48] In Alloway, in 1537, Thome Fayre was instructed by the bailies to prove his allegations against Megge Rankyn whom he had called a 'theif carling and witche carling' who witched 'uther folkis mylk'.[49] At this early date it was Fayre who found himself in trouble and asked to prove his slanderous remarks. While witch persecutions were extremely rare in this period, executions were not unknown, as three women are believed to have been burned as witches in St Andrews in 1542.[50] The town records of Elgin suggest that some women suspected of witchcraft were jailed in 1559 or 1560 but no details are given. Janet Trumbill of Selkirk was accused, in 1561, of casting a spell that caused madness in another woman.[51] In Stirling, in 1562, a mother and daughter were pronounced guilty of witchcraft and banished from the town, under pain of death if they returned.[52]

After 1563, and until the eve of the North Berwick trials in 1590, the evidence begins to mount, with well over a hundred persons investigated for witchcraft. On top of formal prosecutions for witchcraft and sorcery, an unknown number of slander cases was also present in this period. For instance, on 26 November 1563, the magistrates of Arbroath directed that 'Richart Brown sall pass to the chapell the morne, and ask Jonat Cary and Jhon Ramsay, her son, forgyffness for calling her ane she witch and him ane he witch'. In addition, there are occasional references to witches being punished in unofficial sources, such as in Arbroath, May 1568, 'the Counsall decernit that Agnes Fergusson, witch, suld be put in the pit', most likely the dungeon of Arbroath Abbey tower.[53]

A number of these early trials contain evidence of charming and folk healing practices. Jonet Carswell in Edinburgh was tried in 1579 for curing people with concoctions made from black snails, clay and thread.[54] Tibbie Smart was burned on the cheek and sentenced to banishment for various crimes of sorcery and charming. She was accused of causing the deaths of ten people, including a man who had the misfortune to look inside her purse where he saw numerous strange items, such as pieces of salt, coal, thread, barley, and small bones. She used a well-known divinatory practice to locate lost property called 'turning the riddle', which involved balancing a sieve, the 'riddle', on a pair of shears. It was further alleged that she had transformed into the shape of a 'brok' or badger and had been caught by dogs out for a hunt. She was found later on, back in human form, with the tell-tale sign of bite marks all over her face and body. Furthermore, four members of the Findlaw family were accused of consulting with Tibbie to get revenge on their enemy by 'crewell slaughtereis committit be witchcraft and inchantmentis'. Their fate is not known but the Scottish Witchcraft Act did stipulate that consulters of witches, as well as practitioners of witchcraft, were to be punished with death though it is not common to see it put into practice.[55]

The earliest witch-hunt in Scotland, which involved substantially more than one or two individuals, occurred in 1568–9 though very little is known about it.[56] Slightly more is known about the next large-scale hunt which took place in 1577–8 in the Highland region of Easter Ross. In total, six men and twenty-six women were charged with witchcraft. Among them was Kenneth Ower (Coinneach Odhar), the 'Brahan Seer', one of the best-known prophets in Scottish history. He was executed in 1578 as a 'principal or leader of the art of magic', at Chanonry (Fortrose) on the Black Isle. Several others arrested at the same time survived only to face further allegations of witchcraft in the high-profile trial of Katherine Ross, Lady Munro of Foulis, in 1590. Among their crimes, Lady Foulis and others were accused of making 'pictours' – figures or likenesses of individuals – in butter or clay; these were then 'elfshot' by throwing so-called elf arrowheads, or flints, at them. It was further alleged that she had consulted the elf folk.[57]

Some parallels with the Easter Ross cases of 1577–8 and 1590 appear in the account of the Argyll witches, implicated in a conspiracy of murder, in the early 1590s. John Campbell of Ardkinglass was suspected of the assassination of his rival John Campbell of Calder in 1592 and was therefore out of favour with the Earl of Argyll. He approached the widow Margaret Campbell to ask if, through witchcraft, she could bring about a reconciliation with his chief. Margaret cleverly answered that witches could not help him unless they were fully informed of the facts. Ardkinglass came clean, admitting not only his own guilt in the conspiracy but he also named his accomplices. Most of what is known of the plot against John Campbell of Calder is contained within Margaret Campbell's confession which she gave freely and without torture. In the process, she also provided an insight into sixteenth-century witch belief. For instance, second sight is emphasised and the significance of the calendar is revealed; 'all witchcraft is to be practiced [sic] in the begining of every quharter'. Realising that the harvest quarter was fast approaching, Ardkinglass was eager for Margaret to begin as quickly as possible. She duly promised that she would have something to report before Lammas (1 August). Furthermore, when Ardkinglass asked Margaret if witches invoked God or Jesus in their spells, she replied 'that the witches namit God in thair words'.[58]

THE DEVIL'S GREATEST ADVERSARY

In the years immediately following the passing of the Witchcraft Act there was a steady flow of cases, though executions en masse did not ensue. The first mass trial to strike Scotland, in 1590–1, has been, rightly or wrongly, attributed to James VI, Christina Larner arguing that 'educated witchcraft theory was imported from the continent in 1591'.[59] The events surrounding the North Berwick trials – as they have come to be known – therefore reflect, for the first time, the assimilation of educated, continental witch beliefs among Scotland's elite. In particular, the introduction of the Demonic Pact, the Devil's mark, the ability of witches to fly, and witches' gatherings or sabbaths, are all elements that featured strongly in continental witchcraft theory but had not been known in Scotland before James VI encountered these ideas while visiting Scandinavia. The assumption that James acquired this knowledge while in Denmark has been continuously repeated since Francis Legge first suggested it in 1891,[60] though P. G. Maxwell-Stuart has brought this into serious question. He has found no firm evidence that James ever discussed witchcraft during his time abroad and that, even if he had, Danish witchcraft trials were not particularly concerned with either the sabbath or the Demonic Pact.[61] James's hand in all of this is further diminished by Jenny Wormald who has argued that the Demonic Pact was known in Scotland before 1590.[62]

The exact role played by James in the North Berwick trials and, indeed, in Scottish witchcraft beliefs in general, remains nebulous and controversial. If his actions were to be seen as a political ploy, as some have suggested, then it was quite successful. It definitely gained him the publicity his ego would have craved. An English chapbook, *Newes From Scotland* (1591), declared him as Satan's most formidable opponent: 'the witches demaunded of the Divel why he did beare such hatred to the King, who answered, by reason the King is the greatest enemy he hath in the worlde'.[63]

The aftermath of North Berwick must have made an impression upon James, the target of so much diabolical wrath and treachery, that he was inspired to write a book on the subject. James claimed that his motives for writing the book were primarily to refute the ideas of the Englishman Reginald Scot and the Dutch physician Johann Weyer, in his view the two major sceptics of the witch-hunt. In so doing, he set out to prove 'that such divelish artes have bene and are' and to outline 'what exact trial and punishment they merite'. Written in the style of a Socratic dialogue, it is fairly typical of the genre though shorter than most other demonological works of the period. Its defence of continental witchcraft beliefs, its use as a political tool, and the fact that it was written by a king are what mark this text out from the pack, as originality is not its strong suit.[64] *Daemonologie* (1597) is, incidentally, the only treatise on demonology composed by a monarch and was Scotland's entrance on to the European stage of demonological discourse. As this text demonstrates, church reformers were not the only ones worried about the Apocalypse but James, with characteristic arrogance, put himself at the forefront of the last great cosmic battle. James would also have wanted *Daemonologie* to stand as an example of his intellectual and religious capabilities but, as has been plausibly argued, the treatise, 'in genesis and in content', can be read as a testimonial about ideal monarchy.[65]

It is safe to say that King James is a key figure in the history of Scottish witch-hunting. That said, while James was indeed instrumental in bringing about the full absorption of continental witchcraft theory to Scotland's elites, and eventually to the folk at large, it was just as much the pressure coming from the kirk, in its pursuit of a godly society, that fed the fires of

Figure 10.2 *Prenuptial portrait of James VI painted by Adrian Vanson in 1585 and sent to the Danish Court. © Crown Copyright reproduced courtesy of Historic Scotland. Licensor www.scran.ac.uk.*

Scottish witch-hunting. Furthermore, the preconditions for a widespread acceptance and adoption of demonological theory were already present. And this can be evidenced by the demonisation of fairy belief from at least the 1570s, as exemplified in the trial of Jonet Boyman, among others.

JONET BOYMAN

The rise of the demonic can be traced in the Scottish witch trials, particularly through the evidence of fairy belief, but it can also be shown to predate the king's visit to Denmark or the North Berwick trials of the early 1590s. An association between fairies and the Devil was being drawn among some authorities at least twenty years earlier and was, I am suggesting, a precondition that allowed for the full crystallisation of continental witchcraft theory – specifically, the importance of the Devil and the Demonic Pact – so quickly after James's return to Scotland.

The trial of Jonet Boyman is particularly illuminating in this regard, providing evidence of an emerging overlap between witch and fairy beliefs, while representing one of the earliest and most highly detailed of such accounts. Most importantly, this trial supplies confirmation that fairy beliefs, not to mention the accused witches themselves, were undergoing a demonic transformation well in advance of the creation and adoption of a new, learned, witch stereotype, and before the absorption of continental witchcraft beliefs had taken root in Scotland. The so-called 'cumulative concept of witchcraft', as postulated by Brian Levack, was still in its infancy, in a Scottish context at least, and would not fully develop for another decade and a half.[66] This trial is, however, indicative of the demonisation process taking place and the growing awareness of the rise of demonic power infiltrating the world. Furthermore, this account potentially has more to do with contemporary folk belief and charming practice than with intellectual theories about witches and demonology.[67]

The trial of Jonet Boyman is the first Scottish witch trial, so far, for which a detailed indictment has been found and is one of the richest accounts of sixteenth-century Scottish witch and fairy belief as well as charming practices. Condemned as 'ane wyss woman that culd mend diverss seikness and bairnis that are tane away with the faryie men and wemin [changelings]', she was charged with witchcraft, sorcery, charming and diabolical incantation. Proceedings against her were first lodged in 1570 and came to an unfortunate conclusion with her execution on 29 December 1572. It is not certain where Jonet actually came from, one source claiming she was from Ayrshire, but her place of residence is given as the Cowgate, in Edinburgh, in the trial document. Her age is unrecorded though it is known that she was married to William Steill. The record strongly suggests that she was a practising healer, and a fairly popular one at that. Many charmers claimed to have inherited their abilities from a family member, or acquired them from some sort of supernatural encounter. For instance, Christiane Lewingston (1597) from Leith confessed she could cure a variety of ailments and had some psychic ability as a result of information obtained from the fairies via her daughter. In the course of Jonet's confession, she revealed that her ability to heal people was learned, or taught, from a woman in the Potterrow who had once cured her.[68]

The significance of holy or healing wells to everyday life is evidenced in this account. Wells were often regarded as liminal places where the natural and supernatural worlds intersected. Jonet made contact with the other-world at an 'elrich well' on the south side of Arthur's Seat. Here she uttered 'Incantations and Invocations' of the 'evill spreits quhome she callit upon for to come to show and declair' what would happen to her patients. To bring forth the spirits, she would conjure 'ane grit blast' like a whirlwind out of which there appeared the shape of a man who stood on the other side of the well, a further hint at the liminality involved in this ritual. She stood accused of performing this 'diabolicall incantation' to cure a sick man by the name of Allan Anderson. After raising the spirit, she commanded it in the name of the father, the son, King Arthur and 'quene Elspeth', to reveal to her the method of curing Allan. Elaborate instructions were relayed to Jonet who later communicated them to Allan's wife; mostly they involved procedures surrounding washing the ill man's shirt. That same night, on the hour of midnight, there came to the Anderson household a 'grit wind', that shook the foundations of the house, and a 'grit dyn', like the sound of hammers banging on the walls. A herd of horses galloped around the house creating further noise and general disturbance. The couple, terrified by their ordeal, consulted Jonet once again but she offered no sympathy, reproving the man's wife for not following the instructions properly. Her failure to do so would result in Allan being 'ane cripill all his dayes'. The ritual of cleaning the sark [shirt] was once more carried out, this time with the assistance of their servant woman, but must have failed again for, on the second night, the house was plagued, as before, with an almighty din. Though the Andersons' experience was traumatic, it presumably worked, as Allan recovered. However, Only three years later, however, he fell ill again but this time the prognosis was not good.

Jonet was sent for but, unfortunately, she could do nothing to help him this time as it was past Halloween, the time of the year when the 'good neighbours', or fairies, arose, and she had more acquaintance with them on that day than on any other. After Allan's passing, the wife remarried and bore a son with her new husband. Shortly after the birth, Jonet saw her with the newborn but warned her to 'tak the paine to foster that barne for it hes not ane hart and can not life'. It might be guessed that either the child did not have the heart to live or, more likely (since 'hart' in Scots can also mean stomach), it was not hungry enough and was failing to suck or breastfeed. When the child subsequently died, Jonet was asked how she could foretell his fate. She answered 'it had gottin ane blast of evill wind for the moder had not sanit [blessed] it well aneuch' before leaving the house, and so the 'sillyie wychs' – or seelie wichts, another term for the fairies – had found it unsained, or unblessed, and it was 'tane away'. As was common in fairy attacks, they had given the hapless infant the 'blast' and, perhaps, stolen it away to fairy-land. The loss of a child is never easy, and it might be safe to assume that grieving parents took some solace in the explanation that their little one was living on in the realm of the fairies. Jonet said that she had witnessed the evil blast at least twenty times over her career. There may also be overtones here of the changeling phenomenon though this is not specifically mentioned.[69]

The 'evill blast' and whirlwinds created by the fairies seem to have led one unfortunate woman, who lived with her son at Newbattle, to take her own life. The specifics surrounding this incident are vague but Jonet told her interrogators that the woman hanged herself following such an attack. Furthermore, the woman was not allowed burial in the kirk yard, as she was a suicide, but was buried in 'ane litill chapill', though her precise meaning is unclear.

The confession contains quite a lot of details about her life as a 'wyss woman' and some of her charming methods. On one occasion she boiled woodbine leaves in a kettle of water while reciting a prayer; 'Blist Benedicte In the name of ye fader and the holye gost king arthor and dame elspeth'. She also described how she could use a person's sark or shirt to diagnose and cure illness. On the noon hour, she took the shirt to the 'eldrich well' at St Leonard's and would summon a spirit through the recitation of prayers to come and remove the sickness. She describes the fairy man she encoun-tered on one such occasion as 'wele anewch cled . . . wele faceit wt ane baird [beard]'. He stood on the other side of the well from her and, though he seems to have been a good-looking man, when he turned to depart she said he was wasted like a stick when seen from behind.

Halloween was apparently Jonet's time to communicate with the other-world. Despite the fact that all holidays, festivals and saints days had been banned by the Protestant church, it is quite common to find convicted witches referring to significant dates, emphasising the importance of calendar customs in people's daily lives. Bessie Dunlop (1576) spoke of Candlemas, and Christine Douglas (1579), a married woman who lived in Leith, was investigated for conversation with the Devil at Easter.[70] Katherine Ross (1590) highlighted Halloween and Midsummer, while Euphemia Makcalzane (1591), of the infamous North Berwick coven, was indicted, among other things, for attending a gathering at the Fairy Hills, at Newhaven, on Lammas (1 August). Aberdeenshire witch, Margaret Og (1597), was caught by the minister, casting water from a stream over her head and sweeping the dew on the first Monday of the raith (which is the First Quarter of the Year) which he said was 'plane witchcraft and devilry and is one of the chief ceremonies thereof'.[71]

There is fragmentary evidence that Jonet was a recusant, though whether knowingly or unknowingly is unclear as similar suggestive traces are found in several witchcraft and charming confessions throughout the whole period of the witch-hunts. Indeed, it has been argued, that a 'principal source of charms were prayers of the pre-Reformation church'.[72] Some of Jonet's charms involved prayers, one of which began 'Blist Benedicite' an indication of the continued usage of Catholic prayers surviving in folk medicinal practice. The charge she used to summon spirits and fairies, 'in the name of the father, the son, king Arthur and queen Elspeth' is intriguing and might be interpreted as an inversion of the Holy Trinity. The connection between invoking King Arthur, at a well on Arthur's Seat, would suggest that she is referring to Arthurian legend but the personage of queen or dame Elspeth is obscure.

Jonet was pronounced guilty of being a common and notorious witch, charmer and sorcerer. She was burned as a wise woman who knew how to heal diverse sicknesses with a particular ability in curing children that had been 'taken away' by fairy men and women. She was condemned for her conversation, familiarity and speech with the fairy folk, or as her prosecutors put it, evil spirits. The Devil is not specifically mentioned but, at root, her interrogators were almost certainly trying to determine the source of her occult knowledge. Her crimes were against God from whom she had drawn the hearts of the people away but were also against the people whom she stood accused of tricking 'under cullor and pretence of medecine'. While traces of the demonic are undoubtedly present, it is not nearly as intrusive as it would become in a much better-known case that took place only four years later, that of Bessie Dunlop, from Ayrshire, who was strangled and burned in 1576.

The Dunlop trial has been investigated more fully elsewhere (see note 2) so only a few points will be made to illustrate its relevance here. There are numerous instances in Bessie's confession where statements made about fairies and witches overlap. For instance, her contact with the other-world and the source of her healing powers were through her acquaintance with Thomas Reid, a man who had been dead for twenty-nine years and who now lived with the fairies. On the noon hour she was introduced to twelve of his acquaintances from fairyland; the eight women and four men she met were 'gude wychtis that wynnit in the Court of Elfame'. On another occasion, and notably during the birth of her child, she met the queen of Elfland herself who came to her door and predicted the death of her newborn infant. Childbirth was widely understood to be a time fraught with difficulties and dangers, from a purely medical point of view but also, potentially, when women and children were vulnerable to supernatural attacks as well. An interesting passage in the confession seems to suggest discontentment with the new Reformed faith and its aversion to folk belief. When she was questioned for her opinion on the 'new law', she replied that she had spoken with her fairy contact on the matter and he had advised that the new law was not good and the 'old faith', Roman Catholicism, should come back again, though not as it was before. Perhaps Bessie was looking back affectionately to the pre-Reformation days when life was not so risky for someone with her beliefs and talents. It may also be a tiny glimpse into contemporary attitudes, fears and doubts that were circulating among the people who were attempting to come to terms with, and adapt to, the changes taking place around them though not always, at least in Bessie's case, successfully. The fact that Bessie was not blamed for causing harm to anyone, or that her clients included persons of relatively high social standing, did nothing to sway her prosecutors from finding her guilty of using 'sorcerie, witchcraft, and incantatioune, with invocatioun of spretis of the devill; continewand in familiaritie with thame, at all sic tymes as sche thought expedient'. Furthermore, when given the choice to join Thomas Reid and enter the fairy ranks, she refused. Nor did she abjure her faith or reject her baptism. In other words, it was her relationship with fairies, and a ghost, that was now considered criminal behaviour, punishable by death.[73]

CONCLUSION

The death sentences bestowed upon Jonet Boyman and Bessie Dunlop were exceedingly harsh, given that both women were essentially 'white witches' or charmers who never actually hurt anyone. On the contrary, both were consulted, on a regular basis, primarily for their superior healing abilities. What seems to have condemned both of these poor souls to the fire was the fact that they could summon ghosts and were in communication with the fairies from whom they acquired their occult knowledge. The fusion between folk belief and learned witchcraft theory was underway and there was no going back. The demonic seed, so to speak, had been planted and took hold like an unwelcome weed in the garden.

As for James, surely no one man – even though he was a king – could be held entirely responsible for bringing witch 'panics' to Scotland. The conditions had to be right in the first place. Also, it is highly probable that members of the judicial, religious, social and political elites already had some knowledge of the Demonic Pact, and other such continental notions about witches, well before 1590. There would have been other channels of information available to them besides the king's trip to Denmark.[74] I do agree with Lawrence Normand and Gareth Roberts, however, who suggest that 'an important effect of the North Berwick trials and the publications it generated, _News from Scotland_ and _Demonology_, was that it schooled people at various levels of society in a theory of witchcraft and a knowledge of its practices'.[75]

The impact of changing ideas about the nature of witchcraft upon everyday life was immense. As elite society and theological circles took an increasing interest in rooting out diabolical activities in their midst, people at village level had to avert the possible maledictions of witches but also avoid falling under suspicion of witchcraft themselves. Activities and opinions that had once been tolerated, albeit grudgingly, were now punishable offences. It can no longer be assumed, however, that learned ideas about the Devil and educated witchcraft theory in general caused the witch-hunts but rather 'the reverse is much more likely to have been true'.[76] An intermingling of belief, at all levels of society, helped to mould and shape demonic conceptualisations and discourse. Robin Briggs described the European witch-hunts as 'a coalescence between longstanding popular beliefs and the agencies for enforcing social and religious conformity'. Such a statement could easily be applied to Scotland in the last three or four decades of the sixteenth century. The structures of the Protestant church were spreading throughout predominantly lowland regions of the country, and the kirk sessions began, in part, to function as a sort of moral police force, guiding their parishioners away from sin, superstition, unlawful sex and corruption. Meanwhile, both Church and State grew increasingly worried about the possible dangers posed by Satan's trusted minions, the witches, and began to see themselves as involved in a battle to save souls and protect God and country against the forces of evil. Changes taking place within the legal system, the use of torture, harvest failure and plague, are issues that are also of great importance to the way in which witch-hunting evolved.

Notes

1 King James VI and I, *Daemonologie, 1597*, G. B. Harrison (ed.) (London, 1924), p. 2. A version of this paper, 'Rise of the Demonic: Changing Ideas about Witchcraft in Sixteenth Century Scotland', was presented at the *Sixteenth Century Studies Conference*, Geneva, Switzerland, 28–30 May 2009.

2 Lizanne Henderson, 'Witch, Fairy and Folktale Narratives in the Trial of Bessie Dunlop', in Lizanne Henderson (ed.), *Fantastical Imaginations: The Supernatural in Scottish History and Culture* (Edinburgh, 2009), pp. 141–66.

3 Trial of Bessie Roy (1590), Robert Pitcairn (ed.), *Ancient Criminal Trials in Scotland*, 1488–1624, 4 vols (Edinburgh, 1833).

4 Edward J. Cowan, 'Witch Persecution and Folk Belief in Lowland Scotland: The Devil's Decade', in Julian Goodare, Lauren Martin and Joyce Miller (eds), *Witchcraft and Belief in Early Modern Scotland* (Basingstoke, 2008), pp. 71–94.

5 *Miscellany of the Spalding Club*, 5 vols (Aberdeen, 1844–52). See also Cowan, 'The Devil's Decade'.

6 James VI, *Daemonologie*, p. xi.

7 James VI, *Daemonologie*, p. 81.

8 James VI, *Daemonologie*, p. 47.

9 Heinrich Kramer and Jacob Sprenger, *The Malleus Maleficarum*, Montague Summers, trans. (New York, [1486] 1971), part 1, question 2, p. 20.

10 Michael Bailey, 'The Age of Magicians', in *Magic, Ritual and Witchcraft* 3/1 (2008), pp. 1–28.

11 Bailey, 'The Age of Magicians', p. 16.
12 *The Survey of Scottish Witchcraft Database* at www.arts.ed.ac.uk/witches/ provides the most up-to-date figures on Scottish witch trials.
13 Edward J. Cowan and Lizanne Henderson, 'The Last of the Witches? The Survival of Scottish Witch Belief', in Julian Goodare (ed.), *The Scottish Witch-Hunt in Context* (Manchester and New York, 2002), pp. 198–217.
14 Lizanne Henderson and Edward J. Cowan, *Scottish Fairy Belief: A History* (East Linton, 2001; repr. Edinburgh, 2007), esp. chapter 4.
15 Christina Larner, *Enemies of God: The Witch-Hunt in Scotland* (Edinburgh, [1981] 2000), pp. 69, 198.
16 Jeffrey B. Russell, *Lucifer: The Devil in the Middle Ages* (Ithaca and London, 1984), pp. 62–87.
17 Robert Muchembled, *A History of the Devil from the Middle Ages to the Present Day* (Cambridge, 2003), p. 16.
18 Muchembled, *History of the Devil*, pp. 23–4, 35.
19 W. Tod Ritchie (ed.), *The Bannatyne Manuscript*, 4 vols (Edinburgh, 1928–34), vol. 2, pp. 282–3; Priscilla Bawcutt, 'Elrich Fantasyis in Dunbar and Other Poets', in J. Derrick McClure and Michael R. G. Spiller (eds), *Bryght Lanternis: Essays on the Language and Literature of Medieval and Renaissance Scotland* (Aberdeen, 1989), pp. 162–78.
20 Thomas Leys, *Miscellany of the Spalding Club*, vol. 1, pp. 83–4, 97–101.
21 Stuart MacDonald, 'The Devil in Fife Witchcraft Cases', in Goodare, *Scottish Witch-Hunt in Context*, pp. 33–50; Stuart MacDonald, *The Witches of Fife: Witch-Hunting in a Scottish Shire, 1560–1710* (East Linton, 2002), pp. 180–1; Lauren Martin, 'The Devil and the Domestic: Witchcraft, Quarrels and Women's Work in Scotland', in Goodare, *Scottish Witch-Hunt in Context*, p. 77; Joyce Miller, 'Men in Black: Appearances of the Devil in Early Modern Scottish Witchcraft Discourse', in Goodare, *Witchcraft and Belief in Early Modern Scotland*, pp. 144–65.
22 Muchembled, *History of the Devil*, p. 35.
23 On the authorship of the Act see Julian Goodare, 'The Scottish Witchcraft Act', in *Church History* 74 (2005), pp. 39–67.
24 Larner, *Enemies of God*, pp. 55–6. On the Kirk Session see Anne Gordon, *Candie for the Foundling* (Edinburgh, 1992).
25 Henderson and Cowan, *Scottish Fairy Belief*, pp. 110–11.
26 D. Patrick (ed.), *Statutes of the Scottish Church, 1225–1559* (SHS, 1907), pp. 4, 6, 26, 75.
27 Henderson and Cowan, *Scottish Fairy Belief*, p. 108.
28 Henderson and Cowan, *Scottish Fairy Belief*, p. 113.
29 James VI, *Daemonologie*, p. 81.
30 Henderson and Cowan, *Scottish Fairy Belief*, p. 114.
31 Henderson and Cowan, *Scottish Fairy Belief*, pp. 115–16.
32 Stuart Clark, 'Protestant Demonology: Sin, Superstition, and Society c.1520–c.1630', in Bengt Ankarloo and Gustav Henningsen (eds), *Early Modern European Witchcraft: Centres and Peripheries* (Oxford, 1993), pp. 45–81.

33 Bailey, 'The Age of Magicians', p. 19.

34 James VI, *Daemonologie*, p. 66.

35 Larner, *Enemies of God*, p. 1; James VI, *Daemonologie*, p. 81; Robin Briggs, *Witches and Neighbours* (New York, 1997) p. 7.

36 Stuart Clark, *Thinking with Demons: The Idea of Witchcraft in Early Modern Europe* (Oxford, 1997), p. 459.

37 Bailey, 'The Age of Magicians', pp. 22–4.

38 Richard Kieckhefer, *European Witch Trials: Their Foundations in Popular and Learned Culture, 1300–1500* (Berkeley and Los Angeles, 1976). See also Richard Kieckhefer, *Magic in the Middle Ages* (Cambridge, 1989) and Karen Louise Jolly, 'Medieval Magic: Definitions, Beliefs, Practices', in Bengt Ankarloo and Stuart Clark (eds), *Witchcraft and Magic in Europe: The Middle Ages* (Philadelphia, 2002), pp. 1–71.

39 Specific reference is also made to the alchemist John Damian, Abbot of Tongland, Kikcudbrightshire (1504–9), a friend of James IV who, while at court, was a physician, organised morris dances and conducted alchemical experiments. In this poem, Dunbar is mocking his alleged attempts to fly but it is also probably an illustration of human folly and the dangers of sorcery. See, Priscilla Bawcutt (ed.), *The Poems of William Dunbar*, 2 vols (Glasgow, 1998), vol. 1, pp. 114–15, vol. 2, pp. 295–6, 352–4.

40 The paucity of evidence relating to marital status makes it impossible to be accurate so these figures may be impressionistic at best. Lauren Martin and Joyce Miller, 'Some Findings from the Survey of Scottish Witchcraft', in Goodare, *Witchcraft and Belief in Early Modern Scotland*, pp. 51–70.

41 Goodare, 'The Scottish Witchcraft Act', p. 9.

42 For various opinions on the wording of the Witchcraft Act see Larner, *Enemies of God*, pp. 66–7, P. G. Maxwell-Stuart, *Satan's Conspiracy: Magic and Witchcraft in Sixteenth Century Scotland* (East Linton, 2001), pp. 37–8, Laurence Normand and Gareth Roberts, *Witchcraft in Early Modern Scotland: James VI's Demonology and the North Berwick Witches* (Exeter, 2000), pp. 90–1, and on the anti-Catholic context see Goodare, 'The Scottish Witchcraft Act', pp. 8, 12–15.

43 Goodare, 'The Scottish Witchcraft Act', p. 11.

44 Joyce Miller, 'Devices and Directions: Folk Healing Aspects of Witchcraft Practice in Seventeenth-Century Scotland', in Goodare, *Scottish Witch-Hunt in Context*, pp. 90–105.

45 Lizanne Henderson, 'Charmers Spells and Holy Wells: The Repackaging of Belief', in *Review of Scottish Culture* (2007) pp. 10–26.

46 Larner, *Enemies of God*, p. 68.

47 Pitcairn, *Criminal Trials*, vol. 1, p. 66.

48 *Exchequer Rolls*, vol. 16, p. 612, qtd in G. Black, *A Calendar of Cases of Witchcraft in Scotland, 1510–1727* (New York, [1938] 1971), p. 21.

49 Thome Fayre, 1537, *Court Book of the Barony of Alloway*, 4 vols, vol 1, 624, MS. Carnegie Library, Ayr, B6/28/1–4, qtd in Alastair Hendry, *Witch-Hunting in Ayrshire: A Calendar of Documents* (May 1998).

50 Black, *Calendar*, p. 21.

51 *Protocol Book of Sir Ninian Bryden, 1536–1564* (Walter Mason Trust, 1997).

52 *Extracts from the Records of the Burgh of Stirling*, p. 80, qtd in Black, *Calendar*, p. 21.

53 George Hay, *History of Arbroath to the Present Time* (Arbroath, 1876), pp. 129–30.

54 *Canongate Burgh Court Book 1574–77* SL150/1/2, p. 370–3.

55 *Process Notes* JC26/1/13 and JC26/2. See also J. G. Dalyell, The *Darker Superstitions of Scotland* (Glasgow, 1835), p. 373.

56 Michael Wasser has conducted research on the 1568–9 trials but it remains unpublished. Goodare, *Scottish Witch-Hunt in Context*, p. 5.

57 William Matheson, 'The Historical Coinneach Odhar and some Prophecies Attributed to him', in *Transactions of the Gaelic Society of Inverness*, 46 (1968), pp. 1–23; Pitcairn, *Criminal Trials*, vol. 1, III, pp. 192–204; Lizanne Henderson, 'Witch-Hunting and Witch Belief in the Gaidhealtachd', in Goodare, *Witchcraft and Belief*, pp. 95–118; Maxwell-Stuart, *Satan's Conspiracy*, pp. 135–41. For more on elfshot see Henderson and Cowan, *Scottish Fairy Belief*, pp. 77–9, 93–4, Alaric Hall, 'Getting shot of Elves: Healing, Witchcraft and Fairies in the Scottish Witchcraft Trials', in *Folklore*, 116 (2005), pp. 19–36, Hugh Cheape, '"Charms against Witchcraft": Magic and Mischief in Museum Collections', in Goodare, *Witchcraft and Belief*, pp. 227–48, and Hugh Cheape, 'From Natural to Supernatural: The Material Culture of Charms and Amulets', in Henderson, *Fantastical Imaginations*, pp. 70–90.

58 *Highland Papers*, vol. 1, pp. 159–60, 165; Henderson, 'Witch-Hunting and Witch Belief in the Gaidhealtachd', pp. 102–4.

59 Larner, *Enemies of God*, p. 198.

60 Francis Legge, 'Witchcraft in Scotland', in *Scottish Review* 18 (1891), pp. 257–88; A. H. Williamson, *Scottish National Consciousness in the Age of James VI* (Edinburgh, 1979), p. 61.

61 P. G. Maxwell-Stuart, 'The Fear of the King is Death: James VI and the Witches of East Lothian', in William G. Naphy and Penny Roberts (eds), *Fear in Early Modern Society* (Manchester, 1997), pp. 209–25. On Danish witch-hunting see Gustav Henningsen, 'Witch Hunting in Denmark', in *Folklore* 93 (1982), pp. 131–7, and Jens Christian V. Johansen, 'Denmark: The Sociology of Accusations', in Ankarloo and Henningsen, *Early Modern European Witchcraft*, pp. 339–65.

62 Jenny Wormald, 'The Witches, the Devil and the King', in Terry Brotherstone and David Ditchburn (eds), *Freedom and Authority: Scotland c.1050–c.1650* (East Linton, 2000), pp. 170–4.

63 *Newes From Scotland*, 1591 (London, 1924), p. 15; Christina Larner, *Witchcraft and Religion: The Politics of Popular Belief* (Oxford, 1984), p. 15.

64 Stuart Clark, 'King James's *Daemonologie*: Witchcraft and Kingship', in Sidney Anglo (ed.), *The Damned Art* (London, 1977), pp. 156–81.

65 James VI, *Daemonologie*, pp. xi–xii; Clark, 'Witchcraft and Kingship', p. 156.

66 Writing in 1900, Joseph Hansen referred to the 'collective concept' of witchcraft and traced its evolution through the witches' sabbat. See Richard Kieckhefer, 'Mythologies of Witchcraft in the Fifteenth Century', in *Magic, Ritual and Witchcraft* 1/1 (2006), pp. 79–108; Brian P. Levack, *The Witch-Hunt in Early Modern Europe* (New York and London, 1995).

67 See also Henderson, 'Trial of Bessie Dunlop'.
68 Trial of Jonet Boyman, 1572, NAS, JC/26/1/67.
69 For more on the 'blast' and fairy assaults see Henderson and Cowan, *Scottish Fairy Belief*, esp. pp. 78–80, 85–6.
70 *Canongate Burgh Court Book 1574-77* SL150/1/2, pp. 370-3.
71 Pitcairn, *Criminal Trials*, vol. 1, p. 56. The last time Bessie saw Thomas it was the morning after Candlemas; Trial of Katherine Jonesdochter, R. S. Barclay (ed.), *Court Book of Shetland* (Edinburgh, 1967), pp. 38–9; Margaret Og, 'Trials for Witchcraft', *Miscellany of the Spalding Club*, vol. 1, p. 143.
72 Larner, *Enemies of God*, p. 140.
73 Trial of Bessie Dunlop, Pitcairn, *Criminal Trials*, vol. 1, pp. 51–3, 56; Henderson, 'Trial of Bessie Dunlop'.
74 Normand and Roberts, *Witchcraft in Early Modern Scotland*, p. 35.
75 Normand and Roberts, *Witchcraft in Early Modern Scotland*, p. 79.
76 Clark, *Thinking with Demons*, p. vii.

Chapter 11

Glaswegians: The First One Thousand Years

Edward J. Cowan

Kindly Bishop Kentigern, worthy to receive exultant praises,
When you brought light to the people that sat in darkness,
You blazed forth with many a jet of flame, a light set on a candlestick.
Lead us, who sing your praises, into the presence of the lord

INTRODUCTION

This twelfth-century magnificat would have been sung on many occasions throughout the centuries in the great city of Glasgow, but particularly on 13 January, the feast of St Mungo or Kentigern, the city's founding bishop and patron saint.[1] Though there can be no certainty about the date, Mungo is thought to have died in 603. Most dictionaries of saints prefer 612, the year given in the Welsh Annals, the *Oxford Dictionary of Saints* stating, accurately if rather pompously, that 'There are many legends but few known facts about Kentigern: all the sources date from the 11th and 12th centuries and most of them are from the North.'[2] Doubtless the latter would have been deemed more valuable if they had originated in the Home Counties, but saints' lives written some five hundred years after the deaths of their subjects must, in any case, be deemed highly suspect and of little use historically. It is argued, however, that the two surviving *vitae* of Mungo preserve information about everyday life, and attitudes concerning it, in the period at which the lives were composed. They also present the twelfth-century idea of what were believed to be the facts about Mungo's life, the span of which, claiming a little licence, is deemed roughly to mark the beginning of Glasgow's first millennium.

For a number of years now one of the main focuses of my research has been on finding ways to uncover the culture of the folk of Scotland at large. To try, however imperfectly, to recover something of their mindsets and attitudes, to move away from the sometimes overwhelming historiographical obsession with the supposed great and the good of the past, kings and queens, prime ministers and presidents, politicians, generals, achievers, and even saints. Glasgow began as a cemetery allegedly established by St Ninian. It was there that Mungo made his headquarters which later became the site of the magnificent cathedral, the 'dear church' after which Glaschu was named. *Eglwys* 'church', also conveys the sense of community or family, the Glaswegians of my title. The great sixteenth-century Scottish historian, George Buchanan observed that the purpose of history was to introduce our ancestors to us and we to our ancestors. Readers are invited to consider whether they can detect any Glaswegian characteristics in those who lived beside the Clyde during the period comprising roughly a thousand years after the death of Mungo. A sense of continuity was well expressed by Alexander Forbes, Bishop of Brechin in his edition of *The Lives of St Kentigern*:

> The great city of Glasgow . . . now the third city of the empire, numbering (in 1872) a population of 578,705 inhabitants, possessing nearly a thousand ships, exhibiting a tonnage of 444,581, returning with Greenock and Port Glasgow the enormous sum of £2,034,816, 0s 1d as Customs duties, slaughtering 69,499 oxen, 285,549 sheep and lambs, 13,448 pigs, burning 1,227,229,000 cubic feet of gas, exhibiting a rental of £2,327,513, paying duty on 676,590 lbs of tea, and 2,692,456 lbs of tobacco, owes its existence to the earthen rath and wattled church which S. Kentigern erected by the Molendinar stream beside the old cemetery of S. Ninian[3]

THE BIRTH OF A SAINT AND A CITY

The building of the cathedral, that glorious structure, situated on, or close to, the shrine of St Mungo, replacing a timber church destroyed by fire in 1136, probably began soon after and continued for some three hundred years.[4] Between 1175 and 1178 William the Lion had granted Glasgow its foundation charter as a burgh.[5] Two *vitae* or lives of the saint survive from the twelfth century. The first, which exists only as a fragment, was produced by a cleric of Glasgow at the prompting of Bishop Herbert, between 1147 and 1164. The second was commissioned in the 1180s by Jocelin, Bishop of Glasgow,[6] from his namesake, Jocelin, a monk of Furness Abbey in Lancashire. Although the prefaces to both texts mention 'readers' it may be that both were designed to raise support for the refurbishment project. We can imagine that bits of the *Life* were read, declaimed or recited in the marketplace or church before a collection was taken up, including donations in kind which could be sold on, or people were inspired to volunteer their services by donating their labour to the great project. If this is so, we might also wonder which sections were the most popular. The lives may be useless as a source of information on Mungo's actual *vita* but they may have value in reflecting the interests and attitudes of the folk at large in the second half of the twelfth century. After all, though the story rehearsed much that was wondrous, edifying and religiously inspirational, it also had to appeal to everyday experience and concerns, to the recognisable and to the familiar as well as to the exotic. The idea in this chapter is to read it not so much for its content on the saint but as a useful source of social and cultural history, a quarry of information of what 'weegies' thought about their lives and times in the later 1100s.

The fragmentary *Life of S. Kentigern* might more appropriately be named for his mother Thaney whose heroic trials and tribulations form the core of the story as it now exists. The anonymous author thought that, so far as reverence for its saints was concerned, Scotland was 'behindhand, slumbering in negligent sloth'.[7] He found material on Kentigern in 'the little book of his virtues' and in oral communications from the faithful. He apologised for his poor style, invoking Jerome's observation that it is better 'to say true things rudely, than to utter false things gracefully'. Readers (and presumably listeners) should not hold the content in contempt, 'on account of any uncouth names or words difficult to be understood by those who hear, or local designations, where barbarism, as I think, hath rendered rude the tongues of foreign tribes', thus indicating the complex multilingual situation in southern Scotland at this time, a subject almost completely ignored by historians.

Thaney, daughter of King Leudonus or Loth, 'a man half-pagan', was devoted to the Christian cult of virginity, drawing her inspiration from Mary, mother of Christ whose immaculate conception she longed to imitate. When her father learned that she spurned the suit of Ewen, a prince of Strathclyde, he vowed that, if she did not consent to marry, she would be handed over to a swineherd. She chose the latter who turned out to be a chaste and secret Christian. Ewen nonetheless persevered. Having failed to win her with words, gifts, the gently persuasive speeches and latterly the bad-tempered outbursts of her father, the sincere and smitten Ewen sent a woman to act on his behalf only to have her report that 'it were easier to turn stones into wood and wood into stones, than to recall the mind of this virgin from the folly she has adopted'. If Ewen's plight remains all too recognisable, his subsequent actions do not. Vowing to 'touch the knot' of Thaney's virginity, he disguised himself as a female servant, visiting her regularly while she tended her pigs in the field. One day he encountered Thaney beside a fountain where she often washed her hands and from which she sometimes drank. Still in disguise, he asked her to assist him in placing a bundle of wood on his shoulders since there was no man available to help. Having won her trust, he 'suddenly laid hold of her as if in play, and in a moment impregnated her (*fecundavit*), while she resisted the violence with all her might'. Persisting in his shabby ruse, he told her that she need not weep since he was a woman and thus had not known her as a man. 'Am I not a woman like thyself? It is folly to cry for what is done in sport.' Thaney remained in doubt about whether or not she had been defiled because she believed her assailant to be female and chiefly because, states her knowledgeable clerical biographer:

> the tokens of her sex were then beginning to appear in her as in every woman
> at the conception of a child, so that she could not discern the certain sign of
> corruption, although she had suffered pains in the flesh. For at such times the
> membranous structures are naturally relaxed, as well in virgins as in those bearing
> children, and thus the means of defilement always lie more nearly within reach,

whatever that may mean. When her condition became obvious, her father ordered her to be stoned as a whore. The king's men, reluctant to cast the first stone, decided to launch her in a careering chariot from the top of a nearby 'mountain', Traprain Law in East Lothian. Invoking Mary, she emerged unhurt, seemingly reassured that she had indeed been 'made fruitful' by an angel.

Because his subjects were muttering that Thaney's reprieve was due to magic rather than a miracle, Loth decided to consign her to the waves of the sea where God could decide her fate. She was placed in a coracle at Aberlady Bay, known as 'Bay of stinking fish' because so much of their catch was cast away there by over-successful fishermen that the putrefaction resulted in 'a smell of a detestable nature', driving folk away from the place. The Isle of May in the Firth of Forth was a favourite stopping-off point, the reader is assured, for fishermen from all over Britain, as well as from Belgium and France, but no fish remain at Aberlady today for they followed Thaney's coracle over the firth to Fife where she experienced a long and difficult birth. She was tended by shepherds and St Serf who, interestingly, spoke in the vernacular rather than in Latin and who welcomed the newborn babe as 'my dear one', or 'dearest friend' – Mungo. He also handily explained that Thaney's conception was contracted without the taint of fornication though whether he would have convinced twelfth-century mothers may be seriously doubted. Serf believed that the coming together of Mungo's parents:

> excelled in sanctity lawful marriage: seeing that it was the intention of his father to allure the mind of the virgin towards marriage with himself, while the devotion of the mother prompted her by preserving her virginity to avoid the society of men . . . in their meeting lawful love abounded and the virgin devotion was not destroyed . . . Even in law she is not esteemed as defiled who yieldeth not assent to the defiler, but is regarded as a virgin.

Then, as now, such matters were not of everyday experience but they were of everyday interest; a scandal or concern that might today earn five minutes of media notoriety could sustain several centuries of repetition and discussion in the medieval era. Many a Scottish woman must have yearned for the Church to show her such understanding and to have exercised such sophistry with regard to her individual predicament.

Jocelin of Furness, author of the second *vita* was something of an expert in the production of saints, lives, having written accounts of Saints Patrick, Helen, David of Scotland and Waldeve.[8] He sought a better *Life* than that currently used by the cathedral brethren – possibly the full version of the fragment just discussed. In addition, he had consulted a little volume in Scotic, or Irish, a book which he deplored because of obscurities compounded by barbarous language and 'swathed in vile wrappings'.[9] He produced a truly remarkable example of the genre, a *vita* which was political in promoting the diocese of Glasgow as inheritor of the kingdom of Strathclyde or Cumbria,[10] propagandist in attempting to advance Mungo's canonisation and translation,[11] and polemical in fighting battles old and new, noteworthy for its forthright subjectivity but full of colour and local interest.

Part of Jocelin's intention was clearly to blast the past. He condemned the 'stupid and foolish people' of the diocese of St Kentigern who asserted that the saint was conceived and born of a virgin. The monk strenuously denied that there was anything immaculate about Thaney's conception but he did quote some evidence to suggest that a woman could be completely ignorant as to the origins of her pregnancy, citing the repugnant examples of Lot's daughters, the use of mandragora to drug female victims, and the employment of magic. While launching into a rant about carnality and fornication, from which not even contemporary clergymen were immune, he nonetheless condemned Thaney's father for decreeing her terrible death for so simple a sin. His accounts of Thaney's paternal punishments and the birth of Mungo broadly follow those of the earlier life but he etymologises Kentigern as 'capital' or 'chief' lord.[12] His Sunday name thus ironically preserved his secular attributes, notably his royal descent.

RIVER CITY

In his introduction, Jocelin related how he 'wandered through the streets and lanes of the city' in search of information about Mungo whom 'the common people' invoked in time of strife. Glasgow, in the 1180s, must have been tiny though commerce had no doubt been stimulated by the recent establishment of a weekly market, held every Thursday, which was regarded as a day of good fortune. To judge from the *Life*, people were concerned about diseases such as fevers, leprosy, epilepsy, gout, insanity and sterility. In the twelfth century the mad and the possessed were still tied overnight, as they had been in the saint's day, to a great cross which he erected; morning found them cured or dead. Anaesthetics were occasionally used in operations. Death was ever present. The account of the deaths of Mungo and his followers, all dying at the same time, could possibly suggest a visitation of plague. Jocelin has the tale of Mungo's resurrection of a dead cook who rose from his grave briefly to attend church before being swiftly ordered back to his kitchen. He later recounted his post-death visions. Folk expected that their dust 'would be consigned in the womb of the mother of all', and hoped for a place of rest until Judgement Day.

Otherwise the saint's reported miracles were somewhat underwhelming. He supplied unseasonal mulberries at Christmas to spare the embarrassment of the king who had promised a particularly amusing jester any reward he wished. He harnessed a stag and a wolf to the plough and sowed grains of sand which came forth as abundant wheat. Milk poured on to the waters of the Clyde turned into cheese with miraculous properties. A thief who stole a cow was found dead attached to the healthy animal next day. In due course, the bathwater in which Mungo and his disciples willingly and fatally immersed themselves proved to have curative properties when it was swallowed or applied. Jocelin claimed various miracles at his tomb – restoration of sight, hearing and speech, curing of lameness, paralysis, insanity and leprosy – but none of these was specific as to person or date.

An undoubted source of fascination were the sexual activities of Strathclyde's royal family, as in the strange circumstances of Mungo's conception. Later, Jocelin describes the adulterous act now memorialised on Glasgow's city crest.[13] Queen Languoreth falls for 'the perishing beauty' of a young soldier and, proceeding 'from a rash act to a blind love', she presents him with a ring that her husband has given her. Though it is proverbially difficult for 'a cuckold to put faith in one that reveals the failings of a beloved wife and the odium is apt to fall rather upon the informer than the accused', the king, when informed of her actions, becomes reluctantly convinced of her betrayal. He removes the ring from the hand of the sleeping soldier, throwing it into the Clyde. The wife continues to dissimulate but the king has her imprisoned under sentence of death. She, full of repentance, sends a messenger to Mungo who orders him to go fishing, thus landing a salmon with the offending ring in its mouth. The couple are reconciled and live happily ever after while the soldier shoots the craw (that is, he flees). Lest it be thought that Mungo in this case was complicit in defending a faithless wife, a medieval episode of Scottish Television's soap opera *River City* twelfth-century style, it should be recognised that the point of the story is a clumsy replication of Christ's forgiveness of the woman taken in adultery. Unfortunately, there seems to be noticeably little sympathy for the wronged husband.

Mungo seldom hesitated to sermonise in a fire-and-brimstone style worthy of some of his Protestant successors. He memorably lambasted hypocrites and he converted apostates. In Jocelin's eyes, the saint may even have anticipated the Gregorian reforms of the eleventh century as he 'began to overthrow the shrines of demons, to cast down their images, to build churches, to dedicate them, to divide parishes, to ordain clergy, to dissolve incestuous and unlawful marriages, to change concubinage into lawful matrimony, to introduce ecclesiastical rites', all the while striving to establish whatever was consonant with the faith, Christian law, and righteousness.[14]

At Chapter 28 the narrative diverts to condemn violently a gay cleric in quite uncompromising terms. The passage is noteworthy because explicit statements about homosexuality are almost non-existent in Scottish sources, certainly at this early date. Furthermore the issue is still so divisive as to cause certain churches to impale themselves on the issue.

If the sacred canons forbid women, on account of the infirmity of their sex, to which in no ways is blame attached, to be promoted to the rank of priesthood, much more is it our duty to banish from a rank and office so sacred, men who pervert their sex, who abuse nature, who in contempt of their Master, in

Figure 11.1 *Crest of the city of Glasgow showing Mungo at the top with central tree, bell, bird and fish with a ring in its mouth.* © *Glasgow University Library. Licensor www.scran. ac.uk.*

degradation of themselves, in injury of all creatures, cast off that in which they are created and born, and become as women. Nowhere read we of punishment exercising a graver vengeance than against that monstrous race of men among whom that execrable crime first began. Not only did it overthrow those cities (Sodom and Gomorrah), with the inhabitants thereof, with fire, on account of the burning of evil passion, and with sulphur, on account of the stench of that abominable sin, but it also turned them into a place horrid to the sight, full of sulphur and bitumen and horrible smells, receiving nothing living into itself, having indeed on its banks trees that produce fruits externally sound, but inwardly full of smoke and ashes, shadowing forth an image of the torture of hell.[15]

This apocalyptic vision, unsurprisingly perhaps, was shortly followed by the death of the offender, 'cut off by a sudden destruction'. Considerably different is the depiction of Gawain and Yvain joyously holding hands at Arthur's court in the introduction to the romance, *Fergus of Galloway*, composed about 1200. They share a love, 'as great as ever was seen', matching or surpassing that of Achilles and Patroclus. After the quest, Fergus and Gawain run to kiss each other: 'You could have walked slowly for a good four bowshots before they tired of their kissing; those noble knights made as great a fuss of each another as if they were full brothers.'[16] The intention may have been comedic or to emphasise that the Arthurian court was not of the real world, or both, but the tone adopted by the contemporary clerical versifier is non-condemnatory. It is also noteworthy that, in the romance, Fergus's mother calls upon St Mungo while he invokes 'the faith he owes St Mungo' and 'St Mungo at Glasgow'.[17]

According to Jocelin the monk, people were rather spiteful and envious of one another, taking their lead, perhaps, from their rather small-minded rulers, whose advisers were particularly malicious.[18] People were easily diverted from Christian thoughts. Some considered Mungo's mother, Thaney, to be a witch practising magical arts; they feared phantoms and were attentive to prophecy. Folk worried about food, that is, acquiring enough of it, while Mungo fasted for three or four days at a time. He was a vegetarian – except on visits to the great and the good, after which he would diet. He favoured the 'cheapest and lightest foods', such as bread, milk, cheese and butter, abstaining from wine. People rejoiced when, on one occasion, the flooded Clyde, miraculously failed to engulf the royal barns containing stored wheat. The surging waves of the river, almost anticipating the sodden ravages of January 2005, swept the barns on to dry land beside the Molendinar because of the intercession of the saint.[19]

He is said to have only tasted, rather than having taken, sleep, praying and holding vigils throughout the night. To subdue fleshly desires, he bathed naked in fast-flowing, cold rivers, the weather always proving kind. Thus was 'the fire of concupiscence mortified and extinguished', though one frigid day 'when the frost had contracted and congealed everything', he survived his dip to turn frigid when he resumed his clothing, so affording the chance of a parable on human frailty. Not that the latter much troubled Mungo. He once told his disciples that the touch of a most beautiful girl had no effect upon him whatsoever.[20] His needs were not those of ordinary men; what he denied himself, they sought.

The saint was possessed of a very handy garment for one who was patron saint of Glasgow, for his clothes were rain-repellent:

> never in his life were his clothes wetted with drops of rain . . . often standing in the open air, while the inclemency of the weather increased and the pouring rain flowed in different directions like bilge-water, and the spirit of the storm raged around him, he from time to time stood still, or went whither he would, and yet he always continued uninjured and untouched by a drop of rain from any quarter.

As an added bonus, those who hung out with him enjoyed a similar boon.[21] It is noteworthy that St Ninian, who operated in frequently besodden Galloway, enjoyed a divine protection such that, when reading in the open air, even in the heaviest downpours, no rain ever fell upon his book, 'as if he were protected by the roof of a house'. On one occasion, however, 'the pleasant serenity of the weather, becoming obscured by black clouds, poured down from on high to earth those waters which it had naturally drawn upwards'. This little meteorological homily explained that the lighter air arched around Ninian and a companion, 'resisting as an impenetrable wall the descending waters'. But, when Ninian's thoughts strayed briefly, the rain inundated both him and his book.[22]

Jocelin, who should have known about such matters, provides some information about everyday life in a monastery, admittedly one in Wales, rather than in Scotland, but a Kentogernian foundation (St Asaph) nonetheless. Mungo was shown the site by a boar which he rewarded by scratching his head and fondling his mouth. It was important that the abbey should be at a convenient meeting point for intending brothers wheresoever they came from. The ground was cleared and levelled, trees cut down and fashioned to construct buildings of polished wood. Young and old flocked to the new foundation. Middle-class children were brought to be educated. Altogether, 965 individuals (an unbelievably high number) were recruited to be divided into three divisions. Three hundred illiterates were assigned to farming, the tending of cattle and other essential tasks outside the monastery. Another three hundred were given everyday duties within the cloister, performing necessary jobs, preparing food and erecting workshops. The remaining 365, who could read, were appointed to celebrate divine service day and night. Some were made teachers, others the saint's assistants in the execution of his episcopal responsibilities. Some were delegated to pray while many were organised into choirs which performed in rotation.[23]

APOCALYPSE

Curiously, throughout such a triumphant tale, there is a detectable underlying uneasiness about the transitory nature of life, which may reflect contemporary anxieties. Of course, death and ill-health were ever present but even Mungo's great achievements could be overturned as soon as he decided to go off to visit David in Wales and folk reverted to paganism. He predicted that, when St David died, the land would revert to apostasy and Christian law be 'scattered until the appointed time' when it would once again be restored. All this had happened before in the early days, as Christianity rose and fell in the face of successive heathen invasions. According to Jocelin, Strathclyde experienced a veritable doomsday when Mungo withdrew to Wales. The accession of holy King Rhydderch permitted Mungo's return, after a sojourn at Hoddam in Dumfriesshire, rapidly to become the terror of the pagans and missionary to Galloway, Alba and Orkney, yea even unto Norway and Iceland! One of the earliest mentions of Mungo occurs in the inquest into the diocese of Glasgow which David I held about four years before he became king in 1124. Therein it is mentioned that Mungo gave to the thirsty, 'the rich plentitude of heavenly knowledge, ministering spiritual food unto the hungry as a faithful steward'. But, after his death, universal insurrections resulted in the wasting of the whole country so that all good men were banished,

> while divers tribes of different nations poured in from divers parts and possessed the foresaid desolate territory – different in race and unlike in language, living under manifold customs and not easily agreeing among themselves they clung to heathenism rather than the worship of the faith.[24]

There seems to have been some sense in the 1180s that all of this might happen again, that nothing endures except change.

One of the high points of Mungo's career, shortly before his death, was allegedly a visit from St Columba, by no means an everyday event but one full of symbolism in bringing together two of the great figures of early Scottish Christianity. More mundane were the visible signs of imminent death in the aged Mungo which his twelfth-century contemporaries would recognise, such as the 'many cracks' signifying the 'ruin of his earthly house', namely his body, the fastenings of which were withered and ruined. His cheeks and chin sagged, requiring a bandage around head and jaw to disguise his gaping mouth. He spent his final hours advising and blessing his disciples. Close to death, he was visited by an angel who told him that he should die in a warm bath, his disciples submerging themselves in the bathwater to enter the mansions of heaven with their master.

So Mungo passed on but, with regard to the everyday, the language heralding his death is of the greatest interest. When the angelic vision departed, 'a fragrance of wondrous and unspeakable odour in a strange way filled the place and all that were therein'. The vision had appeared, 'while the morning day-star, the messenger of the dawn, the herald of the light of day, tearing asunder the pall of the darkness of night, shone forth with flaming rays'. Medieval people were extremely conscious of light and smell, and Jocelin's *vita* has much of both. Mungo is said to have shone forth in the sunlight of virtue inside his mother's womb to be born, 'an aromatic tree', from the filthy ground of his unfortunate conception. Thaney gives birth to the 'preacher and herald of true light'. God is the Father of Lights. Mungo was like a lamp in a dark place, shedding light 'in the midst of a perverse and wicked generation'. Fergus of Carnock felt a sweetness in his breast 'when the south wind was blowing over his garden so that the odour of its breeze might reach him'. Light, sweet savour and a sweet-smelling cloud accompanied the saint's celebration of mass. Magic represents the deluding of the senses. Thaney was examined by sight and touch to determine whether she

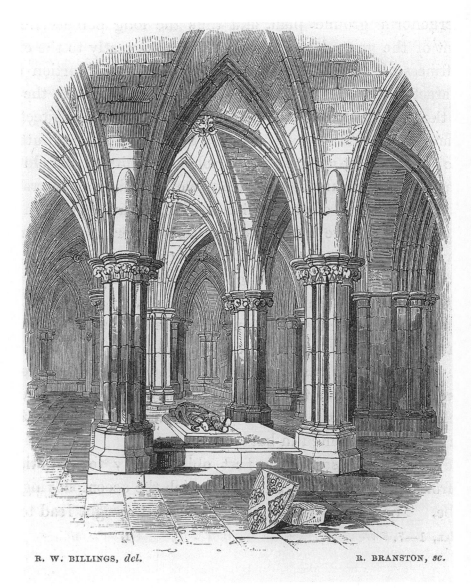

R. W. BILLINGS, *del.*   R. BRANSTON, *sc.*

Figure 11.2   *St Mungo's Tomb in the crypt of Glasgow Cathedral.* © *Glasgow City Libraries. Licensor www.scran.ac.uk.*

was pregnant. The sun's rays are good for healthy eyes, actually improving sight, but can blind the unhealthy. King Maelgwyn, a protesting pagan, was blinded for demanding that Mungo's monks be expelled and his monastery demolished. However, 'on him that sat in outer darkness the true morning star shone, and the external light being for a time taken from him, drew him forth from the darkness and shadow of death into the light of truth'; in other words, Mungo, having blinded him that he might give him light, restored his sight. Smoke is contrasted with flame, stench with brightness. All saints' lives are imbued with the rhetoric of light and, because most ideas about the senses in Christendom were church inspired,[25] it is not to be expected that Scottish notions would be very different from those of any other country. Nonetheless, it can hardly be doubted that the language employed in Jocelin's tirades against the heathen reflects a cosmology of the everyday.

Mungo occupied the same world as Merlin and King Arthur, the subjects of 'poetic songs and histories non canonical'. In his *Life* we can detect the emergence of what would later become the full-blown legend of the Knights of the Round Table. The story of Queen Languoreth and her ring shares certain features with the tale of Guinevere and Lancelot. The last chapter of Jocelin's *Life* introduces a character named Lailoken, a fool who resides in the royal place of King Rhydderch at Partick, and who accurately predicts that, within the year, Rhydderch and another king, Morthec, will perish. Lailoken is to be identified with Merlin who, in other tales and traditions, loses his wits after the battle of Arthuret and who evades a vengeful Rhydderch by seeking refuge in the Forest of Caledon.[26] Curiously, yet another source, Walter Bower's massive *Scotichronicon* (1445) records that Mungo and Merlin died in the same year. According to the story, Mungo met Merlin 'a certain madman naked and hairy' in the wilderness of Tweeddale. The saint brought him back to Christ but the repentant predicted his own death which came to pass at Drumelzier where Merlin died the threefold death, by stoning, impalement and drowning. In this version, Mungo and his followers begin to suspect that Merlin's other prophecies will also come to pass and they are appropriately fearful.[27] The question was – might not Mungo's achievements be overcome in much the same way as those of Merlin? Is the past doomed to repeat itself? Not a very Christian view perhaps but one at which Jocelin possibly hints in his *Life* of the remarkable Mungo, who, as one Glasgow chauvinist delighted in emphasising, was a Christian bishop who blessed ground for Christian burial, 'when Iona was yet an unknown island among the western waves, while St Andrews was the haunt of the wild-boar and the sea-mew, and only the smoke of a few heathen wigwams ascended from the rock of Edinburgh'.[28]

MEDIEVAL GLASGOW

Glasgow Fair was inaugurated in 1197 though, for centuries, people came 'up the watter' for the event which was designed to attract visitors rather than to encourage them to depart elsewhere on holiday. How many came is not known but the fair was regarded as a good time to pay rents and settle disputes. Glasgow seems to have had two centres, one at the cathedral and the other at the cross, but the fair was when the two came together in celebration. It should be remembered that the Clyde represented the true frontier between Highland and Lowland in Scotland. The river brought people from the west coast and the islands but also from Ireland, Galloway and the Solway, the Isle of Man and even further afield. Languages and life-styles would mix on the High Street. It was not for nothing that William the Lion dubbed the cathedral, 'the mother of many nations'.[29] By 1200 those nations included Scots, Gaels, Galwegians, Britons, English, Scandinavians, Normans and Flemings. Glasgow regarded itself as the capital of an ancient kingdom that had once extended through Cumbria to Stainmore in England, a 'special daughter' of the papacy, with a cathedral which was, and is, one of the gems of medieval architecture.

Pilgrimage had always been important economically. Glasgow treasured the bones of Mungo and Thaney, as well as part of the former's hair shirt. It also kept a fragment of the true cross and relics of the Virgin Mary. Trade, however, would become increasingly important. A bridge across the Clyde is recorded by 1286 but, since tolls were probably levied, it is unlikely that the original ford across the river became completely redundant. From the thirteenth century, various trades and crafts appear in the burgh though it can be assumed that some of them, such as miller and blacksmith, had been there earlier. They were soon joined by baker, cobbler, skinner, tanner, dyer and, among others, a female weaver. Also, as has been suggested, the surname Hangpudyng may indicate a specialist in the manufacture of black puddings,[30] or perhaps even haggis. The Fishergate commemorated another important commodity which would include salmon but probably also the harvest of the sea. Although Glasgow has been described as an inland burgh, it is noteworthy that Jocelin's *Life* contains much maritime imagery and one striking evocation of the stench of rotting fish.

Jocelin described how Mungo was bullied at school. When some boys accidentally killed the pet robin of their teacher, St Serf, they blamed the blameless Mungo, fearing 'the blows of rods which are wont to be the great-est torment of boys'. Mungo restored the bird to life, sending it back to a delighted Serf and eventually onwards to its perch on Glasgow's city crest. There it accompanies a tree which seems to derive from another saintly accomplishment. The envy of the pupils led them to extinguish the lamps in the church that Mungo was tending. He thought of quitting the monastery there and then but, instead, he relit the lamps by means of picking a hazel bough which he besought God to ignite, a symbol of the light shining in pagan darkness, akin to Moses' burning bush. The bough miraculously was not consumed but, when planted, a hazel wood grew from it. The 'country folk' in Jocelin's day asserted that even the greenest twig from that grove would instantly ignite 'at the touch of fire'.[31] There was a school in Glasgow from at least the fourteenth century as well as a song school associated with the cathedral. In the Jubilee year of 1450, the Pope decreed that, for folk so-minded, a visit to Glasgow would be as valid as a pilgrimage to Rome. A spin-off was the founding of the university the following year, a notable acquisition for the city, 'a place of renown where the air is mild and victuals are plentiful' in which, it was hoped, the college 'may flourish in all time to come forever'. The declaiming of the foundation bull was a matter of public celebration. Situated in Rottenrow, the new institution had a shaky start, attracting only about twenty students a year. Further public ceremony accompanied the university's removal to a new site in the High Street in 1460. A church service was followed by an elaborate procession, a ceremony, and a banquet, the day concluding with 'some interlude, or other spectacle' to rejoice the people.

The university was, of course, a Church initiative, and several books could and should be written about Glasgow's aggressive ecclesiastics – right up to the present day – though not strictly the business of this chapter. It has been said of Bishop Robert Wishart that his besetting sin was patriotism during the Wars of Independence, a man who was told by the pope of the day that he was a 'rock of offence and a stone of stumbling, prime instigator and promoter of the fatal disputes between the Scottish nation and Edward I'. Wishart was the man who told the Scots that warring against Edward was the equivalent of fighting against the Saracens in the Holy Land.[32] The cause of independence was therefore a crusade. One is reminded of another militant churchman, Archbishop James Beaton (1509–22), who wore a jack, or breastplate, underneath his rochet, discovered by his associate when Beaton beat upon his breast to protest his innocence, and the plates on his body armour could be heard clattering.[33]

In the later fifteenth century there was a kind of intensification of the veneration of Mungo: for example, the building of the Blackadder crypt in the cathedral, Little St Mungo's. Pilgrimage sites still included St Mungo's Cave, St Mungo's bedchamber and St Mungo's Well as well as St Mungo's trees, St Mungo's Spouts and St Mungo's Lane. Later there are references to St Mungo's graveyard, St Mungo's Tree (singular) and something called the 'Freedom of St Mungo',[34] a reference to the liberties and privileges of the burgh jealously guarded against others, such as Dumbarton. It is noteworthy that Glaswegians always seem to have preferred the more affectionate form of Mungo to the rather more learned, one might almost say Sunday name, of Kentigern.

We should not overlook Archbishop Robert Blackadder who made James IV an honorary canon of the cathedral and who thought nothing of inviting the king over to Glasgow for a game of cards. He was the man who negotiated the marriage of the Thistle and the Rose in 1503 between James IV and Margaret Tudor, commemorated by William Dunbar's brilliant poem, which led to the Union of the Crowns a century later. He also drew up the concomitant Treaty of Perpetual Peace and officiated at the royal wedding. He was ambassador to the Spain of Christopher Columbus, to the

Milan of Leonardo da Vinci, and he died on pilgrimage to the Holy Land.[35]
Archbishop Gavin Dunbar of Glasgow became tutor to the young King
James V with whom he would play cachpuyll (tennis) and 'casting eggs to
bikker the castle', chucking eggs at a mark on the castle wall. From tennis
humbler folk were pointedly excluded but they could easily adapt 'bikker
the castle' for their own enjoyment. George Buchanan admired Dunbar's
learning, culture and scholarship. 'Having sat as a guest with Gavin,' he
wrote, 'I envy not the gods their nectar and ambrosia – a feast where was no
vain display, but a table chastely and generously furnished, seasoned with
talk now serious, now with attic wit. As Apollo led the choir of the Muses,
so our host shone above all by his eloquent speech.'[36] This aesthete was
entrusted in 1525 with issuing a curse against the reivers and gangsters of the
Scottish Borders and what he came up with, an extension of the excommunication ban, ran partly as follows:

> I curse yair heid and all the haris of yair heid. I curse yair face, yair ene, yir mouth.
> I curse everilk part of yair body, fra the top of yair heid to the soill of yair feet
> . . . I [curse] yair cornys, yair catales, thair woll, swine, horse, sheep, etc all the
> malesouns and waresouns that ever gat warldlie creatur sen the beginning of the
> warlde to thos mot licht upon thaim. The malediction of God that lichtit upon
> Lucifer and all his fallowis, that straik thaim fra the hie hevin to the deip Hell mot
> licht upon thaim . . . The thunnour and fire-flauchtis that set down as rane upon
> the cities of Zodome and Gomora and brunt thaim for thair vile synns mot rane
> upon thaim. I dissever and partis thaim fra the Kirk of God and deliveris thaim
> quyk to the Devill of Hell . . .[37]

This is the man who sat in judgement of the first Protestant martyr, Patrick
Hamilton, and who dithered over later cases because he had no stomach for
burnings, a man who wonderfully combines in his own being the agonising
indecisions of that most calamitous age of reformation.

EVERYDAY LIFE IN SIXTEENTH-CENTURY GLASGOW

Lesser clerics were just as headstrong as their superiors. In 1510 Thomas
Birkmyre was had up before the chancellor of the archbishopric for using
opprobrious language. Birkmyre told his inquisitor, who wanted to bind
or fasten his feet, in other words to curb his bombastic statements, that he
could not fashion a sheep's heid. 'I sett nocht a fart by you!'[38] When John
Gibson, canon of the cathedral, was setting out on pilgrimage to Rome, he
so distrusted his Glasgow colleagues that he placed all his property in the
protection of the Pope.

From 1573, Glasgow has a rich, if not entirely complete, set of burgh
records, truly a mine of information on its citizens and their everyday lives,
presenting, as their editor J. D. Marwick noted, 'a picture of national character in the manners of the day'. Those earliest records deal with such matters

as horses afflicted with the scab, the exclusion of lepers, and several cases of assault. Margaret Andro, for example, was accused of striking Jonet Tailor and pulling out her hair, 'within the tyme callit of auld the proclamation of Yule girtht (immunity), and now of abstinence'.[39] Throughout, these records generally reveal the council at its corporate best even if the citizens do not always display an equivalent respect for the activities of the councillors. Thus, the council regularly enacted statutes about the price and quality of beer, bread, meat, fish, tallow, candles and so on.[40] Measures were also put in place during recurrent outbreaks of plague. Persons responsible for carrying the disease into the burgh were to be executed. A system of watch was set up, the town's gates guarded by night. Outbreaks of the pest made folk exceedingly wary of strangers and travellers of any kind. Pipers, minstrels, fiddlers and beggars were expelled, the opportunity being taken to cleanse the burgh of unwanted humanity.[41] Normal council business was to remain secret, and penalties were imposed on councillors who blabbed. There was frequent legislation concerning the operation of markets and the containment of such creatures as swine, geese and sheep. In 1577, the council bought back, at a cost of £10, St Mungo's Bell which, before the Reformation, had been rung at funerals. The Protestants banned funerals, considering that there was no scriptural authority for them but public opinion clearly demanded some form of ceremony for the deceased and so they were reinstated along with the bell.[42] It is worth noting that the council took considerable pains to maintain the cathedral in good order. There had been some spoiling of the churches and friaries around 1560, and it was probably just as well that, when Archbishop James Beaton II fled into exile on the Continent, he took with him many of the diocesan muniments, relics and vestments so that some at least were preserved for posterity. There was a false rumour that, in 1578, the Presbyterian firebrand Andrew Melville, of Glasgow University, tried to persuade the magistrates to demolish the cathedral[43] but, in fact, Glasgow's approach to religious reformation appears to have been on the whole rather moderate and thus the cult of Mungo was not forgotten; rather, it may have provided some comfort for those whose inward sympathies remained with the old faith as for those who were somewhat baffled by the new one.

Council dealt with gypsies and tinkers. A perennial concern was the problem of middens and 'fulyie', a word meaning dirt, filth, dung and excrement, commodities which accumulated daily in the streets along with offal and blood discarded by butchers and the stinking waste material scraped off hides by the leathermen. Time and again, Glasgow tried to clean up its act. On 16 July 1608 the council decreed, in conformity with an Act of the Convention of Burghs, that all fulyie was to be cleared within fifteen days and was no longer to be stockpiled, 'be rasoun the samein is nocht only uncumlie and incivill bot lykwayis verie dangerus in tyme of plaig and pestilence, and verie infective of itself' on pain of a £40 fine. Such material and nightsoil were normally sold as manure but, as a result of this legislation, by

4 February 1609 the council had to take measures because there was a shortage; it was being sold to 'unfrie men' who did not dwell in the burgh.[44] Such
'owtintownismen' were forever infringing burghal monopolies; they availed
themselves of the burgh's amenities and facilities but failed to pay their dues
there.

The council was seen to act at its corporate best in times of plague but
also in time of dearth. It was particularly concerned about thirlage, the
grinding of grain in the burgh mills. It scrutinised the weights and measures
used within the burgh and, from time to time, ordered the destruction of
inaccurate vessels of measurement, commissioning potters to manufacture
new ones. There is mention of 'acquavitae pots', probably stills though the
dictionaries do not record them until the eighteenth century.

Above all, the council sought to promote trade. There is reference in 1512
to one, David Lindsay, building a galley in Glasgow.[45] In 1597 we have the
names of the following ships: the James of Glasgow, the Grace of God of
Glasgow, the Pelican of Glasgow, the Lyon of Glasgow, the Marie Gawane
of Glasgow, and the Antilope of Glasgow.[46] Within half a century Glasgow
would see the arrival of the first illegal cargo from the American colonies in
1647, heralding the true beginning of Glasgow's prosperity but, ironically,
also the ruin of her citizens, at least in health terms, when a ship laden with
tobacco and sugar landed in the Clyde.

But Glasgow's strength then, as now, was, of course, its people and, as to
be expected, they crowd the pages of the burgh records. It may be thought
that we find echoes of modern Glaswegians when only a few pages into the
records. Margaret Hamilton is punished for 'rugging Jonet Cowan's hair
casting hir to the erd'. One woman beats up another for calling her 'a priest's
hoor'. A man blasphemes the magistrates. Sabbath breakers are pursued.
Robert Pirry is banished for wounding a bailie with his whinger, or short
sword, and is forbidden to return on pain of losing his right hand; two low-
lifes are accused of attempted rape. Council condemns 'ryotus bancatyng at
brydallis, baptisyng of barnes and upsitting (post-confinement)'. Ninian Swan
is arraigned for hitting Marion Symsoun with his tongs and throwing her to
the ground, and she is also had up for spitting in the said Ninian's face the
same day. For stabbing a nurse, William Ross is scourged and exiled on pain
of hanging should he return. John Kar is found guilty of hitting Katerane Hart
on the mouth with a salmon fish. Two women are banished in 1579 upon
pain of drowning for confessing to having 'mansworn', that is, being guilty
of perjury; in 1595 another woman is threatened with drowning for theft.[47]

Each year the 'Peace of Glasgow Fair' was proclaimed, forbidding any
hurt, trouble, fighting or feuding, and almost every year folk infringed the
peace, even merchants and crafts who should have known better, resulting
in a disarming act. A woman slanders her neighbour by claiming she slept
with her physician but, since nobody believes her, she is placed in the 'gofis',
pillory and branks. Indeed, the council felt it necessary to set up a pair of

jougs at the pillory above three or four steps 'because of the manifauld blasphemeis and evill wordis usit be sindrie wemen'. The Master of Work was instructed that the jougs be 'sure and substantious that they be nocht revin doune and carryit away be evill doaris'. There were complaints that, as a form of recreation, men were using their culverins and pistols to take pot-shots at the doocot, as well as the doos, on Glasgow Green. A couple of Camerons were forced to kneel barefoot and bareheaded at the cross to ask God's forgiveness for attacking John Paton to the effusion of his blood and 'harling and puddling him in ane gutter'. Elspeth Clogy was found guilty of throwing stones at Christian Sauchie 'and byting of hir throuch the arme and latting the piece [of] flesche quhilk scho bait fall in the watter'. David Duncan was done for climbing up on the Toun Cross and breaking it while William Blair was charged with standing on the heid of the cross while playing his pipes.[48]

Not everyone thought the council was doing a great job. Thomas Myln, surgeon, blasted two bailies as traitors and deceivers, speaking slanderously of the town, 'calling it the hungrie toun of Glasgow'. On other occasions, the council complained that it was the target of anonymous 'cokalandis' or lampoons. John Cooper, minister, was similarly treated at Yule when a pasquil (lampoon) was attached to his gate at dead of night containing diverse vain, filthy and injurious words tending to his life, hurt and dishonour. Bad language was not tolerated. The fleshers were accused of using uncomely and absurd language when their customers, honest men's wives, came to purchase meat. Great abuse was said to have been done to honest women by blaspheming bards and scalds. William Bell was accused of blasphemy and contempt towards the dean of guild who was engaged in judging a lining or boundary case. Bell pleaded guilty through 'ovir mekle drink'. *Plus ca change plus c'est la meme chose!*[49]

CONCLUSION

Towards the end of his visitation to Wales, Mungo had a vision of an angel who told him: 'Go back to Glasgu, to thy church, and there thou shall be a great nation and the Lord will make thee to increase among thy people'. *Revertere in Glasgu, ad ecclesiam tuam, ibique eris in gentem magnam, et crescere te faciet Dominus in plebem suam*. The words strikingly associated in this passage are Glasgow, church, nation and people. From Mungo the Dear One, the Dear Church and the Dear Family, the Glaswegians descend; they are all the weans of St Mungo. Jocelin of Furness does not try to conceal the reality that Mungo's Christian beliefs were not of the doctrinaire variety of later ages. Rather he depicts a saint who bestrode the pagan and Christian worlds, fumbling in his interpretation of the biblical and the miraculous, seeking to bring together people of different languages and different cultures, as he established the Mother of Many Nations. He is thus an ideal symbol for twenty-first century Glasgow, a city which transcends creed, colour and political philosophy, and which seeks to flourish by drawing on the strength within diversity, a fitting legacy of,

> Kentigern well-known to all, the kind sun's dawn,
> Lord and ruler of the people of this place.[50]

Notes

1 A version of this chapter was originally presented as the First Annual St Mungo Lecture at the invitation of Liz Cameron, Lord Provost of Glasgow, on 13 January 2005 at the Royal Scottish Academy of Music and Drama.
2 David Hugh Farmer, *The Oxford Dictionary of Saints*, 3rd edn (Oxford, 1992), p. 280.
3 Alexander Penrose Forbes (ed.), *Lives of S. Ninian and S. Kentigern compiled in the Twelfth Century* (Edinburgh, 1874), cv.
4 For a succinct account of the building of Glasgow Cathedral see Stephen T. Driscoll, *Excavations at Glasgow Cathedral 1988–1997* (Leeds, 2002), pp. 1–10.
5 G. W. S. Barrow (ed.), *Regesta Regum Scottorum II The Acts of William I* (Edinburgh, 1971), pp. 245–6; Robert Renwick and John Lindsay, *History of Glasgow*, vol. I, *Pre-Reformation Period* (Glasgow, 1921), pp. 62–3.
6 Norman F. Shead, 'Jocelin abbot of Melrose (1170–4) and bishop of Glasgow (1175–1199)', in *Innes Review* 54 (2003), pp. 1–22.
7 For this and the following discussion see Forbes, *Lives of Ninian and Kentigern*, pp. 123–33.
8 Forbes, *Lives of Ninian and Kentigern*, pp. 312–13; George Mcfadden, 'The *Life of Waldef* and Its Author, Jocelin of Furness', in *Innes Review* 6 (1955), pp. 5–13.
9 Forbes, *Lives of Ninian and Kentigern*, pp. 30–1.
10 Dauvit Broun, *Scottish Independence and the Idea of Britain From the Picts to Alexander III* (Edinburgh, 2007), chapter 5.
11 A. A. M. Duncan, 'St Kentigern at Glasgow Cathedral in the Twelfth Century', in Richard Fawcett (ed.), *Medieval Art and Architecture in the Diocese of Glasgow* (London, 1998), pp. 9–24. See also Alan Macquarrie, *The Saints of Scotland* (Edinburgh, 1997), chapter 5.
12 Forbes, *Lives of Ninian and Kentigern*, pp. 29–41.
13 Forbes, *Lives of Ninian and Kentigern*, pp. 99–102.
14 Forbes, *Lives of Ninian and Kentigern*, pp. 63–6.
15 Forbes, *Lives of Ninian and Kentigern*, p. 86.
16 Guillaume Le Clerc, *Fergus of Galloway: Knight of King Arthur*, trans. D. D. R. Owen (London, 1991), p. 1.
17 Forbes, *Fergus of Galloway*, pp. 8, 14.
18 Forbes, *Lives of Ninian and Kentigern*, pp. 71–2.
19 Forbes, *Lives of Ninian and Kentigern*, pp. 69–70.
20 Forbes, *Lives of Ninian and Kentigern*, pp. 57–8.
21 Forbes, *Lives of Ninian and Kentigern*, pp. 97–8.
22 Forbes, *Lives of Ninian and Kentigern*, pp. 18–19.

23 Forbes, *Lives of Ninian and Kentigern*, pp. 75–81.

24 J. T. T. Brown, *The Earliest Document Relating to Glasgow. The Inquest of David: Facsimile, Text, Translation and Notes* (Glasgow, 1901), pp. 5–6.

25 C. M. Woolgar, *The Senses in Late Medieval England* (New Haven and London, 2006), pp. 5–28. See also A. Roger Ekirch, *At Day's Close. A History of Nighttime* (London, 2005).

26 Myles Dillon and Nora Chadwick, *The Celtic Realms* (London, 1967), p. 270.

27 Walter Bower, *Scotichronicon*, Donald Watt (ed.), 9 vols (Aberdeen, 1987–98), vol. 2, pp. 83–7.

28 Rev. James Primrose, *Medieval Glasgow* (Glasgow, 1913), p. 15. For a recent lavishly illustrated history see Neil Baxter (ed.), *A Tale of Two Towns: A History of Medieval Glasgow* (Glasgow, 2007) which has much information on everyday life.

29 Barrow, *Acts of William I*, p. 327; *mater multarum gentium*.

30 Norman Shead, 'Glasgow: An Ecclesiastical Burgh', in Michael Lynch, Michael Spearman and Geoffrey Stell (eds), *The Scottish Medieval Town* (Edinburgh, 1988), p. 119. It is just possible that the name described a physical condition. 'Puddins' of a different variety were mentioned when, in 1588, Adam Elphinstone, with drawn sword, threatened to lay his victim's 'pudens' (guts) among his feet, J. D. Marwick (ed.), *Extracts From the Records of the Burgh of Glasgow* A.D. *1573–1642* (Glasgow, 1876), p. 122 (hereafter *Glasgow Burgh Records*).

31 Forbes, *Lives of Ninian and Kentigern*, pp. 42–5.

32 Primrose, *Medieval Glasgow*, pp. 51–9.

33 Primrose, *Medieval Glasgow*, p. 169.

34 Primrose, *Medieval Glasgow*, pp. 119–21; Renwick and Lindsay, *History of Glasgow*, vol. 1, pp. 99, 206.

35 Primrose, *Medieval Glasgow*, pp. 127–49.

36 Primrose, *Medieval Glasgow*, p. 249.

37 George MacDonald Fraser, *The Steel Bonnets The Story of the Anglo-Scottish Reivers* (London, 1974), Appendix 1, pp. 333–6.

38 Primrose, *Medieval Glasgow*, p. 156.

39 *Glasgow Burgh Records*, p. 2.

40 *Glasgow Burgh Records*, pp. 25–6.

41 *Glasgow Burgh Records*, p. 29.

42 *Glasgow Burgh Records*, p. 64.

43 *Glasgow Burgh Records*, p. 175.

44 *Glasgow Burgh Records*, pp. 285, 298.

45 Primrose, *Medieval Glasgow*, p. 159.

46 *Glasgow Burgh Records*, p. 187.

47 *Glasgow Burgh Records*, pp. 8–77.

48 *Glasgow Burgh Records*, pp. 88–156.

49 *Glasgow Burgh Records*, pp. 138–332.

50 Bower, *Scotichronicon*, vol. 2, p. 81.

Chapter 12

Marian Devotion in Scotland and the Shrine of Loreto[1]

Audrey-Beth Fitch

INTRODUCTION

Spirituality was an important, indeed crucial, everyday concern of Scottish folk on the eve of Reformation. That Protestant reformers did not always satisfactorily address such worries is indicated by the surviving appeal of the cult of the Virgin Mary well into the sixteenth century. The subject of Marian devotion at the time of the Reformation has not yet been fully explored within the Scottish context. Many historians prior to the 1960s played down the significance of Mary to the laity's spiritual life but, in the 1960s, there arose a new generation of Roman Catholic scholars who began to explore the traditional faith of pre-Reformation Scotland devotion to Mary.[2] My own work emphasises lay demonstrations of Marian devotion rather than the opinions and activities of clerics who were the focus of research in the 1960s.

The Blessed Virgin Mary was a constant companion for most Scots in the later fifteenth and early sixteenth centuries, and devotion to her remained strong after the Reformation of 1560 although, by then, her value officially lay only in her bearing Jesus.[3] Prior to the Reformation, the Scottish Church had acknowledged her as a guide to personal holiness, comforting companion at the hour of death, nurturer and healer of the ill, and protector in daily life. However, Her most important roles, however, were as guide, protector and intercessor at the Day of Judgement,[4] and vernacular devotional works firmly linked her to the saving power of the Cross. Mary's relationship to the Trinity was secure. To a contemporary poet, she was the 'temple of the trinity',[5] and a long devotional prayer, 'The Lang Rosair', referred to her as the 'sepultur of saluacioun' and 'port of paradice'.[6] In the sixteenth century, people increasingly relied on the Passion as their guarantee of salvation, which served only to increase their reliance on Mary who was an indefatigable intercessor on behalf of her human children as well as the loving mother of Jesus.[7] Proof positive of Mary's compassion was her behaviour at the Crucifixion. Imprinted on the lay imagination were images such as the one in Fowlis Easter collegiate church. In this small, intimate church, above the rood screen, there is a richly coloured painting of the Crucifixion. The painter catches well the milling of the crowd around the three crucified men, which makes Mary stand out in her stillness. She stands tearfully at the foot of the Cross, her head averted and bowed, resting on her hand. Mary's emotional response to the dying Jesus, explored so often in Scottish literature and art, encouraged people to develop a similar relationship with him. Without a doubt, it would have been extremely difficult for reformers to weaken the laity's devotion to such a strongly empathetic figure.

THE CULT OF THE VIRGIN

Reforming critics suggested that pilgrimages to Marian shrines indicated that the laity wanted Mary's aid on earth. Her assistance in the afterlife, however, was more than sufficient reason to visit her shrines. Mary's life story led people to rely heavily upon her as 'maist speciall mediatrix for man';[8] God had found her spiritually worthy to bear His Son, she had won His acceptance by participating willingly in the Incarnation; on earth she had enjoyed a close relationship with her son Jesus and therefore could be expected to have great influence over him in heaven,[9] and her spiritual worthiness had been made absolutely clear by her bodily assumption into heaven after death. In fact, to some early modern Scots, Mary was not only supreme intercessor with God, she was actually co-redeemer with Jesus (cf. tree of Jesse imagery gives Mary and Jesus equality).[10] Marian cults, such as Our Lady of Consolation and Our Lady of Loreto,[11] and Marian devotion in general, grew stronger in the socially and politically tumultuous sixteenth century when people feared sudden death by war and epidemic disease. In the sixteenth century, just before the Reformation, despite criticism directed at the cult of Mary, collegiate churches were founded in her honour, and many new prebends, chaplainries, altars and shrines were dedicated to her.

Lay devotion to Mary developed and sustained itself in an environment of intense clerical devotion: for example, the Carmelites and Cistercians.[12] The statues, paintings, retables and other images of Mary in Scottish churches, as well as masses, anthems, prayers and religious processions in her honour, conditioned the laity to consider Mary essential to its spiritual welfare. In particular, there was the litany of Loreto which dated back to the twelfth century, in which Mary was celebrated as a 'mystic rose'.[13] Marian rose imagery appeared in Scottish poetry and art. Mary was described as a pure rose, 'rose intemerat',[14] and as a 'rose Intact' who was the laity's greatest help in time of need,[15] and many illustrations in devotional works and carvings in churches used the rosary or other rose imagery to remind the viewer of Mary. Preachers validated Mary's intercessory role and parish priests reinforced the laity's belief that she was approachable and extremely effective as an intercessor. Lay authorities supported the Church in its defence of Marian devotion. In 1541, James V promulgated an Act of Parliament demanding that Mary be worshipped and honoured, and that prayers be addressed to her so that she might intercede with God, the Son and the

Figure 12.1 *Mary nursing Jesus, from a panel painting of the Trinity, Fowlis Easter collegiate church. A. Fitch.*

Holy Ghost. The government deemed Mary's intercession essential to the welfare and prosperity of the king, queen and their successors, and to the maintenance of peace, unity and concord between James V and all Christian princes.[16] Two years after this Act of Parliament, James V's widow, Mary of Guise (1515–60), later regent of Scotland, indicated that she shared her late husband's outlook, making a pilgrimage on foot to the shrine of Our Lady of Loreto 'praying for peace among her lords with the realm of England'.[17]

OUR LADY OF LORETO

In an article on Glasgow Cathedral published in 1966, David McRoberts looked briefly at the cult of Our Lady of Loreto. It was a cult which grew to prominence in Scotland in the 1520s and 1530s and led to the founding of a shrine in 1533 at Musselburgh, Midlothian, on the southern coast of the Firth of Forth, the same shrine which was visited by Mary of Guise in 1543.[18] The cult of Our Lady of Loreto was based upon a belief that the house of the Blessed Virgin Mary had been moved after the fall of Acre in 1291 to Dalmatia, modern-day Croatia, before moving in 1294 directly west across the Adriatic Sea to Loreto in Italy (in the region of Marche; Loreto lies three miles inland and fifteen miles south of Ancona).[19] The shrine was officially recognised by Pope Julius II at the turn of the sixteenth century, and visits to Rome made by Scottish clerics may help to explain the importation of the cult to Scotland; McRoberts ascribes the origin of the Scottish cult of Loreto to Scottish ecclesiastics and pilgrims residing in Rome, noting that clerics founded the shrine at Musselburgh and also a church dedicated to Our Lady of Loreto at Perth. The widespread popularity of the cult, however, may at least be partially attributable to Scottish traders who had close links with the Continent. Scottish trading links to Flanders were particularly strong, a staple being established in Bruges by the end of the fourteenth century, and remaining in Flanders throughout the early modern period. It was common for Flemish religious enthusiasms to find their way into early modern Scottish craft and merchant guilds without a prominent cleric first having introduced the idea: for example, the Holy Blood cult.[20] Thus, in 1526, before the clerical foundations of Perth and Musselburgh, the socially prominent goldsmiths of Edinburgh sent one of their number to Flanders to obtain an image of 'our Lady of Lorriee'. By obtaining an image of Our Lady of Loreto, the goldsmiths demonstrated their devotion to Mary, their desire to venerate her image, and their acquaintance with continental Marian cults.[21]

Another example of lay support for the cult of Loreto comes from Perth. On 28 December 1528, James V granted land, dwellings and wasteland to cleric Edward Gray (Sir) founder of a church dedicated to the Blessed Virgin Mary of Loreto.[22] In 1536, the king survived a storm at sea en route to France, and expressed his gratitude to Our Lady of Loreto by walking from

Stirling to the Musselburgh shrine, a distance of some 40 miles.[23] In May of 1538, while aboard ship, he offered two crowns to Our Lady of Loreto.[24] The king's association of Our Lady of Loreto with success at sea is unsurprising. In the Scottish vernacular version of the prayer 'O Clementissime' she is referred to as the 'sterne [or star] of the sey', 'bowsum [willing] gidder of schip brokin' and 'port of saluacioun' to souls wracked with self-doubt and urgently needing her assistance in preparing themselves spiritually for death. The mariners of Leith, Edinburgh's port, took Mary as their special patron, and founded a church in her honour in 1483; the town's seal depicted Mary and the baby Jesus in a galley at sea.[25]

This chapter focuses on the Loreto shrine at Musselburgh because its popularity made it the target of criticism before and after the Reformation. In 1533, Thomas Doughty (Douchtie), allegedly a hermit of the Order of S. Paul, or 'hermit of Mt Sinai', returned from the Holy Land with a statue of the Blessed Virgin Mary.[26] One chronicler even declared that Doughty had been held captive by the Turks in the Holy Land before returning to his homeland, this claim no doubt adding lustre to Doughty's reputation.[27] On 27 January 1534, the bailies, burgesses and community of Musselburgh gave Doughty and his successors at the shrine land on which to build a perpetual chapel, cell and garden. The community of Musselburgh must have been pleased to have been given the opportunity to profit from such a shrine and may also have been moved by religious zeal although this is not made explicit in the foundation document.[28] From Doughty's perspective, Musselburgh would have been a good site for the shrine as it was on an important transport artery – the Firth of Forth – and it was located in one of Scotland's most densely populated regions.

Once the shrine was set up, it proved to be immensely popular. Its popularity may have been due in part to contemporaries' understanding that the hermit of Loreto had received the image of Our Lady from Heaven. According to Bishop of Ross, John Leslie, the divine origin of the image, plus the shrine's reputation for miraculous healing, led to its veneration by a great number of people.[29] Sir David Lindsay (?1486–1555) criticised people who went to the shrine. Lindsay was a pre-Reformation courtier, poet and playwright whose opinions were well known in his own time, and even better known after the Reformation, thanks to the availability of cheap print copies of his works and a strong demand for them. Lindsay reported in his work *The Monarche*, written and published in 1554, that a multitude of men and women went 'flynagand on thare feit, Under the forme of feynit [pretended] sanctytude, / For tyll adore one image of Loreit', and he sneered that they even kissed the 'claggit [besmeared] taill' of the hermit at the shrine.[30] Lindsay was convinced that 'fowl fornicatioun' was the purpose of the pilgrimage, rather than piety.[31] He believed that all pilgrimages could lead to 'wantounnes', particularly in women.[32] Thus he warned men not to allow their wives and daughters to go on pilgrimage, vowing that he had seen 'gud wemen' return in sin and shame, having succumbed to lust while on their journey.[33] Poet Alexander Scott (c.1530–c.1584) supported Lindsay's contention that pilgrimage might be merely an excuse for a lover's tryst. In his poem 'Of May', written prior to the Reformation, he declared that one of the joys of the month of May was the journeying of maidens to Loreto to meet their lovers.[34]

Although Sir David Lindsay was not keen on pilgrimage of any sort, he was forced to admit that many of his contemporaries believed in its efficacy as a means of gaining salvation and remedy from earthly harm. They went from town to town visiting saints' images, praying and making offerings.[35] A similar view to Lindsay's was expressed by Londoner, William Patten, who took part in the English foray into Scotland in 1548. He wrote to Sir William Paget, comptroller of Edward VI's household, that Scotland was in 'servile thraldome and bondage', worshipping idols, making offerings to wax images, setting up candles to saints in every corner, clacking rosary beads in the pews and offering prayers for the cure of disease.[36]

Critics of shrines and the cult of saints held the upper clergy and preaching friars responsible for leading the laity astray with stories of miracles, teaching through images, and not acting to quell the laity's natural credulity and superstition. But the clergy defended its use of images. Images were teaching tools, 'books for the unlearned',[37] and clerics rigorously defended the notion that saints, especially Mary, effectively interceded for humanity. But Sir David Lindsay did not agree with the clergy that images of saints were merely 'books' for the unlearned. He believed that laypeople's devotion to saints readily turned to idolatry, and he held the clergy responsible for the persistence of misguided lay attitudes and behaviour.[38] The shrine of Loreto, with its image of Mary and apparently conscienceless founder, Thomas Doughty, was singled out by Lindsay, Knox and other critics as a particularly egregious example of shrines which were set up with the sole purpose of fleecing the laity and which did nothing to aid the search for salvation.

THE PROTEST OF REFORM

Prominent Protestant reformer, Alexander Cunningham, Lord Kilmauris and later Earl of Glencairn, attacked the friars, and Doughty in particular, in a poetic 'epistle' in which Doughty, the 'hermit of Loreto' warned his Franciscan brothers that they all had been found out by the 'Lutherans'. They were now known to be idolatrous, hypocritical heretics and lazy idlers sent by Satan, people who believed that their clerical garb would save them rather than Jesus' Passion. They were wolves in sheep's clothing, seeking to devour people and keep them from knowing Jesus, and thereby closing the gates of Heaven against them. Undaunted by his unmasking, Doughty informs the friars in the epistle that he plans to move his image of Mary to Argyll in the west to whip up enthusiasm through the performance of 'miracles', which he hopes will then lead to the founding of a new church.[39] The epistle was a robust attempt by Kilmauris to undercut the credibility of the popular Musselburgh shrine. John Knox's inclusion of the epistle in his *History of the Reformation in Scotland* brought Kilmauris's opinions to a wide readership and set his own stamp of approval on Kilmauris's condemnation of the Franciscans and his linking of them to hermit Thomas Doughty.

Despite the negative publicity received by Doughty, even devout Protestants found it difficult to convince some family members to boycott the shrine. In 1558, good Protestant Robert Colville, laird of Cleish in Fife, was forced to follow the servant of his Catholic wife, Francisca Colquhoun, to the chapel of Loreto to prevent the servant from making an offering, of gold and her mistress's sark (undergarment), to ease Lady Cleish's labour pains.[40] Praying to Mary for assistance in childbirth was traditional. In the *Actes and Monuments*, John Foxe recorded that Helen Stark had been accused of heresy for calling on God rather than on Mary during childbirth, and for denying that God had chosen Mary to be mother of Jesus because of her merits.[41] In 1542, pregnant Mary of Guise walked 7 miles from Edinburgh to Loreto. The queen had lost two children in infancy, within a few hours of each other, and the shrine was believed to miraculously heal the ill. Mary of Guise must have believed that making a pilgrimage to Loreto would help to ensure the survival of her unborn child; three years previously she had made a similar pilgrimage to the shrine of St Adrian in the Isle of May, a shrine noted for its success in assisting barren women.[42]

When the laird of Cleish arrived at the chapel in pursuit of his wife's servant, he found a large number of people from the nearby counties of East and West Lothian, the Merse and Tweeddale. The higher clergy apparently had announced that a miracle was to occur at the shrine, an event for which the laity had turned out in large numbers.[43] The suspicious laird waited to watch this miracle in which a blind man's sight was restored. Once the miracle had taken place, the laird hired the newly sighted man as his servant and then interrogated him in private. He learned that the 'cure' was a hoax, a false miracle organised by male clerics with the tacit approval of the nuns of the convent of the Sciennes outside Edinburgh, for whom the man worked as a shepherd. The Protestant author of this tale, William Row, was out-raged that the common people had been misled in such a fashion; the alleged 'miracle' had led them to believe that the 'ceremonies' associated with it were effective, and they had even given the man money. To make matters worse, the man had publicly blessed the holy family, saints, priests and friars for having effected the 'cure', thereby contributing to the audience's mistaken belief that the heavenly family and saints were in the habit of collaborating with the clergy.[44]

This story of a Loreto miracle is found in William Row's continuation of his father John's *The Historie of the Kirk of Scotland* which itself was based on the papers of William's grandfather, the first John Row (c.1526–80). Given the evidence upon which it is based, *The Historie* is a fairly reliable expression of one man's understanding of the religious changes taking place in mid-sixteenth-century Scotland, though there certainly is some interpretative commentary from his son and grandson, both of whom were Protestant ministers. John Row's conversion to Protestantism was striking, as it appears to have happened extremely quickly in 1558, soon after he returned from Rome where he had spent the previous eight years. As a canon lawyer and newly appointed papal legate, his mission in Scotland was to help prevent the spread of Protestantism. Instead, he ended up as a strong supporter of the Reformed cause and a powerful member of the early Protestant Church establishment.[45] It has been suggested that it may well have been the false miracle at the Musselburgh shrine which finally turned him against Catholicism, and the prominence given to this incident in William Row's contribution to the *Historie* tends to support this interpretation. Yet it must be noted that William Row himself credited his grandfather's quick conversion 'to the trueth' to his disputations with persuasive reformers, such as John Knox, rather than to the Loreto miracle.

Nevertheless, it is worth asking why John Row chose to record the details of a miracle at the Loreto shrine rather than a miracle at another popular pilgrimage site, such as Tain in the north-east (on the Dornoch Firth) dedicated to St Duthac, or Candida Casa (Whithorn) in the south-west (on the Solway Firth), dedicated to St Ninian.[46] It is also worth pondering the reasons for William Row's interest in the tale; as a member of seventeenth-century Protestant society, one might have expected him to ignore the details of a miraculous cure in the immediate pre-Reformation period.

John Row's interest in the tale appears to have arisen from his own sense of outrage that clerics in his own day were getting away with lying to people in such a blatant fashion. He appears to have been worried about the popularity of this particular shrine, and to have found its clerical leaders unusually corrupt. The shrine was founded at a time when criticism of the cult of saints was mounting, so one might have expected people to have stayed away from a new Marian shrine,[47] yet this was not the case. Furthermore, the shrine was close to the capital and other population centres, and was not far from pockets of Catholic resistance such as Angus to the north. Thus, the shrine may have been understood by Row and other Protestant leaders to pose a particular threat, unlike shrines in far-flung parts of the country, such as Tain and Candida Casa.

Marian devotion had been on the increase in the decades prior to the Reformation of 1560, and it was by no means non-existent in the seventeenth century. An incident from the pre-Reformation period helps to demonstrate just how contentious the subject of Marian devotion could become. A Scot doing time in a French galley in the mid-sixteenth century reacted violently when a painted image of Mary was thrust at him upon his arrival in Nantes. John Knox, his fellow prisoner, reported the man's words as follows: 'Truble

me nott; such an idole is accursed; and tharefoir I will not tuich it.' When
the image was thrust in his face, the man threw it in the river saying: 'Lett
our Lady now sail hirself: sche is lycht aneuch; lett hir learne to swyme.'[48]
William Row's exploration of the Loreto shrine, and evidence of tension
between Marian supporters and detractors, suggest that Mary's supporters were just as committed as her detractors, and that her challenge to the
reformed cause was deemed much more serious by contemporaries than the
cults of national saints, however ancient or popular.[49]

   William Row's relating of the story of the false cure was intended to
undercut post-Reformation faith in the miracle-working power of saints'
shrines in general, not just Marian shrines. John Row's personal conversion
to Protestantism may or may not have been inspired by this false miracle but
the story of the miracle reveals that the cult of Mary did not merely wither
and die soon after the Reformation. Hence, false miracle stories, such as
the one recorded by William Row, could be used by Protestant leaders and
ministers to convince their seventeenth-century contemporaries of the right-
ness of the Protestant triumph and the need to resist the pull of old shrines
as well as the blandishments of Counter-Reformation Jesuit priests. From
the time of the Reformation, the Protestant leadership had had constantly
to exhort the general populace to give up its reliance on saintly intercession; the assembly of Lothian, whose territory included Loreto, expressed
concern in 1581 that people persisted in making pilgrimages to wells, crosses
and images, and in celebrating saints' festivals.[50] Matters had not improved
by 1587 when the General Assembly of the Church of Scotland recorded
that Lothian, Merse and Teviotdale were full of practising Catholics and
priests and that there were 'many superstitious pilgrimages and keeping of
holy days'.[51] Publication of such books as Sir David Lindsay's *The Monarche*
(1580) and John Knox's *History of the Reformation in Scotland* (1586/7) aided
the Protestant leadership as it sought to draw people away from the old
ways.

THE SURVIVAL OF THE CULT

The strength of post-Reformation devotion to saints is unsurprising given
pre-Reformation attitudes. Attempts before the Reformation to convince
people to pray only to Jesus and God had sometimes been met with violence. John Foxe recorded in his *Actes and Monuments* that in Perth in the
1540s burgess Robert Lamb had been set upon by a crowd, mostly women,
who objected to his open criticism of a friar's sermon about the efficacy
of prayers to saints.[52] Lamb was later sentenced to death for dishonour-
ing the Blessed Virgin Mary and the saints, among other crimes.[53] John
Wedderburn's mid-sixteenth-century collection of reforming ballads, entitled *The Gude and Godlie Ballatis*, claimed that the 'simple people' preferred
to put their faith in saints' images rather than in the promises of an unseen

God.[54] Thus, the exhortation to the laity in the *Catechism* of 1552 to pray devoutly to saints was merely reinforcing existing behaviour and, when the provincial council of 1559 complained that there was less than total reverence for saints in the realm, it was arguing from the perspective of a Church hierarchy which had every reason to expect its flock to be devout followers of the 'holy ones'. Saintly images and stories were prominent in lay devotional life and in Church imagery and practice,[55] and only gradually was the Reformed Church able to eradicate devotional practices associated with saints and their miracles.[56]

Row's tale about the laird of Cleish and the shrine of Loreto was also an attempt to undercut the credibility of Catholic clerics practising in the post-Reformation period, whether native priests or Jesuit missionaries, as these men were proving immensely effective in providing a focus for recusancy. His claim that clerics staged miracles as a means of securing the common people's allegiance to Catholicism implied that, without such tricks, Catholicism would fail.[57] He also appears to have wished to use the tale to advise women about their proper role in the religious life of the community. Just as the laird of Cleish's wife had refused to convert to Protestantism alongside her husband, so too other early modern women refused to accept the authority of the Protestant male leadership. In 1616, the General Assembly of the Church of Scotland accused women of arranging for Jesuit and other Catholic priests to educate their young children in the Catholic faith.[58] By organising religious instruction for the young and thereby harbouring the priestly enemies of the new faith, women were interfering in the new, entirely male, religious authority structure. Because they no longer had the option of entering a convent, women's leadership activities were confined to the home. Consequently, it is unsurprising that it is in this context that women drew criticism from the authorities. A desire to remind his own society that women should not hold positions of religious authority may have been part of the reason for William Row's critical comments on the nuns of the convent of St Katherine of the Sciennes because, at first glance, it makes little sense to judge them so harshly for having allowed the false miracle to take place at Loreto when it was a male clerical elite that engineered the miracle. Destroying the reputation of these nuns was not easy, however, as they had been well known for their integrity. The convent had been founded in 1517, only a few decades before the shrine of Loreto, and it was difficult to find evidence of impropriety or impiety in an institution so recently founded by the pious Lowland ladies of Seton, Bass and Glenbervie.[59] James V claimed that they spent their days praying to Mary and worshipping God,[60] and even critics of the clergy, such as Sir David Lindsay, were forced to admit that morally the nuns were beyond reproach.[61] John Leslie, writing in the 1570s, declared with a touch of bitterness that it was St Katherine of the Sciennes' reputation as the best convent in Scotland that had made it the target of the reformers' destructive wrath.

CONCLUSION

It can fairly be said that the shrine of Our Lady of Loreto in Musselburgh, Scotland, helped to form the religious understanding of post-Reformation Scots as well as those living when the shrine functioned as a legitimate pilgrimage site. The shrine, founded only twenty-seven years before the Reformation, represented the power of Mary to command the love and devotion of the laity from the least commoner to the king, and for some, the power of Mary to effect miracles. In consequence, the shrine and its founder, Thomas Doughty, were the target of reforming criticism both before and after the Reformation. Discussions of sixteenth-century Scottish lay faith, and the everyday popularity of various rituals and institutions, surely must now take into account the commitment to Mary felt by many Scots. Scholars of post-Reformation Scotland might now ask themselves whether they have explained how Marian devotion was channelled in the Protestant period, rather than merely asking whether people remained 'Catholic' or converted to 'Protestantism', and viewing Marian devotion as an indication of this. One avenue of enquiry might be to explore whether Mary's roles as healer on earth and protector at the Day of Judgement were transferred to her son in the Protestant period, in which case there should be evidence of a change in people's understanding of Jesus' nature and function, a change which might be partially attributable to lay spiritual imperatives as well as to a changed theology. The hereafter and the salvation of one's soul remained a source of everyday anxiety and of profounder import than the arguments of the Reform. Whatever the case, a better understanding of Marian devotion and of shrines such as that of Musselburgh, can only enrich our understanding of lay religion as it was transformed in the Reformation period.

Notes

1 Unfortunately Audrey-Beth had not fully completed this chapter before her tragic death. The editors hope to have retained the spirit and integrity of the original and properly to have interpreted the notes. See now Audrey-Beth Fitch, *The Search for Salvation: Lay Faith in Scotland, 1480–1560*, Elizabeth Ewan (ed.) (Edinburgh, 2009).

2 The studies by such Catholic scholars as David McRoberts, John Durkan and Mark Dilworth complemented the work of Gordon Donaldson and his circle of students who came to dominate Scotland's universities in the 1970s and 1980s. Donaldson's work emphasised the institutional, political and economic aspects of pre-Reformation Scottish religion although, later in life, he did develop a stronger interest in interior faith, publishing *The Faith of the Scots* (London, 1990), a survey of Scottish faith from earliest times to the twentieth century.

3 John Gau, *The Richt Vay to the Kingdom of Heuine*, A. F. Mitchell (ed.) (Edinburgh and London, 1888), p. 101.

4 Benedicta Ward, *Miracles and the Medieval Mind: Theory, Record and Event 1000–1215* (London, 1982), p. 162.

5 William Dunbar, 'Ros Mary: Ane Ballat of Our Lady', in William Mackay Mackenzie (ed.), *The Poems of William Dunbar* (Edinburgh, 1932), I.19, p. 175.

6 'The Lang Rosair', in J. A. W. Bennett (ed.), *Devotional Pieces in Verse and Prose, from MS. Arundel 285 and MS. Harleian 6919* (Edinburgh, 1955), p. 327.

7 Bennett, *Devotional Pieces*, p. 330.

8 Bennett, *Devotional Pieces*, p. 330.

9 Richard Bauckham, 'The Origins and Growth of Western Mariology', in David F. Wright (ed.), *Chosen by God: Mary in Evangelical Perspective* (London, 1989), p. 145.

10 For example, Bennett, *Devotional Pieces*, p. 332 ('tre of lif'), and p. 330 ('maist speciall mediatrix for man'), and Bauckham, 'Origins and Growth of Western Mariology', p. 157.

11 David McRoberts, 'Notes on Glasgow Cathedral', in *Innes Review* (Glasgow, 1966), pp. xvii, 42–4.

12 The Carmelite houses in Scotland were those of Aberdeen, Banff, Berwick, Edinburgh (Greenside), Inverbervie, Irvine, Kingussie, Linlithgow, Luffness, Queensferry and Tullilum, those of Inverbervie, Linlithgow and Queensferry being fifteenth-century foundations. The Cistercian nunneries in Scotland in the sixteenth century were those of South Berwick, North Berwick, Eccles, Coldstream, Haddington, St Bothan's, Manuel and Elcho, and the Cistercian monasteries were those of Balmerino, Coupar Angus, Culross, Deer, Dundrennan, Glenluce, Kinloss, Melrose, Newbattle, Saddell and Sweetheart. Thus, it can be seen that the Carmelite and Cistercian orders were in Scotland in force, and that they had a countrywide presence, providing a constant source of Marian imagery and devotion. See Ian B. Cowan and David E. Easson (eds), *Medieval Religious Houses Scotland*, 2nd edn (London and New York, [1957] 1976), pp. 72, 135, 144.

13 Anne Winston-Allen, *Stories of the Rose: The Making of the Rosary in the Middle Ages* (University Park, PA, 1997), p. 88.

14 William Dunbar, 'Ros Mary: Ane Ballat of Our Lady', in Mackenzie, *Poems of William Dunbar*, p. 176.

15 Anon, 'Ane Ballat of Our Lady', in W. A. Craigie (ed.), *The Asloan Manuscript: A Miscellany in Prose and Verse*, 2 vols (Edinburgh and London, 1923–5), vol. 2, p. 245.

16 T. Thomson and C. Innes (eds), *The Acts of the Parliaments of Scotland*, A.D. *MCCCCXXIV*–A.D. *MDLXVII*, 12 vols (Edinburgh, 1814–75), vol. 2, p. 370.

17 Rosalind K. Marshall, *Mary of Guise* (London, 1977), p. 141.

18 McRoberts, 'Notes on Glasgow Cathedral', p. 42.

19 Jenny Wormald, *Court, Kirk and Community: Scotland 1470–1625* (London, 1981), p. 47.

20 For example, Scottish merchants took part in the Holy Blood pageant in Bruges, and the cult of the Holy Blood soon became popular with merchant guilds in

Scotland. McRoberts, 'Notes on Glasgow Cathedral', p. 44, Wormald, *Court, Kirk and Community*, pp. 47, 91, I. F. Grant, *The Social and Economic Development of Scotland Before 1603* (Westport, CT, 1930), pp. 331–3, and Ian D. Whyte, *Scotland Before the Industrial Revolution: An Economic and Social History c.1050– c.1750* (London, 1995), p. 51. Archbishop Blacader introduced the cult of Our Lady of Consolation in the early sixteenth century.

21 NAS GD1/482/1, fo 7r. Further north in the booming eastern port of Aberdeen, St Mary's College, later King's College, recorded an image of 'our Lady of Lorett' on one of its 'tables'. Inventory of 1542, in Francis C. Eeles, *King's College Chapel Aberdeen: Its Fittings, Ornaments and Ceremonial in the Sixteenth Century* (Edinburgh, 1956), p. 44.

22 McRoberts, 'Notes on Glasgow Cathedral', pp. xvii, 42, and James Balfour Paul and John Maitland Thomson (eds), *Registrum Magni Sigilli Regum Scotorum: The Register of the Great Seal of Scotland*, [Hereafter RMS] 11 vols (Edinburgh, 1883), vol. 3, no. 722, p. 157.

23 John Leslie, *Historie of Scotland*, qtd in David Laing (ed.), *The Works of John Knox*, 6 vols (Edinburgh, 1846–64), vol. 1, pp. 76, 150.

24 James Balfour Paul (ed.), *Compota Thesaurariorum Regum Scotorum: Accounts of the Lord High Treasurer of Scotland*, 11 vols (Edinburgh, 1877–1916), vol. 7, p. 24.

25 Charles Carter, 'The Arma Christi in Scotland', in *Proceedings of the Society of Antiquaries of Scotland* 90 (1956–7) p. 73, and R. M. Urquhart, *Scottish Burgh and County Heraldry* (London, 1973), p. 247. The close association of Mary with the sea continued into modern times. The 'Dawn Prayer of the Clanranald', sung at sea, referred to her as the fair maiden of the sea, and a traditional Highland poem, 'Prayer to Mary Mother', requesting that Mary 'pilot them at sea' just as she guided them on shore, in Bennett, *Devotional Pieces*, pp. 83–4, 89, 91, 281, and Alexander Carmichael (ed.), *Carmina Gadelica: Hymns and Incantations*, 6 vols (Edinburgh, [1900] 1940), vol. 3, no. 255, p. 125.

26 McRoberts, 'Notes on Glasgow Cathedral', p. 44.

27 T. Thomson (ed.), *A Diurnal of Remarkable Occurents that have Passed Within the Country of Scotland since the Death of King James the Fourth till the Year MDLXXV* (Edinburgh, 1833), p. 17.

28 RMS, vol. 3, no. 1403, pp. 309–10.

29 John Leslie, *The Historie of Scotland*, E. G. Cody (ed.) and James Dalrymple (trans.), 2 vols (Edinburgh, 1895), vol. 2, p. 253.

30 Sir David Lindsay, *The Monarche* ('Ane Dialogue betuix Experience and ane Courteour, Off the Miserabyll Estait of the Warld'), in Douglas Hamer (ed.), *The Works of Sir David Lindsay of the Mount 1490–1555*, 4 vols (Edinburgh, 1931), vol. 1, p. 278; Carol Edington, *Court and Culture in Renaissance Scotland: Sir David Lindsay of the Mount* (Amherst, MA, 1994), p. 224, and Harry G. Aldis, *A List of Books Printed in Scotland Before 1700* (Edinburgh, 1904), no. 24.

31 Lindsay, *The Monarche* in *Works*, p. 278.

32 Lindsay, 'Kitteis Confessioun', in *Works*, vol. 1, p. 126.

33 Lindsay, *The Monarche* in *Works*, vol. 1, pp. 278–9.

34 Alexander Scott, 'Of May', in Alexander Scott (ed.), *The Poems of Alexander Scott*

c.*1530*–c.*1584* (Edinburgh, 1952), p. 35. cf. William Dunbar, 'The Tretis of the Tua Mariit Wemen and the Wedo', in Mackenzie, *The Poems of William Dunbar*, p. 86.

35 Lindsay, *The Monarche* in *Works*, pp. 268–70.

36 William Patten, *The Expedicion into Scotlande of Prince Edward, Duke of Somerset*, London, 1548, NLS Adv. MS 28.3.12, fos 57v and 61r–v.

37 For example, Ninian Winzet, 'Certain Tractates together with the Book of Four Score Three Questions', in James King Hewison (ed.), *Certain Tractates together with the Book of Four Score Three Questions and a Translation of Vincentius Lirinensis*, 2 vols (Edinburgh, 1888–90), vol. 1, pp. 123–4, and David Patrick (intro. and notes), *Statutes of the Scottish Church, 1225–1559* (Edinburgh, 1907), p. 126, 174.

38 Lindsay, *The Monarche* in *Works*, vol. 1, pp. 268–9.

39 Alexander, Lord Kilmauris, later Earl of Glencairn, 'Ane Epistle Direct Fra the Holye Armite of Allarit to his Brethren the Gray Freires', in Laing, *The Works of John Knox*, vol. 1, pp. 72–4. Note that the first edition of Knox's *History* was c.1586. The MS (or those parts of it including the poem) have been dated 1566–71. Poem thought to have been written as early as 1540. See, for example, *Dictionary of Scottish Church History and Theology* (Edinburgh, 1993), p. 367.

40 William Row, *The Coronis; Being a Continuation of the Historie*, B. Botfield (ed.), 2 vols (Glasgow, 1842), vol. 1, pp. 204–5. Francisca was the daughter of Patrick Colquhoun of Drumskeath, see James Balfour Paul (ed.), *The Scots Peerage*, 9 vols (Edinburgh, 1904–5), vol. 2, p. 569.

41 John Foxe, 'Actes and Monuments', in Laing, *The Works of John Knox*, vol. 1, p. 524. cf. Gau, *The Richt Vay to the Kingdom of Heuine*, pp. 101–2.

42 Leslie, *Historie of Scotland*, vol. 2, p. 253; Marshall, *Mary of Guise*, pp. 78, 82, 86–7, 96–7.

43 Row, *Historie of the Kirk of Scotland*, vol. 1, p. 205.

44 Row, *Historie of the Kirk of Scotland*, vol. 1, pp. 206–7.

45 Row, *Coronis*, pp. 205, xxxi–xxxii.

46 Letter to Julius II, in Robert Kerr Hannay and R. L. Mackie (eds), *The Letters of James the Fourth 1505–1513* (Edinburgh, 1953), pp. 182–3; cf. Walter Macfarlane, *Geographical Collections Relating to Scotland*, Arthur Mitchell (ed.), 3 vols (Edinburgh, 1906), vol. 1, p. 255. The Marian shrine and well of Fetteresso, Kincardineshire, just west of Stonehaven, which James IV had declared to be famous for its many miracles and the pilgrimage destination of 'multitudes of the faithful'.

47 David McRoberts, 'Material Destruction Caused by the Scottish Reformation', in David McRoberts (ed.), *Essays on the Scottish Reformation 1513–1625* (Glasgow, 1962), pp. 417–18 (1533), and D. Hay Fleming and James Beveridge (eds), *Registrum Secreti Sigili Regum Scotorum* [hereafter RSS], 8 vols (Edinburgh, 1936), vol. 3, no. 636, p. 95 (1544).

48 Laing, *Works of John Knox*, vol. 1, p. 227, and David F. Wright, 'Mary in the Reformers', in David F. Wright (ed.), *Chosen by God: Mary in Evangelical Perspective* (London, 1989), pp. 163, 164, 168.

49 Leslie J. Macfarlane, *William Elphinstone and the Kingdom of Scotland 1431–1514: The Struggle for Order* (Aberdeen, 1985), p. 234.

50 T. Thomson (ed.), *Acts and Proceedings of the General Assembly of the Kirk of Scotland from the Year MCLX (The Booke of the Universall Kirk of Scotland)* [hereafter BUK], 4 vols (Edinburgh, 1839–45), vol. 2, pp. 535–6.

51 BUK, vol. 2, p. 720.

52 Foxe, 'Actes and Monuments', in Laing, *Works of John Knox*, vol. 1, p. 523.

53 RSS, vol. 3, no. 611, p. 92.

54 Iain Ross (ed.), *The Gude and Godlie Ballatis* (London, 1940), no. 12, p. 30.

55 John Hamilton, *The Catechism of John Hamilton*, Thomas Graves Law (ed.) (Oxford, 1884), and David Patrick, *Statutes of the Scottish Church, 1225–1559* (Edinburgh, 1907), p. 174.

56 Gordon DesBrisay, 'Catholics, Quakers and Religious Persecution in Restoration Aberdeen', in *Innes Review* 47 (autumn 1996), pp. 143, 145, and, for example, BUK, vol. 2, pp. 715–19, 724 (1587), and vol. 3, pp. 829–30 (1592) and 1047–50 (1608). Part of the problem was that powerful Catholic nobles carried on protecting practising Catholics (for instance, Gordons of Huntly).

57 Row, *Coronis*, vol. 1, p. 205.

58 BUK, vol. 3, p. 1120 (1616).

59 George Seton, *A History of the Family of Seton*, 2 vols (Edinburgh, 1896), vol. 1, pp. 94–106.

60 Robert Kerr Hannay and Denys Hay (eds), *The Letters of James V* (Edinburgh, 1954), pp. 232–3.

61 Cowan and Easson, *Medieval Religious Houses*, p. 152, and McRoberts, 'Material Destruction Caused by the Scottish Reformation', p. 419.

Annotated Bibliography

INTRODUCTION: EVERYDAY LIFE IN MEDIEVAL SCOTLAND

So far as is known, this volume represents the first attempt to provide a wide survey of everyday life in medieval Scotland, a challenge that most commentators have hitherto avoided owing to the absence of relevant sources. A number of studies make valiant attempts to include a chapter or two on 'the peasantry' or 'the burghs' but, as a topic, the everyday has not yet entered the historiographical mainstream. General surveys that contain some useful pointers are W. Croft Dickinson, *Scotland from the Earliest Times to 1603* (Edinburgh, [1961] 1965), A. A. M. Duncan, *Scotland. The Making of the Kingdom*, Edinburgh History of Scotland vol. 1 (Edinburgh, 1975), Ranald Nicholson, *Scotland. The Later Middle Ages*, Edinburgh History of Scotland vol. 2 (Edinburgh, 1974), Alexander Grant, *Independence and Nationhood: Scotland 1306–1469* (London, 1984), and Jenny Wormald, *Court, Kirk and Community: Scotland 1470–1625* (London, 1981). A useful treatment of source material is Bruce Webster, *Scotland from the Eleventh Century to 1603* (London, 1975).

A good impression of how everyday lives were lived is to be found in the dated, but still useful, I. F. Grant, *Social and Economic Development of Scotland before 1603* (Edinburgh 1930) – truly a pioneering work. A brief, but sound, modern treatment is Peter Yeoman, *Medieval Scotland: An Archaeological Perspective* (London, 1995). For everyday life in monasteries see Derek Hall, *Scottish Monastic Landscapes* (Stroud, 2006). There is also a hint of dirt and stench in Elizabeth Ewan, *Townlife in Fourteenth-Century Scotland* (Edinburgh, 1990) as in M. Lynch, M. Spearman and G. Stell (eds), *The Scottish Medieval Town*. There are some hints of everyday life in S. G. E. Lythe, *The Economy of Scotland 1550–1625* (Edinburgh, 1960) and in Part 1 of S. G. E. Lythe and J. Butt, *An Economic History of Scotland 1100–1930* (Glasgow and London, 1975) now overtaken by R. A. Dodgshon, *Land and Society in Early Scotland* (Oxford, 1981) and Ian Whyte, *Scotland before the Industrial Revolution: An Economic and Social History c.1050–c.1750* (London, 1995).

Scottish medieval historiography is largely concerned with monarchs and aristocrats who, of course, led their own everyday lives. A selection of studies offering some pointers would include Jennifer M. Brown (ed.), *Scottish Society in the Fifteenth Century* (London, 1977), K. J. Stringer (ed.), *Essays on the Nobility of Medieval Scotland* (Edinburgh, 1985), Jenny Wormald,

Lords and Men in Scotland: Bonds of Manrent 1442–1603 (Edinburgh, 1985), Louise Olga Fradenburg, *City, Marriage, Tournament Arts of Rule in Late Medieval Scotland* (Madison, 1991), Alexander Grant and Keith J. Stringer (eds), *Medieval Scotland: Crown, Lordship and Community. Essays presented to G. W. S. Barrow* (Edinburgh, 1993), Edward J. Cowan and R. Andrew McDonald (eds), *Alba: Celtic Scotland in the Medieval Era* (East Linton, 2000), Steve Boardman and Alasdair Ross (eds), *The Exercise of Power in Medieval Scotland c.1200–1500* (Dublin, 2003) and Cynthia J. Neville, *Native Lordship in Medieval Scotland. The Earldoms of Strathearn and Lennox, c.1140–1365* (Dublin, 2005).

Evidence for the recovery of the everyday is more readily available from the fifteenth century and almost abundant for the sixteenth, especially in the period of the Reformation which was as much concerned with social reform as it was with religious transformation. The available literature is quite voluminous but particularly helpful in pursuit of our topic are, Michael Lynch, *Edinburgh and the Reformation* (Edinburgh, 1981), Ian B. Cowan, *The Scottish Reformation: Church and Society in Sixteenth-Century Scotland* (London, 1982), Margaret Sanderson, *Scottish Rural Society in the Sixteenth Century* (Edinburgh, 1982), Frank D. Bardgett, *Scotland Reformed: The Reformation in Angus and the Mearns* (Edinburgh, 1989), James Kirk, *Patterns of Reform: Continuity and Change in the Reformation Kirk* (Edinburgh, 1989), Michael Graham, *The Uses of Reform: 'Godly Discipline' and Popular Behaviour in Scotland and Beyond, 1560–1610* (Leiden, 1996), Julian Goodare, *State and Society in Early Modern Scotland* (Oxford, 1999) and Margo Todd, *The Culture of Protestantism in Early Modern Scotland* (New Haven and London, 2002). An excellent study which truly explores Scottish everyday life is Margaret H. B. Sanderson, *A Kindly Place? Living in Sixteenth-Century Scotland* (East Linton, 2002).

Some of the most illuminating sources on everyday life are literary. For some indication of the potential see R. D. S. Jack (ed.), *The History of Scottish Literature*, vol. 1, *Origins to 1660* (Aberdeen, 1988) and Ian Brown (ed.), *The Edinburgh History of Scottish Literature*, vol. 1. *From Columba to the Union* (Edinburgh, 2006). An attempt to investigate the mindset and beliefs of Scottish people is Lizanne Henderson and Edward J. Cowan, *Scottish Fairy Belief: A History* (East Linton, 2001).

CHAPTER 1: LANDSCAPE AND PEOPLE

The physical environment of medieval Scotland is not terribly well served compared with its political, religious, cultural and more recently, its economic history. A. A. M. Duncan, however, did write a chapter on 'The Land' in his volume of The Edinburgh History of Scotland, *The Making of the Kingdom*, as far back as 1975. G. W. S. Barrow similarly introduced his book *Kingship and Unity* (1981) with a chapter on 'Land and People', though this was focused primarily on the south-east. Michael Lynch devoted a chapter to 'Land and People', albeit before AD 400, in his *Scotland. A New History* (1991). And I did something similar in *Scotland from Prehistory to the Present* (2001). The land was also implicitly dealt with by David Ditchburn and Alastair Macdonald in the first, largely economic, section of their chapter on medieval Scotland in *The New Penguin History of Scotland* (2001). Most work on the medieval environment, however, has tended to be done by non-historians. *Scotland after the Ice Age* (ed. K. Edwards and I. Ralston) contains work by archaeologists, palaeoecologists, soil scientists and geographers, and examines everything from climate, rocks and soils to what grows in and on the land until about AD 1000. Woodland history is particularly advanced in Scotland and there is a preliminary section on the state of Scottish woodlands up to 1500 in *A History of the Native Woodlands of Scotland* (T. C. Smout, A. MacDonald and F. Watson, 2005). With a rise in interest in environmental history, however, innovative work such as R. Oram and P. Adderley's 'Lordship and Environmental Change in Central Highland Scotland *c*.1300–*c*.1400', *Journal of the North Atlantic* vol. 1 (2008), pp. 74–84, is beginning to appear in certain journals.

CHAPTER 2: THE WORLDVIEW OF SCOTTISH VIKINGS IN THE AGE OF THE SAGAS

Books on the Vikings appear annually. All of them contain helpful sections on everyday life. One of the first of a sequence of beautifully illustrated studies is Bertil Almgren (ed.), *The Viking* (London, 1966) in which drawings are included as well as photographs to splendid effect. More modest but right on topic is Jacqueline Simpson, *Everyday Life in the Viking Age* (London, 1967), a lively text which demonstrates why Viking everyday life is much better documented than that of most other early peoples. A ground-breaking study is Gwyn Jones, *A History of the Vikings* (Oxford, 1968). Peter Foote and David M. Wilson, *The Viking Achievement. The Society and Culture of Early Medieval Scandinavia* (London, 1970) marked something of an achievement for the authors who produced what might still be regarded as one of the best and most comprehensive studies on the subject although it has been somewhat overtaken by more recent research, especially on archaeology. A distinguished pupil of Foote and Wilson is James Graham-Campbell, *The Viking World* (New Haven and New York, 1980). Else Roesdahl, *The Vikings* (London, 1987) is particularly strong on the Scandinavian homelands, offering something of a corrective to the anglocentric tendency of some other studies. Peter Sawyer (ed.), *The Oxford Illustrated History of the Vikings* (Oxford, 1997) complements James Graham-Campbell et al., *Cultural Atlas of the Viking World* (Abingdon, 1994). John Haywood, *Encyclopaedia of the Viking Age* (London, 2000), which closely followed his *The Vikings* (Stroud, 1999), is a handy guide to the subject, as is the same author's *The Penguin Historical Atlas of the Vikings* (London, 1995). R. Chartrand, K. Durham,

M. Harrison and I. Heath, *The Vikings: Voyagers of Discovery and Plunder* (Oxford, 2006) explores the question of Viking violence and warfare, while Paddy Griffith, *The Viking Art of War* (London, 1995) delivers the promise of its title. Stefan Brink (ed.) *The Viking World*, in collaboration with Neil Price (London, 2008) is a rather massive collection, so long in the making that some of its contents were a little dated by the time it appeared.

Books on Scotland include F. T. Wainwright (ed.), *The Northern Isles* (Edinburgh, 1962) a pioneering work which rightly places Orkney and Shetland at the crossroads of the Scandinavian world, supplemented by Alexander Fenton and Hermann Pálsson (eds), *The Northern and Western Isles in the Viking World: Survival, Continuity and Change* (Edinburgh, 1984). There is useful historical discussion in Alfred P. Smyth, *Warlords and Holy Men: Scotland AD 80–1000* (London, 1984) which should now be read alongside Benjamin Hudson, *Viking Pirates and Christian Princes: Dynasty, Religion, and Empire in the North Atlantic* (Oxford, 2005) and Alex Woolf, *From Pictland to Alba 789–1070* (Edinburgh, 2007). The best monograph by far is undoubtedly Barbara E. Crawford, *Scandinavian Scotland* (Leicester, 1987). Colleen E. Batey, Judith Jesch and Christopher D. Morris (eds), *The Viking Age in Caithness, Orkney and the North Atlantic* (Edinburgh, 1993) presents an excellent collection of essays on the subject. During the last thirty years or so, archaeology has figured significantly in publications about Viking studies in Scotland. Anna Ritchie, *Viking Scotland* (London, 1993) is a clear-eyed survey of the Scottish Viking archaeology, as is James Graham-Campbell and Colleen E. Batey, *Vikings in Scotland. An Archaeological Survey* (Edinburgh, 1998), an invaluable summary of excavation and investigation. See, too, the impressively illustrated Olwyn Owen and Magnar Dalland, *Scar: A Viking Boat Burial on Sanday, Orkney* (East Linton, 1999). There is considerable Scottish focus in A. Forte, R. Oram and F. Pedersen, *Viking Empires* (Cambridge, 2005).

For the saga period *Orkneyinga Saga* is essential. The standard modern English translation is Hermann Pálsson and Paul Edwards, *Orkneyinga Saga. The History of the Earls of Orkney* (London, 1978) which should be supplemented with Alexander Burt Taylor *The Orkneyinga Saga: A New Translation with Introduction and Notes* (London and Edinburgh, 1938), a more strained translation but one accompanied by very useful notes. Barbara E. Crawford (ed.), *St Magnus Cathedral and Orkney's Twelfth Century Renaissance* (Aberdeen, 1988) provides an excellent collection of essays on the context of *Orkneyinga*, as does Olwyn Owen (ed.), *The World of Orkneyinga Saga. 'The Broad-Cloth Viking Trip'* (Kirkwall, 2005). Tom Muir, *Orkney in the Sagas. The Story of the Earldom of Orkney as told in the Icelandic Sagas* (Kirkwall, 2005) is a straightforward retelling of the saga together with Orcadian references in other sagas. For a discussion of the end of Scandinavian rule in the Hebrides and of *Hakon's Saga* see Edward J. Cowan, 'Norwegian Sunset – Scottish dawn: Hakon IV and Alexander III', in Norman H. Reid (ed.), *Scotland in the Reign of Alexander II 1249–1286* (Edinburgh, 1990), pp. 103–31.

On sagas and medieval Icelandic literature see Carol J. Clover and John Lindow (eds), *Old Norse-Icelandic Literature: A Critical Guide* (Ithaca and London, 1985), Rory McTurk (ed.), *A Companion to Old Norse-Icelandic Literature and Culture* (Oxford, 2005) and Jónas Kristjánsson, *Eddas and Sagas. Iceland's Medieval Literature*, trans. Peter Foote (Reykjavik, 1997).

CHAPTER 3: SACRED AND BANAL: THE DISCOVERY OF EVERYDAY MEDIEVAL MATERIAL CULTURE

The international nature of this material is emphasised by the fact that many of the best publications deal with material from other countries. Most obvious are pilgrim badges, some of the best catalogues covering material from the Netherlands; the two volumes of *Hielig aan Profaan* (Rotterdam 1993 and 2001 respectively) show a range of pilgrim badges which have stylistic parallels this side of the North Sea as well as some secular examples.

The panoply of medieval personal objects is well covered in the Museum of London catalogue 'Dress Accessories *c.*1150–1450' (London, 1991) and, together with 'Object and Economy in Medieval Winchester' (Oxford, 1990), give a useful insight into the wide array of material culture widely used throughout the British Isles. For this material in a Scottish context 'Excavations in the Medieval Burgh of Aberdeen' (Edinburgh, 1982) and 'Excavations in the Medieval Burgh of Perth' (Edinburgh, 1987) are useful guides to the use of this material in Scotland, at least in an urban context. For a more rounded – and regional – picture there is a glut of recent excavation reports published in what are popularly referred to as the 'backlog' editions of the *Proceedings of the Society of Antiquaries of Scotland*; these are double volumes of the Proceedings published from 1995 to 2000.

A useful discussion of the high-quality jewellery can be found in 'Mediaeval European jewellery' (London, 1992) and finally, for an overall view, the recent and authoritative 'Gold and gilt, pots and pins: possessions and people in medieval Britain' (Oxford, 2005) is highly recommended.

CHAPTER 4: THE FAMILY

The following four works, chosen from many, help to set the European scene although they say all too little about Scotland. A selection of useful studies on the wider view of marriage in Europe, while including little or no material on Scotland, would include Georges Duby, *The Knight, the Lady and the Priest: The Making of Modern Marriage in Medieval France* (London, 1985), Jack Goody, *The Development of the Family and Marriage in Europe* (Cambridge, 1983), Kenneth Nicholls, *Gaelic and Gaelicised Ireland in the Middle Ages* (2nd edn, Dublin, 2003) and Christopher Brooke, *The Medieval Idea of Marriage* (Oxford, 1989). See now Elizabeth Ewan and Janay Nugent (eds), *Finding the Family in Early Medieval and Modern Scotland* (Aldershot, 2008).

The following four articles illustrate aspects of the Scottish story. The first two are not nearly as well known as they should be. A. E. Anton, '"Handfasting" in Scotland', *Scottish Historical Review* 37 (1958), pp. 89–102, R. W. Munro, 'The clan system – fact or fiction?', in Loraine Maclean of Dochgarroch (ed.), *The Middle Ages in the Highlands* (Inverness, 1981), pp. 117–29, W. D. H. Sellar, 'Marriage, divorce and the forbidden degrees: canon law and Scots law', in W. N. Osborough (ed.) *Explorations in Law and History: Irish Legal History Society Discourses, 1988–94* (Dublin, 1995), pp. 59–82, and Jenny Wormald, 'Bloodfeud, kindred and government in early Modern Scotland' *Past and Present* 57, pp. 54–97.

CHAPTER 5: 'HAMPERIT IN ANE HONY CAME': SIGHTS, SOUNDS AND SMELLS IN THE MEDIEVAL TOWN

The study of everyday life as a whole in medieval Scottish towns is not well developed but many works include discussions of aspects of the topic. Some excellent nineteenth-century local histories, such as Alexander Maxwell, *Old Dundee* (Edinburgh, 1890), used court records extensively to recover the lives of ordinary people. The publication of M. Lynch et al. (eds), *The Scottish Medieval Town* (Edinburgh, 1988) and M. Lynch (ed.), *The Early Modern Town in Scotland* (London, 1987), both with essays including aspects of daily life, encouraged modern urban history in Scotland. E. Ewan, *Townlife in Fourteenth-Century Scotland* (Edinburgh, 1990) examines a range of towns. Recent histories of towns usually include relevant chapters or sections – E. P. Dennison et al. (eds), *Aberdeen Before 1800* (East Linton, 2002) and E. P. D. Torrie, *Medieval Dundee* (Dundee, 1990) are good examples. Margaret Sanderson, *A Kindly Place? Living in Sixteenth-Century Scotland* (East Linton, 2002) provides an evocative picture of ordinary people's lives in Edinburgh (and elsewhere). Many essays in B. Harris and A. R. MacDonald (eds), *Making and Unmaking of the Kingdom* (Dundee, 2006) vols 1 and 2, incorporate the most recent urban research into their examinations of Scottish life. Urban women's lives are examined in essays in E. Ewan and M. M. Meikle (eds), *Women in Scotland c.1100–c.1750* (East Linton, 1999).

With the relative lack of documentary evidence, historians also draw on literary, art historical and archaeological evidence. Priscilla Bawcutt, *Dunbar the Makar* (Oxford, 1990) includes a detailed evocation of Dunbar's Edinburgh. Many essays in edited collections, such as T. van Heijnsbergen and N. Royan (eds), *Literature, Letters and the Canonical in Early Modern Scotland* (East Linton, 2002), provide lively pictures of daily life. The work of John McGavin and Eila Williamson on early Scottish drama, building on Anna Jean Mill, *Mediaeval Plays in Scotland* (New York, 1924), has produced important articles on leisure and other aspects of life in small towns, for example J. J. McGavin, 'Drama in Sixteenth-Century Haddington', *European Medieval Drama* 1 (1997). Town sports also figure in John Burnett, *Riot*

Revelry and Rout. Sport in Lowland Scotland before 1860 (East Linton, 2000). Architectural and archaeological evidence of medieval buildings discussed in such works as A. T. Simpson and S. Stevenson (eds), *Town Houses and Structures* (Glasgow, 1980) has helped scholars recreate the material culture of everyday life. Urban archaeology, much of it appearing in *The Proceedings of the Society of Antiquaries of Scotland* (*PSAS*), has been a crucial source of information shedding light especially on those who rarely appear in the records. Skeletal evidence, discussed in works such as J. A. Stones (ed.), *Three Scottish Carmelite Friaries* (Edinburgh, 1989), can shed new light on disease and other stresses of daily life. Scottish archaeologists have made their findings accessible to wider, readerships through works such as Peter Yeoman, *Medieval Scotland* (London, 1995). Russel Coleman, 'The archaeology of burgage plots in Scottish medieval towns: a review' *PSAS* 134 (2004), surveys much recent work in urban archaeology. The publications of the Scottish Burgh Survey are invaluable in providing syntheses of recent historical and archaeological findings on material culture, health and other conditions of life in individual towns. A fine recent example, which also provides a model for community involvement in producing its own history, is E. P. Dennison and S. Stronach, *Historic Dunfermline* (Dunfermline, 2007).

CHAPTER 6: PLAYTIME EVERYDAY: THE MATERIAL CULTURE OF MEDIEVAL GAMING

For the wider context of play in general and its cultural importance the two key opposed texts are Johannes Huizinga, *Homo Ludens: A Study of the Play Element in Culture* (Boston, 1950) and Roger Callois, *Les Jeux et les hommes* (Paris, 1958). For the wider board games context, two works by H. J. R. Murray – *A History of Chess* (Oxford, 1913) and *A History of Board Games Other Than Chess* (Oxford, 1952) – are, though in need of revision in several places, still of huge value. They can be usefully combined with David Parlett's *The Oxford Book of Board Games* (Oxford 1991), the journal *Board Game Studies* (for details see www.boardgamestudies.info and Irving Finkel (ed.), *Ancient Board Games in Perspective Papers from the 1990 British Museum Colloquium with added contributions* (London, 2007).

For the European, medieval social context around board games and play, the insightful analysis by Arno Borst, *Medieval Worlds: Barbarians, Heretics and Artists* (Oxford and Cambridge, 1991) is highly recommended. For a comparative overview of the range of board games and other play forms from medieval England, Compton Reeves, *Pleasures and Pastimes in Medieval England* (Stroud, 1995) remains useful.

Turning to the specifically Scottish context, a new introduction to the gaming material of the first millennium AD is provided by Mark Hall, *Playtime in Pictland: The Material Culture of Gaming in First Millennium AD Scotland* (Rosemarkie, 2007). Significant new archaeological studies of specific assemblages of gaming equipment include the graffiti boards from Inchmarnock: Chris Lowe (ed.), *Inchmarnock. An Early Historic Island Monastery and its Archaeological Landscape* (Edinburgh, 2008); the gaming pieces from medieval Perth: Mark Hall, 'Cultural Interaction in the Medieval Burgh of Perth, Scotland 1200–1600', in G. Helmig, B. Scholkman and M. Unterman (eds), *Medieval Europe Basel 2002 Preprinted Papers*, vol. 1 (Hertingen, 2002), pp. 290–301; and the Lewis chessmen: David Caldwell, Mark Hall and Caroline Wilkinson, 'The Lewis Hoard of Gaming Pieces: A Re-examination of their Context, Meaning, Discovery and Manufacture', in *Medieval Archaeology* 53 (2009), pp. 155–203. The earliest account of the Lewis pieces remains very useful: Frank Madden, 'Historical remarks on the introduction of chess into Europe and on the ancient chessmen discovered in the Isle of Lewis', in *Archaeologia* XXIV (1832), pp. 203–91.

CHAPTER 7: WOMEN OF INDEPENDENCE IN BARBOUR'S *BRUCE* AND BLIND HARRY'S *WALLACE*

The Wallace and Bruce wars together represent one of the defining moments in Scottish history. As such they have figured prominently in the nation's historiography since the fourteenth century. Indispensable primary sources are John Barbour, *The Bruce*, edited with translation and notes by A. A. M. Duncan (Edinburgh, 1997), which is full of insights deriving from the editor's lifetime study of the subject. A companion text for the other hero of independence is Blind Harry, *The Wallace*, Anne McKim (ed.) (Edinburgh, 2003) but for textual notes it is necessary to consult M. P. McDiarmid (ed.), *Harry's Wallace*, 2 vols (Edinburgh, 1968–9). One of the great Scottish scholarly achievements of the past generation is Walter Bower, *Scotichronicon*, D. E. R. Watt (ed.) 9 vols (Aberdeen and Edinburgh, 1989–98); vols 6 and 7 deal with the period providing, like the other volumes, parallel texts in Latin and English with full notes. Also important are E. L. G. Stones (ed.), *Anglo-Scottish Relations 1174–1328 Some Selected Documents* (Oxford, 1965) and E. L. G. Stones and Grant G. Simpson, *Edward I and the Throne of Scotland 1290–1296. An edition of the record sources for the Great Cause*, 2 vols (Oxford, 1978). All of the following studies point researchers towards other indispensable sources Scottish, English and Irish.

On Wallace see Andrew Fisher, *William Wallace* (Edinburgh, 1986) and Graeme Morton, *William Wallace, Man and Myth* (Stroud, 2001) as well as the rather different approach of Fiona Watson, *Under the Hammer: Edward I and Scotland 1286–1306* (East Linton, 1998). Edward J. Cowan (ed.), *The Wallace Book* (Edinburgh, 2007) offers a distillation of recent research.

G. W. S. Barrow, *Robert Bruce and the Community of the Realm of Scotland* (Edinburgh, [1965] 2005), is undoubtedly the leader in the field but remains light on the post-Bannockburn period, though the author has made many other important contributions to the topic in the form of articles. His *Robert the Bruce and the Scottish Identity* (Edinburgh, 1984) tackles an important issue, as does A. A. M. Duncan, *The Nation of Scots and the Declaration of Arbroath (1320)* (London, 1970), while A. A. M. Duncan (ed.), *Regesta Regum Scottorum V The Acts of Robert I* (Edinburgh, 1988) is a superb guide to every aspect of the king's reign. More recent studies include Colm McNamee, *The Wars of the Bruces. Scotland, England and Ireland, 1306–1328* (East Linton, 1997) and the same author's *Robert Bruce, Our Most Valiant King and Lord* (Edinburgh, 2006). Sean Duffy, *Robert Bruce's Irish Wars. The Invasions of Ireland 1306–1329* (Stroud, 2002) usefully helps fill a gap. Correctives to the Bruce cult are to be found in Alan Young, *Robert Bruce's Rivals: The Comyns, 1212–1314* (East Linton, 1997) and Amanda Beam, *The Balliol Dynasty 1210–1364* (Edinburgh, 2008). For the second phase of the wars see Michael Penman, *David II 1329–71* (East Linton, 2004).

Two studies which look at ideas during the period are Sir James Fergusson, *The Declaration of Arbroath* (Edinburgh, 1970) and Edward J. Cowan, *'For Freedom Alone': The Declaration of Arbroath 1320* (Edinburgh, 2008). For general treatments of the period see Ranald Nicholson, *Scotland: The Later Middle Ages* (Edinburgh, 1974), Alexander Grant, *Independence and Nationhood: Scotland 1306–1469* (Edinburgh, 1984), Michael Brown, *The Wars of Scotland 1214–1371* (Edinburgh 2004) and R. James Goldstein, *The Matter of Scotland: Historical Narrative in Medieval Scotland* (Lincoln and London, 1993).

Needless to say there is no study of everyday life during the Wars of Independence but the situation on the study of women in the Middle Ages is greatly improving, for which see the excellent bibliography in Elizabeth Ewan and Janay Nugent (eds), *Finding the Family in Medieval and Early Modern Scotland* (Aldershot, 2008).

CHAPTER 8: EVERYDAY LIFE IN THE HISTORIES OF SCOTLAND FROM WALTER BOWER TO GEORGE BUCHANAN

By far the easiest way to become familiar with what chroniclers actually say about the everyday is to read them: Walter Bower's *Scotichronicon* (Aberdeen and Edinburgh, 1987–98), John Mair's *History of Greater Britain* (Edinburgh, 1892) and John Bellenden's *Chronicles of Scotland* (Edinburgh, 1821) are all reasonably accessible although new readers might find Bellenden's Scots quite dense. Interpretations of that material or guides to its extraction are much harder to identify because comment, like the texts themselves, has generally been focused on the 'big' issues of politics, identity, and historical narrative. However, Jenny Wormald, *Court, Kirk and Community: Scotland 1470–1625* (Edinburgh, 1981) uses both Bellenden's and Mair's work to illuminate the documentary account of Scottish life (see esp. pp. 41–55); she also discusses their political vision in the light of accounts and other records. Whereas Wormald is most interested in the descriptions of the realm provided by the chroniclers, in *Theatricality and Narrative in Medieval and Early Modern Scotland* (Aldershot, 2007), John McGavin discusses everyday practice and assumptions that underpin Bower's and other chroniclers' narrative of particular events. Taken together, these volumes demonstrate ways in which the chronicles can be used to piece together everyday experience.

CHAPTER 9: DISEASE, DEATH AND THE HEREAFTER IN MEDIEVAL SCOTLAND

Few Scottish texts relating exclusively to issues of health, disease and death have come down to us from the Middle Ages. Instead, most evidence relating to these topics is embedded in other types of source, especially saints' Lives, in which ailments and their miraculous cures are detailed, or charters conveying sources of income to the Church to pay for masses and prayers for the spiritual welfare of the dead. Important examples of the former are the Latin *Vita et Miracula S Æbbe Virginis* and *Miracula S Margarite Scotorum Regine*, and the Scots *Legend of St Ninian* which detail over eighty examples of physical and mental maladies and the cures effected for them; see *The Miracles of St Æbbe of Coldingham and St Margaret of Scotland*, (ed. and trans.) R. Bartlett (Oxford, 2003); W. M. Metcalfe (ed.), *Legends of the Saints* (Edinburgh, 1896). Among the few specifically medical texts to survive is *A nobyl tretyse again ye Pestilens*, a short essay giving advice on the prevention and treatment of plague. Based on a fourteenth-century Latin treatise by Sir John de Mandeville, it was circulating in Scotland in the early fifteenth century and survives translated into Scots in the records of Kelso and Paisley Abbeys; see *Liber Sancte Marie de Calchou*, 2 vols (Edinburgh: Bannatyne Club, 1846). Unlike England or the Continent, Scotland has no substantial contemporary narrative accounts of the epidemics of plague that swept across Europe in the fourteenth and fifteenth centuries. There are short accounts of the 1349 epidemic and recurrences of the plague in the *Gesta Annalia* component of the Latin *Chronica Gentis Scotorum*, attributed to John of Fordun, and in the epic *Scotichronicon* of Abbot Walter Bower of Inchcolm; see *John of Fordun's Chronicle of the Scottish Nation*, (ed.) W. F. Skene, vol. 2 (Edinburgh, 1872), and Walter Bower, *Scotichronicon*, (ed.) D. E. R. Watt and others (Edinburgh, 1996). More detail of how the authorities attempted to regulate disease and control its spread can be read with specific reference to leprosy in the late twelfth-century *Laws of the Four Burghs*, the late thirteenth-century *Gild Statutes* from Berwick, and parliamentary legislation from 1428; see *The Acts of the Parliaments of Scotland*, (ed.) T. Thomson (Edinburgh, 1814), and *Records of the Parliaments of Scotland*, 1428/3/9 at www.rps.ac.uk. The earliest regulations for control of plague in Britain, dating from 1456, can be read in the *Records of the Parliaments of Scotland*, 1456/7. The best modern overview of the impact of plague on Scotland is still J. F. D. Shrewsbury's *History of Bubonic Plague in the British*

Isles (Cambridge, 1971) although there are nowadays many questions over the identification of the disease. For a wider range of diseases and their treatment, the most substantial work is J. Comrie's magisterial *History of Scottish Medicine*, 2 vols (London, 1932), and Helen Dingwall's identically titled book (Edinburgh, 2003) is a first-class, accessible updating of our understanding. Discussion of the physical evidence for the health and diseases of medieval Scots is embedded in a host of published archaeological reports, among the most substantial of which relate to the excavation of medieval cemetery sites. For example, see A. Cardy, 'The Human Bones' and D. A. Lunt and M. E. Watts, 'The Human Dentitions', in P. H. Hill, *Whithorn and St Ninian: The Excavation of a Monastic Town 1984–91* (Stroud, 1997), and O. Lelong and J. A. Roberts, 'St Trolla's Chapel, Kintradwell, Sutherland: The occupants of the Medieval burial ground and their patron saint', *Scottish Archaeological Journal* 25:2 (2003), pp. 147–63. For attitudes to death and the hereafter, and for the preparations made for a 'good death', the two most recent works are R. D. Oram's 'Lay religioisty, piety and devotion in Scotland c.1300 to c.1450', *Florilegium* 25 (2008), pp. 95–126, and A.-B. Fitch's *The Search for Salvation: Lay Faith in Scotland 1480–1560* (Edinburgh, 2009) both of which deal with the later medieval period; there is no similar detailed work for the pre-1300 period.

CHAPTER 10: 'DETESTABLE SLAVES OF THE DEVIL': CHANGING IDEAS ABOUT WITCHCRAFT IN SIXTEENTH-CENTURY SCOTLAND

The best general overview of the Scottish witch-hunts remains Christina Larner, *Enemies of God: The Witch-Hunt in Scotland* (Edinburgh, [1981] 2000) though see also two fine collections of essays, Julian Goodare (ed.), *The Scottish Witch-Hunt in Context* (Manchester and New York, 2002) and Goodare et al. (eds), *Witchcraft and Belief in Early Modern Scotland* (Basingstoke, 2008). Brian Levack, *Witch-Hunting in Scotland* (New York and London, 2008), is strong on the legal aspects of witch-hunting, while Julian Goodare, 'The Scottish Witchcraft Act', in *Church History* 74 (2005) provides a much needed look at the Scottish witchcraft legislation. Though not primarily based upon sixteenth-century evidence, Stuart MacDonald's case study *The Witches of Fife: Witch-Hunting in a Scottish Shire, 1560–1710* (East Linton, 2002) is useful, as is Lizanne Henderson and Edward J. Cowan, *Scottish Fairy Belief: A History* (East Linton, [2001] 2007), which contains a good deal of evidence on folk belief garnered from witch trials, and Lizanne Henderson, *Witchcraft and Folk Belief at the Dawn of Enlightenment: Scotland, c.1670–1740* (Basingstoke, 2011). Few works specifically target the sixteenth century but an exception is P. G. Maxwell-Stuart, *Satan's Conspiracy: Magic and Witchcraft in Sixteenth Century Scotland* (East Linton, 2001), and Edward J. Cowan, 'Witch Persecution and Folk Belief in Lowland Scotland: The

Devil's Decade', in Goodare et al., *Witchcraft and Belief in Early Modern Scotland* (Basingstoke, 2008), pp. 71–94.

An excellent primary source on sixteenth-century elite attitudes to witchcraft is King James VI and I, *Daemonologie, 1597* (London, 1924). There are numerous sources for witch trials but Robert Pitcairn (ed.), *Ancient Criminal Trials in Scotland*, 4 vols (Edinburgh, 1833) contains some of the major trials and is a good starting point, as is the online resource, *The Survey of Scottish Witchcraft Database* at www.arts.ed.ac.uk/witches/.

On James VI and his role in the witch-hunts see Stuart Clark, 'King James's *Daemonologie*: Witchcraft and Kingship', in S. Anglo (ed.), *The Damned Art* (London, 1977), P. G. Maxwell-Stuart, 'The Fear of the King is Death: James VI and the Witches of East Lothian', in W. G. Naphy and P. Roberts (eds), *Fear in Early Modern Society* (Manchester, 1997) and Jenny Wormald, 'The Witches, the Devil and the King', in T. Brotherstone and D. Ditchburn (eds), *Freedom and Authority: Scotland c. 1050–c. 1650* (East Linton, 2000). An important early study on the North Berwick trials is Edward J. Cowan, 'The Darker Vision of the Scottish Renaissance: the Devil and Francis Stewart', in I. B. Cowan and D. Shaw (eds), *The Renaissance and Reformation in Scotland* (1983), pp. 125–40, and in more recent years, Laurence Normand and Gareth Roberts, *Witchcraft in Early Modern Scotland: James VI's* Demonology *and the North Berwick Witches* (Exeter, 2000).

For comparisons with the Jonet Boyman trial, see Lizanne Henderson, 'Witch, Fairy and Folktale Narratives in the Trial of Bessie Dunlop', in Lizanne Henderson (ed.), *Fantastical Imaginations: The Supernatural in Scottish History and Culture* (Edinburgh, 2009) and Emma Wilby, *Cunning Folk and Familiar Spirits* (Brighton, 2005).

The complex role of the Devil in Scotland is an understudied topic but see Stuart MacDonald, 'The Devil in Fife Witchcraft Cases', in Goodare, *Scottish Witch-Hunt in Context*, pp. 33–50, and Joyce Miller, 'Men in Black: Appearances of the Devil in Early Modern Scottish Witchcraft Discourse', in Goodare et al., *Witchcraft and Belief in Early Modern Scotland*, pp. 144–65.

CHAPTER 11: GLASWEGIANS: THE FIRST ONE THOUSAND YEARS

A new edition of the Life of Kentigern or Mungo is badly needed. Currently we have to make use of the antiquated Alexander Penrose Forbes (ed.), *Lives of S. Ninian and S. Kentigern compiled in the twelfth century* (Edinburgh, 1874). Also lacking is any book-length academic study of the saint. All we have are one or two 'wee bookies' such as Hubert L. Simpson, *Saint Mungo (Kentigern) The Patron Saint of Glasgow* (Glasgow and London, 1918) and Reginald B. Hale, *The Beloved. St Mungo Founder of Glasgow* (Ottawa, 1976). Fortunately there are some excellent articles on the saint, such as A. A. M. Duncan, 'St Kentigern at Glasgow Cathedral in the Twelfth Century', in

Richard Fawcett (ed.), *Medieval Art and Architecture in the Diocese of Glasgow* (Leeds, 1998), and chapter 5 of Alan Macquarrie, *The Saints of Scotland* (Edinburgh, 1997). An informative exploration of the life of the author of the *vita* is Norman F. Shead, 'Jocelin abbot of Melrose (1170–1174) and Bishop of Glasgow (1175–1199)', *Innes Review* 54 (2003), pp. 1–22, who also explores the origins of Glasgow in his 'Glasgow: An Ecclesiastical Burgh', in Michael Lynch, Michael Spearman and Geoffrey Stell (eds), *The Scottish Medieval Town* (Edinburgh, 1988). An in-depth context for the development of the saint's cult is provided by Dauvit Broun, *Scottish Independence and the Idea of Britain from the Picts to Alexander III* (Edinburgh, 2007), chapter 5. On the building of the cathedral see Stephen T. Driscoll, *Excavations at Glasgow Cathedral 1988–1997, The Society for Medieval Archaeology Monograph* 18 (Leeds, 2002).

An invaluable publication is J. D. Marwick (ed.), *Extracts from the Records of the Burgh of Glasgow* A.D. *1573–1642* (Glasgow, 1876), complemented by Rev. James Primrose, *Medieval Glasgow* (Glasgow, 1913) and Robert Renwick and John Lindsay, *History of Glasgow*, vol. I, *Pre-Reformation Period* (Glasgow, 1921). All of these publications shed interesting light on everyday life as does the lavishly illustrated Neil Baxter (ed.), *A Tale of Two Towns. A History of Medieval Glasgow* (Glasgow, 2007).

CHAPTER 12: MARIAN DEVOTION IN SCOTLAND AND THE SHRINE OF LORETO

Contributed by Ted Cowan

One of the great strengths of the late Audrey-Beth Fitch's approach was her sound grasp of European historiography, thus providing a comparative context for her investigation of lay faith in Scotland. She made good use of such studies as Philippe Aries, *Hour of Our Death* (New York, 1981), Robert Scribner, *For the Sake of the Simple Folk: Popular Propaganda for the German Reformation* (Cambridge, 1981), Marina Warner, *Alone of All Her Sex: The Myth and Cult of the Virgin Mary* (London, 1985), Bernard Hamilton, *Religion in the Medieval West* (London, 1986), John Bossy, *Christianity in the West 1400–1700* (Oxford, 1987), Robert Whiting, *The Blind Devotion of the People: Popular Religion and the English Reformation* (Cambridge, 1989), Eamonn Duffy, *The Stripping of the Altars: Traditional Religion in England 1400–1580* (New Haven, 1992), Anne Clark Bartlett, *Male Authors, Female Readers: Representation and Subjectivity in Middle English Devotional Literature* (Ithaca and London, 1995) and Donna S. Ellington, *From Sacred Body to Angelic Soul: Understanding Mary in Late Medieval and Early Modern Europe* (Washington, 2001).

Relevant Scottish studies are D. McRoberts (ed.), *Essays on the Scottish Reformation* (Glasgow, 1962), Gordon Donaldson, *The Faith of the Scots* (London, 1990), John Malden, *The Abbey and Monastery of Paisley* (Renfrew,

1993) and Michael F. Graham, *The Uses of Reform: 'Godly Discipline' and Popular Behaviour in Scotland and Beyond 1560–1610* (Leiden, 1996). To these should be added Margo Todd, *The Culture of Protestantism in Early Modern Scotland* (New Haven and London, 2002) and Margaret H. B. Sanderson, *A Kindly Place? Living in Sixteenth-Century Scotland* (East Linton, 2002). For further bibliographical information see Audrey-Beth Fitch, *The Search For Salvation: Lay Faith in Scotland 1480–156*, Elizabeth Ewan (ed.) (Edinburgh, 2009).

Notes on the Contributors

Rebecca Boorsma graduated from the University of California, Berkeley with an honours degree in History and Political Science. Shortly after, she completed her MLitt in Scottish Cultural Heritage at the University of Glasgow (Dumfries Campus). Her research interests include the Scottish Wars of Independence, Scottish popular culture, and the Ruthwell Cross.

Stuart Campbell has worked in public-sector heritage organisations in the United Kingdom and United States and currently works in the Trove Units in the National Museums Scotland.

Edward J. Cowan, Emeritus Professor, formerly Professor of Scottish History at the University of Glasgow and Director of the university's Dumfries Campus, previously taught at the Universities of Edinburgh and Guelph, Ontario. A fellow of the Royal Society of Edinburgh, he is much in demand as a speaker, journalist and broadcaster, and has been a Visiting Professor in Australia, New Zealand, Europe, Canada and the United States. His most recent publications are *The Wallace Book* (revised edition 2010), *For Freedom Alone: The Declaration of Arbroath 1320* (revised edition 2008) and *Folk in Print: Scotland's Chapbook Heritage* (2007). He is currently working on a book on the Arctic Scots.

Elizabeth Ewan is University Research Chair and Professor of Scottish Studies and History at the University of Guelph, Guelph, Ontario, Canada. Among her publications are *Townlife in Fourteenth-Century Scotland* (1990), *Women in Scotland c.1100–c.1750* (1999), *The Biographical Dictionary of Scottish Women* (2006), and *Finding the Family in Medieval and Early Modern Scotland* (2008). Her current research interests include gender and crime in fifteenth- and sixteenth-century Scottish towns, the life of a late medieval Edinburgh woman, and masculinity in Scotland c.1400–c.1600.

Audrey-Beth Fitch, before her untimely death in 2005, was Associate Professor of History at the California University of Pennsylvania. She graduated with a BA History, University of Toronto, a BEd, University of Calgary, and PhD, University of Glasgow. Her book, *The Search for Salvation: Lay Faith in Scotland 1480–1560*, edited by Elizabeth Ewan, was published posthumously by John Donald in 2009.

Mark A. Hall is currently employed as the History Officer for Perth Museum & Art Gallery where he is chiefly responsible for curating the archaeology collection (notable for its medieval excavation assemblages from Perth). His interest in medieval material culture focuses principally on the cult of saints, gaming and reception studies (especially cinematic portrayals of the medieval past) on which he has published in several journals and books.

Lizanne Henderson is Lecturer in History at the University of Glasgow (Dumfries Campus). She is co-author, with Edward J. Cowan, of *Scottish Fairy Belief: A History* (2001; 2007), editor of '*Fantastical Imaginations*': *The Supernatural in Scottish Culture* (2009) and author of a monograph *Witchcraft and Folk Belief at the Dawn of Enlightenment: Scotland c.1670–1740* (2011). She has published articles on the Scottish witch-hunts, charming, ballads, and Scotland's connections with the transatlantic slave trade. She is currently editing *The Routledge Companion to British and Irish Folklore*. She has lectured on cultural history and folklore in Europe, Canada, America, and Australia.

Richard D. Oram is Professor of Medieval and Environmental History, and Director of the Centre for Environmental History and Policy at the University of Stirling. He has published widely on aspects of the late medieval and early modern environment in Scotland, the medieval Scottish Church, and noble society and culture in medieval Scotland.

Nicola Royan is Lecturer in Medieval and Early Modern Literature in the School of English Studies, University of Nottingham. She has published widely on the literature of fifteenth- and sixteenth-century Scotland, with a particular focus on historiography and other political writings. She is Editorial Secretary of the Scottish Text Society and a Trustee of the Scottish Medievalists. She is currently editing the *Edinburgh Companion to Scottish Literature 1400–1650* and writing on the poetry of Gavin Douglas.

David Sellar is Lord Lyon King of Arms and an Honorary Fellow of the School of Law at the University of Edinburgh. He has written extensively on Scots law and Scottish history, including legal history and family history and origins.

Jenny Shiels, who sadly passed away in 2009, published research on prehistoric Cypriot pottery. She worked in the Treasure Trove Unit from 1999 and was instrumental in expanding the role of the Treasure Trove system to reflect the nature of medieval objects being discovered.

Fiona Watson is a medieval and environmental historian, formerly a senior lecturer at the University of Stirling and Director of the Centre for

Environmental History, a joint venture with the University of St Andrews. In 2006 she left academia to become a writer and broadcaster. She has published four books: *Under the Hammer: Edward I and Scotland* (1997); *Scotland: A History* (2000); *A History of the Native Woodlands of Scotland* (with T. C. Smout and Alan MacDonald, (2005) and *Macbeth: A True Story* (2010). She has also presented numerous programmes on Radio Scotland, as well as a major BBC TV series, *In Search of Scotland*, in 2001.

Index

Boyman, Jonet (witch), 231, 233,
244–8
Braidfute, Marion, 180
Braudel, Ferdnand, 1
Briggs, Robin, 249
Britons, 187
Bronze Age, 68
brooches, 71–2, 74, 75, 113
Brough of Birsay, 42
Bruce, Robert, king of Scots, 2, 15,
169–81, 201
Bruce, The, 169–81
Bruges, 275
Brusi, earl of Orkney, 38, 47, 53
Buchan, 92
Buchanan, George, 9, 185, 191, 192,
194, 255, 268
Buckle, Henry, 102
Buckquoy, 41, 43, 147
Buittle, 13
bull-baiting, 125
bullion, 68
burgesses, 109–10
burghs, 67, 69, 76, 86, 109–32
burials, 43, 78, 80, 118, 134, 197–8,
203–4, 207, 218, 219, 220,
269
burnings, 58, 61, 268
butchers, 269
Bute, 150, 151, 152, 156, 158
Byzantium, 50, 63

Cairston, 197
Caithness, 37, 41, 42, 45, 54, 61
calendar customs, 16–17, 32, 227,
241, 246
Advent, 189
Beltane, 120, 122
Candlemas, 17, 120, 246, 253
Christmas, 48, 57, 58, 261
Corpus Christi, 120, 128
Easter, 16, 246
Good Friday, 11, 61
Halloween, 16, 20, 227, 245,
246

Lammas, 241, 246
Lent, 125, 189
Michaelmas, 17
Midsummer, 246
Quarter Days, 241, 246
Rogation Sunday, 32
Rood Fair, 16
St John's Day, 12, 16, 17
Shrove Tuesday, 121
Yule, 16, 119, 122, 124, 125, 269,
271
calps, 32
Calvin, John, 234
Calvinism, 235
Campbells, 93
Canongate, 122
canon law, 90, 91, 95, 96–9
cannibalism, 8
Carlisle, 12, 14, 17
Carlyle, Thomas, 62
Carmelites, 275, 285
Carrick, 32, 92, 190
castle, 154, 156
Carver, Robert, 118
Catholics, 8, 283
celibacy, 261
cemeteries, 197, 204, 214
Chalmers, George, 36
chapmen, 111
charming/charmers, 133, 226, 230,
236, 238, 240, 244
Chaucer, Geoffrey, 160, 215
childbirth, 20, 45, 46, 133, 177, 226–7,
245, 247, 257, 263, 280
children, 8, 10, 19, 43, 95, 179, 197,
198, 200
China, 63
Chisholms, 93
chivalry, 172
chronicles, 185–7, 188
Church, 9, 10, 16
Cistercians, 275, 284, 285
Clan Chattan, 94
Clan Donald, 92, 93
Clan Dougall, 92